D1548119

PSYCHOLOGY'S CRISIS OF DISUNITY

Philosophy and Method for a Unified Science

Arthur W. Staats

PRAEGER SPECIAL STUDIES • PRAEGER SCIENTIFIC

Library of Congress Cataloging in Publication Data

Staats, Arthur W.
    Psychology's crisis of disunity.

    Bibliography: p.
    Includes index.
    1. Psychology—Philosophy.   2. Psychology—
Methodology.   I. Title.
BF38.S676   1983   150'.1   83-2154
ISBN 0-03-063289-7

To my supportive friends.
And to those who cherish the beauty, simplicity,
and power of discovering that this is an
orderly, principled world.

Published in 1983 by Praeger Publishers
CBS Educational and Professional Publishing
a Division of CBS Inc.
521 Fifth Avenue, New York, New York 10175 U.S.A.

© 1983 by Praeger Publishers

3456789   052   987654321

Printed in the United States of America
on acid-free paper

Preface

I consider psychology to be a science, but a not yet fully developed science. The lack of development I refer to is not just quantitative: lack of development in a quantitative sense simply requires doing more of the same in the present case of multiplying experiments, innovating apparatus, obtaining new findings, formulating additional theories, and the like. I believe, rather, that psychology as a social science is qualitatively different from the advanced natural sciences in lacking certain characteristics the latter sciences display. The characteristics are so central that without them, no matter how much psychology progresses in what it has been doing, it will never become a full-fledged science.

Psychology's present state has developed within the general framework involved in its original revolutionary separation from philosophy. That first revolution was to gain acceptance as an independent science. This framework required abundant scientific products, which psychology has produced at an accelerating rate. Now a new revolution is needed because the resulting flood of knowledge inundates this field and the knowledge is chaotic. Without organization the products of the science remain inconsistent, competitive, unrelated, and without meaning. Today's psychologist is bewildered by all but a small corner of the fragmented science; only by specialization can meaning be gained. Excessive diversity destroys the efficiency of research and practice. New empirical-method-theory findings no longer advance the science or profession, for they merely add to the confused complexity. Psychology's body of knowledge lacks the organization, meaning, and power of the unified knowledge of the natural sciences. Centrally, a disorganized body of knowledge can never be recognized to be scientific in the full measure of the word.

Neither the framework of psychology's original revolution nor that of

the field of the philosophy of science has provided an understanding of the special problems of the modern, disunified science. Thus, it is not understood that psychology, in addition to lacking a methodology for creating unified knowledge, has developed characteristics that *prevent* the achievement of unity; disunity is produced even where unity already exists or could be attained easily. The primary obstacles to achieving the enormous benefits of unified science lie in *not recognizing* psychology's ubiquitous disunity, its characteristics that promote and hang on to disunity, and its need for a counteracting philosophy and methodology of unity.

The optimistic message in the present work, nevertheless, is that what psychology has achieved in its 100 or so years of self-conscious striving does provide the raw materials for making the leap to the status of a unified science. I believe that psychology is ready for the revolution to the unified state that must inevitably occur, for there is now a deep tension in psychology produced by its disorganization. It is not that the task of turning the disorganized raw materials into something generally meaningful is a small task. Quite the contrary, a large investment is demanded. But that effort will not be expended until there is a revolution in thinking about what psychology is and can be. We need to see what it is that organized sciences have and that disorganized sciences do not — what is different in the two cases. We must also see that unification of a modern disunified science requires methodological and philosophical developments. These are the considerations the present work attempts to begin.

The philosophy and methodology that is developed herein thus aim to provide a framework for making sense of what psychology is and can be, what psychology must do to become a full science. Since psychology is a social science the philosophy that is proposed has relevance for the consideration of additional disciplines such as sociology, anthropology, political science, economics, and history as well as the relationships of the social sciences. Finally, as an indigenous philosophy that differentiates social and natural science, it is hoped the present work will provide new directions for the development of the philosophy of science.

This work has consumed much time devoted to its context of discovery and less but nevertheless considerable time to working out its present form of expression. In the latter work I wish to express appreciation to the Social Science Research Institute of the University of Hawaii, to its Director Donald M. Topping, and to Deane Neubauer, Dean of the Social Sciences, for freeing half of my time for research during the past two years. This enabled me to achieve completion of this work earlier than would otherwise have been the case. I wish also to thank Nina Horio for help in tracing some difficult bibliographic materials and to Roberta Fong for secretarial help of the highest order. The Social Science Research Institute also contributed help in the preparation of the present manuscript.

I wish also to add a special word of appreciation here. In the past few years there has been a gathering of individuals who have worked to develop the unified theory framework that is called social behaviorism or paradigmatic behaviorism — to establish the manner in which such a comprehensive framework can be heuristic theoretically, experimentally, and in the clinic, school, and home. Foremost among them is Aimeé Leduc of Laval University, who has established the first center of such activities in Quebec, Canada, in a most extraordinary way leading a group producing a range of important works. Another very active research group is led by Jean Rondal of the University of Liege, Belgium in his work on language development. Leonard Burns of the University of Connecticut has conducted studies in behavioral assessment, intelligence, and cross-cultural psychology. Ian Evans of the State University of New York at Binghamton is taking a leading role in integrating social behaviorism works in conceptually-based presentations. Paolo Meazzini, a leading Italian psychologist, at the University of Rome, in addition to his own important contributions, has made social behaviorism an influential approach in his country, and Karl Minke and Elaine Heiby at the University of Hawaii, in experimental and clinical psychology, respectively, are special contributors to the growing group. Dr. Minke, in addition to his original research, is editing the *International Newsletter of Social Behaviorism*. George Eifert at the University of Frankfort is conducting original research and contributing new analyses in understanding anxiety. Such efforts support the fruitfulness of a particular general, unified theory. Although the present study is not concerned with particular theories, the support of the above efforts gives strength to the possibility that unified approaches can be developed. I wish thus to give thanks to those who provide that support.

Acknowledgments

The author wishes to thank the following authors, publishers, and agents for permission to quote from copyrighted material or personal communications:

Pages 261–63 excerpted from "Methods for integrative reviews," by Gregg B. Jackson in *Review of Educational Research*, 1980, Volume 50, pp. 438–460. Copyright 1980, American Educational Research Association, Washington, D.C.

Page 213 excerpted from a personal communication by Richard Jessor of August 25, 1980.

Pages 30–31 excerpted from "Comment," by Sigmund Koch in the *American Psychologist*, 1978, Volume 33, pp. 637–639. Copyright 1978, American Psychological Association, Washington, D.C.

Pages 235–36 excerpted from "Epilogue," by David Krech in *Toward Unification in Psychology* (Edited by Joseph R. Royce). Copyright 1970, University of Toronto Press.

Pages 60–62, 81 excerpted from *The Structure of Scientific Revolutions* by Thomas S. Kuhn. Copyright © 1962 by the University of Chicago. By permission of the publisher and the author.

Pages 167–68 excerpted from "Priorities in scientific research," by Robert K. Merton in the *American Sociological Review*, 1957, Volume 22, pp. 635–659. Copyright 1957, American Sociological Association. By permission of the publisher and the author.

Pages 75–76 excerpted from "Introduction," by Frederick Suppe in *The Structure of Scientific Theories*. Copyright © 1977 by the Board of Trustees of the University of Illinois. By permission of the University of Illinois Press as publisher.

Pages 138–39, 174 excerpted from *Human Understanding* by Stephen Toulmin. Copyright 1972 by Princeton University Press. By permission of the author.

Contents

Part I
States and Stages of Science

Chapter 1

Crisis of Disunity

There are many special characteristics that separate humankind from the rest of the animal world. Like other animals humans can behave, but unlike others can also step back and consider what they have done. Such considerations themselves can involve a productive and original symbolic level of activity that can then serve as a guide to later actions. We can describe the philosophy of science in these terms, for this type of study consists of stepping back and considering what scientists have done. Almost always, however, it is the activities and products of natural scientists that are the objects of consideration. Usually the highest forms of scientific development provide the basis for formulating a philosophy of science. Such philosophies of science may later be used as models when one is interested in considering general concerns in the social sciences. But this process involves some problems. The philosophies of science drawn from the natural sciences are more likely to be directly applicable to the natural sciences because they are first-hand. Such philosophies are second-hand for the social sciences, to the extent that the characteristics and problems of the social sciences are different from those of the natural sciences. Although there has not been much in the way of contemporary philosophy of science that has been sufficiently functional for psychologists to use as a central guide in constructing their theories and pursuing their work, the efforts to adapt philosophical positions to the social sciences has not usually been received positively by philosophers of science. We can see this in the following examples.

Kuhn's philosophy emerged from and is meshed into intricate debates in the philosophy of science about change, growth, rationality, knowledge and history. None of this is alluded to by Studdert-Kennedy [1975], so his

3

book has no philosophical weight. It does not use Kuhn to connect debates about the social sciences with debates about the natural sciences, and hence its "application" of Kuhn is jejune.

My explanation is that professionalism is substituted for scholarship. Studdert-Kennedy's book belongs to a curious sub-field: methodological discussions within political science. These discussions are curiously out of kilter with the philosophical material they derive from, much as are similar discussions in psychology. Dimly perceiving that their first-order work is leading them into philosophy, political scientists and psychologists turn to that field for guidance. Used to looking for findings and results, they try to see what the latest thing in philosophy is. Depending on who they talk to or what they dip in to the result is quite often unsatisfactory simply because they have failed to grasp that most issues in philosophy are in perennial debate, and that frequent mention of a person or idea by no means signals an agreed result or finding. It is thus no surprise that a good deal of what is discussed is warmed-over positivism. The worry is over *operationalizing* concepts, about using empirical concepts and theoretical concepts and devising bridging laws or intermediate variables, etc. (Jarvie 1979, p. 102).

A similar criticism is expressed in the following, this time with respect to the work of an important figure in psychology.

It seems to be characteristic, but unfortunate, of science to continue holding philosophical positions long after they are discredited. Thus, for example, Skinner's radical behaviorism, which insists on operational definition, came into prominence and dominated behavioral psychology well after most philosophers had abandoned the doctrine of operational or explicit definitions (Suppe 1977b, p. 19).

I have raised this point to introduce several concerns. First, as this criticism indicates, at least some specialists in the philosophy of science consider the social scientists who have dealt with relevant topics to be naive and poorly prepared to make a contribution. The statement by Suppe, for example, indicates pointedly that one of psychology's most dominant approaches is considered by philosophers of science to be passé, behind the times. Such evaluations would suggest that psychologists should drop their interest in warmed-over positivism, operationalizing concepts, using empirical concepts and theoretical concepts, and so on in accordance with Jarvie's statement already referred to. The fact is, however, that what psychologists should do to advance their science is not well indicated by the field of the philosophy of science. In introducing the nature of the present work let me put into perspective philosophy of science's tendency to reject philosophical positions of social scientists, as well as the absence of a framework in the philosophy of science that could be used to guide the development of the social sciences, specifically psychology.

There was an earlier time when the philosophy of science/psychology relationship was closer. When I was a graduate student in the early 1950s, stimulated by the second-generation behaviorists, there was a hot-bed of concern with the philosophy of science, or at least part of it. This was an outgrowth of the mission of behaviorism (see Boring 1950; Mackenzie 1977) to make itself a science in the mold of the natural sciences and also, one might add, an outgrowth of a methodology that was rejecting the subjectivistic orientation of traditional psychology. Behaviorism influenced the development, at least slightly, of the early character of logical positivism (Mackenzie 1977), but in return logical positivism had a marked effect upon the philosophy of science that was developed by the later behaviorists. Behaviorism, or learning theory, became concerned with constructing scientific theories and with stating the methodology of how this was to be done, and with analyzing theoretical structures already in place in psychology in terms of the principles of the philosophy of science. The learning theorists, who composed the nucleus of this group of philosophers of science of psychology, all developed variations of logical positivism and/or operationalism with which to treat and approach psychology. Much attention was paid to objective definition of terms and with how one could be concerned with internal cognitive events and still define one's terms with external, objective observations — that is observations of stimuli and responses. The focus of concern became such concepts as intervening variables (concepts defined solely by stimuli and responses) and hypothetical constructs (which were concepts that included surplus meaning besides the objective stimulus-response meaning) (MacCorquodale and Meehl 1948; Marx 1951; Spence 1944; Tolman 1951). There was analysis of the types of laws that could be formulated to relate events isolated in psychological research. The types of laws involved were said to define the characteristics of the theories based upon such laws. For example, it was said that there were S-R (stimulus-response) laws that related environmental (cause) and behavioral (effect) events. Then there were said to be R-R (response-response) laws involving events that were both effects. For example, in the field of psychological testing, psychological test performance (one type of response) is used to predict later behavior (another type of response). Both responses are effects of the same causes, so one response can be used to know about the other, but not to explain the other. These R-R laws were considered as non-explanatory correlations rather than as the cause-and-effect S-R laws (Spence 1944).

Others of that bygone era were concerned with additional general methodological issues concerning the way psychology was to go about its science. B. F. Skinner, for example, in his methodological approach, emphasized the empirical part of logical positivism. Formal theory and the method of deducing experimental hypotheses from formally stated theoretical bodies were rejected (see Skinner 1945, 1950, 1961). Psychology was not to be concerned with theory dealing with the events that might underlie the learning of behavior, but rather was to be concerned with observable stimuli and observable responses and the laws of conditioning. Clark Hull, on the other hand, emphasized the search for classic, formal theory like that of the natural sciences. He saw his task as composing a formal theory to account for the various empirical relationships that had been found to exist between stimuli and responses in studying the processes of conditioning. An elaborate structure of precisely defined concepts, related by mathematical functions, was employed by Hull to explain learning, and supposedly human behavior in general. The experimental program was to be deduced from this axiomatized theoretical structure using formal hypothetico-deductive methods (see Hull 1943, 1961). Importantly, thus, the philosophy of science of these men was functional in their work as scientists in psychology.

The theories of such men as Edward Tolman, Edwin Guthrie, Clark Hull, and B. F. Skinner dominated experimentally oriented psychology during the 1940s and 1950s. But the heyday of the grand learning theories passed. The competition between the theories and their attendant philosophies of science and of theory construction did not provide a basis for continued development. Many of the conceptual analyses remained, however, and continue to be employed. Most psychologists today, for example, are aware of the importance of the methods of definition of terms in the study of behavior. A term representing a mental process that is inferred to exist in the individual — the inference based solely on the observation that the individual behaves in a particular manner — is seen to provide less information than a term that is defined by observations that the behavior occurs only when the organism has been subjected to certain antecedent environmental conditions. Statements that are based upon observations of the correlations between test performances and later behavior are seen to be different than statements that indicate that if the individual receives experiences of a certain kind his later behaviors will be of a certain kind — and so on — the latter being a cause-and-effect statement. That the lessons of the era were retained and continue to appear in contemporary works may be seen in the quotations of I.C. Jarvie and Frederick Suppe already presented. There was continuity even though interest in the areas of scientific psychology switched from grand theories to that of studying relatively narrow experimental facts with methodological precision and to constructing small but methodologically sophisticated microtheories (see Marx 1970).

Thus, the framework of logical positivism and operationism proved useful in the development of psychology. Although the philosophy of science has changed its character, and no longer holds logical positivism (also called the Received View) in the same esteem as it once did, this does not mean that the elements that were drawn from this philosophy no longer have any utility for a science such as psychology. Criticisms of psychology that are based upon the changing interests of the philosophy of science are misdirected — criticism should grow out of the needs of the science itself for furthering its development. It is interesting that Suppe clearly recognizes that a philosophy of science should be valuable to the practicing scientist (1977b). But this criterion does not apparently function when a social science is involved.

Philosophers of science may be correct, however, in criticizing psychology for not continuing a systematic interest in examining its field in terms of its general scientific characteristics. While concern with logic and empirical definitions (the interests derived from logical positivism) may be important, we can readily see that such considerations do not provide a methodological framework by which to guide the science in solving many of its problems. As will be further indicated there is a crisis in psychology that involves issues very different from those that are related to operational definitions and the tenets of logical positivism. While there is a crisis of confidence in the path being followed by contemporary psychology, there has been no new or systematic philosophy of science — produced either by philosophers of science or psychologists — that has indicated what the problems of the science are or that has pointed a way toward their resolution.

In beginning this chapter I quoted the critical comments of the philosophers of science concerning the philosophical positions of social scientists to indicate one additional point. The criticisms, and their tone and manner, express an underlying, but general, evaluative posture, one that deprecates the social scientists' views of science. It is clear that many philosophers of science consider general statements about the nature and problems of science to be their special province. That is not an unreasonable expectation, at least in certain senses. As specialists in the study of science, their knowledge of science should be at the forefront of advancement. But there is something additional that requires consideration when it comes to psychology. The major philosophies of science are based upon the study of the natural sciences. If it is indeed the case that sciences progressively change as they go from their early stages to later stages, then a philosophy based upon the study of the contemporary advanced science may omit concerns of central importance to the science that is not advanced. It is the present view that this disjunction is indeed involved, and that this possibility has not been considered. And that means that there are characteristics of the contemporary, but less advanced, science that are not well-understood and thus are not being dealt with appropriately by the philosophy of science. If these are central characteristics and central problems then important issues to the science may be involved.

THE GUIDING FRAMEWORK

As will be indicated at greater length in later chapters, in dealing with the concerns of this book, logical positivism has been criticized in part because it restricted its interests to the formal theories that some sciences produce. And there are characteristics of science, other than formal theories, that are important and, as we shall see, crucial in the consideration of the social sciences. In addition to the formal theories of a science, a more general guiding framework involving other constituents may play a central role.

Thus, to illustrate this concept for the purposes employed here, we have described the philosophical positions of the second-generation behaviorists in their development of elements of logical positivism and operationalism for psychology. Those behaviorists, it should be noted, were primarily engaged in constructing general theories of learning. Each of the prominent behaviorists (for example, Tolman, Hull, and Skinner) thus constructed a specific, personal theory whose purpose was to account for the many facts established in the experimental psychology of learning, to project new directions of animal learning research, and to account eventually for all types of behavior, including that of humans.

The important point here is that in addition to the formal theories of these behaviorists, there were other aspects of the guiding framework that were not as formal or explicit. One positive aspect of the guiding framework was the value placed on the construction of large, formal, and general theories. We can see this clearly by the fact that this feature has since died out. The science became disenchanted with the competitions between the great theories, with the work generated within the theories, and with the strategy of constructing great theories. As we will see in the statements of contemporary psychologists, the era of the classic learning theories left a legacy of distrust of general-theory efforts that persists today, although those theories were constructed in the 1930s and 1940s and began to die out in the 1960s.

To continue, however, one of the central aspects of psychology since its inception has been its insistence that the methods of the natural sciences could be applied to the subject matter of psychology. Thus one of the primary goals of psychology has been to prove that it is a science. This part of the framework has set a very high value on the ability to obtain objective data, in the manner of the experimental sciences. The conduct of experiments, the acquisition of precise and systematic data, the construction of new apparatuses and laboratories, all of these are valued in and of themselves. It should be noted that the collapse of the big, second-generation behavioristic theories of such men as Tolman, Hull, and Skinner had the effect of enhancing this experimental focus. More emphasis was then placed upon experimentation for its own value, without regard to its significance for general theory. Another effect was to shift concern in psychology from large to much more limited theories. The science has since been urged to adopt a microtheory approach — one that is to be concerned with narrowly defined problems that can be explored systematically and with precision, yielding microtheories with classic, if limited, dimensions (see, for example, Marx 1970). In addition, there are philosophies such as Skinner's (see 1950) and his followers (see Bayes 1980; Sidman 1960) that have said with great force and influence that the path to advancement in our science is through obtaining more data — that the construction of theory is a precarious process at best and must be preceded by strong experimental knowledge. The scientist is told by this philosophy that the road to progress is not through theoretical endeavor.

> The hypothesis [and theory generally] can be useful but, very possibly at least in the first stages of a science — as is the case with psychology, for example — much less so than which we generally believe. For a theoretical model and the hypotheses generated by it to be fruitful we must first obtain a great quantity of data if we hope that this hypothesis is not to rest upon air. In disciplines that still do not possess much basic data and in which there exist few functional relations that have been securely established, it is likely to be more advantageous that the investigator devote the valuable time that has been conceded him on this earth to a systematic exploration of unknown areas rather than to the construction of allexplaining theoretical models capable of generating numerous hypotheses that, on their own, may be the source of uncountable empirical investigations that not only rob the investigator of his own time but also that of many of his colleagues. As Claude Bernard has indicated, "It is better to know nothing than to have fixed ideas based on theories whose confirmation we look for constantly, paying no attention to all that is not in accord with the theories" (1865 p. 71) (Bayes 1980 p.91. trans. from Spanish).

This provides a clear example of one of the columns of the framework that drives contemporary psychology. It says forcefully that we should not attempt to construct omniexplicativo theory, theory yielding general explanation.

I cannot begin to explicate in this introduction the characteristics of the guiding framework or frameworks that are functional in psychology, nor is it my mission to do this generally for the science of psychology. Only some of these characteristics will be of interest here, but the concept of the guiding framework has been mentioned by way of introduction, and also by way of suggesting that the framework that is presently acting in psychology has its good and its bad parts. On the one hand the framework of psychology is and has been very successful. There are large numbers of psychological scientists in our culture, operating in various social institutions — and this attests to the value of their skills. The field is recognized by the science establishment as being a science — if perhaps not fully by some — and the science secures support which, if not of the highest level, is considerable in scope and quantity. Psychology has shown its ability to accelerate production of mountains of empirical findings, with ever-increasing precision and sophistication. As scientists go, psychologists are sophisticated in the knowledge of science and in the methodology of science as applied to their field. Albeit in its early stages, there is also ample proof that the empirical methods, principles, and procedures of the basic science have significance for solving problems of the natural world. Psychological knowledge from the basic science has been applied to designing equipment, solving organizational problems, obtaining social information, treating individual and social problems of behavior, and so on. While far from monumental in importance at this point, the possibilities have been shown. Thus it can be said with good reason that the knowledge achievement of the science has been considerable and it is valuable, and thus that the framework that has guided the efforts that have gained that knowledge is itself valuable.

THE CRISIS

But that does not mean, necessarily, that the science is operating under the best possible framework, that the framework is complete, that there are not deep and central problems in the science, or that there is not a deep and widespread dissatisfaction with the science, with its products, and implicitly with the framework that results in those conditions. I would suggest here, and will suggest in much greater length further on, that there is a large and important area of defect in the present-day framework that guides our science and, moreover, that from this defect springs a deep and widespread dissatisfaction with our science and its framework and its products. This dissatisfaction mounts to the tension of a crisis, yet its cry is mute because the characteristics of the science involved are still implicit and there has been nothing solid upon which to pin the blame for the problems. While there are innumerable expressions of this dissatisfaction, and we will see examples of it in various places in this study, there has been no systematic analysis of its roots. Let me exemplify this expression of that general dissatisfaction.

> Social psychologists once knew who they were and where they were going. The field's major scientific problems were obvious, and means to solve them were readily available. Particularly during World War II and the two subsequent decades, the total number of social psychologists increased rapidly, exciting new research discoveries were often reported, and theoretical developments seemed to promise dramatic advances in the understanding of human behavior.
>
> . . . During the past decade, . . . many social psychologists appear to have lost not only their enthusiasm but also their sense of direction and their faith in the discipline's future. Whether they are experiencing an identity crisis, a paradigmatic crisis, or a crisis of confidence, most seem agreed that a crisis is at hand. . . .
>
> These widespread self-doubts about goals, methods, and accomplishments are by no means unique to social psychology. Similar doubts have been expressed recently within many other areas of psychology, particularly the closely related fields of personality research [Carlson 1971; Fiske 1974], developmental psychology [Wohlwill 1973], and clinical psychology [Albee 1970; Farberow 1973]. Serious self-questioning has developed simultaneously in the other social sciences, including sociology [Gouldner 1970], anthropology [Hymes 1972], and economics [Roberts 1974] (Elms 1975, pp. 967-68).

Without knowing what it is or how to address it, Alan Elms nevertheless has given us an astute description of the crisis that is of the present concern, and has indicated also something about its generality in our science. Moveover, he has included also a hint that the crisis involves an absence of direction. Let me begin to focus the problem a bit by saying that as abundant as the products of the science are, we cannot see where we are going, or even that we are advancing. We are obtaining great masses of knowledge, but somehow that does not resolve the problem, for the knowledge does not seem to make us more knowledgeable, in the way that we would expect. We do scientific work in the specific, but our efforts seem to be just additional elements in a fund of theory, findings, and method that we already do not know what to do with. A central aim of psychology as a science has been to produce scientific findings, that is findings obtained with the sophisticated methods of science. But the success in that endeavor has brought us a further problem, that of finding some meaning in the deluge of theory, fact, and method that has resulted. There is presently no clearly discernible path or character to the development of the science's knowledge. Additional expressions of various psychologists in this regard will be indicated further on. Psychologists in general, as well as psychology's leaders, cannot see where the science is headed, or that it is progressing on the path. The typical psychologist cannot even get a feel for what his science is about, because the materials in it are so diverse and disorganized.

DISUNITY IN PSYCHOLOGY

In the present view there is a crisis in psychology. That is the theme of the statement by Elms that was quoted above. But Elms, as well as the others who have made similar statements, have not described what it is that the crisis is about. Elms says maybe it is "an identity crisis, a paradigmatic crisis, or a crisis of confidence." But that does not tell us what we need to know, that is, what the crisis is, the characteristics that produce the crisis, and the changes that must be made in our science to resolve the crisis.

It is the purpose of the present work to deal with these topics. I might indicate that although this book will appear in one fell swoop, it did not arise in that manner. The observations and ideas expressed here grew out of some special experiences that I have had relevant to these concerns for the past 30 years. The present book is not focally concerned with specific theories. Only in the next to the last chapter will a brief mention of my own theory be presented, as an example of a framework of theory methodology within which to establish unity of study in psychology by means of comprehensive theory. It is relevant to mention, however, that it was in the process of forming that unified theory that the present view of psychology as a science was formulated. The by-products of my work to establish a general, unified theory in psychology provided serendipitous conditions for me to observe the characteristics of psychology with respect to unification. Centrally, the mission of forming a general, unified theory contrasts with the dominant character of the guiding framework of contemporary psychology. Psychology is not and really has never been oriented toward the creation of unity or integration of knowledge in its various areas and interests. There is not a powerful part of psychology devoted to this effort; few, if any, psychologists are concerned with establishing unified theory, and the preponderance of psychology is in fact opposed to such endeavors. Even in the days of the grand theory there was no interest in effecting unification, and no program for doing so. I state these things here definitively, although later discussions will deal with the issues more substantively. At this point I merely refer to some of my early impressions, for it was those impressions that formed the context of discovery and led me to examine the matters involved more closely.

To continue, the serendipity in my experience is that my mission confronted me with characteristics of our science that are not seen by the special-area-oriented psychologist whose work coincides with the separatistic characteristics of the science. That is, in attempting to formulate and promulgate a unified theory in our science, I began to experience how important the divisions of the science were, how the divisive nature of psychology overrode and actually prevented progress towards unified theory. My experience has been, that the science is resistive to the consideration and assessment of general theory; the science does not have a model for what a general theory is. A general theory appears to be equated with a textbook survey, such as would be found in a book in introductory psychology. For this reason, a general theory that treats different areas is considered not to be a theory in the heuristic sense ordinarily accorded real theories. The fact that there are few, or no, other theories to use as comparisons prevents systematic consideration of a general theory, and the latter does not provide an atmosphere conducive to the development of general theories.

This treatment is extended to the subtheories in a general theory. They are not evaluated in the usual way. That is, the subtheory will not be taken out of the general theory and be compared to and evaluated along with other theories in the special area. The special-area psychologist appears reluctant to refer, as an authority source, to the subtheory in a general theory. Perhaps this is because a general theory is equated with introductory textbook treatments, rather than with theory with heuristic quality and one would hesitate to quote a textbook as the source of ideas for original work in a specialized area. The special-area psychologist may also devalue the subtheory because it is associated with other theories in the general theory — other theories with which he is unfamiliar and hence does not think highly of.

These were only personal observations and I will not dwell on them here because I am more interested in certain general things about our science. The main significance of the impressions is the way in which they sensitized me to consider the nature of our science with respect to its unification or integration. These impressions alerted me to other observations of the disparity and competitiveness in psychology. For example, adherents of one theory did not seem to know the position of the opposing theory, and this was true of the most sophisticated works. Similar concepts might be expressed by antagonistic theorists, but the similarity was lost in the commotion of the strife. As a graduate student I began to notice this — because my orientation toward science even then was to establish relatedness in knowledge. However, generally there seemed to be no desire to bring things together — only to demarcate one concept, principle, theory, or analysis from another. Theorists with similar viewpoints seemed motivated by the same spirit of competition with each other, even when the competition served to weaken their common theory with respect to a really different, actually opposing theory. I saw this most clearly in the competition between the learning theories of such men as Hull, Skinner, and Tolman. These theorists and their followers appeared to me to be more interested in opposing each other than in forming a general theory that could then be employed to consider the problems in other areas of psychology, a general theory that would do a better job than nonlearning positions of an oppositional sort.

These and many other observations and impressions made me wonder about the separatistic characteristics of psychology that were involved. I felt that this separatism was even more pronounced when one crossed special areas of study. It was enhanced even more when major divisions in the social sciences were involved. Very frequently, I would read things in one area of psychology, or of another social science, that could be dealt with very well within principles from another area — but which were not. The separatism appeared to me in such cases, and there were many, to be disadvantageous to the science areas involved, in very fundamentally important ways that will be indicated later.

I was, and am, convinced that psychology is a science in its basic character along various lines that I deemed important. But psychology seemed to have a character that was different than other sciences like physics, and chemistry, or biology and its divisions. These advanced sciences currently displayed less separatism, more unity, than my science. In my view of theory in science it was important to state a theory in as general a manner as possible: to generalize principles in the sense of showing the various events and areas for which they are relevant. The nature of psychology appeared to interfere with this. Moreover, my experience with the science told me that the separatism in psychology was a great and general drawback to it, much more important than could be seen in the consideration of specific theories. Confinement to specialty knowledge, a universal characteristic of the contemporary psychologist, did not reveal the central matters involved. Very generally in the science there was no recognition of the worth of a unifying theory of whatever scope, of the need to develop a methodology for unifying efforts, or of the need to consider the topic. Overwhelmed by the very abundance of conflicting, isolated knowledge in psychology, members of the science took this arrangement to reflect its true nature — that increased specialization was the only answer to the problem of diversity.

In the present view, psychology is a science with very powerful tools. It has the sophisticated skills of an advanced science. It can and has produced ingenious apparatus. It has fine experimental ability, and has developed experimental methodology to a high degree. It has a fund of empirical fact — complex, abundant, and wide-ranging. It has many important conceptual elements, and theoretical endeavors of varying degrees of generality. As a consequence of this development, psychology has produced an abundance of theory-fact-methodology products and is capable of producing much more, a superabundance.

The present thesis, centrally, is that we are being drowned in the sea of our own scientific products. We cannot handle that which we have already produced in a way that would make for some general meaning. Yet with each passing month we are faced with a new deluge of knowledge. The crisis in psychology is that of the modern, disunified science that has the tools for disparate knowledge production but not the tools by which to turn disparate knowledge into organized, consensually accepted knowledge. It should be noted that this characteristic of disunity has been recognized before, its generality guarantees that it will not escape unseen. As will be indicated further on, various opinions have noted in one way or another the lack of unity displayed within psychology, and the other social sciences as well. But these notations have been incidental, not systematic considerations. And it is not until one has made a systematic study that the central importance of the topic can be seen. My serendipitous experiences, however, gradually over a period of years, led me to be concerned about unity-disunity in psychology, which in turn led me to more careful examination of the circumstances involved. This consideration has shown me that what is involved is not an interesting although minor characteristic, but instead pertains to matters that have revolutionary importance, hence the title of the present work.

The work thus deals with lack of unity of psychology, with what the lack of unity consists of, with what its sociological and substantive effects are, with the philosophy the disunity engenders and how further disunity is affected by the philosophy, with the inefficacies produced by the disunity and its philosophy, and focally with steps that are necessary to move psychology to a more advanced state as a unified science. These considerations, it is hoped, will reveal new things about a science that has not yet progressed to the state of the advanced, unified sciences. These considerations also provide a basis for confronting the task of composing a methodology for advancing from the disunified to the unified state, to becoming an advanced science.

Realization of the aim of dealing with the characteristic of disunity in psychology requires utilization of literature that is relevant in elaborating the analysis. The first part of the book presents concepts and descriptions from the history and philosophy of science that can be helpful in establishing the general background and context of discourse. Thomas Kuhn, for example, has drawn attention to several things that are significant in the present conception. Thus, he has briefly described the early disorganized state of the natural sciences. However, his treatment of that early state is just a brief mention, in the service of elaborating his concept of the paradigm and of the manner in which science changes through competitions between paradigms (a paradigm being similar to a general approach to an area of study in a science).* The brevity of treatment of the early states of the natural sciences is reasonable since the problems of disorganization are no longer important in these sciences. Nevertheless, as Chapters 2 and 3 will indicate, some of the materials describing those early states are relevant to the present concerns because psychology still faces the problems of a science in early development. It may also be noted that a by-product of this consideration is the demonstration that descriptions of the natural sciences can be significant for understanding the social sciences.

Chapter 2 begins by indicating that psychology began with the philosophy that it was a natural science. Logical positivism later provided a more systematic view of what it meant to be a natural science, of the goals to be striven for as such, focusing on the characteristics of the most advanced theories of the natural sciences — their axiomatic-mathematic characteristics, and the specific manner of their experimental definition of theoretical terms. After dominating the philosophy of science for a long period it finally became recognized that logical positivism was not the final method with which to understand science. It may be added that there is more to science than logic and fact. Moreover, problems that are important to the social sciences do not come into view when one's model of science is adopted from the natural sciences, as has been the fashion. Although there are similarities between the natural and social sciences, there are also differences, and a philosophy of science — such as logical positivism — that is descriptive of advanced parts of the natural sciences cannot be expected to deal with all of the needs of a social science such as psychology. The answer is not a rejection of the logical positivism/natural science position en masse and a retreat to opposing, subjectivist philosophies for the social sciences, as influential works have suggested. Rather, the present view is that there are characteristics of psychology that are not found in the natural sciences, and that must be studied first hand. While there are aspects of the natural sciences that are pertinent to psychology and the other social sciences, and logical positivism had its fruitful products, there are new currents in the philosophy, history, and the sociology of science that have not been dealt with that are important to its present and future development.

Chapter 3 substantively demonstrates that the focus on logic and fact was too narrow. In more contemporary periods, *weltanschauungen* philosophies have said that science is accomplished within broad conceptual perspectives that determine largely what will be done, found, and ac-

---

*The concept of paradigm is employed here, but there are various terms that have been used that essentially stand for the same phenomena — for example, concepts from the works of other philosophers of science (such as Darden 1974; Shapere 1977; or Toulmin 1972) as well as the concept of *zeitgeist* introduced into psychology by Boring (1950).

cepted in the science. One weltanschauung approach is that of Kuhn, who has introduced the term paradigm to stand for the generally accepted theory-problem-method-apparatus framework of an area of study in a science. He also suggested that there is a prescientific state before a science area attains a paradigm. There has been much confusion concerning whether or not psychology (and the other social sciences) have paradigms and thus are like the natural sciences. The confusion arises because there is little understanding of the nature of psychology with respect to what it means to have a paradigm, and there has been no systematic development of what a paradigmatic science is. The present view is that there is a dimension in science of central importance, the dimension extending from disorganization of knowledge to organization of knowledge. At the beginning, sciences have little or no organization to their bodies of knowledge. Then organization begins in specialized areas of study culminating in the formation of a paradigm. As the science progresses, more and more of its areas become paradigmaticized, which is part of becoming a unified science, but only part. It is also important that the several paradigms of a science display theoretical coincidence with one another, in a progressive manner, rather than remain discrepant. Moreover, it is important that there be a growing coincidence and complementarity in the methods and goals of the different areas. The paradigmatic science will also include an explicit or implicit philosophy that is consistent across its specific area interests for the working scientist. An essential aspect of this philosophy is the belief in the unity of the science, a consequent search for unity, and methods for attaining unity of knowledge. In the present view, psychology and the social sciences have not advanced very far in their progression to a unified science, even to the level of having attained paradigms in the specific areas of study. Moreover, neither logical positivism or the new weltanschauungen philosophies have provided a conceptual framework by which psychology can make progress in this most central aspect of science. It is thus necessary to provide a philosophical foundation by which to consider psychology in terms of its unity, and on the basis of this consideration to advance a methodology for dealing with the problems of creating unity in the contemporary preparadigmatic (disorganized) science. These are respectively the concerns of the following two parts of the present work.

The second part of the book develops the previously introduced concepts in the context of considering psychology as a preparadigmatic, or pre-unified, science. The contemporary opinions on this topic — without a basis in systematic consideration — have been inconsistent. Chapter 4 thus describes in some detail the preparadigmatic nature of psychology. The science is seen to have no or virtually no unified areas (paradigms); rather it has innumerable islands of disconnected, conflicting, competitive knowledge. Various dimensions of divisiveness are described. It is suggested that the preunified characteristics of science, that have only been incidently studied by scholars in an historical way in the natural sciences, can be studied as contemporary phenomena in psychology (and seemingly the other social sciences). There are new implications involved in this analysis for the disciplines that study science.

Kuhn's mention of the preparadigm period of science has referred briefly to the disorganized state of knowledge that is involved. Detailed and systematic consideration is needed, for the matters are relevant to contemporary sciences, not just to historical interests. Chapter 5 utilizes materials in the sociology of science to differentiate the preunified from the unified science. Thus, for example, the description of the early priority battles in the natural sciences can be seen to reveal characteristics of the competitive social organization and competitive practices of preparadigmatic and early paradigmatic science. The chapter proposes that there is a progression in the character and results of competition as the science advances from the preunified to the unified state. The characteristics involved, although of a social nature, have profound effects on the substantive aspects of science.

Chapter 6 uses this framework to consider more deeply the effects that preunified competitiveness has upon substantive characteristics of psychology. Examples are provided of how important conceptual materials and empirical findings are maintained as separate, distinct, and competitive bodies of knowledge, when those materials could be presented in a unified, coherent way. The preunified science of psychology is described as artificially diverse, with different standards for relating and unifying knowledge than are found in the advanced, paradigmatic, natural sciences.

Chapter 7 deepens the picture by indicating that there is a philosophy concerning the unity of the science that is part of the preunified science. It is not an explicit systematic philosophy, because the philosophy of science that is overtly dominant is that based upon the natural sciences, and the natural sciences are unified, paradigmatic sciences. Nevertheless, when statements of prominent psychologists are examined it can be seen that the philosophy herein called preparadigmaticism is descriptive of the disorganization of the science, and the philosophy legitimates and prescribes disorganization. Preparadigmaticism in its strong form states that disunity is the basic nature of psychology, and that this must be accepted. Since a philosophy of science is prescriptive, and preparadigmaticism provides no foundation for unifying endeavors in the preparadigmatic science, it is important to introduce a unificationist philosophy for the preunified science — which is a purpose of the present work.

The third and last part of the book introduces consideration of methodological issues relevant to the modern preunified science and describes means for creating unified theory out of the disorganized knowledge in such a science. Chapter 8 indicates that unification of knowledge in psychology necessitates the development of methodological goals and skills that are not presently operative in the science. If, as is the thesis of this book, the knowledge of the science is artifically disorganized because of the preunified nature of the science, then potentially monumental progress may be attained by solving the problems of the disorganization of knowledge. This first presentation of these topics, as derived from the preceding analysis of the preunified science of psychology, is seen as a call for systematic attention to the important methodological problems involved.

Chapter 8 deals with creation of unification in subareas of knowledge in psychology. Chapter 9 deals with a methodological approach to the creation of large structures of unified knowledge. The discussion suggests that the traditional fields of study in psychology are related to each other and that an aim of psychology should be the creation of unified theory structures interrelating the fields and explicating their relationships. There are both same-level and hierarchical relationships between presently separated areas of knowledge. In the latter case one field (or area) will be basic to another and the latter will in turn be basic to yet another field. The methodology outlined composes a general approach to construction of comprehensive, unified theory in psychology, independent of the particular theory approach that is employed.

Chapter 10 concludes by discussing the implications of the preceding analyses of psychology for the development of the science as a unified — paradigmatic — science. In the present view psychology has in its years as a productive preunified science acquired knowledge — factual, theoretical, of apparatus and method — that can provide the foundation for a unified science. These elements are of great importance, which is disguised by the fact that the elements are now considered as inconsistent, disorganized, competitive, and mutually debilitating. With a unificationist philosophy, with a methodology for creating unification, with the creation of unified theory and the use of that which is presently available, it is suggested that psychology has the elements now by which to make revolutionary progress toward becoming a unified science. Such developments have yielded immense power in other sciences, and there is reason to believe this will be the case in the social sciences such as psychology. It is the purpose of the present book to deal with these topics.

Chapter 2

More to Science than Logic and Fact

I have said that there is a crisis in psychology and that it is a crisis of disunity. There remains the task of developing that thesis as well as the paths by which to treat the problems involved. Such matters are the stuff of a philosophy of science of psychology — in the area that is of concern. In developing these matters it will be the better part of reason to relate them to the extent possible to relevant developments in other fields of study that deal with the characteristics of science. As will be touched upon in later discussions, although science has sometimes been considered solely in terms of the formal methods of study that it uses and the formal theories that it creates, there is much more to science than that. For one thing, the general conception regarding the area of study of interest to the science, and the general conception of how that study should be conducted, may be of central importance in guiding the form the science takes. Sometimes the general conception is explicitly announced and accepted. But there may also be circumstances in which the guiding conception, or at least parts of the guiding conception, are not explicit or are not expressed formally. Yet they may nevertheless be operative characteristics of the science that still have a guiding role. We will be interested in both types.

PSYCHOLOGY AS A NATURAL SCIENCE

Perhaps the best example of how a philosophy can guide a science is given by the conception that was effective in launching the development of the field of psychology. Psychology as an independent science is just over 100 years old. Prior to that time the study of what would now fall within the field of psychology would have been considered to be a part of philosophy. The natural sciences previously had made their individual separations from the "mother," natural philosophy. And the success of the natural sciences was apparent. From philosophical musings, and informal, naturalistic methods of observations, they had grown even by the late nineteenth century to be imposing bodies of method and knowledge.

It is no wonder that formation of psychology should attempt to follow the same pattern, and do so within the same philosophy of science framework that was so successful for the natural sciences. And that is what psychology's premier historian has said about Wilhelm Wundt, the recognized founder of the science. "It is quite reasonable, then, that Wundt should also have felt the need for stressing the fact that psychology too, as physiological psychology, is a science" (Boring 1950, p. 319). Anthony Giddens has more generally described this same process for the social sciences of sociology, anthropology, economics, and history.

> Both Comte and Marx wrote in the shadow of the triumphs of natural science, and both regarded the extension of science to the study of human conduct in society as a direct outcome of the progressive march of human understanding towards man himself. . . . An end to mystery, and an end to mystification: This is what Comte and Marx alike anticipated and strove for. . . . [They sought] to bring into being a science of society which would reproduce, in the study of human social life, the same kind of sensational illumination and explanatory power already yielded up by the sciences of nature (Giddens 1976, pp. 12–13).

It is interesting to note also the great similarity in this thinking to that which was involved in the later establishment of behaviorism in psychology, as will be indicated by quoting a passage of John Watson in the next section. To continue, however, Murray Levine has described the dynamic of making psychology into a natural science in a different way that has significance in the present context. "[O]ne can also make a good case that the 100-year-old collective decision, about what psychology's method was to be was, at heart, a political and social decision designed to give the newly emerging field of psychology independence from philosophy, and standing with the earlier developed physical sciences" (1974, p. 662). It should be stressed that while this decision, this conception of what psychology should be, can be stated very simply, it had far-reaching effects upon the characteristics of psychology. Some of these effects are of concern to us, for it has been recognized that the "classic view of the natural sciences" as the model for psychology "survives more or less intact as the contemporary, dominant view" (Sampson 1978, p. 1332).

The fact is that the idea that psychology should be a science in the mold of the natural sciences was pretty much an extrapolation in the crucial time of the formation of the science. It was by no means clear that there was a subject matter in the area that could be productively approached through the use of natural science methods of study. Pretty generally, psychology was thought of as the study of the mind, or consciousness. And the mind is ineffable, like the soul. The latter is the appropriate concern of religion, not science. The mind also could be something to speculate on, but was it of the stuff that lends itself to the methods of observation that had been shown to be so successful in the natural sciences? How does one observe, measure, and do experiments on something that cannot be observed?

The early experimental psychologists began to answer this question in different ways. While the workings of the mind could not be directly observed, perhaps indexes of the mind could be employed. Thus, for example, one might present different tasks to the subject that presumably demanded different mental processes. One might then measure the length of time involved and if there were differences one would have a measurement of the duration of the different mental processes. Measurement could be considered one step toward experimental specification. Similarly, one could hope to conduct experiments involving presentation of various stimuli to the human subject, presumably with different effects upon the mind, using the subject's report of his mental experiences to specify the contents and the working of the mind. One could also conduct experiments on animals and humans that involved presenting different circumstances and noting what the systematic effects were on the organism's behavior. One could infer from the circumstances that had been presented and from the behavior the organism displayed what the mental processes were that determined how the organism behaved.

Many experiments were conducted that would fit into such types of methodological strategies. Many experiments are conducted today that we could also see as examples, although the conceptual, methodological, and apparatus elements would be much more advanced now. Stated in simple terms, the original model of natural science involved systematic study of psychological events through the conduct of formal experimentation to verify one's conceptual or theoretical formulations. The methods of the conduct of the experimentation were very important, and it was important that this experimentation meet the standards of objectivity that would be acceptable to the more advanced sciences.

THE SOPHISTICATION OF BEHAVIORISM
AND LOGICAL POSITIVISM

Thus many experiments were conducted in the framework that has been briefly outlined. But that is not to say that there was complete satisfaction with the methods that were employed and the findings that resulted. This was not an argument with the conception that psychology was to be like the natural sciences. However, there was dissatisfaction with accepting the study of something that is ineffable and thus not susceptible to the methods of objective and direct observation. Watson said very clearly that Wundt's mind (consciousness) was simply a substitution for the religious term soul (Watson 1930, p. 3). Moreover, there was dissatisfaction with much of what was resulting from the study of the mind. The method of having subjects introspect on their own mental processes particularly seemed not to be objective on the one hand, and on the other to be producing conflicting, unstable results. "[It was] felt that the 30 odd barren years since the establishment of Wundt's laboratory had proved conclusively that the so-called introspective psychology of Germany was founded on wrong hypotheses — that no psychology which included the religious mind-body problem could ever arrive at verifiable conclusions" (Watson 1930, p. 4).

In the second decade of the twentieth century the weaknesses of the approach of studying the mind through introspection were made apparent by the inconsistencies produced. Another general conception thus arose that rejected part of the guiding framework, that part that set the study of the mind as the task of psychology. Considering psychology as a science was not at issue, that remained as the central guide, but a new framework began to be constructed about that foundation, as we can see in the words of John Watson, himself one of the central builders.

> [The behaviorists] decided either to give up psychology or else to make it a natural science. They saw their brother-scientists making progress in medicine, in chemistry, in physics. Every new discovery in those fields was of prime importance; every new element isolated in one laboratory could be isolated in some other laboratory; each new element was immediately taken up in the warp and woof of science as a whole. . . . The behaviorist asks: Why don't we make what we can *observe* the real field of psychology? . . . You will find, then, the behaviorist working like any other scientist. His sole object is to gather facts about behavior — verify his data — subject them both to logic and to mathematics (the tools of every scientist) (Watson 1930, pp. 5–6).

We can see the similarity here to the previously presented description of Comte's and Marx's interest in making the social sciences into natural sciences. Rather than the mind being the focus of study in psychology, Watson declared that the two essential elements to be dealt with were the environment (analyzed into stimulus events) and behavior (analyzed into response elements). Studying these elements would not involve inferences concerning an ineffable, subjective, evanescent mental process. Stimuli and responses were objective, publicly observable, manipulable events — hard facts.

Interestingly, this turn toward the observable specification of the

things in which psychology should be interested coincided with a very harmonious development in the philosophy of science. Mackenzie (1977) has
suggested, as a matter of fact, that psychology gave some impetus to the
philosophical development. The philosophical development was logical
positivism. First, however, it is relevant to mention the philosophy of
positivism itself, which was the progenitor. As was indicated in the first
chapter, humans can not only act, they can step back and consider how
they have acted. A philosophy of science can be constituted of observations
of what scientists do, and positivism may be considered one of the early
such descriptions. The statements of Watson (and those that Giddens refers
to Comte and Marx) were those of a simple positivism, which is that science
is based on observation, on fact.

> [Behaviorism] may never make a pretense of being a *system*. Indeed
> systems in every scientific field are out of date. We collect our facts from
> observation. Now and then we select a group of facts and draw certain
> general conclusions about them. In a few years as new experimental data
> are gathered by better methods, even these tentative general conclusions
> have to be modified. . . . Experimental technique, the accumulation of
> facts by that technique, occasional tentative consolidation of these facts
> into a theory or an hypothesis describe our procedure in science. Judged
> upon this basis, behaviorism is a true natural science (italics added) (Wat-
> son 1930, pp. 18–19).

As Watson's statement indicates, the preoccupation of positivism is
that science is to be composed of observations and observational methods.
Observations in this philosophy of science were considered sacrosanct,
purely objective, the last arbitor of scientific issues. Later, however, this
philosophy of science was developed also to analyze systematically what
was considered to be the other central realm of science, theory. Theory was
considered to be a neutral language, with logical characteristics that could
be analyzed separate from empirical concerns. The goal of the theorist (or
philosopher of science) was to examine theory, to help put it in its correct
form — which was an axiomatic form in which there are basic assumptions
or principles from which propositions are derived according to the rules of
logic or mathematics. Some terms in a scientific theory will be defined by
observable events. When the terms in the theory are given such empirical,
factual definitions (according to the rules of operational definition), the
propositions that result are then statements about the happenings in the
empirical world. Establishing such theories is what science consists of, according to logical positivism, and the philosophy of science was to be concerned with improving these elements of logical analysis of theory and the
rules of definition or correspondence of terms in the theory with empirical

observations. Questions that did not involve things in one of these two realms were considered to be irrelevant to science and the philosophy of science.

The tenets of logical positivism were applied to the problems of psychology by various members of the science and some philosophers of science. Gustav Bergmann and Kenneth Spence (1941), for example, wrote on the topic of how theoretical terms in psychology must be linked to observations — the concern of operational definition — and how this affected theory construction in psychology. In doing so they analyzed different theoretical orientations in psychology. The following statement indicates the influence of logical positivism and operationism on psychology theories.

> A number of psychologists, Tolman (1951), Skinner (1931), and Stevens (1939), stimulated by the writings of Bridgman (1928, 1936), have centered their efforts largely on the *empirical component* of scientific method. Under the watchword of operationism, they have carefully considered and laid down the requirements [concerning observability] that scientific concepts must fulfill in order to insure testability and thus empirical meaning. The second aspect, the *formal (theoretical) component* of scientific endeavor has been brought to the forefront in psychology principally through the writings of Hull (1937, 1939, 1940–41) and Lewin (1938, 1940) (Bergmann and Spence 1941, p. 1).

To elaborate on this development in psychology, Skinner's approach was once called descriptive behaviorism. The term indicated Skinner's concern with observable stimuli and observable responses, and the description of the relations between the two. For Skinner the essence of psychology was to be explication of the relationship $R = f (S, A)$, where R refers to a response and S to the stimulus whose presentation results in the occurrence of the response, and A refers to other variables that affect the strength of the response that is elicited when the stimulus is presented.

> The study of the reflex, then, leads to the formulation of two kinds of law. The first are laws describing correlations of stimulus and response.... Secondly, there are laws describing changes in any aspect of these primary relationships as functions of third variables.... It is difficult to discover any aspect of the behavior or organisms that may not be described with a law of one or the other of these forms (Skinner 1931, pp. 457–58).

Skinner's positivistic philosophy of science has been very much in harmony with that of John Watson's original behaviorism and Bridgman's operationism, when Skinner has stated his philosophy. Skinner has been concerned with the definition of the terms he employs in his learning theory. He has criticized the interest in formalizing theory, rejecting the use of the systematic hypothetico-deductive methods that involve deriving hypotheses from a formal theory as the inspiration for the conduct of experiments (see preface of Skinner 1969). Skinner has promulgated the method of experimentation, using his apparatus, in which reinforcement (reward) variables are manipulated and the effects upon the rate of occurrence of a simple response are charted. His methodology was said to be that of progressively increasing the generality of empirical principles via experimentation—a completely inductive enterprise (Skinner 1945, 1950, 1959, 1961, 1963, 1969, 1975) that is still part of contemporary psychology (see Bayes 1980).

Tolman also was centrally concerned with the observational or operational definition of terms, and in fact his approach was sometimes called operational behaviorism. Tolman's methodology involved the attempt to bring behaviorism back to the consideration of cognitive activities — those activities that Watson, and later Skinner, eschewed as a proper subject matter for an objective psychology. Behaviorism was based upon observable events and this was the justification for outlawing cognitive concepts. And logical positivism had laid down the laws for the observational definition of terms in a scientific theory. Those who were interested in mental events had to meet those specifications. To circumvent the rejection of internal, cognitive events Tolman introduced the concept of the intervening variable to psychological considerations (1936). The intervening variable methodology outlined a strategy for objective definition of inferred cognitive events. "[M]ental processes, whether they be those of another or of ourselves, will figure only in the guise of objectively definable intervening variables" (Tolman 1950, p. 88). "Or (to borrow a phrase from William James) the sole 'cash-value' of mental processes lies, I shall assert, in their character as a set of intermediating functional processes which interconnect between the initiating causes of behavior, on the one hand, and the final resulting behavior itself, on the other" (Tolman 1951, p. 88).

Hull (1943) and his co-worker Spence (1956, 1960), continued the interest in the methodology of the definition of intervening concepts, moving in the direction of applying the methodology not to mental processes but to more basic concerns such as habit and drive. The approach was formalistic and depended very centrally on the elaborate use of intervening variables in the theory construction task. The task was to formulate a general theory that would precisely describe the relationships of the independent variables (or causes), such as stimulus presentation in conditioning, deprivation of food, the massing of conditioning and hence work, and the like, upon the dependent variables (or effects) such as the strength of the organism's behavior. The intervening variables (theoretical terms) included learning (or habit strength), drive, inhibition, and so on. These intervening variables were defined solely by the independent variables and dependent variables. For example, habit strength was defined by such independent variables as number of conditioning trials, the intensity of the stimuli involved in the conditioning, and so on. As another example, drive (motivation) was defined by time of deprivation of the reinforcing (rewarding) stimulus that is relevant to the conditioning. The relationships of the intervening variables were also an integral part of the theory — for example, habit strength and drive were seen to combine in a multiplicative way to yield another intervening variable that was related by other mathematical functions to yet other intervening variables. Finally the combination of intervening variables would yield mathematical predictions concerning the strength of behavior that the organism would display in the relevant situation — that is, the amplitude of the organism's response, the probability of occurrence of the response, and so on. The theoretical structure, relating the antecedent events to the consequent behavioral indexes of learning, was impressively complex.

As this description indicates, the theory was in statement precise, objective, and mathematically sophisticated. The strategy was to make assumptions concerning the mathematical functions relating the independent variables to the first-line intervening variables. Mathematical functions relating these intervening variables to each other to produce second-line intervening variables were posited. The specification of the second-line intervening variables could then be used to project the mathematical function leading to the predicted behavior variables. The various assumed functions were established on the basis of the best available evidence and then the strategy was to derive experimental hypotheses from the theoretical body and to conduct relevant parametric studies to refine the mathematical functions. The deduced hypotheses and their experimental exploration were done to more precisely establish the functions. The program was described as hypothetico-deductive in nature. The theory was axiomatized. The use of the language of mathematics was integral. Hull's theory followed the criteria of logical positivism and the model of the advanced theory described for the natural sciences, and is perhaps the best known, most general use of the methodology of logical positivism in psychology. This was the most advanced form of theory in that era of the logical-positivist approach as applied to psychology. Hull's conception became a forceful model of what theory was, or should strive to be, in psychology. It gave marked impetus, for one thing, to the conduct of precise, controlled studies to improve the mathematical functions involved in the theory — in a manner that would initate the characteristics displayed in the natural sciences. As a general model it is influential in experimental psychology today.

S. S. Stevens (1939, 1951) was another psychologist who accepted the logical-positivist analysis of science and scientific theory, and who felt that the emphasis on operational definition made by Bridgman was of central importance to the development of theory in psychology. Stevens indicated the necessity of distinguishing the two realms of science, the formal (or theoretical) and the empirical (real world) realms of events. He stated that problems arose when these two were not distinguished and their independence indicated. Thus, one problem occurred when it was felt that mathematics developments — developments in a formal system — could only be made if it could be shown that the relationships depicted in the mathematical statements had real-world counterparts. For example, there was at one time resistance to admitting the study of negative numbers to mathematics, on the grounds that there were no negative events in nature. It may be added that another problem occurs when it is assumed that any statement that can be derived from a formal system has truth value for the real world. As a consequence of this misplaced faith, theoretical bodies have had great prestige and their implications have been followed in areas that did not apply. Numerologists, for example, derived statements from number analyses, presuming the statements to apply to worldly events when this was untrue. Examples of such errors will be given further on in the context of making other points. A fundamental concern of Stevens was with the appropriate linking of the formal theory elements with appropriate empirical events in the act of measurement in psychological study.

THE PASSING OF LOGICAL POSITIVISM

In the philosophy of science, logical positivism was the dominant view for several decades, providing the standards for what constituted science and what could be considered to be scientific theory. But cracks in the monolith began to appear, in various areas of consideration. For one thing, there was criticism concerning the sacrosanct nature of observations. It became clear that facts are not even facts, at least as the final anchoring bastion of authority, uncontaminated by theory influences (Popper 1963; Hanson 1967, 1969; Kuhn 1962; Feyerabend 1970 a, b; Lakatos 1970). Imre Lakatos provides a clear example that facts are a mix of theory and observation in a manner that must temper the empiricist's view of the ultimate objectivity of his or her criteria.

> Galileo claimed that he could 'observe' mountains on the moon...and that these 'observations' refuted the time-honoured theory that celestial bodies are faultless crystal balls. But his 'observations' were not 'observational' in the sense of being observed by the — unaided — senses: their reliability depended on the reliability of his telescope — and of the optical theory of the telescope — which was violently questioned by his con-

temporaries. It was not Galileo's — pure, untheoretical — *observations* that confronted Aristotelian *theory* but rather Galileo's 'observation' in the light of his optical theory that confronted the Aristotelians' 'observations' in the light of their theory of the heavens (Lakatos 1970, p. 98).

Moreover, the world is composed of an infinity of events that we can observe. By what means do we choose to observe certain of these events as those that are crucial in the construction of our scientific theories? Skinner, as an example of a simple positivist, says we must build psychological science by making observations, and his own research was largely restricted to the study of how reinforcement (reward) scheduling affected the rate of response of rats and pigeons in a simple experimental situation. But determining that this type of observable event is the central datum for a science of psychology rests upon theoretical grounds. Nature does not thrust the types of events to be specially studied upon the scientist — there is selection involved, and that is based upon a conceptual framework. Although Skinner does not grant this in his methodological statements, the importance of the study of reinforcement is based on a conceptual body that had a long history of development in empirical-theoretical efforts of early philosophers; as we can see in preceding concepts in the classic philosophies of hedonism, in the utilitarian hedonism of Jeremy Bentham, and in the pleasure principle of Freud, and so on (see Staats 1975). Accidental discoveries of phenomena do occur, of course. But by and large science operates in a constructive way, guided by previously established conceptual frameworks. As we will see, it is important that we consider these in our concern with psychology as a science.

Furthermore, the other major province of logical positivism came under attack. Logical positivism's view of scientific theory was drawn from observation of the products of the natural sciences — actually, those areas in the natural sciences that were the most developed towards axiomatic, mathematical theoretical structures. Whether or not this type of scientific theory could be considered to be representative of that which should exist in all areas of science came into question. This topic is of special interest in the present development, and will be discussed additionally a bit further on. What I want to indicate at this point is that logical positivism fell onto bad times in the philosophy of science. Moreover, that disenchantment spread to psychology, where opponents of the psychological approaches that were based in logical positivism gathered their voices of criticism.

Opponents of Psychology's Natural Science/Logical Positivism View

When there is a crisis in some social institution or area of human endeavor it is typical to question the foundation or basic system of the institution or area involved. This can apply to the structures that occur in science as in other social endeavors. It has been said that there is in psychology today a crisis and we might thus expect that the foundations of the science have come into question. Sigmund Koch has been one of the most vehement critics of the framework that has guided psychology, as can be seen from the following passage, which rejects the original and basic rationale that has justified the formation and conduct of psychology.

> Ever since its stipulation into existence as an independent science, psychology has been far more concerned with being a science than with courageous and self-determining confrontation with its historically constituted subject matter. Its history has been largely a matter of emulating the methods, forms, symbols of the established sciences, especially physics. In so doing, there has been an inevitable tendency to retreat from broad and intensely significant ranges of its subject matter, and to form rationales for so doing which could only invite further retreat (Koch 1961, p. 629).

Koch (1981) has stated that psychology is not an independent science, separated from philosophy. He says that attempts to treat the field in this manner have been ill-advised, involving the ludicrous characteristics of scientism, that is, the rejection of meaningful investigation in favor of studying trivia in a manner that gives the appearance of science. He states that psychology should be more concerned with earnest speculation on the imponderables concerning human nature that have bewitched humankind through the milennia. Koch questions the ability of psychology to work within the framework of the natural sciences if it is to deal with its centrally important subject matter.

> If empirical decidability (which, incidentally, itself cannot be *decided in advance*) is the criterion for bounding the meaningful, one then has a perfect rationale for selecting for study only domains that seem to give access to the generation of stable research findings. If any domain seems refractory to conquest by the narrow range of methods (usually borrowed from the natural sciences and mutilated in the process) held to be sacred by the work force, then, obviously, *meaningful* questions cannot be asked concerning the domain, and that domain is expendable. If one cannot achieve stable findings when the dependent variable is of "subjective" cast, then eliminate such data and concentrate on behavior (Koch 1981, p. 122).

With heavy irony, Koch thus says that the essential aspects of human nature cannot be studied by the methods of natural science, and that those who follow the natural science approach can do so only by ruling out of study those centrally important things for which their methods are not suited. The end result is a hodgepodge of trivialities. Willem van Hoorn (1972) is another example of a philosophically oriented psychologist who has concluded that the model of science that psychology has followed is incorrect, referring to E. G. Boring's influential position.

> Boring and his fellow-scientists modelled psychology after an ideal of natural science. . . . Perhaps one of the reasons operationism failed in psychology is due to the fact that psychology is not a natural science (van Hoorn p. 26).

Erwin Esper, an historian of psychology, has also cautioned against the view that the characteristics of the natural sciences can serve as a model for psychology in saying "[T]he history of psychology reveals over and over again the pathetic eagerness of psychologists to adopt *analogically* the current fashion in physics or chemistry; well-known historical examples are the psychical mechanics of Herbart and the mental mechanics and mental chemistry of the Mills" (Esper 1964, p. 9). The important point here, however, is to indicate that there is a well formed opinion that considers psychology not to have the characteristics of a natural science (see also Gergen 1973; Giorgi, Knowles, and Smith 1979; Sampson 1978), in general. Gergen (see Gergen, Greenberg, and Willis 1980) considers psychology to be an historical science, rather than a natural science, and the knowledge of psychology to be relativistic rather than to involve progressive advancement toward empirical truth or reality. There are also those who are more detailed in their criticism in specifically challenging the appropriateness of employing logical positivism as a philosophy of science for psychology. Koch has radically rejected the developments in psychology that were guided by logical positivism and operationism.

> That happy interval commenced in the early 1930s and may, in modified form, still be with us to this very day. The mark of the Age of Theory . . . was that all activities were to be subordinated to production of a "commodity" called "theory" in a *quite special sense defined by the Age.* . . . The overarching cosmology of this interval was based on a loose melange of vaguely apprehended ideas derived from logical positivism, operationism, and neopragmatism. . . . In continued epistemopathic effort. I have succeeded — at least to my own satisfaction — in demonstrating the dysfunctionality of each statute in the Age of Theory code (Koch 1981, p. 261).

It is interesting that some of Koch's criticisms of logical positivism as it was and is applied in psychology coincide with my own criticisms, although my views and Koch's are in basic opposition in other respects. We can see also very general criticism of the logical-positivistic view of scientific theory for the social sciences in general, expressed in the following words.

> Beside the seeming certainties of [Newtonian physics] the achievements of
> the social sciences do not look impressive.... However, a sort of yearning
> for the arrival of a social-scientific Newton remains common enough,
> even if today there are perhaps many more who are sceptical of such a pos-
> sibility than still cherish such a hope. But those who still wait for a New-
> ton are not only waiting for a train that won't arrive, they're in the wrong
> station altogether (Giddens 1976, p. 13).

Giddens thus says that a philosophy of science (logical positivism) based
upon the type of science engaged in by Newton is a misleading guide for
the social sciences. The present view, however, is that logical positivism is
not an all-or-nothing type of phenomenon. There have been many positive
effects of logical positivism on psychology, and these continue to exert their
effects. The philosophy, however, has also had errant influence on the field.
And, most centrally to the present concerns, there are very important
lacunae in logical positivism as a philosophy by which to guide the development of psychology as a science. Significant parts of the present work attempt to fill in these lacunae, but other matters must be discussed first, for
example, the disadvantages of accepting the extreme view that the natural-
science/logical-positivism/behaviorism view of psychology should be completely rejected.

Discarding the Baby with the Bath Water

As has been indicated in chapter 1, there are philosophers of science
who rather completely reject psychologists who still employ elements of the
logical positivism/behaviorism methods of science. Two quotations were
presented in the first chapter that criticized writings in the social sciences
for their concern with the rules of definitions, that is, the manner in which
theoretical terms are defined by observations. Logical positivism has become passé in the philosophy of science. Therefore social scientists who
employ elements of that philosophy are discredited. Let us examine the result of that approach.

In the present view criticism of psychology for its concern with definitions is misguided, for psychology faces special problems of the definition
of its concepts. There is the problem of observational specification of behavioral or mental processes that reside within the individual and that cannot be directly observed. Watson (and Skinner) solved this problem by ruling the study of such processes out of the realm of a scientific psychology.
Tolman, another behaviorist, was not willing to dispense with the possibility of studying such processes. He felt it must be done, but in an obective
way. He took the lead in introducing the methodology of the intervening
variable (1936). In essence he said that internal states could be defined appropriately, if the definition involved antecedent stimulus conditions as

well as consequent behavioral outcomes. Thus, for example, the internal emotional state of anger might be defined by certain antecedent conditions and the resulting angry behavior of the individual. Hull (1943) developed the methodology in elegance and complexity and in experimental stipulation with his theory of learning, which involved intervening variables such as habit strength, drive, inhibition, excitatory potential, momentary excitatory potential, and so on, all in the context of basic animal conditioning studies.

Spence (1944) provided important contributions to this general framework by stipulating that there are different types of theoretical terms or constructs in psychology. There are theoretical constructs, like the term learning, that are defined by the fact that providing certain training experiences for an organism will result in certain changes in the organism's behavior. What is involved is a cause-and-effect relationship and a multitude of studies have been conducted that specify in detail the way that manipulations of the environmental experiences can have a variety of lawful effects upon the behavior of the organism.

As Spence indicated, however, the type of theoretical term that we illustrate here is different from other terms that are employed in psychology. Let us take the example of intelligence. We have various observations that people differ with respect to the goodness of their behavior in many situations. In school some children learn easily, some with difficulty. Some people's behavior in various life situations has the same quality: they solve problems well, they reason well, they express themselves well, they put two and two together well, and so on, and other people do such things less well. Intelligence tests have been devised to measure this quality, which is assumed to be an internal quality, process, or structure that people have that determines their external behavior. The point here, however, is that the term intelligence does not have the same type of meaning as the term learning. Learning is defined by cause-and-effect relationships of events. Intelligence is not. There are no systematic manipulations of causal events that result in altering the learning ability, reasoning ability, and so on, that people take to be a reflection of intelligence. The study of intelligence has more substantially involved systematic research on the manner in which intelligence test results are predictive of the performance of individuals in other life situations. These are the findings that give intelligence its primary meaning — that is, that high test-intelligence scores are predictive of high academic performance in school, and so on.

It should be noted that the two types of theoretical terms — learning and intelligence — have different properties. The term intelligence, and the investigations involved in the definition of the term, can give us prediction (albeit not perfect prediction). If we know the individual's intelligence we can predict school performance. But we cannot with the information given by the term intelligence do anything about affecting school performance. The term intelligence does not provide information concerning what conditions can be manipulated to produce high intelligence (although there are claims that the causes of intelligence are either genetic or environmental) and better performance in school and other places. It should be noted that there are terms in psychology that have even less specification of causative events. Let us take the example of the term readiness as it occurs in educational psychology. It has been observed that children can be taught things easily at one age that they will learn only with great difficulty, or not at all, at an earlier age. The theoretical term readiness has been invoked to explain this age-related difference. Readiness has traditionally meant that there is some biological maturation process that develops with age, and that some level of maturation must be reached before the child is capable of learning particular things. Biological maturation, thus, is inferred to be the causative agent, but this cause is not firmly specified by observation of actual maturational events that enhance learning. Without introducing additional information (for example, by tests to measure children's readiness), we cannot obtain even prediction from this theoretical term, not to mention the ability to do something about the child's ability to learn.

There are thus different types of concepts in psychology, and they have different properties. When we say that the child is doing well in school because of learning — and the concept of learning refers to a specified program by which to establish prereading skills in the child — the statement has different potential properties than when we say that the child is doing well in school because she is intelligent, or because she has reached the necessary stage of readiness.

This type of analysis is helpful in theory construction. And the analysis contributes in providing methods by which to evaluate different theories in psychology, by which to indicate what the properties of different theories are, and to indicate the types of knowledge that different methods of study will provide. Arguments and competitions between theoretical orientations occur because the proponents of the theories do not recognize the differences that theories can have on the basis of the manner in which the terms in the theories are observationally defined. The fact is that the differences in theories that arise through the methodology by which the terms in the theories are defined, are not universally understood in psychology, or in our general language. Since much of the theory in psychology is very close to the common language, with all of its ambiguities and weaknesses, it is important that students in psychology receive training in the variations in theory, and the principles of theoretical construct definition — regardless of the fact that these topics are no longer in vogue in the philosophy of science. Logical positivism still retains such important guides.

Relative Realism

As another example of discarding the whole when only a part has been criticized, let me refer to the criticism that observations cannot be considered to be the pure, objective, independent events that constitute the bedrock of science in general and psychology in particular. Methodologists in psychology and the other social sciences have jumped on the philosophers' criticism of logical positivism's concept of the purity and independence of observation as a means of criticizing the natural science approach in general (Weimer 1979). Discrediting methods for psychology that are based on observation, because observations cannot be perfectly objective and independent, is misguided. In the present view, we do not have to assume that the empirical world is capable of being known objectively, without taint by one's conception, in a certain and pure manner, before we can take an empirical position and recognize observations as a fundamentally important source of knowledge. The present conception of the growth of scientific knowledge admits the interaction of theory and observation always. Moreover, it states that this is the basic form of knowledge acquisition. Individuals with different conceptions observe different things, for example. And what constitutes empirical fact will change over time, with a change in conception. Thus, our conceptions influence selectively which events we will observe and how we will interpret them. Science issues, certainly in psychology, are rarely capable of being settled through resort to some consensually accepted realm of observable fact. Of the many theory controversies in psychology, I cannot recall any that were resolved by the science through observational proof; however, these disclaimers and criticisms do not suggest that observations are not a fundamental underpinning of science.

In brief, the present view is that humans began their knowledge quest with poor conceptions and made poor observations. But added experience led to the rejection of some aspects of the conception and the support of others. Through this conceptual improvement it was possible to make better observations. The two realms are in continuous, progressive interaction in producing a progressively refined fund of knowledge — a fund that is not without error, that contains distortion, that is idealized, and that is never a perfect knowledge mirror of the world. Although not much space can be devoted to these questions of epistemology in this study, the principles in this simple statement reflect a view that is basic to the present approach, as will be seen in some of the later discussions. It should be noted that hermeneutic philosophies, concerned with understanding, versus the empiricism of the natural sciences, have described a process that has similarities to the conceptual-observational interaction view outlined above. "[T]here is an acknowledgement of . . . the 'hermeneutic circle': that no description free from 'interpretation in the light of presuppositions is possible'" (Giddens 1976, p. 52). The method of hermeneutics involves the idea that one enters an area of study, such as historical study or literary interpretation, with language skills that involve presuppositions, but that the study can yield interpretations that allow one to change those presuppositions, and those changes allow one to improve one's additional study of the area, which again works back to improve one's interpretations, which again improve one's study, and so on. "All understanding demands some measure of pre-understanding whereby further understanding is possible," states Giddens in describing the hermeneutic circle of Hans-Georg Gadamer and Martin Heidegger (Giddens 1976, p. 56).

The present view, to give it a name, represents a *relative realism*. It accepts that there is a real world that can be known, at least in part, through observation. This is not to say that the observation is entirely true or complete, or that it ever will be perfect, uncontaminated by one's conception or beliefs. Nevertheless, we as individuals come to know, in some imperfect sense, something about the real world, and science has developed special methods for improving that knowledge in certain areas. In general we are capable of progressively improving our observations, and we have much evidence of science's ability to do this. It is comforting, it may be noted, to have support from modern philosophers who assert freely in present times a philosophy of realism that is close to that used by working scientists.

> Underlying most contemporary work on the growth of scientific knowledge, as well as work on the nature of theories, . . . is the basic assumption that science can and does yield knowledge descriptive of how the world really is. . . . Thus a strong commitment to . . . realism is characteristic of the new philosophy of science today . . . (Suppe, 1977c, p. 652).

Separating the Wheat from the Chaff

It is not the present intention to deal systematically with such topics here. Rather two examples have been given that the natural-science/logical-positivism approach should not be discarded in toto because some of its parts are in error, or partially in error. A general approach such as logical-positivism, or the behaviorism that has incorporated parts of logical positivism, consists of many elements. There can be productive parts of a general conceptual structure mixed in with parts that are nonproductive, or even in error. In fact this is the usual case. When a field has a number of such general positions, frequently there will be overlap in the elements of the positions. Even though, as will be seen, two general positions may be considered to be quite different, opposite, and in competition, they may nevertheless overlap in part on the basis of common elements. There is a tendency in sciences such as psychology, for reasons that will become more clear later, for general positions or theories to be considered as a whole, and to be accepted or rejected as a whole. Various effects derive from this process, it is suggested. For example, using the present case, logical positivism was accepted as a whole for a period by a majority of those in relevant fields. Competitive positions were not held in the same esteem. On the basis of its inadequacies, logical positivism is being rejected, again as a whole. But, if the philosophy contains important elements, as is the present view, then at some later point down the road those elements will appear in a new conceptualization. In the interim, opposing positions may hold the stage, since they too contain valuable elements that were set aside during the period logical positivism dominated. We have many such cyclical phenomena in psychology, for example, nature versus nurture positions, behavioristic versus cognitive positions, and so on.

What this amounts to is throwing the baby out with the bath water, in a manner that retards progress in the science, for it would be much more effective if productive elements from opposing approaches could be joined, rather than having oscillation involving repeated total acceptances followed by total rejections. (This methodology will be elaborated on in the last part of this book.) The opinions that have been quoted above in criticism of logical positivism are pretty much absolutist in character. Whereas logical positivism was once completely accepted by many in the social sciences, now it is being completely rejected by many. Does that mean that it had no positive effects and thus that it presently has no positive effects upon the social sciences? Clearly, in the present view, the philosophical and methodological analyses of psychologists that were made within the natural-science and logical-positivist and operationist framework contributed valuable guides to important aspects of psychology.

It should be clear, for example, that the natural-science model was eminently successful as the general framework for beginning the development of the science. It produced the active search for methods and apparatus by which to establish reliable empirical findings in the systematic study of psychological phenomena. The productivity of psychologists in the pursuit of empirically based study is very evident. Abundant knowledge has been produced and this has included the development of extensive and sophisticated experimental methodology as well as apparatus and technological products. From a sparse set of phenomena that were investigated, psychology has advanced to the study of a large number of behavioral events in various areas. The number and extensity of topics and findings has necessitated the formation of many subparts of the science, and many suborganizations. There are numerous meetings to report the studies conducted, and psychology requires a large number of journals and books within which to publish the findings. And logical positivism and operationism have contributed to this growth, by supporting the natural science orientation and by more particular contributions. Rather than discarding the positive elements in the natural-science/logical-positivism position along with the rest, it would be better to make a discriminating analysis. With this in mind, there are several weaknesses of the logical-positivist position, as it is relevant for psychology, that should be considered in the present context. These are the types of elements that should be discarded. Realizing what should be discarded can give a better appreciation of what needs to be developed in a philosophy of psychology. The present criticism is thus conducted with a constructive goal in mind, rather than one calling for total rejection.

AN EMPTY TANK, BAD PARTS, AND AN OUTMODED DESIGN

It has not been the intent to deal with logical positivism and its positive effects on psychology in a specialized way, and the same pertains to criticism. However, there are several deficiencies in the general position that are specially relevant to the present work.

Axiomatization: The Criterion Characteristics

Logical positivism as a philosophy of science was based upon the observation of the most advanced areas of science, such as the mathematicized treatments of physics, as can be exemplified in Newton's theory of gravitation. Although this type of theory constitutes only a small part of the theory that exists in science generally, logical positivism reached conclusions that were thought to apply to all of science. We can see the absolutist doctrine that was embodied in logical positivism in the words of Suppe. "The Received View [logical positivism] was advanced by its proponents as an adequate explanation of scientific theories — the claim being that if a theory does not admit of a canonical [axiomatized] reformulation meeting the conditions of the final version of the Received View, it is not a genuine scientific theory" (1977b, p. 64). In the words of a psychologist, "The stature of a science is commonly measured by the degree to which it makes use of mathematics" (Stevens 1951, p. 1). Thus, this philosophy of science set forth a dichotomy, that between scientific theory — which was axiomatic and mathematic and employed formal logic — and all lesser symbolic structures.

This categorization of theory, and the understanding that lay beneath the categorization, constituted an error for the great part of science, including the social sciences. Thus, for example, Skinner originally did not consider his conceptual works to be theories, presumably because he accepted the dichotomy of his fellow logical-positivist behaviorists. Moreover, for the same reason, presumably, he was led to generally criticize theory in psychology, although what he was really criticizing was the type of theory that was composed on the basis of the criteria of logical positivism, specifically Hull's theory. Skinner's criticism of theory — because it was made in a general rather than specific sense — tied his followers to a methodology that avoided theoretical analysis, believing that science advances solely by experimentation and technology. My personal experience with various operant behaviorists, until very recent times, has been that Skinner's most important works, which were actually theoretical analyses, were considered to be conjectural, not theories (presumably because of their informal nature), and were not the valuable part of his approach. Skinner's acceptance of the logical-positivist description of theory confined his approach to a misunderstanding of what constituted theory in psychology.

We can see the same acceptance of logical positivism's definition of theory, and the dichotomy involved, in the words of two modern methodologists in sociology.

> Finally, it is frequently contended that there are, strictly speaking, no systematically related propositions in sociology that even begin to conform to a theory. There are no firmly established laws of social behavior, no integrated sets of universally acknowledged and empirically documented sets of propositions from which to posit new relations for study or predictions. When the usual criteria are applied to our ideas, they fall so short of meeting them that it would be frivolous to dignify the ideas as theories (Black and Champion 1976, p. 54).

There are, of course, many conceptual structures — theories — in sociology. Yet they cannot be identified as theories, according to this statement, only in a frivolous way. But such frivolity would not provide much impetus for examining nonaxiomatized conceptual structures with the same seriousness that is reserved for dealing with "real" theories. Moreover, the approach tells one that the path of advancement for a conceptual structure is being put in axiomatic form, regardless of whether or not the structure's imminent needs would be fulfilled in this way. These are legacies of logical positivism, and they are not productive.

> The axiomatic method in effect is a method for introducing order into an already well-developed body of knowledge; in particular, fruitful axiomatization of a theory is possible only if the theory to be axiomatized embodies a well-developed body of knowledge for which the systematic interconnections of its concepts are understood to a high degree. Without

these conditions being met, any attempt at axiomatization will be premature and fruitless (Suppe 1977b, p. 64).

Logical positivism examined a small part of the various fields of science, and on the basis of this small part set criteria that were to apply to all of science. But its criteria did not apply productively to all of science. In this sense the philosophy was arrogant and elitist. Rather than providing a framework within which to study methods for improving theory in the undeveloped social sciences, logical positivism contributed to a denigratory view of the social sciences, saying in effect that theories in these areas were not scientific and should not be considered. It may be added that there are many scientists in psychology who have accepted the criteria of logical positivism as the *sine qua non* of real science and who also deprecate the parts of psychology that do not meet those criteria. It is well to recognize such views as parochial, and unproductive in terms of contributing to the solution of most of the problems of sciences such as psychology. Most of the conceptual structures in psychology do not meet the criteria of a logical-positivist analysis. Logical positivism, in terms of serving as a guiding framework for theory construction in psychology, did not deal with the scope of theory concerns in science. And in claiming that it did it was in error. Let us consider briefly two areas that are needed to broaden the scope of consideration of theory in psychology.

Scientific Progress Versus Science Dichotomization

There is an implicit effect of logical positivism's dichotomization of theory that is important herein. In dividing theory into two categories — axiomatic on the one hand and nonscientific on the other — logical positivism does not lay a reasonable basis for considering the manner in which sciences progressively advance. A philosophy of science should have a function in helping guide the conduct of science. Without a conception of progressive development, logical positivism could not provide a framework by which to guide the development of sciences that needed development. Logical positivism could not indicate, for example, what the theory needs were of sciences that did not have theory that could be axiomatized. Its attention transfixed by advanced, axiomatic theory, it did not systematically concern itself with earlier or less-developed forms of theory and the problems of theory that can reside in areas of science before they develop axiomatic theory. Moreover, its lack of concern with the progressive development of science left the door open for philosophies saying that science is not progressive, that there are no criteria for evaluating progress, that there is relative change but that what develops in science cannot be considered an advancement over knowledge that existed before.

The present view is that it is important to have a conception of progressive development in science. Science loses much of its significance and
becomes a mere game without a notion of progress. Moreover, scientific
knowledge loses major status as a conception of the world — in its competition
with other conceptions, such as religious and methaphysical conceptions — unless it provides the conviction that it is a means of progressively improving
knowledge of the world, a means that nonscientific approaches may not
have. There are important points to be discussed in this area, within the
present position, but this is not the place. However, a notion of progress in
science is important in the present thesis — because one type of such progress is the focus of interest — and a few words should be said on the topic.

To elaborate, in the present view there are various gradations of theory, not just the dichotomy of axiomatization versus no-axiomatization.
Any symbolic system, whose statements are applied to events considered to
occur in the world, is a theory. And theories should be defined by function — that is, by whether or not they are serving in the role of a theory. The
individual's language thus serves as a theory for him (Staats 1968). It is a
symbolic system that has terms that are considered to stand for events in the
world. And the individual uses his language to understand events, to predict events, and to attempt to manipulate or effect these events. It is important to realize that there are dimensions of advancement in theory even
on the common language level, as the following example indicates.

> The Jivaro Indians of South America are said to have no concept of death
> from infection or disease. The Jivaro man, on learning of the death of a
> relative is likely to say, "This is the result of evil spirits set into the body of
> the relative by a Shaman at the instigation of so and so." He has no term for
> virus infection or disease. His behavior, as mediated by his language sequ-
> ence, will be different than the Christian who says, "It was the will of God
> who moves in mysterious ways." And both behaviors will be different
> than that which is mediated by the language sequence of a third man who
> says, "It was the result of a flu infection complicated by pneumonia be-
> cause he got out of bed too soon." (Staats 1968, p. 188).

This analysis went on to stipulate that the theories involved in natural
language progressively improve, as a function of improved observations,
methods, and other things that will be touched upon. This analysis was
part of an early interest of the author's in analyzing how science progresses
on the basis of learning, over generations of scientists as well as during the
individual's career (Staats 1963). In that account examples were taken from
history to indicate early forms of logic and early forms of definition of theoretical terms. Both examples were taken from an 1899 work by A.D.
White that describes the manner in which the Christian religion has clashed
with science. As part of this he includes examples taken from the Middle

Ages, of terms that are defined by supernatural monsters: "the basilisk kills serpents by his breath and men by his glance...," "the 'cockatrice' of Scripture... 'drieth and burneth leaves with his touch, and he is of so great venom and perilous that he slayeth and wasteth him that nigheth him without tarrying'" (1955, Vol. I, pp. 33-34). These statements are not made in jest, but were writings of advanced thinkers of the time, about things they considered to be real. We thus see that the standards of empirical definition of terms in the Middle Ages were not the same as those which are practiced today by individuals engaged in the systematic study of the world, or even in eduated common-language discourse.

The same is true of the standards of logic that were once followed by the foremost thinkers of the time. White gives the following example of the logic that was employed in times past for generating expectations concerning events of the world.

> Josephus argued that, since there are twenty-two letters in the Hebrew alphabet, there must be twenty-two sacred books in the Old Testament.... Hilary of Poitiers argued that there must be twenty-four books, on account of the twenty-four letters in the Greek alphabet. Origen found an argument for the existence of exactly four gospels in the existence of just four elements. Irenaeus insisted that there could be neither more nor fewer than four gospels, since the earth has four quarters, the air four winds, and the cherubim four faces... (White 1955, Vol. II, p. 296).

The use of numerological reasoning about worldly events involved very complex examples where the logical (numerological) analysis was extensive. Scholarly and scientific derivations of hypotheses employ a different logic today than the numerology that was the custom in those early times. This is also true of the methods of inquiry that are employed in gaining knowledge, as White further describes in reference to the Middle Ages again.

> Then, too, there was established a standard to which all science which did struggle up through this atmosphere must be made to conform — a standard which favoured magic rather than science, for it was a standard of rigid dogmatism... The most careful inductions from ascertained facts were regarded as wretchedly fallible when compared with any view of nature whatever given or even hinted at in any poem, chronicle, code, apologue, myth, legend, allegory, letter, or discourse of any sort which had happened to be preserved in the literature which had come to be held as sacred (1955, Vol. I, p. 376).

Today we would not regard terms referring to monsters, the logic of numerology, and the methods of dogmatism to be scientific in nature, but these elements were employed typically by intellectual authorities of earlier times. It has been the present author's view that what is involved is a progression in science, from such early beginnings in inquiry, to those that pertain today (see Staats 1963, pp. 245-58). In equating language with theory a progressive concept is introduced. Theory is not restricted to that which is axiomatic and mathematical. Theory is that which functions in the role of theory. Theory is on a continuous dimension, beginning with common language statements that claim to relate to events of the world in a manner expressing some knowledge of those events (Staats 1968). This conception provides a basis for considering all types of theory, and for concern with advancing the quality of all types of theory.

This view of theory, it should be noted, is supported by statements of modern philosophers of science (see Suppe 1977c, p. 708). As another example, Feyerabend has made a statement that deserves quotation for its similiarity to the present view (Staats 1968b, pp. 184-91). It is interesting to cite this agreement, since many of Feyerabend's views are at odds with the present position in other respects. In this area, however, Feyerabend considers theory to include "ordinary beliefs (for example, the belief in the existence of material objects), myths (for example, the myth of eternal recurrence), religious beliefs, etc. In short, any sufficiently general point of view concerning matter of fact will be termed a theory" (1965, p. 219).

The present view, to indicate briefly that it constitutes a general view of science, also holds that all aspects of science can be considered to progress. As has been indicated (Staats 1963), the principles involved in that progress are the principles of learning. Individual scientists learn in their careers how better to make observations, how better to devise and state general methods of observation, how better to construct theories along various dimensions, how better to organize science to promote the goals of science, and so on. And this learning continues over generations of scientists. Each generation begins with the advantages of knowledge that have been established by preceding generations. Thus, science is progressive and cumulative. This occurs on the basis of the principles of learning (Staats 1963). When there are two alternative methods—for example, religious dogmatism of the type described by White versus the methods of systematic observation—and one produces more advantageous outcomes, individuals exposed to the two alternatives and their results will learn to use and value the more valuable method.

The present view is not that there is a perfect and inexorable march toward better and better science. The results and implications of alternatives are not always easy to see. Frequently in science wrong alternatives are chosen and adhered to for a time, for various reasons, some of which will be discussed later. In the long run, however, wrong alternatives reveal themselves for what they are. Because of the nature of science—which is oriented toward accomplishing its goals of better knowing and dealing with the events of the world.— alternatives that produce no progress or that are less good than other alternatives will come to be characterized as such. The present author, among others (see Staats 1964b), has noted that science is a self-correcting enterprise. It may be said that self correction, along with its other goals, gives science its long-term progressive nature.

This conception of progress in science through the individual and group learning of scientists (see Staats 1963, 1968b, 1971a), it should be noted, is both rejected by and supported by analyses made by philosophers of science. It is true that philosophers such as Kuhn (1962) and Feyerabend (1970) have been considered to view changes in science as such, but not necessarily of a progressive nature. (Kuhn 1970b, has denied the charge.) Such views are considered to be relativistic: to suggest that knowledge in science does not take place as an inexorably closer and closer approximation to truth (reality), but to involve changes that are not necessarily better. This view is very much like the cultural-relativism position that human cultures and language are quite different, but this does not imply that one is better than the other. (This position with respect to language has been rejected in the present approach, see Staats 1968b, pp. 184–91.)

Support for a progressive view of science, however, is given by such philosophers of science as Stephen Toulmin (1972) and Dudley Shapere (1979). Toulmin has employed evolutionary principles as the explanatory mechanism by which progressive change takes place in science. According to this conception men with natural inventiveness introduce innovations into science that represent new variations. Disciplinary selection then occurs such that only certain of the variations of one generation will be passed on to the next generation. It is a drawback in the present view to employ evolutionary principles by which to describe any aspect of human skill development since the actual principles are those of learning.

Shapere's view is even more like that which was advanced in the present approach. Shapere is also concerned with relativism's challenge to the notion of progress in science. Thus, for example, Shapere describes the opposition in views between presuppositionists who believe that science functions by certain fundamental, unchanging, assumptions that serve as criteria by which to judge science and its progress, and relativists who believe that there is no real ground for judging science or progress in science. Shapere's position is that there is indeed change in science and that it involves more than the discovery of new facts and theories. Like the present view (Staats 1963, 1968b), Shapere recognizes that science changes in its methodology and logic as well. Moreover, in close agreement with the present view (Staats 1963, 1968b), Shapere sees that changes are progressive and depend upon experiencing the success resulting from use of certain methods in comparison to use of others. He very clearly agrees that the progressive change of science, even in these metascientific features, is due to learning (Shapere 1979). The present author (1963, p. 258) suggested generally that what are usually called the assumptions of science, or the scientific method, are not really assumptions, but are conclusions that have been learned. Scientists in the past have found that such things as publicly verifiable observations, the maintenance of skepticism, the rejection of authority, tradition, and dogma, and so on, have been successful in the search for knowledge of nature. Shapere also shares that view, saying at one point, "Like so much else we have considered, the role of doubt in inquiry, too, is learned" (1979, p. 50).

It is not the intent of the present work to provide a full philosophy of science of psychology (although it is the present position that it is important to do so; see also, Rechea 1980). However, the question of the progress of science is very relevant to the present topic, because a primary purpose of the present work is to describe a central type of progress in science, a change that is so fundamental that it can be considered revolutionary, and one that psychology has not yet undergone. For that reason, the position of progress in science, versus relativistic change, should be understood. This topic has been stressed, moreover, as one criticism of logical positivism because it restricted itself to the consideration of the most advanced of theories, leaving out of systematic consideration lesser theories. It was thus of little use for much of social science, which needs methods for producing progressive development of preaxiomatic theory. The present view corrects this by indicating the progressive nature of science, and the fact that there are theories of various levels of advancement. This has been emphasized, because later chapters will deal with problems in psychological theory, and ways of solving those problems, that are quite different from the concerns of logical positivism with axiomatization and the observational definition of theoretical terms.

More to Science than Logic and Fact

The name logical positivism was employed to label two primary concerns of the philosophy of science: the logical analysis of theory, and the analysis of the empirical foundation of theory. Through the prism of logical positivism science was considered only in terms of its theoretical realm and its empirical realm. One of the corrections to the influence of logical positivism that was needed, thus, was the recognition that it does not contain "everything that we always wanted to know" about science or the philosophy of science. It has become increasingly apparent within the areas of the history of science (Kuhn 1962, 1970), the sociology of science (see Merton 1973; Hagstrom 1965; Ravetz 1971) and the philosophy of science (Feyerabend 1970a,b; Burian 1977; Toulmin 1972; Lakatos 1971; Musgrave 1974; Shapere 1977; Suppe 1977b,c) that there are factors to consider in the study of science that are not to be found in the logical analysis of the structure of a theory and the relationship of the theory to its empirical support.

The evidence for this has of course been there for all to see, even in the period when logical positivism held its sway. For example, early in my career (see Staats 1963), when my knowledge of the general characteristics of science was derived from the works of logical positivists, I nevertheless was struck by the impressive work, already mentioned, that detailed the manner in which theological values and ideas influenced the development of the various sciences (White 1899). White's account describes the effects of Christian theology on various aspects of physics, chemistry, biology, geology, astromony, archaeology, anthropology, meteorology, and so on. This account suggested to me how the background conceptions that scientists held influenced what they would do and what their theoretical positions would be in their scientific work. As a student in psychology I had even before that time become acquainted with E.G. Boring's concept of the zeitgeist in his history of psychology (1950), which he described as cultural "habits of thought" that would determine the things that scientists would discover and the manner in which they would accept discoveries at any particular time. This mention is not in defense of Boring's historiography, which has been criticized (see Koch 1981; O'Donnell 1979; van Hoorn 1972), but to illustrate that his concept of zeitgeist includes recognition of the extra-theory and extra-empirical influences on scientific development.

We can see similar ideas in others' conceptions. Another related concept may be seen in what has been called the Whorfian hypothesis in the study of language. Benjamin Whorf hypothesized that the nature of one's *language* determined one's thought and perceptions of the world (see Whorf 1956). Thus, for example, some languages contain concepts that others do not and this produces a different view of the world among those employing different languages.

Such conceptions can be employed to understand that what scientists theorize about, and indeed what they observe itself, is subject to factors not included in the simple study of their theories or their observations. A number of modern philosophers of science have thus indicated that observations are much more than just fact (Popper 1963; Hanson 1967, 1979; Kuhn 1962; Feyerabend 1970; Lakatos 1970). Lakatos's example from the history of science, in indicating that the rejection of Galileo's telescopic observations of the mountains on the moon — versus the traditional belief that the moon was a perfect sphere — was not a rejection of fact, but of theory-fact. Galileo's observations called for a belief in the instrument that was employed, the telescope. Why would one place any more trust in a telescope than a kaleidoscope? Accepting the observations of a telescope as providing information about the moon requires either extensive experience with the telescope, confirmation by others in whom one has trust, or understanding of the construction of the instrument and the theory of optics involved. When none of those are available telescopic observations are not facts.

As another example of nontheory, nonfact aspects of science, Toulmin (1972) has indicated that there are decisions made in science that are crucial, but that cannot be considered to have involved deductions from theories. Toulmin (1974) has said that such decisions, which are rationale, while not of the formal, logical type considered exemplary of advanced science, nevertheless may be based upon experience and may demand a grasp of the present and past and an extrapolation to the future. The original decision that psychology should model itself after the natural sciences was that type of decision — not a theoretically derived proposition, but crucial to the direction taken by the field.

Finally, Kuhn (1962) has probably been most influential in recent times in bringing attention to the fact that science consists of more than formal theory and fact. As will be indicated at greater length further on, Kuhn has posited that there are constellations of method, theory, apparatus, beliefs, and so on — which he calls a paradigm — that are involved in the direction of science and its change. Very clearly he recognizes that there is more to science than logic and fact.

This general view is widely held now, helping to contribute to the demise of the dominance of logical positivism as a philosophy of science. The present work will focus on matters that are considered crucial in the development of psychology as a science; matters not involving axiomatic theories and methods of empirical investigation. Decisions concerning the path that the science should take in its further development will be introduced. However, the decisions do not derive from a specific theory, but rather from consideration of the characteristics of psychology as a science, and how they compare to the characteristics of other sciences.

The Generalization Problem: Is Psychology Like a Natural Science?

We have seen how some scientists have been anxious to establish the similarity of psychology to the natural sciences. For them the characteristics of the natural sciences are thought to transfer to psychology (and the other social sciences). Logical positivism shared these expectations, at least as an ideal, while at the same time most such philosophers of science would have believed, and do now believe, that psychology as presently practiced does not approach that ideal. On the other hand, as has been indicated, there are many who consider psychology (and the other social sciences) to be quite different types of sciences from the natural sciences. Logical positivism has not provided a conception which has settled this question, and as a consequence this leaves the way open to deny that psychology is a science and should be developed in a manner appropriate to the advanced sciences. The problem cannot be dealt with in detail here, but a few words should be said to indicate the present position.

In the present view psychology can be like the natural sciences in certain very basic ways. It can seek knowledge of the worldly events in which it is interested through the methods of observation-theory of science — be these mental (or cognitive), or be they overt responses to environmental stimuli. It can progressively improve its observation-theory-method knowledge, as can any natural science. The same basic methodological concerns are relevant, for example, concerns with skepticism and avoidance of dogmatism, with public and repeatable observation, and with obtaining laboratory control.

But there are many characteristics of the natural sciences that do not generalize to psychology and the social sciences. We have seen how the expectation that theory must be axiomatic is inappropriate for the social sciences. In general, we must expect that there are parts of the natural sciences that will generalize. Moreover, and more importantly herein, we might also expect that there will be aspects of psychology and the other social sciences that will be different from the natural sciences and different from each other. The present work will deal with problems of psychology that are no longer problems in the natural sciences, and with other characteristics of psychology that the natural sciences never had or will have. There are differences in sciences; astronomy, for example, unlike physics, ordinarily cannot perform laboratory, manipulative experiments. Psychology, a social science, is more like physics in that a prominent part of its knowledge is derived from laboratory experimentation. Astronomy, however, generally includes theory that in its axiomatic-mathematical nature is like that of physics in a way that is not characteristic of theory in psychology. In considering history as a science, as another example, we have to realize that history cannot include laboratory manipulations as a source of knowledge. Moreover, history does not ordinarily have direct observation of the events in which it is interested, having to rely upon the interpretive observations of those reporting those events, with all the weaknesses that this may involve. Obviously there will be differences in the theory-observation-method of these several areas of inquiry, yet there may be certain basic similarities also in the knowledge-seeking endeavor of each.

The important thing here is to take a rational, understanding approach, rather than a dogmatic, closed, and elitist approach. The goal of science is not to make silk purses out of sows' ears. There may be limits on a science's characteristics, imposed by the nature of the events dealt with. Thus, the goal of science must be to develop methods by which to maximize the knowledge output that can be derived from the limited input that can be obtained from contact with the worldly events in any particular area of study. Expertise in the endeavor can be expected to result from systematic efforts to study the realm involved. We can expect progressive improvement in theory-observation-method types of knowledge, in comparison to the knowledge provided by less systematic methods of other approaches, in whatever area of study is involved. The limits of the goodness of that knowledge will ultimately be imposed by the nature of the worldly events studied in the particular area.

When we enter a new area of study it makes sense to use as much as possible what others have found. For example, if in some other area of study it has been found successful to assume the events involved are natural — in contrast to supernatural — then that is something we will want to try in the new area. It makes sense to extrapolate in this way, if we realize that we are doing so in a state of ignorance and we may be wrong, and if we are thus sensitive to disproof and rejection. We make errors in generalizing that which is inappropriate. We make errors in not generalizing that which would be appropriate. It should be noted that this applies equally well to those who feel that natural science's methods and philosophy should not be generalized to the study of human behavior. It is my experience that their convictions are frequently based on their views of human behavior, for example, religious views, metaphysical views, and so on, rather than on the systematic study of whether the generalization of natural science methods is appropriate. In so doing they are generalizing their methodology from a conceptual body also, and that may also be inappropriate or appropriate.

The major point here is that we can expect similarities and differences between sciences. The more basic the feature of science treated, the more widely the feature can be expected to be general. All sciences utilize observations of worldly events, for example, in obtaining knowledge of the world. All sciences are concerned about the goodness of those observations. When we get into particular ways of achieving good observations, however, we can expect methods to have characteristics idiosyncratic to the nature of the events dealt with. The same can be expected to be true of theory, that is, similarities of a basic sort as well as differences in other features.

Logical positivism said in essence that science, all science, should exhibit the features of science, and those features were those of axiomatic theory, and so on. This position does not provide a foundation for productively considering the differences and the similarities of features across sciences — a consideration that might be enlightening. As will be indicated, a prominent difference that occurs between the social sciences and the natural sciences concerns the extent of unity and organization of knowledge that these two classes of science have. We cannot gain a philosophical impetus to systematically investigate that difference from logical positivism, although in the present view crucial matters are involved. It is important that a philosophy of science for any of the social sciences provide a basis for systematic concern with the differences between sciences, without accepting the extremist position that the social sciences and natural sciences are entirely different and that generalization from the study of the natural sciences is inappropriate.

The Failure to Organize and Give Direction to the Science

As will be elaborated in a later chapter, in psychology there are various conceptual schisms that divide the science into warring factions. One long-standing division has been termed the nature-nurture issue: whether the characteristics of human behavior are determined by biological conditions of genetics and biological development, or by the conditions of learning produced by the environment. While resolution of such an issue may be a theoretical problem, there are philosophical questions involved in whether or not such issues should be taken to indicate that psychology contains elements that are irreconcilable — incommensurable, to use the term employed by Kuhn (1962) and others, Koch (1981) — or whether we have a philosophy that such issues are to be resolved, a philosophy that provides some methodological directions to take in such unifying tasks. Later discussions will deal with whether or not we should assume that there are approaches in psychology that are incommensurable, doomed to remain different from each other and isolated, although they pertain to the same realm of events.

Related to this issue is the larger issue of the unity of science and, hence, the unity of psychology. Logical positivism included an interest in unified science, and this included a method for attaining unified theory in science. The method was that of theory absorption, called theory reduction or reductionism. The more general theory would simply absorb the less general theory. Less basic sciences, like the social and biological sciences, would eventually be reduced to more basic sciences, that is, to biochemistry, to chemistry, and ultimately to physics. But logical positivism's reductionism did not solve the problems of nonunity within psychology itself, and in the present view this remains as the paramount problem in the science, as will be treated focally here. Thus, a very central weakness of logical positivistic approaches was that they did not present a positive program, a methodology, by which psychology could make organized sense out of its multiple products and diverse theories and methods of approach. The natural-science/logical-positivism philosophy has taken psychology a long way toward the production of a rich body of scientific knowledge. But there remains the question of what all that knowledge means, and logical positivism has not indicated how that question is to be answered.

A BUILDING VIEW

The present view of science is that it is a complex activity engaged in by many people and the products of scientific activity are therefore numerous and diverse. The present view is that human skills in general are learned, and that includes those that are relevant to science.

> Man develops. . . as he learns in an historical or phylogenetic sense. That is, we may look upon the history of man as a species as the acquisition of a great variety of behavioral skills through the principles of learning. The original acquisition of any skill may be seen as a laborious, time-consuming, imprecise process—like the trial-and-error learning that Thorndike investigated. One can see, historically, this slow and uncertain development in any area of complex behavioral development—music, athletics, religion, business rules, government, language, science, and so on.
>
> It is important to note that the refinement of such skills involves the advances of the individuals involved at any one point, plus the general or group advancement that has preceded them. A youngster learning to high-jump today does not go through the various stages in the development of the contemporary skill that were necessary in the historical development, which involved the successive learning of many men. He begins with the maximal point of development that has been achieved to that point. The variations in the skill that he makes are made from a higher point of skill than a youngster in the preceding generation. As a result, the picture we get of such a progression is one of systematic advancement.
>
> The major point here, however, is that man develops his skills phylogenetically—as a species or group, over the generations (Staats 1971, pp. 294–95).

Part of this view, as has been indicated, is that science is cumulative, which is to say that it is a building process. This is easy to see, but it is frequently overlooked by specialists who become entranced by other things, such as the individual creativity of scientists.

The natural-science/logical-positivism view of psychology played a dominant role in the science, but it is now being rejected en masse. It is important to criticize such a philosophy, for that can lead to constructive development. But, as has been indicated, there is a tendency to accept or reject complex intellectual structures as if they were monoliths. Rather they are composed of elements. The building process must be to separate the wheat of useful structures from the chaff of those parts that are weak, nonfunctional, and disadvantageous, as well as to add on new and needed structures that have not been built before.

Logical positivism failed because it yielded and yields what it has had to offer, and now has no further lines to guide new directions. It was part of the natural-science conception of psychology that gave impetus to the pro-liferation of science products and that continues to drive psychology. It continues also in such areas as helping provide a framework by which to an-alyze theory and to inspire formal theory-construction methods.

But its theory principles suffer from general inadequacy and do not apply to the great majority of theory structures in psychology. And the theory prin-ciples do not tell us what we have to do to obtain better theory in our sci-ence. Logical positivism does not tell us how to solve our problems of con-troversy, divisiveness, and fragmentation in psychology. The philosophy does not indicate paths by which we can get a meaningful picture of what psychology is, or of how its multitudinous products and specialties relate to one another. Logical positivism has not indicated what are the important characteristics of the science that must be improved. It does not recognize, characterize, or project solutions for the crisis that is experienced in psy-chology. The philosophy no longer provides a projection for the science, other than to say that it should continue to improve upon the theory and re-search that it is conducting.

These are reasons that the philosophy of science should be criticized. In such cases the expected path for critics with opposing philosophies is to exploit the demonstrated weakness by completely defeating the philosophy that is down (see Giddens, 1976; Koch, 1978, 1981; van Hoorn, 1972; Weimer, 1979), creating a swing of the pendulum to the opposite extreme. In the present view, however, the answer to the problems of psychology are not to be found in the resurgence of subjectivist philosophies. The answer is not to be found in attempting to demolish in its entirety the basic natural science philosophical framework. Let us realize, rather, that the frame-work has been very productive because of positive features, but that the framework has lacked essential ingredients. Logical positivism can be seen as inadequate because it has run out of gas, because it contains bad parts that need replacement, and because it does not steer well anymore and thus lacks the features that are needed to project directions for the development of today's psychology (and that of other social sciences).

In the present view the answers to the problems of psychology's crisis will not emerge from analyzing logical positivism using presently available philosophical conceptual tools. Rather, we must go directly to analysis of the science itself. There are problems with the characteristics of psychology as a science that must be scrutinized in and of themselves. This is a job for a firsthand analysis, not one that derives from a philosophy of the natural sci-ences, that is merely extrapolated to psychology and the other social sci-ences — although we can use many of the descriptions from the natural sci-ences in the task that lies before us. This conclusion derives from the view that psychology and the other social sciences have characteristics that the natural sciences do not have, either at the present time or at any time. There are new currents in the philosophy, history, and sociology of science that can be employed in analyzing characteristics of psychology that have not been dealt with and that are important in its present and future development.

Chapter 3

Unity and Proliferation in Science

It has been said that one of the weaknesses of logical positivism was its focus upon only two aspects of science: the logical analysis of theory, and the ways by which empirical terms in theory are defined by observations. As has been indicated, there has been a growing recognition that this framework is too narrow to consider the various aspects of science that are of interest. Such individuals as Stephen Toulmin, Thomas Kuhn, N.R. Hanson, Karl Popper, Paul Feyerabend, and David Bohm recognize that other things than formal theory and formal fact were important in science, as the following statement by Frederick Suppe indicates clearly.

> ...Rather [than logical positivism], what is required is an analysis of theories which concerns itself with the epistemic factors governing the discovery, development, and acceptance or rejection of theories; such an analysis must give serious attention to the idea that science is done from within a conceptual perspective which determines in large part which questions are worth investigating and what sorts of answers are acceptable; the perspective provides a way of thinking about a class of phenomena which defines the class of legitimate problems and delimits the standards for their acceptable solution. Such a perspective is intimately tied to one's language which conceptually shapes the way one experiences the world. In short, science is done from within a *Weltanschauung* or *Lebenswelt*, and the job of philosophy of science is to analyze what is characteristic of scientific *Weltanschauungen*, what is characteristic of the linguistic-conceptual systems from within which science works. Theories are interpreted in terms of the *Weltanschauung*; hence to understand theories it is necessary to understand the *Weltanschauung*. Such a *Weltanschauungen* approach to analyzing the epistemology of science obviously must pay considerable attention to the history of science and the

sociological factors influencing the development, articulation, employment, and acceptance or rejection of *Weltanschauungen* in science. As such, the concerns of the philosophers of science overlap those of the historian and the sociologist of science (Suppe 1977b, pp. 126-27).

The most widely known weltanschauung approach, at least outside of the specialized fields of the history-philosophy of science, is that of Kuhn's paradigm (1962). Kuhn held that organized traditions of scientific research that constitute normal science are integrated by and develop from paradigms. Paradigms consist of generally accepted scientific achievements that indicate what the problems of the science are and how they should be studied. The achievements include the laws, the theories, the applications, and the instruments of science as well as methodological and even metaphysical commitments. The paradigm also determines the methods and standards of problem-solution and the problems that the scientists in the science consider important and acceptable, guiding their actions of selection and evaluation and criticism. Paradigms thus determine science by providing the guides for normal science activities. Normal science consists of working to validate and to elaborate its paradigms and to make them more clear and precise. There is paradigm determination of the movement of science also through another mechanism. Paradigms may develop instabilities because they lead to insoluble problems, their predictions contain inexplicable errors, and so on. In such a case a new paradigm may arise and for a time there will be a paradigm clash. This is eventually resolved in the direction of one of the paradigms, in which case the activity of normal science resumes. The paradigm clashes are considered to result in the revolutionary changes that occur in science. As has been indicated, Kuhn's original position was a relativistic one. He did not indicate that the clashes were resolved in favor of the winning paradigm because it was superior in truth-value, but indicated rather that more subjective events were involved (Lakatos and Musgrave 1970; Scheffler 1967).

Kuhn's concept of the paradigm has been criticized on a number of grounds. As will be referred to later, his approach has been criticized because the model of science involved is that of conformity, at least in the normal science period, while a contrary view emphasizes the need for creative proliferation and diversity in science (Feyerbend 1970a). Another criticism is that the paradigm concept is circular. The concept arises as a description of science, but then it is turned around and the paradigm is said to be a cause, an *explanation* of how science operates (Shapere 1971). That is, Kuhn originally said that before a paradigm arose in an area of science there was chaos. Then a paradigm would form. When the paradigm did arise it would change the nature of the field, bringing order and direction and cooperative endeavor, where there had been none. In this and other senses the paradigm was given causal properties. Following the criticism, however, Kuhn retracted his view that the paradigm had such properties (1977, pp. 294-95). A better resolution of this issue lies in the realization that human achievements may be both causes and effects. As an example, it has been said that human intelligence consists largely of learned skills. The skills are thus the effects of experience, and intelligence should be studied as an effect. But once the child has acquired intelligence skills they become the foundation for yet more complex intellectual learning. Intelligence, thus, has a causative role in determining the intellectual skills the individual will further acquire (see Staats 1971a; Staats and Burns 1981). The same can be said of any human achievement, including the paradigm. The paradigm can be considered to be an achievement — a complex constellation of achievements, actually — and in this sense can be considered an outcome, an effect, of an extensive array of scientific activities. But once the paradigm has been attained, it can serve in the role of a cause, by guiding future developments in the science. Logical positivism is itself an example of such a cause-*and*-effect principle. Logical positivism was an intellectual accomplishment that was derived from the study of the natural sciences. But it was posed as a philosophy for the social sciences, and it guided efforts that took place in the social sciences, and in so doing it was a cause.

It is not the purpose of the present discussion to make a full presentation of the criticisms of Kuhn's views of science. One additional criticism is of relevance here, however, that is, that Kuhn's concept of paradigm has so many definitions that it becomes a muddle. Margaret Masterman (1970), a supporter of Kuhn, has outlined the 21 definitions that Kuhn has given of the paradigm. In the present view, as has been indicated, science is a complex event. There is theory, observation, observational technique, apparatus, and method. There are broader conceptual frameworks in which these are embedded. There are organizational characteristics that affect the nature of the science and of the subparts of the science, such as interest areas, formal divisions, schools, journal organizations, and so on. As we will see there are sociological effects on science, as well as the more familiar ones involving theory and fact. The important point, as Shapere (1971) has indicated, is that the multiple definitions Kuhn gave of the paradigm made it coincident with science itself. This also made the concept circular. It actually stood for science, but was used to explain science. As will be indicated in a moment, this complexity and lack of clarity in the definition of the term paradigm does not provide a sure basis for its use in understanding the various sciences, such as psychology.

To continue, however, Kuhn in developing the concept of the paradigm, also described briefly the state before the science field has attained a paradigm — an area of concern that will be of great importance in the present work, as will be developed later. The period before the paradigm was described as a primitive development, in which there were many competing schools, each trying to prove itself the correct approach. Masterman (1970) later elaborated this conception to include three categories of science, that is, nonparadigm science, multiple-paradigm science, and paradigm — (or dual-paradigm) science. Nonparadigm science refers to the primitive, disorganized state of prescience acquisition of knowledge. Multiple-paradigm science refers to "that state of affairs in which, far from there being no paradigm, there are on the contrary too many" (Masterman 1970, p. 74). This state contains much of the achievements of full science, but is divided into subparts, each of which "defined by its technique is so obviously more trivial and narrow than the field as defined by intuition, and so grossly discordant with one another, that discussion on fundamentals remains, and long-run progress (as opposed to local progress) fails to occur" (Masterman 1970, p. 74). Masterman does not indicate how the competing schools of the preparadigm science are to be distinguished from the competing paradigms of the multiple-paradigm science. In the present view, as will be indicated, they are not fundamentally different. Masterman's third category is named dual-paradigm science. This refers to the fully advanced state of science in which there is in the particular area one guiding paradigm in the normal condition and two antagonistic paradigms during the periods of revolutionary change.

In the vacuum left by the demise of logical positivism's influence, Kuhn's work has had much popularity in the social sciences, including psychology. Despite that popularity, however, Kuhn's view has not produced additional clarity in understanding those sciences. In psychology, for example, there are those (Barber 1976; Buss 1978; Gadlin and Ingle 1975; Kruglanski 1976; Palermo 1971; Weimer and Palermo 1973) who consider the science to contain paradigms and to thus be like the advanced sciences. Theodore Barber (1976), to illustrate, treats Skinner's form of operant behaviorism as a paradigm. He considers the same to be true of the cognitive approach and the psychoanalytic approach. The term paradigm has been used rather widely in psychology applied to such schools, and writers suggest there are paradigm clashes, and so on, between the opposed approaches. From such an analysis one would never derive the proposition that the paradigms in psychology represent a different state of affairs than those of the natural sciences. Yet if one examines the circumstances more closely one finds that Skinner's approach, the cognitive approach, and psychoanalytic theory, as examples, do not have a consensus of support within the science, or even within the area or areas of interest to which each is addressed. They are competitive schools, not paradigms — *an essential aspect of a paradigm as considered here is the consensus it inspires.*

On the other hand, some have suggested at least superficially that psychology is a preparadigmatic science (Briskman 1972; Elms 1975; Macken-

zie 1977; Staats 1968a, 1975, 1978, 1980, 1981; Tibetts 1975; Yates 1975).
Alejandro Dorna and Hernan Mendez state that "La evidencia nos informa
que no existe ni ha existido un paradigma aceptado por la comunidad
científica en psícologia; por el contrario, tan solo podemos enumerar una
cierta cantidad de enfoques que se disputan la supremacia" (1979, p. 62).
This translates to say that the evidence tells us that a paradigm accepted by
the scientific community does not exist and never has existed in psychology;
on the contrary, we are only able to enumerate a certain quantity of approaches that fight among themselves for supremacy.

Thus, there are two opposing views concerning the state of psychology
as a science: whether it has paradigms and is hence a paradigm science, or
whether it is a nonparadigm science or a multiple-paradigm science. The
fact is that there has not been a systematic consideration of this conflict of
interpretations, or of the general problem area. There has been no systematic treatment of the characteristics of psychology as a science containing
paradigms or as one that does not. There is presently little understanding of
what is involved for the science that has or has not attained the advanced
state of a paradigm science.

The ambiguity of the term paradigm has simply maintained ambiguity in the understanding of social sciences such as psychology. It may be noted as well that the ambiguity concerning the concept of the paradigm has
permeated also other social sciences besides psychology. To elaborate,
Kuhn (1977) in his conceptualization distinguished exemplars from the disciplinary matrix (or paradigm). The exemplars were considered to be subparts in the disciplinary matrix. The disciplinary matrix consisted of ideas,
theories, beliefs, and so on, shared by the members of the professional discipline, while the exemplars consisted of the problems and problem solutions, apparatuses, and methods that are found in the generally accepted
works of the discipline, as in textbooks. These ideas have been employed also in characterizing psychology (see, for example, Paniagua 1981) as well as
the social sciences, but they have not clarified the ambiguity that exists, as
can be seen by a recent controversy in sociology. Both sides of the controversy refer to Kuhn's concepts. Yet the scholars cannot agree upon how
these concepts apply to sociology, as indicated in the two expressed opinions.

> . . . Eckberg and Hill and I disagree on which of Kuhn's definitions of a
> paradigm is best suited to the analysis of sociology. They prefer his later
> definition of a paradigm as an exemplar. In spite of the fact that he later
> rejected it, I prefer Kuhn's earlier definition of a paradigm as a disciplin-
> ary matrix. . . . Eckberg and Hill are virtually unassailable in their con-
> tention that the paradigm concept has been misused by those who have at-
> tempted to apply it to sociology. . . . However, [i]f we were to take both

Kuhn and Eckberg and Hill literally, we would end up with hundreds, or maybe even thousands, of paradigms (Ritzer 1981, p. 245).

Ritzer and others continue to adhere to the paradigm-as-disciplinary matrix definition, while performing analyses which do not even fit the criteria for disciplinary matrices. In Ritzer's case, we now believe this is because he does not understand what a paradigm is or does (Hill and Eckberg 1981, p. 250).

In conclusion, it is suggested that despite the popularity of Kuhn's philosophy of science, it has not led to a consensual understanding of the social sciences, even in the areas of interest that are directly applicable to the philosophy.

Paradigm Argument Is a Side Issue

Kuhn's major theme involved the concept of the paradigm. The paradigm was seen to be the centrally important determinant of the course of science. When the paradigm first arises in an area of study it unifies the work in that area. The paradigm then determines the state of the course of normal science. And the character of the science changes when a new paradigm arises that clashes with the old. The result of this clash is a revolutionary change in the area of study. These are concepts and principles that have been focused upon and criticized in the philosophy of science.

The concepts of the paradigm and of paradigm clashes and of scientific revolutions have weaknesses, as critics have indicated. More importantly, however, the approach falls short because it does not focus on the most significant matters involved, at least if one is interested in a science such as psychology. Although some of the criticisms of Kuhn's concept of paradigm and the dynamics of change in science are well-taken, neither the original concepts nor the criticisms indicate what it is that we need in order to better understand the path of development that psychology, or sciences that are like it, should take in their advancement.

Contrary to the typical concern, in this study the central contribution of Kuhn's analysis resided in the descriptions that he made of areas in the natural sciences when they were in their early stages of development. These descriptions provided a frame of reference with which to compare the descriptions that the present author had made of psychology over his years as a practicing member of the science community. Finding similarities between the contemporary science of psychology and the state of the natural sciences at a much earlier time provided clues concerning the nature and the problems of psychology. Thus, in the present view the most important part of Kuhn's work was his historical description of the early natural sciences and their development toward unity. It was necessary to abstract the elements in Kuhn's work that were important in this context, since the focus in his work was of another kind. Moreover, it was also necessary to compose a conceptual analysis that would present those elements in a manner that was relevant to the task of considering the characteristics of psychology.

CHARACTERISTICS OF EARLY NATURAL SCIENCE

The thesis to be developed in the present work concerns the character of psychology with respect to its unity-disunity. The author's many years of working in the science convinced him that this character of psychology was central in the science's contemporary operation, and it would be central in the advancement of the science. This thesis can be developed by utilizing and developing some of the materials presented by Kuhn, in comparing psychology to other sciences. Of primary importance is Kuhn's description of some of the characteristics of early natural science. The descriptions are not elaborate or lengthy, and thus can be quoted here.

> The history of electrical research in the first half of the eighteenth century provides a more concrete and better known example of the way a science develops before it acquires its first universally received paradigm. During that period there were almost as many views about the nature of electricity as there were important electrical experimenters, men like Hauksbee, Gray, Desaguliers, Du Fay, Nollett, Watson, Franklin, and others. *All their numerous concepts of electricity had something in common* — they were partially derived from one or another version of the mechanico-corpuscular philosophy that guided all scientific research of the day. In addition, *all* were components of real scientific theories, of theories that *had been drawn in part from experiment and observation* and that partially determined the choice and interpretation of additional problems undertaken in research. Yet though all the experiments were electrical and though most of the experimenters read each other's works, their theories had no more than a family resemblance. . . . History suggests that the road to a firm research consensus is extraordinarily arduous.
>
> History also suggests, however, some reasons for the difficulties encountered on that road. In the absence of a paradigm or some candidate for paradigm, all of the facts that could possibly pertain to the development of a given science are likely to seem equally relevant. As a result, *early fact-gathering is a far more nearly random activity* than the one that subsequent scientific development makes familiar. . . .
>
> But though this sort of fact-collecting has been essential to the origin of many significant sciences, anyone who examines, for example, Pliny's encyclopedic writings or the Baconian natural histories of the seventeenth century will discover that *it produces a morass.* One somehow hesitates to

call the literature that results scientific. The Baconian "histories" of heat, color, wind, mining, and so on, are filled with information, some of it recondite. But they juxtapose facts that will later prove revealing (e.g., heating by mixture) with others (e.g., the warmth of dung heaps) that will for some time remain too complex to be integrated with theory at all. In addition, since any description must be partial, the typical natural history often omits from its immensely circumstantial accounts just those details that later scientists will find sources of important illumination. . . . Moreover, since the casual fact-gatherer seldom possesses the time or the tools to be critical, *the natural histories often juxtapose descriptions like the above with others, say, heating by antiperistasis (or by cooling), that we are now quite unable to confirm.* Only very occasionally, as in the cases of ancient statics, dynamics, and geometrical optics, do facts collected with so little guidance from pre-established theory speak with sufficient clarity to permit the emergence of a first paradigm.

This is the situation that creates the schools [preparadigms] characteristic of the early stages of a science's development. No natural history can be interpreted in the absence of at least some implicit body of intertwined theoretical and methodological belief that permits selection, evaluation, and criticism. If that body of belief is not already implicit in the collection of facts . . . it must be externally supplied, perhaps by a current metaphysic, by another science, or by personal and historical accident. No wonder, then, that in the early states of the development of any science different men confronting the same range of phenomena, but not usually all the same particular phenomena, describe and interpret them in different ways. What is surprising, and perhaps also unique in its degree to the field we call sciences, is that such initial divergences should ever largely disappear.

For they do disappear to a very considerable extent and then apparently once and for all. *Furthermore, their disappearance is usually caused by the triumph of one of the pre-paradigm schools, which, because of its own characteristic beliefs and preconceptions, emphasized only some special part of the too sizable and inchoate pool of information. . . .* To be accepted as a paradigm, a theory must seem better than its competitors, but it need not, and in fact never does, explain all the facts with which it can be confronted.

[T]he Franklinian paradigm . . . suggested which experiments would be worth performing and which, because directed to secondary or to overly complex manifestations of electricity, would not. Only the paradigm did the job far more effectively, partly because the end of interschool debate ended the constant reiteration of fundamentals and partly because the confidence that they were on the right track encouraged scientists to undertake more precise, esoteric, and consuming sorts of work. Freed from the concern with any and all electrical phenomena, the united group of electricians could pursue selected phenomena in far more detail, designing much special equipment for the task and employing it more stubbornly and systematically than electricians had ever done before. *Both*

*fact collection and theory articulation became highly directed activities.
The effectiveness and efficiency of electrical research increased accordingly* . . . (italics added) (Kuhn 1962, pp. 13–18).

There are various points that should be abstracted in this description,
for they coincide with points that have emerged in the present analysis of
psychology, points that will be considered further on in describing
contemporary psychology. First, as compared with the paradigm period,
the preparadigm period is characterized by randomness of endeavor, of
poorly guided fact-gathering and theoretical development. In the realm of
observations, there are important facts mixed with insignificant facts;
there are reliable facts and unreliable facts, with little distinction. The result is a morass that is uninterpretable without some guiding conception
that provides a basis for selection, evaluation, and criticism. Different people concoct different guiding conceptions, which yield schools of thought.
Very importantly, in the present view, there is commonality to the various
schools, conceptually and methodologically, and in the facts addressed.
But, as will be indicated later, the commonality goes unnoticed. Finally,
however, the initial divergence in views disappears. There is a triumph of
some preparadigm school, which seems better than its competitors in some
way, and in attaining consensus becomes a paradigm. The irreversibility of
unification of the paradigm may be mentioned here as an important in-
stance of a progressive dimension in science development.

It may be added that the school that later provides the basis for a paradigm development is not recognized before the fact. Although the school
has the potential for emerging as the paradigm, in the morass that Kuhn
describes this could not be seen by most scientists. In any nonparadigm area
or science, there may exist a preparadigm, perhaps in inchoate form, that
will later on be developed to paradigm status through its ability to produce
paradigmatic consensus. I wish to advance the hypothesis for the science or
science area that is presently in the nonparadigm stage. It is a purpose of
this book to indicate some of these implications.

As will be indicated, the present conception is that there are contemporary preparadigmatic sciences, and that psychology is one of them.
The characteristics of the preparadigmatic science, moreover, have thus far
only been hinted at through the use of historical materials. Much greater
understanding of the preparadigmatic science should be obtained by systematically studying contemporary preparadigmatic sciences. If there are
important differences between preparadigmatic sciences and paradigmatic sciences, then casual consideration is not sufficient. We must understand the nature of the preparadigmatic science, since almost all of what
we know of science has been based on the paradigmatic, natural sciences.
The next chapter will deal with some of the characteristics of psychology as

a preparadigmatic science and later chapters will consider how these characteristics affect the efficacy of the conduct of the science. What has only been hinted at in the brief historical accounts is that there are large differences between preparadigmatic and paradigmatic sciences that involve social workings and more importantly concern the substantive and methodological efficacy of science. At this point, however, it is appropriate to develop a bit more the conceptual framework to be employed in the succeeding analyses.

PREPARADIGMS AND PARADIGMS, PREPARADIGMATIC AND PARADIGMATIC SCIENCES

It has been indicated that psychologists (and other social scientists) have utilized concepts from Kuhn (1962) in ways that are inconsistent with one another. One reason is that psychologists have simply lacked a characterization of their science that would allow them to accurately employ the concept of the paradigm. In addition, however, Kuhn's account did not include the distinctions that are necessary in order to apply his concept to a science such as psychology, and his use of the concept of paradigm was not clear. Kuhn originally described the early period of science that has been quoted above as one means of defining his term paradigm. That is, he began by indicating what science was like before it had a paradigm. In essence, in the process of showing the importance of the paradigm to science, he indicated that before the paradigm there was chaos. When the paradigm arises the science area is transformed; it becomes organized, the chaos is replaced. For Kuhn, at least at first, the paradigm produced this remarkable transformation. This was for Kuhn a primary indication of the causative qualities of the paradigm. Once the paradigm has transformed the science area, it never returns to its nonparadigm state.

Thus, Kuhn made a sharp distinction between the schools that existed in the nonparadigm science and the paradigm that ultimately would arise. But Kuhn's definition of the paradigm was criticized. Moreover, members of the present-day sciences of psychology and sociology, as has been indicated, describe their sciences as having paradigms, even when there is more than one such paradigm in the same area of study (which should be an indication that schools rather than paradigms are involved). Masterman, as has been indicated, does not differentiate between multiple paradigms that are competitive with each other and paradigms that have attained a consensus in the science area. Under the pressure of criticism, Kuhn also changed his conception of the paradigm. He stated that "Whatever paradigms may be, they are possessed by any scientific community, including the schools of the so-called preparadigm period" (1977, p. 295). It thus remains necessary to

make a distinction between the paradigmatic science and the preparadigmatic science, and the difference between preparadigms and paradigms is
part of the distinction.

Preparadigms and Paradigms

One of the reasons why the paradigm concept of Kuhn was not understood and was criticized was that it did not specify the different types of
events that such a concept must concern. There are sociological, substantive, and philosophical differences between preparadigms and paradigms.

Sociological Definition of the Preparadigm-Paradigm Shift

To begin, sociological characteristics are important in original paradigm formation. That is, it is proposed that the presence of a paradigm period, in comparison to a preparadigm period, can be specified through
historical sociological study. In the preparadigm period there are various
groups of scientists, each group with internally shared commonality, competing with one another, criticizing one another, not well understanding
one another, and so on. There are numerous cases in science that can be so
described, where this sociologically defined state has given way to another
state, the paradigm state. In this state the competitive groups become dis-
solved in the service of a larger group. Viewed externally it can be seen that
the conflict, competition, misunderstanding, and it may be added rivalry,
lack of communication, and so on, disappear in the paradigmatic science
area. Rather, a common guiding purpose is displayed within the larger
group that was formerly only displayed among the members of the smaller
schools, but not between them. The work in the paradigm may then be described as cumulative and cooperative; achievements relating constructively, rather than competitively and destructively, come to be emphasized.
Kuhn's (1962) historical descriptions provide evidence of such sociological
groupings and their changes. This is a very productive aspect of Kuhn's
work. The fact that a school (preparadigm) displays such constructive,
cumulative, cooperative endeavor within its own group does not make it a
paradigm, for at the same time the school will be in vigorous competition
with other schools in the same area of the study. The members of a school,
as a consequence, work in a different type of science than do the members
of a paradigm.

This phenomenon is important to consider solely on the sociological
level. That is, aside from whether or not Kuhn assumes a relativistic approach to science, the sociological evidence of preparadigm and postpara-
digm organization of science is significant. Competition, rivalry, lack of
communication, lack of cooperation — the elements of preparadigm con-

flict — refer to a social organization inconsistent with constructive, cooperative, building types of activities. It is true that it is important in science to clarify discrepancies in views such that differences are revealed and subjected to investigation. However, it is also true that constructive interrelations in science, where the findings of one scientist then constitute a part of the foundation for the work of another, are also very important. For such constructive occasions to take place, however, various relationships among scientists are necessary. For example, on a basic level, scientists must apprise themselves of others' works, there have to be means to which the scientist has access by which to do so, the scientist also has to utilize others' works, not suppress such works and otherwise fight against them. To maintain constructive interchange, moreover, it is necessary that scientists give recognition to each other's work, otherwise communication suffers, as does the continuity of the science, and willingness to exchange findings. Conditions that promote rivalry of the type that has a purpose of attacking the position of another group of scientists are likely to negatively affect science advancement in terms of the cooperative interactions mentioned above. When a combative relationship exists that is unnecessary, and this relationship constitutes an obstacle to the building type of relationship, then the combative relationship constitutes an obstacle to the effective conduct of the science. It has been generally suggested (Staats 1968a, 1975, 1977, 1980, 1981) that there is a loss of efficacy of psychology that is produced by conditions of oppositional rivalry, as will be elaborated further on. This characteristic has been noted by Mackenzie in describing the classic learning theories of behaviorism.

[A] major part of the theoretical and experimental work performed by the proponents of each theory constituted an attempt to show that their theory's answers were right and that a competing theory's answers were wrong. The attempt to do in a rival, or to avoid being done in, was often the principal factor behind the introduction of new apparatus (Mackenzie 1977, pp. 18–19).

Kuhn's description of the preparadigm period was not extensive, and he did not focus his attention on the sociological effects of the preparadigm on the functioning of science. However, it is suggested that this is one of the most important implications that may be drawn from the historical description of the early stages of the presently advanced sciences. If there are sciences today that are still in the early stages, the preparadigm stage, of science *then it is important to understand the sociological processes that affect the progress of these sciences*. If psychology, for example, is a preparadigm science, and if there are sociological differences between paradigm and preparadigm sciences, then comparative studies should be possible that would isolate the characteristics involved. An analysis suggests systematic study comparing the preparadigm and paradigm sciences for the sociological characteristics that the analysis predicts, as well as for the effects these characteristics have on the science. Material presented in later chapters will elaborate on this topic, indicating its importance to science.

To continue, however, there are further sociological specifications of the paradigm. Kuhn (1962) has said, for example, that paradigms, once formed, prevent reversion to the preparadigm state of the science area. Although there may be a number of schools or preparadigms (competing groups of scientists) in the area of study prior to the paradigm state, once the paradigm has arisen the field never moves back to the rivalry, lack of communication, and misunderstanding of the earlier phase. One may ask what are the sociological mechanisms that implement this social organization. And what are the advantages of the paradigmatic state such that reversion to preparadigmaticism never occurs? Does the organization, for example, change to produce scientific societies when a paradigm has achieved consensus? Do such societies promote communication? Are publication media formed? Do educational circumstances change from the preparadigm to the paradigm state? Does the philosophy of science change? What are the means by which the social organization changes in moving from the preparadigm state to the paradigm state? Kuhn includes one suggestion (1962) in stating that in the preparadigm state scientific ideas were expressed in books, whereas after the formation of a paradigm, scientific works are then published in articles addressed to other specialists in the science, rather than to the world at large. And, centrally, is the sheer fact of scientists working constructively together a major aspect of the enhanced productivity shown in paradigmatic science areas? Perhaps the importance of the sociological nature of the paradigm is independent of the substantive nature of the paradigm. As an example, it is interesting to wonder if a sociological consensus behind any of the preparadigms in the field of electricity would not have seen an enhanced productivity of the scientists Kuhn described, leading ultimately to the same end result.

The above analysis, in any event, hypothesizes that there are interesting phenomena of a sociological sort to be studied in specifying the paradigm stage as distinguished from the preparadigm stage of science. Moreover, it says that it would be significant, especially, to conduct such a study in a manner that would help to characterize the differences in present day sciences that might fall into the two categories. An essential part of the study would be to establish the relative advantages provided by the two states of social organization. Centrally, although before the fact it might be a task to differentiate preparadigms from paradigms on a substantive basis, sociological factors can aid in that differentiation.

Substantive Definition of Preparadigm-Paradigm Shift

One purpose of the present discussion is to make clear the different dimensions involved in the specification of preparadigms and paradigms. Sociological specifications are involved, and these should be separated conceptually from substantive specifications. That is, the paradigm is not defined solely by the cooperative-versus-competitive behavior of the various scientists involved; however, what the differences are exactly in the substantive structures of the preparadigm and the paradigm have not been specified. That type of knowledge will only be gained by systematic study, which has not been made yet. Kuhn makes brief reference to some characteristics that are of interest in the present context. They are of interest because they agree with the observations that I have made of my own science. Centrally, Kuhn has suggested that "there is commonality to the various schools." Although the various schools contain many elements that differ, and although the schools may be in sharp conflict and competition and rivalry, which prevents a cooperative endeavor, nevertheless they contain much in common. This is a crucial principle for psychology.

Conversely, the preparadigms will also contain elements that are not valuable. There will be misleading, unconfirmed facts (Kuhn refers to the "heating by antiperistasis"). There will also be concern with things that are too complex to be considered at the time. There are other elements in preparadigms that can be considered unproductive in terms of establishing a paradigmatic path of continuous progress. In the next chapter I will refer to the many studies published on paired-associate learning that are trivial, unimportant facts. The same is true of the many superfluous studies of reinforcement schedules. A small percentage of experimental studies in most areas will turn out to be germane to the ultimate development of psychology.

I have quoted Kuhn's passage and abstracted two principles — that preparadigms will contain common elements and that they will contain different materials, some of which will later come to be known as incorrect and worthless or obstructive. The two principles are ones that I have abstracted from my study of the science. On the basis of this study I would add that different, even opposing, approaches (preparadigms) in psychology, when examined in principle, can be seen to overlap. Sometimes concepts are even taken from each other, but similar elements that are part of opposing preparadigms will not be recognized as being similar. The differences in the structures of which they are a part will dictate that the similarity is not recognized. The same is true of the other characteristic of preparadigms, that they contain materials that are incorrect and inappropriate. All the various preparadigms in psychology contain elements that will ultimately prove to be valueless and obstructive in terms of the paradigm that later develops in the particular area of study.

We would expect these characteristics from the previously presented conception of the progressive development of science. To recapitulate, a number of people begin studying systematically in some area of the empirical world. They commence with a very unclear conceptual understanding of the events involved. They will ordinarily have a religious or mystical view, at least at the beginning, and their techniques of gathering knowledge will be poor. As they systematically study the subject matter, however, they will begin to gather observations, some of which will be accurate, or relatively so. The observations that are made will be interpreted in terms of the individual's conceptual system. This process will make for similarities and differences in the preparadigms that eventuate — observations of the events of the world will produce some similarities, for example, while the differences in background beliefs, theories, superstitions, or whatever, will produce idiosyncratic differences.

In a state where there are a number of such preparadigms, establishing a paradigm will involve the sifting process of selecting that which is true and discarding that which is useless and misleading from the knowledge fund that is presented by the various preparadigms in an area. This must involve the work of a theorist or a number of theorists cumulatively performing the task. The paradigm that results in such a case can be expected to have many features from the knowledge provided by the various preparadigms. As I will elaborate in the third part of the book, I would expect the valuable elements that can be employed in the formation of a paradigm to be among those that have been common to the several preparadigms. Although this cannot be expected to hold in all cases, typically the principles that will ultimately prove to be durable in the construction of a paradigm of lasting development are those principles that the scientists from the various preparadigms have found to be compelling in nature. I have referred to these as heavyweight products (Staats, 1963).

Much of what is involved in any preparadigm established under the aegis of an incorrect view, will not be basic and not be valuable. The paradigm, thus, will be simpler, more clear, and more succinct than any of the preparadigms, a central reason it is more valuable to the scientist than the multiple preparadigms that together include the necessary constituents, but embedded in an exceedingly complex structure that appears as a consequence to be a mish mash. The paradigm is more simple because many of the mistaken beliefs and superfluous elements of the preparadigms will have been discarded, including unnecessary problems of study, unnecessary methods of study, as well as unnecessary concepts, and an incorrect overall theory. More will be said of these matters in later chapters. It is because the paradigm is a superior framework, which can provide the basis for continuing progress, that insures the science area will never revert to its former divisive state. These are the present hypotheses.

Philosophical Definition of the Preparadigm-Paradigm Shift

I will not say much on this topic, because it will be dealt with more deeply in the discussions to follow. The point is that the methodology and the philosophy of science of the preparadigm scientist can be expected to differ from those of the paradigm scientist. Briefly, the guiding philosophical framework of the preparadigm scientist will be that of winning the preparadigm conflict. His concepts of science will be determined by what he experiences. Experiencing difference and competition, he will take such a state of affairs to be the inevitable characteristics of his science. He will learn a methodology likely to lead to success within the science as he sees it to be characterized.

The paradigmatic scientist, having different experiences, will have a different view of his science. He will also learn a different methodology for conducting science, at least in certain respects that are relevant to preparadigm and paradigm science activities. Aspects of a paradigm methodology for psychology will be discussed in the last part of the present work.

Preparadigmatic Science and Paradigmatic Science

It has been said the concept of the paradigm was ambiguously defined. Moreover, there has been no systematic definition of the paradigmatic science. And there has been no distinction of the concepts of paradigm and paradigmatic science. These weaknesses have underlain some of the confusions in applying the concept of the paradigm to the social sciences. It is constructive to make the necessary distinctions in developing the present conceptualization.

As indicated by the example of Kuhn excerpted earlier, the definition of the paradigm involves areas of a science, rather than a whole science. Kuhn's examples characterizing preparadigm-to-paradigm development involved areas like the study of electricity and light and visual optics. Yet, on the basis of these examples of paradigms, sciences are considered as having reached the paradigm stage. There is an ambiguity involved in this lack of distinction of the paradigm from the paradigmatic science. Does the presence of one paradigm in a science area make the science paradigmatic? Or are the two concepts not coextensive? If the differences between paradigmatic sciences and preparadigmatic sciences are important — and as will be indicated it is the present thesis that they have central importance for considering the development of preparadigmatic sciences — then it is essential to understand these differences. In the present view this must involve consideration of the paradigmatic science, not just the paradigm. Without a concept of the paradigmatic and preparadigmatic science, social scientists have not known how to categorize and to consider the characteristics of their own science. That is the basic reason why there is disagreement in the social sciences in this area. Actually, the concepts of the preparadigmatic and paradigmatic science have much greater importance than the concept of the paradigm.

To begin the clarification, the concept of the paradigm refers to limited-area concerns within a science. In physics, in the context of paradigms, such areas as physical optics, electricity, and mechanics have been described (Kuhn 1962). In psychology we have areas of concern like personality, learning, communication, reading, social interaction, attribution, learned helplessness, and many more. Likewise, Ritzer says that, employing Eckberg and Hill's concept of the paradigm as an exemplar, "within one substantive area in sociology — occupational sociology — we could identify such paradigms (following the model of status attainment) as job satisfaction, alienation, commitment, role conflict, professionalization, and innumerable others" (Ritzer 1981, pp. 245-46). Only confusion results from attempting to characterize a science by reference to such diversity.

One definition of a paradigmatic science would be that a paradigmatic science contains paradigms. That seemed to be Kuhn's first approach. Accordingly he rejected psychology and the social sciences from consideration as paradigm sciences because he felt they lacked paradigms. His later view (Kuhn 1970a,b), however, stated that preparadigms were also paradigms — and thus the basis for distinguishing paradigmatic sciences from preparadigmatic sciences was lost. In the present view, although the preparadigm may have some of the constituents a paradigm does, it does not have other characteristics described herein that underlie obtaining a consensus and maintaining it. So preparadigms are not paradigms. Masterman (1970) makes the mistake of thinking that the social sciences have paradigms — hence her classifying the social sciences as multiple-paradigm sciences — but psychology does not have paradigms. It only has preparadigms, as will be indicated. The present view disagrees with Kuhn's approach in yet another way, for in any event it is not the presence of a paradigm in a science that makes the science paradigmatic. Having a paradigm, or paradigms, is an important feature separating paradigmatic sciences from preparadigmatic sciences. This is a necessary characteristic, but it is not the only one.

Let us elaborate this by stipulating that the paradigmatic science must include paradigms, content areas in which a consensus has been reached concerning theory, philosophy of science, methods, findings, problems, and so on. This requires additional specification, however. To illustrate, if in the great scope of a science like psychology one could show that there was one paradigm, or perhaps several, or even more, would one conclude that the science was paradigmatic? What if the largest proportion of the areas of study in the science were in a preparadigmatic state, with chaotic controversy concerning methods, problems, philosophy, findings, theory, and so on? If this was the case, it might be difficult to justify considering the science to be paradigmatic in comparison to other sciences where the majority of the areas with which the science was concerned were paradigmatic. Thus, it is suggested that a science is not paradigmatic until it has a large proportion of paradigmatic development in its various areas. Sciences that show a preponderance of preparadigmatic area conflict and chaos in competing theories, methods, problems, and so on, across various area-concerns are not paradigmatic sciences. Perhaps an even more precise way of indicating this concept would be to say that there is a dimension in moving towards being a paradigmatic science, a dimension involving the proportion of areas in the science that have paradigms. The absence of paradigms, or the existence of only very few paradigms, would indicate that the science was not paradigmatic.

This, it is suggested, is an important characteristic of science: the proportion of paradigm areas. But the characteristic still does not get at the heart of what makes a science paradigmatic. Thus, a science could have developed some paradigms, but each could be in conflict with the others, on very basic matters. The several paradigms could follow a different philosophy of science, different experimental methods, different and conflicting theories, and the like. Such a state would not represent a paradigmatic science.

To continue, it is suggested that although separate paradigm developments are essential in a science and contribute toward the science's advancement to the paradigmatic level, as individual paradigms they do not constitute the paradigmatic science. The paradigmatic science consists of a broad framework that encompasses and unifies a major number of paradigms so that they are related in a general interest in a generous aspect of the natural world. The broad framework of a paradigmatic science also includes various specific methods of observation and experimentation that are mutually consistent and recognized as complementary within the general methodology of the science. The paradigmatic science includes a philosophy of science, explicit or implicit, that is consistent across the various specific area-interests of the scientists working in the science — consistent in terms of methods, problems, theory, and so on. One essential aspect of this philosophy — a belief in the unity of the science — is so central it will be described more fully in a later chapter. The paradigmatic science also has a theoretical structure that is consistent across many of the area paradigms included in the science. The theory may not serve a heuristic function for all the paradigms in the paradigmatic science, but it will ordinarily not be opposed by, rivaled by, or invalidated by the theoretical developments in the several paradigms. The theory of the science may in fact involve more than one theoretical body, but again there will ordinarily not be mutual invalidation but rather eventual continuity or complementarity will be expected.

This must be qualified in several ways, of course. For example, at research frontiers there may be unanswered questions that pose problems for the general science theory as well as for the specific paradigm involved. There may also be bodies of knowledge — theory, findings, methods, and so on — that are not related to one another. It is, however, the mark of the paradigmatic science to believe typically that at some later date the bodies of knowledge will be interrelated. But, of course, there may be conflicting theories, approaches, or strategies, until the conflict is resolved. In general, it is suggested that the various examples of paradigms in the science of physics referred to by Kuhn *do not* define the paradigmatic science. It is *the general unification and continuity of method, theory, philosophy, problems, and so on, that make the science paradigmatic.*

Furthermore, in the present view there is a development involved, organized along a dimension, from the primitive to the advanced stage of paradigmatic science. At the primitive level various individuals are simply interested in various aspects of their world. They make observations, they devise methods of study, they make theories, and they formulate a philosophy of how to go about things in general. These products of various men are idiosyncratic and in conflict with each other in the various characteristics. Preparadigms may organize around such opposing approaches. Advancing further, certain preparadigms, in their competitions, ultimately put together a body of elements that can undergo continuous development and that are superior enough to be generally adopted. These are paradigms. Still the different paradigms may be in conflict, or at first they may simply remain unrelated. When they are joined into a large framework composing an important part of the science, along with the development of a common philosophy and so on, the science can be said to be paradigmatic. There is always a dimensional characteristic involved, however. There is a more or less state of being a paradigmatic science. Sciences could be described on a dimension of how paradigmatically unified they are. It may be added that it is conceivable that one day there will be a very large paradigmatic formulation that will include all of science — and well-known scientists and philosophers have proposed this unity of science as the ultimate goal, as will be indicated in the next section.

In any event, the present conception is that paradigms alone do not make a paradigmatic science. It is only when paradigms are placed in a framework that establishes continuity between the paradigms that there is an organized, paradigmatic science. When this has occurred, the science has an organized, building characteristic. The students in the science are trained in the various paradigms. Yes. But they are also trained in the general science, its philosophy, its methodology, its theory, and so on, as well as in the special problem areas. The individual scientist may develop special skills for his paradigmatic area, skills unimportant to other paradigmatic areas, but these skills are added on to the general foundation that he has acquired from the paradigmatic science. As will be indicated, this and other things do not pertain to the preparadigmatic science, or only at a much reduced level.

At this point, it is relevant to briefly outline what psychology would need to develop in order to become a paradigmatic science. To begin, within the multifarious areas of the science, one requirement would involve change in many cases from a state where there are competing approaches within the same specialized area of study to a state where there would be one consensually accepted paradigm in the area. A paradigm would be reached, for example, in the field of social interaction (with its subparts involving attraction, prejudice, leadership, conformity, communication, and so on) when there was consensus concerning the approach (theory, methods, problems, philosophy, and so on) to be followed. The same would be true for personality, child development, learning theory, reading, intelligence, memory, information processing, psychotherapy, abnormal psychology, and many more. In addition, however, paradigmatic science status for psychology would involve attaining the state where many of its areas developed paradigms.

But that alone would not make psychology a paradigmatic science. It would be necessary that the various paradigms were not in competition with one another. It would be necessary also that there be an overall conceptual-methodological-philosophical umbrella that related at least a good portion of the various paradigms to each other in a harmonious, unified, and frequently productive and heuristic manner. And, as a later chapter will indicate, there would be the overall philosophy of the paradigmatic science, which is different than that of the preparadigmatic science in important features. This is an essential characteristic that must be given separate treatment. In any event, the preparadigmatic science is being defined here also by the absence of paradigmatic science characteristics. As will be dealt with prominently herein, there are also preparadigmatic characteristics themselves that must be understood in order to understand the preparadigmatic science. In fact, a major thrust to the present work is to define directly the modern preparadigmatic science of psychology.

With this as the standard, it will be the task of the next chapter to begin to consider psychology in terms of its paradigmatic character, or lack of such. For it should be suggested, even from this preliminary description, that psychology in no manner approaches the paradigmatic state described above. The present account, however, has also touched upon the issues of unity as a characteristic of and a goal of science. These issues are centrally germane to the present work and consideration of the issues is necessary in developing this work. For the preparadigmatic to paradigmatic advancement is essentially that of attaining organization and unity in the science versus the competition, rivalry, and chaotic disorganization that existed before. The movement from the preparadigmatic state to the paradigmatic science state, it should be stressed, is such a momentous development for the science that we may apply the term revolution to the process.

UNITY OF SCIENCE, REDUCTIONISM, AND THE WELTANSCHAUUNGEN VIEWS

Unity of science, although it may be a question of contemporary interest and controversy, is not a new concept. As Stevens (1939) indicated, Leibnitz in 1666 displayed a concern with attaining unified science. Leibnitz proposed creation of "*a general method in which all truths of reason would be reduced to a kind of calculation . . . a sort of universal language or script*" (Stevens 1939, p. 41) (italics added). Neurath (1937) introduced into the Vienna Circle of logical positivists the idea of a unified basis of science and the *International Encyclopedia of Unified Science* was begun. Stevens summarized the logical positivist view of the unity of science as including (1) unity of its logic and syntax, (2) distinction of the formal (theoretical) and empirical aspects of science, (3) recognition that logic and mathematics are simply symbolic statements, (4) recognition that empirical statements have meaning only when there is a concrete procedure for testing them, (5) recognition that the truth of an empirical proposition is never absolutely proved, only made more likely, and (6) recognition of the fact that all scientific sentences must be in a physical language—that is, pertain to physical happenings—which commits psychology to being behavioristic (Stevens 1939, pp. 42–43). This view, it may be stressed, is not a program to use in the task of creating unity of science. To continue, however, the goal of unity of science has been accepted by philosophers of science of a logical-positivist persuasion very generally (Braithwaite 1955; Reichenbach 1951), the following being one example.

> The aim of scientific explanation throughout the ages has been *unification*, i.e., the comprehending of a maximum of facts and regularities in terms of a minimum of theoretical concepts and assumptions. The remarkable success achieved, especially in the theories of physics, chemistry, and to some extent recent biology, has encouraged pursuit of a unitary system of explanatory premises (Feigl 1970, p. 12).

Such statements of philosophy, as is typical, are derived from observation of what occurs in science. There have been many cases in science where unification has been achieved via theories that brought together previously separated elements of knowledge. Newton's theoretical works have been employed as examples many times. "Newton's principle of gravitation . . . provided a theoretical integration of such laws as Kepler's concerning planetary motions, Galileo's law of falling bodies, laws of the tides and so on" (Spence 1944, p. 48).

Reductionism

Philosophy of science descriptions, however, typically give rise to prescriptive treatments, and the present case is no exception. One of the aspects of logical positivism has been its program for achieving unity. The method is called theory reduction, or reductionism. As Suppe (1977) indicates, according to the logical-positivism view, scientific progress occurs in several ways. In one very important way, "various disparate theories, each enjoying high degrees of confirmation, are included in or *reduced* to, some more inclusive theory" (italics added) (Suppe 1977b, p. 53). In this view the most important type of scientific progress is seen to result from reduction. Suppe has very succinctly summarized the logical-positivist position.

> . . . Once a theory is accepted, then, scientific progress concerning it is of the second sort, consisting of attempts to expand TC [the theory and its content] to a wider scope—that is, in the production of TC', TC'', and so on. Each of these expanded versions of TC is a new theory. . . . [The C in the above term may be taken to refer to the descriptions of the phenomena that the theory T treats.] This expansion of the scope of a theory is a form of *theory reduction*. Nagel characterizes such reduction, thusly, "the laws of the *secondary science* [TC'] employ no descriptive terms that are not used with approximately the same meanings in the primary science [TC]. Reductions of this type can be regarded as establishing deductive relations between two sets of statements that employ a homogeneous vocabulary" (Nagel 1961, p. 339). Essentially the same form of reduction is involved if TC is expanded to a wider scope of augmenting the theoretical principles T by additional ones which use the same theoretical terms as TC, thus obtaining T'C or T'C' [the term T'C indicates change in the principles of the theory and T'C' indicates both change in the theory as well as change in the events to which the theory is addressed]. . . . Thus the development and expansion of a theory is via this first form of theory reduction, and consists in the replacement of TC by closely related, more comprehensive theories.
>   Scientific progress sometimes involves a second form of theory reduction which occurs in science when a theory TC is absorbed into a more inclusive or comprehensive theory—for example, the reduction of thermodynamics to statistical mechanics or the reduction of Kepler's laws to Newton's dynamics. "The phenomenon of a relatively autonomous theory being absorbed by, or reduced to, some more inclusive theory is an undeniable and recurrent feature of the history of modern science" [Nagel 1961, p. 337]. When the conditions are met all of the laws and observable

consequences of the secondary theory can be deduced from the primary theory, and so the secondary theory has been reduced to, or incorporated into, the primary theory. As such the reduction is "the explanation of a theory or a set of experimental laws established in one area of inquiry, by a theory usually though not invariably formulated in some other domain" [Nagel 1961, p. 338] (Suppe 1977b, pp. 54–56).

Anti-Reductionism

The methodology of reductionism has very general implications, as we can see from the following statement.

> It . . . would not be very surprising if the hopes, held for a long time, that chemistry can be reduced to physics, were to come true, as indeed they seem to be doing. . . .
> It is also conceivable, though less likely, that we may one day have *good reduction* of biology, including physiology, to physics, and of psychology to physiology, and thus to physics (Popper 1972, pp. 290–94).

The implication of reductionism for social science, of course, is that social science is expendable. The suggestion is that there is a hierarchy of sciences, with the most general and important science being that of physics. In due time psychology will disappear into physiology and then into physics. The process implies that the area or theory to be reduced is weak, or valueless, or redundant. It would hardly be promising to be identified with such a subservient science. It is thus no wonder that there have been various expressions against the concept of reductionism in psychology. "Skinner's approach . . . rejects even the logical possibility of a reductionism" (Verplanck 1954, pp. 308–09). Skinner's philosophy, it may be added, does not provide the basis for extending behavioral psychology upward to link with the other social sciences, or downward to link with physiological psychology, physiology, and so on. And his philosophy has been influential in psychology. There are other influential psychologists who, although of different theoretical persuasions, have been just as adamantly opposed to reductionism. Gestalt psychologists, to give one more example, were in good part identified by this characteristic. A primary tenet of their study of human behavior was that the whole was greater than the sum of its parts. The idea was that human acts could not be explained by resort to analysis of constituent, more elementary, processes. Explanation could only be gained by understanding the process as a whole (Boring 1950). This represents not only a denial of reductionism to other sciences, but of reductionism even to more elementary areas of study in psychology.

It is interesting to note, in giving this analysis more breadth, that the other social sciences also contain anti-reductionistic sentiments, and that these are frequently addressed not to the natural sciences or to the biological sciences, but to psychology. It has been said many times in various social sciences that the particular science involved is not reducible to psychology. White has said that history, like sociology, deals with social concepts and therefore should not be reduced to psychology (1943, p. 12). Gellner (1956) has applied to history and sociology the Gestalt argument against analytic conceptualization of human behavior. In sociology it has been suggested that there are emergent social phenomena that are basic in and of themselves, not reducible to other disciplines. "Since [the] essential characteristic [of social phenomena] consists in the power they possess of exerting, from outside, a pressure on individual consciousness, sociology is not a corollary of psychology" (Durkheim 1927, pp. 124–25). The same type of functionalism has pertained in anthropology (Wallace 1962, p. 2). Mandelbaum (1955, pp. 306–07), in stating a nonreductionistic position, argues vigorously against psychologizing and for the uniqueness of emergent social concepts and principles, and he warns of an attempt to unify the social sciences within one set of concepts and basic principles, as well as one philosophy of science.

Weltanschauungen Concepts of Unity

It can be seen from this brief indication that there is not unanimous agreement with the reductionistic program of unification. It may be added that the logical-positivism view of unity of science, as based upon a physicalistic common language with axiomatic logical analysis, has been rejected in contemporary philosophy of science (Suppe 1977). Nevertheless, this rejection does not extend to the description of science as progressing towards unity. We can see the same recognition of the importance of generality and unity in the statements of philosophers of science not identified with the orthodox (logical-positivist) approach. Lakatos (1970), for example, gives emphasis to the role of research programs in the development of science, research programs that give the science organized unification. The same is true of Toulmin's (1972) disciplines, Shapere's (1977) domains, and Lindley Darden's (1974) fields — which conceptually are analogous to Kuhn's concept of the paradigm, which we will see has been criticized for its suggestion that science should be unified.

It is productive here to also indicate something about Shapere's notions, because they are in agreement with later discussions to be made concerning unification in psychology. Shapere develops his notions in the context of examples in physics.

> Thus there were strong grounds for believing that electricity and magnetism constituted distinct subjects for investigation, for which different explanations were to be given. Nevertheless, in spite of these clear differ-

ences, reasons accumulated over the succeeding two or three centuries for *suspecting* that these differences might prove to be superficial, and that there was some deep relationship to be found between electrical and magnetic phenomena. . . .

The phenomena of electricity, particularly in the nineteenth century, also came more and more to be connected with chemical phenomena; and, through this association of electricity with chemistry, the suspicion — growing gradually into an expectation or even a demand — arose that a unified theory of electricity and matter should, in some form, be sought. . . .

The relations between electricity and light underwent a similar development. Faraday's demonstration of the effect of a magnetic field on the plane of polarization of a light ray provided one sort of consideration leading to the belief that there was a deeper relationship to be sought between magnetism and hence, because of the developments summarized above, electricity and light (Shapere 1977, pp. 519–21).

This passage contains an implicit point that has not been abstracted for consideration. What is being described is the conviction of the scientists of the time that later discoveries would show unity. They believed in the unity of their subject matter even before it was shown to exist. The importance of this belief will be indicated further on. At this point it is germane to use this passage to indicate why it is that philosophers of science stress that science has the goal of unity. They do so because that is the way scientists behave — and in describing that behavior they abstract a prescriptive principle that science should strive for unified knowledge. "Such cases [as the above] are common in the history of science: . . . we find a general trend toward unification" (Shapere 1977, p. 527). Shapere, it may be noted, aided by the vantage point of historical description in the natural sciences, characterizes primitive stages of science by the inability to see such unity. This is like the present characterization of the nature of psychology. Because unity has not generally emerged in psychology, at least as recognized, the goal of unity can only be a projection for this science rather than a conclusion based on historical demonstrations.

Criticism of Paradigmatic Unity:
The Principle of Proliferation

We have seen that there have been opponents of the logical-positivism view of the value of unity of science and of the method of reductionism in attaining such unity. The same is true of the weltanschauung view of the value of unity, as we can see by referring to critics of Kuhn's approach. Like Lakatos's research programs, Toulmin's disciplines, Darden's fields, and Shapere's domains, Kuhn's concept of the paradigm also contains a philosophy of unified endeavor in science. In fact the concept of the paradigm had the effect of raising once more in the philosophy of science the question of the value of the unity of science.

> . . . Yet it was precisely the unity, and the controlling status, of paradigms that constituted the appeal and the challenge of Kuhn's original view: the contention that there was a coherent, unified viewpoint, a single overarching Weltanschauung, a disciplinary Zeitgeist, that determined the way scientists of a given tradition viewed and dealt with the world, that determined what they would consider to be a legitimate problem, a piece of evidence, a good reason, an acceptable solution, and so on (Shapere 1971, p. 707).

As has been indicated, however, the appeal of this view was not universal. And some of the criticism was directed against the idea that there is and should be a paradigm that directs the work of scientists in a unified manner during the normal science phase. The paradigm conception suggested to some philosophers of science that science normally operates in a conformist way, directed by the paradigm, as the following statement by Feyerabend indicates.

> . . . More than one social scientist has pointed out to me that now at last he had learned how to turn his field into a "science" — by which of course he meant that he had learned how to *improve* it. The recipe, according to these people, is to restrict criticism, to reduce the number of comprehensive theories to one, and to create a normal science that has this one theory as its paradigm. Students must be prevented from speculating along different lines and the more restless colleagues must be made to conform and "to do serious work." *Is this what Kuhn wants to achieve?* Is it his intention to provide a historico-scientific justification for the ever growing need to identify with some group? Does he want every subject to imitate the monolithic character of, say, the quantum theory of 1930? Does he think that a discipline that has been constructed in this manner is in some ways better off? That it will lead to better, to more numerous, to more interesting results? (Feyerabend 1970a, pp. 198–99).

Popper (1970) also rejected Kuhn's notion of normal science. For Kuhn, normal science consisted of unified work within the paradigm, conducted in a puzzle-solving manner, in a manner to elaborate and substantiate the paradigm. To Popper that was the work of the applied scientist, not the creative scientist, who is ever skeptical, ever looking for new approaches.

> Finally, since theories can only be falsified and not confirmed, Popper views it as being unjustified for science to maintain one theory to the ex-

clusion of all others. Rather, theories are conjectures, and science ought to proliferate theories as much as possible, subjecting a wide variety of theories to possible empirical falsification. Indeed, it is exactly this proliferation of a variety of theories which is responsible for the growth of scientific knowledge. Science should not be a closed society dogmatically tied to single theories or conjectures; it ought to be an open society (Suppe 1977, p. 170).

We see in this statement the presentation of a principle that is antagonistic to the quest for unity that has been described herein, the principle of proliferation. Feyerabend has elaborated this principle in the present context and drawn its implications as an antagonist of unity in science.

I am sorry to say that I am quite dissatisfied with what Kuhn has to offer on this point. . . . [H]e steadfastly emphasizes the dogmatic, authoritarian, and narrowminded features of normal science, the fact that it leads to a temporary 'closing of the mind' (Kuhn 1961a, p. 393) (Feyerabend 1970a, p. 205). . . . What is needed [in Kuhn's view] is the acceptance of *one* theory and the relentless attempt to fit nature into its pattern (Feyerabend 1970a, p. 202).

. . . [S]cience must use a principle of tenacity together with a principle of proliferation. . . . Proliferation means that there is no need to suppress even the most outlandish product of the human brain. *Everyone may follow his inclinations* and science, conceived as a critical enterprise, will profit from such an activity (Feyerabend 1970a, p. 20).

. . . [I]nvent and elaborate theories which are inconsistent with the accepted point of view, even if the latter should happen to be highly confirmed and generally accepted (Feyerabend 1970b, p. 26).

The principle of proliferation is thus set in opposition to the idea that unity should be sought in science. As will be indicated further on, this is an unfortunate opposition, because the principle of proliferation is important as a guide to scientific activity, as is the goal of unity of science. Before indicating how these two principles can be reconciled, another aspect of the philosophy that is opposed to the search for unity will be described, that of incommensurability. Interestingly, Kuhn is the author of the concept of incommensurability — which is used by some to oppose the search for unity — although Kuhn's concept of the paradigm has been taken to be in support of the unified, organized direction of science.

Kuhn (1962) said that the paradigm dictates the view the scientist has. The paradigm determines what problems will be considered to be significant. The paradigm determines what facts are important, as well as what will be considered as a fact. Theoretical terms and the meanings given to the terms will be determined by the paradigm. The important point, however, in the present context is that different paradigms, even when directed to the study of the same realm of events, will produce different views of the world. There will not even be agreement on what constitutes facts, methods, philosophies, general strategies, and so on. Moreover, Kuhn indicated that different paradigms are incommensurate — their elements cannot be placed in conjunction with one another so as to be meaningful to one another. The scientists in different paradigms will not be able to communicate with one another.

> The proponents of competing paradigms are always at least slightly at cross-purposes. Neither side will grant all the non-empirical assumptions that the other needs in order to make its case. Like Proust and Berthollet arguing about the composition of chemical compounds, they are bound partly to talk through each other. Though each may hope to convert the other to his way of seeing his science and its problems, neither may hope to prove his case. The competition between paradigms is not the sort of battle that can be resolved by proofs. . . . In the first place, the proponents of competing paradigms will often disagree about the list of problems that any candidate for paradigm must resolve. Their standards or their definitions of science are not the same (1962, p. 147).

In essence the concept of incommensurability has stimulated a philosophy that says that incommensurability is an expected characteristic of science — that it is incorrect to expect unification generally in science. There are new voices in psychology that state that science is intrinsically incommensurable, on a very broad and general basis. Koch (1978, 1981), for example, says that psychology is by nature to consist of separated fields, and separate bodies of knowledge within the same field. The acceptance or rejection of this philosophy is of great moment in the development of the science, and later discussions will return to this topic, on the basis of the foundation that is being presented here.

One point that should be made now is that in the philosophy of science there is not unanimity with respect to the concept of incommensurability. Lakatos (1970), Popper (1970), and Toulmin (1970) have criticized the view. The arguments have already been given herein to some extent. That is, various philosophers of science have rejected the irrationality and relativism entailed in Kuhn's approach. Kuhn, in the face of such criticism, has modified his position to suggest that incommensurability is not absolute and that some translation can occur (1970). However, the concept of incommensurability requires much more consideration than this, in treating the topic of unity in a preparadigmatic science such as psychology.

For one thing, it is suggested that the concept of incommensurability was developed in the context of the natural sciences. Yet incommensurability cannot be seen in its full development, or its importance realized, when one considers only paradigmatic science. Although there are cases of incommensurability in paradigmatic science, when there are clashes between an old and a new paradigm, it is not until one looks at the preparadigmatic science that one can realize in great scope what is involved. As will be described in the next chapter, in the preparadigmatic science there is incommensurability between theories large and small, between specialized fields of study, between bodies of fact, between apparatus modes, between methods of research and theory construction strategies, and between philosophies of science. Moreover, there are many different separated knowledge entities formed on the basis of these elements. This means that there is much, much incommensurability. In fact, the preparadigmatic field may be most aptly described, perhaps, by its lack of communication. It has been said that incommensurability cannot be seen fully in the paradigmatic science. This also pertains to the effects of incommensurability. When intercommunication is low in a field, we may also be interested in what this does to the science. If the effects are a problem, we may also be interested in asking how incommensurability can be reduced in the science. That is the situation that pertains in psychology. Special treatment will be required to establish understanding of what is involved, as later discussions will indicate.

We have seen that there are contemporary voices in the philosophy of science that have spoken against unity of science. There is the idea that a philosophy must stress proliferation of theory in science, against the stultification that may be produced by theories and paradigms. And there is the idea of incommensurability; that there are in science theories and paradigms that although they pertain to the same realm of events are intrinsically incommensurable. Each of the incommensurable positions involved may be equally valid, but they cannot be brought into relationship with one another. This philosophy puts a positive value on the fact that psychology is disunified and that its manifold separate parts have not been interrelated.

To some extent these views arose as a response to the restrictiveness of the philosophy that preceded more contemporary approaches, the philosophy of logical positivism and its narrow views of the unity of science. However, the opponents of unity have not resolved the schism between unity and proliferation, between whether science should strive to be unified and organized, or whether science should simply proliferate diversity. In the context of the natural sciences the issue is not of overwhelming importance, because the natural sciences long ago solved their problems concerning unification. Regardless of what the philosophers conclude, natural scientists strive for generality and unity, and they have rules of science work that promote unity. But for sciences that have not attained the level of advancement of the natural sciences, the issue is still of overwhelming importance, and there is no philosophy that resolves the issue or, equally importantly, presents methodological guides to follow in implementing the resolution. The following section will indicate that both proliferation and the search for unity are important to science. The trick is to realize under what circumstances the one or the other is called for.

UNITY AND PROLIFERATION:
THE PHASE PRINCIPLE OF RELATIONSHIP

The value of creating ever more general theory and of unifying previously separated bodies of knowledge is very evident as a sign of progress of science. A few words should be said of this circumstance. For one thing generality and unity of science are related to a very general value in science, that of the search for parsimony. It has been generally accepted that, other things equal, the more simple a theory is in science the better. Parsimony has very functional qualities in science. That is, the utility of a theory rests in good part on its ability to organize knowledge on the most general level possible (Braithwaite 1955; Reichenbach 1951). Our understanding is increased in its scope, when our knowledge is organized within the same theoretical language, which means that it is easier for us to grasp and incorporate. On the other hand, the smaller the range of the theory, the larger the number of the theories necessary to deal with the events of our natural world. Different theoretical languages require time and effort to learn. And there is a limit to how many can be learned by one individual. The necessity of learning multiple theory languages makes the task of the scholar, the student, and the practicing scientist more difficult. On the other hand, the theory that combines, unites, and organizes an extensive range of events provides us with increasing conceptual ability, to the extent of its generality, partly through the simplification it provides. We can learn about many things with relative ease, within one theory language. This is true when the theory organizes descriptions of empirical events, and it is true when it organizes other theoretical efforts. A theory that relates and encompasses several theoretical formulations provides a more general theory, and this is to be sought, for its utility in these senses. If nature is organized, interconnected in its parts, with general laws, then a goal of science must be to produce theory that reflects these characteristics. Such a theory is more valuable than a number of part theories, even though they are equally true, because simplicity is tremendously functional. Each unnecessary theory, also, typically produces inefficiency in terms of increased competitiveness, loss of communication, possibly competitive social organizations, and so on. One of the important characteristics of science is its building character, as will be indicated later, and this character depends upon the communication and cooperation that is yielded by unity and organization.

Additional functions of theory may also be expected to be increased by an increase in the generality of the theory involved. When different areas of empirical findings or of theoretical statements are united by a new, general theoretical statement, additional heuristic products ordinarily result. Thus, a theory showing the relationship between two heretofore separate areas of empirical research may suggest that principles already found in one of the areas, but not yet found in the other area, may be relevant. The principles can thus serve as hypotheses for new investigations in the other area.

It should be noted, in addition, that a theory that deals with several areas will ordinarily require characteristics that were not necessary in the separate area theories. The general theory will ordinarily thus have additional principles, or more generally stated principles, than the individual theories. The general theory will thus function as a better device for instigation of new investigations in each area, and perhaps in areas not yet studied at all.

Because of the tremendous power that is gained through achieving unity in science, it is important that the search for unity not be displaced by philosophies that devalue unity. On the other hand, we can recognize that the call for proliferation is not without value also. Popper and Feyerabend have addressed a real problem for science. There are numerous cases in the history of science where a viewpoint, a theory, or a paradigm has become a tradition, and as such has stifled innovative and productive approaches that were inconsistent with the tradition. We all know of discoveries that were delayed greatly in acceptance because they differed from a science tradition. Feyerabend refers to quantum theory as an example of a monolithic theory. Perhaps the most inclusive example is that which A. D. White (1955) has dealt with, the many-fronted battle of various early areas of science to free themselves from the oppressive tradition of Christian theology.

Since Feyerabend and others who similarly resist the idea of unity in science have such an important point to make — the injunction to be innovative in the face of tradition — on what basis can this idea be contested in the defense of unity in science? The injunction to look for the different is incorrect when it is made in a general sense, without specification concerning its selective suitability, a qualification that demands an historical and dynamic perspective. In the present view there are circumstances in science that undulate. In brief statement, there are phases in science when the call to freedom, to proliferation, is an essential ingredient for progress. There are other phases, however, where the productive guide is not proliferation, but rather is the goal of unity of view.

To elaborate one type of phase, the present author has considered that theories have a career, rather than a fixed role, in their impact on science. The concept of the career has been applied to the changes in a theory that take place over time.

> . . . Lakatos is perhaps the most important of a large number of philosophers who have argued that the career of a theory is, at least sometimes, more important than the formal relations between evidence claims and theoretical postulates at any stage of the theory's history. Relevant factors here include, arguably, the theory's ability to accommodate auxiliary hypotheses, its capacity to reshape itself under competitive pressure or in the face of experimental difficulties, its success in predicting facts before they are discovered, etc. These factors are not included in traditional models of theory evaluation — and their inclusion requires a significant departure from the spirit of logicism. This departure is necessitated by the fact that a theory, considered as a product, does not always reflect the intricacies of its career. To understand its career, one must compare materials taken from different stages of its development, materials not included in the finished structure of the theory nor in the totality of evidential claims (Burian 1977, p. 8).

This statement has been selected because of its agreement with the present view. The present purpose of considering the changing career of a theory, however, is not that of examining theory itself, but rather the effects of the theory's career on what is a productive philosophy of science. That is, it is suggested that a theory (or paradigm) has a changing role in the context of a science, and a philosophy of science must include principles that recognize that there are such changes. To elaborate, in line with the ideas of progress in science that have already been expressed, it is suggested that a theory emerges from a context. It is not important in this consideration whether the theory is the product of one man's ideation or whether it is more appropriately described as a joint or group effort. The context consists of the level of advancement at that particular time, that is, the conceptual content, the unsolved but interesting problems, the apparatus, the empirical findings available, and the current theory or theories, and so on. The new theory is constructed within this context. Having the benefit of the full context at that particular time, including the theory or theories that then prevail, the new theory will ordinarily be an improvement upon what has gone before. The past theory, let us say, will have been in existence for some time. Although during that time it will have made the types of adjustments that Burian describes above, its basic nature will have been formulated within the context that pertained at the time of its origin, and its basic nature will be limited by that context. The old theory is a structure containing elements that limit its ability to profit from the new context that has built up in its period of reign.

The new theory has all of the advantages. It has the advantages of access to all the productive elements in the science field, many of them that have stemmed from or have been included in or made possible by the old theory. It should come as no surprise then that new theories are ordinarily improvements and that they come to replace older theories. As an example, very briefly stated, there was a context for the findings and theory of such men as Ivan Pavlov and Edward Thorndike. That is, there was a conceptual context that involved concern with the association of ideas in the one case, and in the other case with pleasure and reward. The associationistic idea that when stimuli were presented together the response to one would be associated with the other was part of the context within which Pavlov's findings and interpretations took place. Moreover, associationism gave his findings contextual significance. The same was true with Thorndike's experimental specification that pleasure, or reward, did indeed have expected effects upon learning and behavior. Hedonism provided a context for interest in such findings. Theories were formed around the findings and the conceptual elements provided in each case by the context. And these theory developments of Pavlov and Thorndike then gave impetus to production of much additional research and theory which then added up to a new context. At a later time in this development the resulting context provided a new foundation for theory development, and the second generation of behavioristic or learning theories began to emerge. At this point the context included both Pavlov's classical conditioning and Thorndike's instrumental conditioning and related experiments and concepts. Both of these were principles of learning, or association. The new context thus included a new problem, how the two types of learning were to be related to one another. This context and its special problem gave rise to the second generation of behaviorism. There were alternate solutions to the problem and the context gave rise to multiple efforts. Some theorists stated that all learning was of the Pavlovian, associative type (for example, Edwin Guthrie), some stated that all learning was of the reward variety of concern to Thorndike (for example, Clark Hull), and some said there were two types of learning (for example, B. F. Skinner). These theories, as individual theories and as they composed a theoretical context, influenced further developments, which along with many other developments, ultimately led to a new context. This brings us to contemporary times when the new context has begun to give rise to a new generation of theory (see Staats 1975). This has been the analysis underlying the present author's use of the concept of the first, second, and third generation of behaviorism (see Staats 1968b, 1975).

The point in the present argument, however, is that a theory at its birth is ordinarily an advance. It profits from what has gone before, and it has capabilities that surpass the theories that have gone before. The theory, because of this advancement, then makes a contribution to the development of the science. In doing so it sets a process in motion that will ultimately result in the theory's demise. That is, it creates a new context, which includes all of the knowledge which it possesses, but not all of the theory's weaknesses. Because the theory was born at an earlier time, in the context of more primitive problems and concerns, it has basic features that are limiting. (See Lakatos 1971, for a related concept, that of the "degenerating stage" in the evolution of a research program, where it ceases to lead to new discoveries.) The new theory is born of a truer vision. The context has changed. It no longer stresses the problems and concerns that existed and gave impetus to the earlier theory. Thus, as an example, a theory in the third generation of behaviorism may not accept the central concern of the second generation with the controversy over whether all learning was Pavlovian, Thorndikian, or both. The new theory can accept other concerns as central, and it can thus provide a structure to guide progress in new directions (see Staats 1968b, 1975). The old theory, at this point in time, cannot provide the new leads that are necessary. Even when it has been patched to take better account of the new context, the old theory has become an obstacle to progress.

Now, with reference to the problem at hand, on the basis of the above analysis, it is suggested that various principles in the philosophy of science may be more or less relevant depending upon the phase that pertains to the science. The development or career of a theory, as described above, is an undulating one. A theory is born, it enjoys enhanced productivity over what existed before, but it produces a new context, which in turn provides the basis for creation of a new theory. Then, with respect to the theory at the end of its career, what was at first an advancement later becomes an obstacle to further progress. The influence of the old theory holds back the acceptance of the new, more progressive theory. The old theory has status, it has supporters, it has organizational strength and can project its achievements widely. It commands attention and allegiance. Against this power the new theory is relatively weak and cannot project its efforts, gain supporters and support, and so on. The power of the old theory even holds scientists back from recognizing how inadequate it is, and from looking for better solutions.

The point of emphasis here is that *an injunction to proliferation and innovation has a different value depending upon in what stage of the process the science finds itself.* In a period just after introduction of a new theory with greatly enhanced heuristic value—a theory that maximally has drawn upon the context in its formulation, a theory markedly in advance of what has existed—the call for proliferation, for innovation inconsistent with the reigning view— a demand for difference for the sake of difference —may have little value. It may provoke useless and wasteful actions. At this point there is nothing new in the context to provide a foundation for productive innovation in the way of theory.

At the other end of the cycle, however, the call may have great value.

The theory has now stimulated much work whose products constitute a new context. In this phase the theory, now old, is no longer making maximal use of the available context. Worse, it has features limited by the context that prevailed at the time of its birth. Its vision is narrowed and it misdirects important efforts in the science. The problem is now to break away from the restrictive blinders the outworn theory imposes. The call for proliferation, for innovation, for the freedom to be different now is central. The call is especially important because old theories are entrenched and difficult to dislodge. Thus, science includes phase processes with respect to the important values of unity and proliferation, and a philosophy of science should contain principles that recognize the phase process. Without such recognition the philosophy's role as a guide is weakened.

Freedom-Versus-Unity, and Paradigmatic Development

The points that have been made in the preceding analysis have special significance when considering preparadigmatic and paradigmatic states of science. Here, again, a temporal consideration of the relevance of proliferative-freedom versus creative-unity philosophies is very important. What to recommend depends very much on the phase of science involved.

To elaborate, as we can abstract from Kuhn's description of the early stages of the natural sciences, and as will be indicated herein with respect to psychology, the preparadigmatic stage of a science is one of great individualistic proliferation of theory and other aspects of science. There are disparate views, disparate findings, disparate methods, and so on. There is a paucity of unity. There is a morass of fact and theory and method. There is no agreement on general goals. There is little communication.

In contrast, in the paradigmatic phase of science the picture is drastically changed. There is unity of purpose, of theory, of methods, of problems, and of findings. When a paradigm has been accepted it pretty well guides the activities of the scientists in the field of the theory's purview. There is less individualism and more organized, cooperative activity.

When considered over these two stages of science, the exhortation to proliferation of views, and so on, has a variable value. In the phase concept of unity-proliferation, a central problem of the well developed preparadigmatic science is its proliferation. There is no need to provide further impetus to the proliferation approach to science. In fact such impetus, as will be indicated, serves a deleterious purpose and is a major obstacle to progress. On the other hand, in paradigmatic science the principle of proliferation and the call for freedom and innovation may be a valuable addition to a philosophy of science that does not recognize the fact that theories and paradigms can be stultifying. The conclusion is that our philosophy must recognize the differing needs of science, if it is to be productively prescriptive. To do so the philosophy of science must include principles that are descriptive of the differing preparadigmatic-paradigmatic developmental characteristics of the sciences, as well as of differing states of theory involving their inception, growth, and decline.

METHODOLOGY OF UNIFICATION

Reductionism was the methodology proposed by logical positivism for producing unity of scientific theory. This method was stated in terms relevant for axiomatic theories, where one was reduced to the other. The same method was proposed by behaviorists whose aim was to create axiomatic theory in psychology (Spence 1944).

This methodology was based upon a philosophy that saw scientific theory to be axiomatic in form. The present view of theory, however, and the concept of theory careers, as well as the concept of the preparadigmatic-paradigmatic progression, provide a different basis for considering methods of creating unification. As the next chapter will begin to describe, psychology as a preparadigmatic science does not have axiomatic theories. It has many, many idiosyncratic varieties of theory, with great incommensurability. It has findings concerning great varieties of phenomena, ordinarily considered to be inheritantly different from one another. It has a variety of different methods of study that are competitive, each claiming to be the true way to develop the science, and each rejecting the others.

The problems of organizing this chaotic mass of knowledge are enormous — and the mass grows by leaps and bounds with each passing month. Yet there has been no systematic attempt to broach the problems involved, to construct a philosophy of unification for the preparadigmatic sciences, and to formulate methods by which to achieve unification of theory, findings, and research methods. There are different theories in psychology, each of which has developed on an idiosyncratic basis with respect to terminology, observations, apparatus, and research methods, but which contain within them much that is common to one another in principle. Two theories, for example, may contain the same principles, or overlap in important parts, yet the actual unity can be obscured by idiosyncratic elements, as will be indicated in later discussions. Now, in the science it would be exceedingly important to show the relationship between the theories. This would simplify the science. Where there formerly had been different principles — frequently thought to be the basis of opposing theories — the science would see the principles were the same and that they pertained to a variety of phenomena. When there are multitudinous such examples in a science, the loss in the classic simplicity of the unified science may be monumental.

There are other types of cases in which unity should be actively pursued in psychology, but is not because of the lack of development of its philosophy of science, and because of the lack of methods for obtaining unity. These are topics for more specialized treatment, however, which will be the purpose of later chapters. After adding a few concluding remarks, I will move into consideration of the characteristics of psychology as a preparadigmatic science. Following that I will return to the topic of producing unified theory in our preparadigmatic science, as part of the present philosophy that it is this means by which the science will make the tremendous leap that changing to a paradigmatic science will represent.

Further Clarification

These several sections have been intended to serve several purposes. A brief description of the manner in which science progresses from disunity to unity has been presented. Various concepts have been invoked in referring to unity and they need to be reconciled with each other within the general understanding of what unity of science is, the role unity serves in science, what its functions are, the manner in which it is appropriate to strive for unity, as well as the manner in which it is not appropriate to do so. Unity of science means different things to different people because special characteristics that are not intrinsic to the description have been attached to it. Thus, for example, unity of science within logical positivism meant establishing a common logic and physicalistic language, which would serve as the basis for axiomatizing all scientific theories and thereby creating unity. This approach would have meant the subordination of all areas of study to methods and characteristics that were not appropriate. Moreover, the strategy involved was that of the grand theory displacing less basic theories. In rejecting these special characteristics, some contemporary philosophers have rejected others that are not inherently part of those characteristics, for example, the general notions of unity of science.

Some of the rejection of the goal of unity of science, it is suggested, rests upon the use of absolutist approaches. Thus, to recognize the importance and the power of unification in scientific study should not imply that this is the *only* important principle by which to describe scientific progress. Moreover, acceptance of unity should not mean that unification is to be sought at every stage or step of science, or in every area of science and in complete form. It has been suggested here that the search for unity of science is especially relevant depending upon the preparadigm-paradigm characteristics of the science. This may be further broken down, since it is not suggested that unity is to be sought centrally in every preparadigmatic science at every point of development. Before unity can be sought it is necessary to have a body of knowledge that permits unification. This may depend upon the prior development of many observations, various apparatuses, many experimental facts, and various theoretical concepts and theories.

The first impetus provided to a new field through a philosophy of science may, because of this, be a proliferative injunction that induces work to develop the diverse findings that are needed. (Shapere 1977 has also recognized that a field has to be ready for unification.) Additionally, at another stage in science, when the area of study has been guided by a theory for some period such that the theory is now stultifying, it may not be important to stress unification. It may be necessary to cast aside the old unified theory to be able to generate a new theory of even greater unifying value or of other productive characteristics. In a science at this stage of development, where the power of unified theory is well recognized, a principle of proliferation may be more relevantly stressed, to give impetus to progress.

The same absolutist trend, it is suggested, has led to rejection of the importance of unification in other respects; there is a philosophy in opposition to unification efforts in the social sciences, including psychology. This philosophy has been especially opposed to reductionism. It is suggested that this stems from the recognition that certain ideas of theory reduction involve subjugation or subordination. Opposition to such reduction can be seen clearly in some of the statements already quoted. For example, M. G. White (1943) was concerned for the status of history unless it could discover terms unique to its area of study. Other social scientists have fought the idea that societal facts could be reduced to principles of individual behavior, insisting that there were emergent qualities associated with societal facts.

In the present view such positions require consideration. Before the fact, one cannot tell to what extent societal facts and principles of individual behavior can be related. The extent to which principles of individual behavior can be elaborated to account for societal facts has not been systematically studied and the possibility is still moot. One's position on this question must reside on other grounds than that unification has been tried and found wanting, or that it has been tried and found to be eminently successful.

If acceptance of the principles of individual behavior as the basis for explanation of other social sciences meant that psychology was to become the preeminent science in the social sciences — that sociologists, political scientists, and so on, would be secondary scientists, or perhaps completely expendable — then resistance to such a reductionist position would be understandable. One would be unlikely to have much enthusiasm for an approach that would legislate one's own science out of existence, or markedly weaken it. The same would be true with respect to psychology and physiology. Learning theorists or personality theorists would not have much enthusiasm for a suggestion, before the fact, that their area of study was really unessential and would ultimately be replaced by study of neurophysiology.

Combinations of fields of study under a unified theory does not necessarily imply such dislocations. As has been indicated, the general trend of unification is for earlier theories to be important constituents of later, more general theories. Science elements that have been substantiated are not thrown out. It is the task of the more general statement to include those elements, and their theory and method counterparts. The behavioral facts of the field of learning, as substantiated as they are, will not be overturned by any theory, whether it is physiological or not. The area is of undeniable importance in and of itself. As another example, societal facts and concepts, in the present view, even if included within a theory based upon principles of individual behavior, would not lose their great importance (Staats 1975). The type of theory unification that has been proposed for the social sciences (Staats 1975, 1981), states that there should not be status differences in unification. Each field contributes to the other — heuristic and explanatory movement from one field to the other is to be expected. Thus, it is mutually heuristic to consider how the study of behavior via learning principles relates to the biological level of study. For example, there is continuity in considering that the principles of learning are general to animal behavior because they are adaptive and thus have been attained and retained according to evolutionary principles (Skinner 1966; Staats 1963, 1971, 1975). The point is that when such unification takes place no loss to either area is to be expected, any more than there has been between physics and chemistry, which are becoming unified. More will be said of methods for constructing such unified theory in chapters 8, 9, and 10.

UNIFICATION IN DEVELOPING A PHILOSOPHY FOR PSYCHOLOGY

One of the purposes in presenting the various diverse opinions of philosophers of science has been to demonstrate that diversity. Philosophy of science is itself a complex field, with preparadigmatic characteristics. There are in this field many concepts, some seemingly opposite and opposed, others unrelated, and there are various general viewpoints associated with individuals and groupings. There is thus not even agreement in describing the existing, developed natural sciences. There are not likely to be agreed-upon philosophies for an incompletely developed science. How could there be, when the characteristics of the science cannot be clearly seen because of the chaos that is exhibited by preparadigmatic sciences? Philosophers of the preparadigmatic science must construct their philosophy through their own vision. It must be expected that there are important and useful materials to be drawn from the philosophy and history and sociology of the natural sciences. But the task of the preparadigmatic philosopher of science is that of abstracting from the philosophy of the natural sciences that which is productive. Doing this, as we have seen for the present case, may involve resolving some of the issues that reside in the philosophy of the natural sciences, guided by the philosophy that one has obtained from the preparadigmatic science. In doing this, various characteristics of particular views in the philosophy of the natural sciences need to be discarded, and other pieces need to be selected and retained, and still others require innovation. The problem is to fit together a framework for presenting the view that has been arrived at in the study of the preparadigmatic science itself.

It should be emphasized that this must be done from the perspective of the science involved, and with an intimate, general, and creative understanding of the characteristics of the science. Since no systematic characterization of the undeveloped or preparadigmatic science is available, this must be provided by the philosopher from intimate experience with the science. Most of the philosophy of science has been written in description of the natural sciences. Some portion of this material must be thought to be in response to features particular to the sciences involved, features that will not be repeated in other sciences. The philosophy of science of a social science, thus, may be expected to have features that are not pertinent to natural sciences, or are no longer pertinent, as well as features that show continuity. This has been the strategy in the present effort; the approach has been that a philosophy of science for psychology must begin with a general conception of the science. The formulation can then be strengthened by concepts selected from the products of the general philosophy, history, and sociology of science. There has been no philosophy of science for the preparadigmatic science. There have not been scientists in the preparadigmatic science of psychology, for example, who are unified theorists (in the sense developed here) as well as philosophers of science in interest. And there have not been philosophers of science who have devoted themselves to the very large task of becoming unified theorists in psychology, capable of viewing this disparate science in the framework of unified versus disunified science.

At this point, the conceptual basis has been laid for the consideration of psychology. The thesis is that psychology has characteristics that mark it as a preparadigmatic science, that these characteristics are handicaps in the progress of the science, and that, as later chapters will reveal, they are anachronistic. The nature of psychology and the philosophy it typically produces are the heritage of the past, but they represent a powerful stultifying shackle for which there is rather unified, paradigmatic acceptance. The present situation calls for a proliferative philosophical formulation of a contrasting type, which the present work aims to provide.

Part II
Psychology's Disunity

Chapter 4

Psychology: A Disorganized Science

Psychology, at least in major part, has been concerned focally with developing itself as an independent, experimental science for over 100 years. This effort has involved great advances in various areas that are usually important to a science. Psychology has advanced from modest beginnings in experimental apparatus and methodology to specialized concerns with the logic, statistics, and design properties of psychological research. Beginning with rudimentary methods such as introspection, and so on, psychology has advanced to include many different methods for the study of a variety of phenomena. To illustrate, from the simple measurement of reaction times, apparatus in psychology has advanced to the use of complex computers for studies ranging from conditioning in animals to computer-assisted instruction for children.

A corresponding increase has taken place in such things as the number of experiments that are published in psychology, the number of experimental findings that are available, and the number of theories that are dealt with. Some of its theories are sophisticated in their use of mathematics, logic, and statistics. Organizationally, psychology has grown from the state where Wilhelm Wundt, about 100 years ago, was considered to be the first member of the independent science of psychology to the point of being a science and profession; in the United States alone psychology includes a membership in excess of 40,000. Psychology has advanced organizationally to fit these numbers, now including a number of divisions within the main organization of the American Psychological Association as well as various other organizations that are devoted to different aspects of psychology. The number of journals in psychology has grown proportionately, to the point where psychology appears to have more journals than many other science areas.

Moreover, the scientific skills of the psychologist have been found to be useful in various aspects of the society, and the application of psychological knowledge has burgeoned in recent times. Why is it then that there is some question concerning whether or not psychology can be considered to be a science? As will be indicated later, many philosophers of science, as well as others, indicate they do not believe that psychology is a science. One of the main goals of scientific psychology has been to have the field accepted as a science — a science with all the necessary characteristics — and it is therefore important to psychology to consider all of the lines of development that are involved in becoming a science. Many of the features of science — for example, those of apparatus and methodology, theory, experimental findings, scientific organization and publication, application of findings, and so on — have been achieved by psychology and progress in further development in these areas is a matter of systematic attention. If there is some characteristic that has not been considered, however, then it would be important to isolate this characteristic and to begin to systematically deal with that dimension of development. It is a central feature of the present book to do just that, as the present chapter will begin to indicate.

Let us consider what can be called paradigmatization in this context. It has been said earlier in this work that there is a progression from the preparadigmatic science to the paradigmatic science. Masterman (1970) has further divided Kuhn's two-stage dimension from preparadigmatic to paradigmatic science into the three stages already described. She further states the following about the psychological, social, and information sciences, which she considers multiple-paradigm sciences.

> Here, within the sub-field defined by each paradigmatic technique, technology can sometimes become quite advanced, and normal research puzzle-solving can progress. . . . Thus multiple-paradigm science is full science, on Kuhn's own criteria; with the proviso that these criteria have to be applied by treating each sub-field as a separate field (Masterman 1970, p. 74).

As was indicated in the previous chapter, however, Masterman in this same passage states that multiple-paradigm sciences such as psychology fail to make long run progress and each subfield is trivial and narrow. These characteristics hardly seem appropriate in the description of a full science. There are positive aspects to Masterman's view but also errors. She recognizes the progress that psychology and the social sciences have made from the very early stages of science, and recognizes, moreover, that sciences such as psychology can achieve scientific characteristics, at least in some measure. This is a more correct view of psychology and the social sciences than has been accorded these fields by some of the other philosophers of science.

Nevertheless, Masterman has not correctly characterized psychology. She makes the same error concerning paradigms that was indicated in the last chapter, that is, she assumes that when a number of scientists in a particular area of study accept a common theory-method-apparatus-problem definition of the area this constitutes a paradigm. The present view is that such an assemblage does not constitute a paradigm *if there are other competing assemblages of scientists-and-approach, in the same area of study.* The assemblage, moreover, does not constitute a paradigm if it does not relate to other assemblages in the science, or appear to relate to some general understanding of the science, after it has had a sufficient time to establish such relationships. When there are multiple competing approaches within a particular area of study (an area in which there has never been an accepted paradigm), or when approaches consider each other's work irrelevant, each group of scientists with a common approach represents a school or preparadigm, not a paradigm.

In psychology there are no, or very few, paradigms. (Perhaps a field like physiological psychology represents a paradigm. Since it draws its foundation from a paradigmatic area, biological science, it has a uniformity of approach in large part.) The groups of scientists we see working within a common approach almost entirely represent schools. Within the same area of study the schools are in competition. Most usually, moreover, there are more than two schools in any area of study. Typically the schools in an area will have differences in world views, in their philosophy of psychology, in their understanding of theory and research, and so on — characteristics that add to their opposition.

There are cases of the type that Masterman appears to be describing, where there are no competing schools in an area of study. This occurs, however, because the opposing views consider the area of study itself to be inconsequential and unrelated to the task of psychology, and therefore do not enter and compete in the area. Thus, for the psychoanalytically oriented clinical psychologist the study of animal learning customarily is trivial and irrelevant. The fact that psychoanalytic theory has not seriously presented a theory to compete with the learning theories that treat the study of animal learning should not be taken to indicate that psychoanalytic theorists accept learning as an important contributor to the understanding of human behavior, but only as a sign of deep incommensurability. What might appear to be a lack of discord may only reflect such very basic incommensurabilities. Actually, that is the very general circumstance between the multiple "paradigms" in psychology. In some cases work in an area appears to arise on the basis of development of an experimental technique, as will be indicated further on, and the findings in the area center around the experimentation and remain unrelated to any other work in the science. This may occur even though on face value one might expect the area to be related to other areas in the science. Again, however, the knowledge produced remains isolated on the one hand while, on the other hand, still competitive with other conceptual-methodological approaches.

PARADIGMATIZATION AND SCIENCE

Masterman's statement was quoted because it states that psychology, and the social sciences, are indeed sciences, because in the sub-fields of these sciences "technology can be quite advanced, and normal research puzzle-solving can progress." One must thus ask why it is that psychology is not generally considered to be a science by many philosophers. To the psychologist employing scientific methods and making local progress in the study of some subfield of psychology, it comes as a rude and frustrating experience to find that scientists and philosophers in the natural sciences typically do not consider psychology to be a science (for example, Popper 1963, p. 34).

Why? It is the present thesis that the reservations concerning the scientific status of psychology stem from its characteristics with respect to unification (paradigmatization). The knowledge of psychology is disorganized, in conflict. These characteristics are very real; they are important characteristics with respect to the development of a science; and they are different from those of the more advanced natural sciences. It is because of the importance of the characteristics, and their susceptibility to development through the procedures of science, that the present work aims to open the topic and call for systematic consideration.

My argument is that a prominent feature of a science that has attained a high level of technological development still resides in whether or not it presents an organized body of knowledge. This is not to say that there may not be parts of the science that do not integrate well into the large body of the science. There may also be parts of the science that do not tie together well, and that may even be inconsistent. Nevertheless, a prominent characteristic of the advanced sciences, and a goal toward which they strive, is organized knowledge, knowledge that is consistent and continuous.

Let us say that there are two sciences equally advanced with respect to scientific method. Each has advanced apparatus and experimental procedures by which reliable observations can be made. The statements made in each science are equally operationally sound. But one science has a set of statements that are organized. It has a philosophy of science that justifies the various experiments that are conducted under its rubric, and justifies as well the various methods employed. The other science, however, does not have these characteristics. The methods and findings in one area of the science will be challenged by scientists in another area or be considered irrelevant, and typically there will be competitive approaches within the various areas of study in the science. There will be disagreement about philosophy, about general methodology, and about what the essential problems of the science are. The findings and the conceptual elements of the science are antagonistic and unorganized, even competitive.

The former science will be considered to be much more advanced than the latter. In comparison, the former will be considered by many to be a science, and the latter not to be a science — an area with many of the trappings of science, but still not a science. In the present view, as will be further elaborated, the organized science has attained a higher level of development, is a more efficacious science in various ways, and deserves to be considered in those terms. The less organized science, on the other hand, and this reveals a motivation of the present book, would benefit from seeing the difference between organized and disorganized science, for recognition of the difference should be the first step towards systematic concern with and ultimate progress in developing from the disorganized to the organized state. Science is not simply the generation of knowledge, the development of apparatus and research skill or of methodological sophistication. It is the generation of these things in a way that provides a body of organized knowledge about an important part of our world. *Psychology is not considered to be a science by many because it has not attained the ability to present an organized body of knowledge.* Moreover, the importance of the goal of organization for the science has not been recognized in psychology, or indeed by students of science outside of psychology.

Does psychology have the accoutrements of science, that is, theory, apparatus, methodology, experimental findings, scientific bodies, and media of publication? Yes, in abundance. Psychology has the constituents in these respects. However, abundance itself can add to the problem, if it results in complexity, confusion, competition, and chaos — when the need is for simplication and organization. In considering these matters it is pertinent to describe briefly some of the general areas of knowledge within which the diversity of psychology contributes to its disorganization. The separation among the various aspects of psychology stems from various sources and reasons which will only be revealed in complete form by a systematic history of psychology. It is relevant here, however, to give the reader an opportunity to get a feel for the disorganization of psychology.

EXPERIMENTALISM-GOVERNED SEPARATISM

Wilhelm Wundt has been recognized as the first self-conscious psychologist and the founder of psychology as an independent science. It is interesting to note that the concern with making psychology a science commenced at the beginning. "It is quite reasonable, then, that Wundt should also have felt the need for stressing the fact that psychology too, as physiological psychology, is a science. Even today psychologists have not ceased to be self-conscious about the scientific nature of psychology" (Boring 1950, pp. 319–20). This is an important point, as will be elaborated further on.

The history of science reveals in great clarity the importance that systematic investigation has had in the development of scientific knowledge. Many important scientific developments waited on or stemmed from the development of the means for such investigation. For many people science has become identified with the means and methods of observation and experimentation. The present section will suggest, however, that the value placed upon experimentation in a science area may itself contribute to preparadigmatic characteristics of the science. Experimentation may be conducted for experimentation's sake, simply because the methods employed generate reliable, scientific findings, without consideration of what the findings mean in terms of constructing a unified approach, even within a relatively demarcated area. It is important in understanding the preparadigmatic nature of psychology to understand something about this dynamic. The fact is that examination of the journals in psychology reveals that there is a profusion of experimental findings, but these findings constitute an unorganized, chaotic bunch. Research findings make sense, for the most part, only to the specific area of research involved.

To understand this dynamic in psychology, which may be referred to as experimental scientism (or experimentation for its own sake), one must recognize some of the historical factors involved in the origin of psychology as a science. Psychology had to break away from the parent, the field of philosophy, as had other sciences. In this development psychology was called on to demonstrate that it could be a science. This was not accepted as obvious, since, by the time psychology began, the natural sciences had already acquired characteristics that readily identified them as sciences. Thus, an early and continuing struggle for psychology has been to gain recognition among the established sciences that it too is a science.

As a consequence one of the strongest values inherent in the development and the present state of psychology has been its emphasis upon experimentation and its prowess as a laboratory science. This has included an emphasis on developing experimental methodology and apparatus. This value can be seen early in the description of the work of one of the progenitors of experimental psychology.

> Ebbinghaus' systematic views are not important. Here his tolerance within the experimental field became eclecticism. . . . He accepted the psychology that had proved itself amenable to experimentation, but he had no fervid convictions on anything but *experimentalism* (italics added) (Boring 1950, p. 392).

Several points may be made with respect to this statement. First, eclecticism, in the sense concerned with the present case, represents a focus on the doing of science—the methodology and apparatus and appearance of science—rather than on the meaning and content of what the doing produces. The greatest effect of this characteristic is in not demanding that studies fit into some larger context or conceptual framework, in not providing a philosophical rationale giving impetus to comprehensive theory, or to efforts to integrate the various experiments in the field. Eclecticism is not a step in the direction of unified theory. Quite the reverse. The eclectic is not concerned about theory. His interest is in the products of various approaches, which he uses depending upon circumstances. In the field of experimental psychology, eclecticism means an emphasis upon experimental refinement at the expense of other considerations, such as unity of theory. Thus, for example, there are high and explicit standards with respect to the methodology employed in articles published by the journals of the American Psychological Association. Yet, as the next section will show, studies within a particular approach may be published over a period of many years and number in the hundreds, without the conglomeration of knowledge having to show some coherence and meaning either within its own sphere or in relationship to other bodies of knowledge in the science. In terms of the appearance of science, it may be noted that, other things being equal, a work that utilizes scientific apparatus, logic, or mathematics (as in complex statistical analysis) will receive a more ready reception than a work that does not. There are explicit criteria for the methodological worth of a study, and none for meaning and significance. The important thing here is that experimentalism by itself gives impetus to multiplication of experimental studies, and thus constitutes a proliferation principle rather than one that impels the science toward organization and unification. In any event, the concern with establishing psychology as a science, and with developing the accoutrements of psychology to resemble the physical sciences has had, and continues to have, a strong effect upon the field. Not only is experimentation—the demonstration of reliable cause and effect relationships—central to experimental psychology, but the methods of experimentation and other visible appearances of research are considered of central importance *in and of themselves*. At this point an example will be given of how this guiding framework can produce inefficiency and waste, in very large measures, in psychological science.

Verbal Learning: A Case in Experimental Psychology

The case to be used in illustration concerns the field of rote verbal learning, which until recent years was one of the most viable, productive, experimental areas of psychology. The field stemmed from the work of

Hermann Ebbinghaus. Ebbinghaus employed the loose philosophy of the mind as the conceptual foundation for his work. The associationists of his period considered that the contents of the mind were formed through the association of experiences. Ebbinghaus was interested in experimentally establishing the characteristics of the mental processes of memory. He found that the association and retention of verbal experience, using non-sense syllables as the material learned, could be manipulated depending upon how the syllables were presented. Ebbinghaus' experiments established a set of experimental procedures along with a loose conceptual framework that together gave impetus to the generation of a very large number of studies by other experimental psychologists. As one example, Ebbinghaus varied the time between learning the associated syllables and their recall, and ascertained what the effect on memory was. Since his time there have been multitudes of studies whose aim is the specification of the associationistic characteristics of the mental process of memory involving verbal materials. As examples, the experimental task might be one of pre-senting pairs of digits simulaneously, one in each ear, testing the effects upon memory of the time interval between pairs (Broadbent 1954; Hellige, Cox, and Litvak 1979). The experimental task might vary the number of letters in the stimulus to be learned, the order of presentation of the stimu-lus, and the mode of recall (Kellas and Butterfield 1971). The extent to which words are retained when the subject is performing another task, versus the task when his instructions are to learn the words, has been stud-ied (Zerdy 1971). The manner in which two materials learned, one after an-other, affects the retention of each (proactive and retroactive inhibition) has been the topic of a multitude of investigations. The manner in which sleep after learning materials affects memory of the materials affects has been studied many times (Jenkins and Dallenbach 1924; Ekstrand, Sulli-van, Parker, and West 1971). The variation of conditions under which the subject associates lists of paired nonsense syllables have been involved in countless studies.

The multitudinous studies conducted in this area constitute science, at least in their methods and the reliability and replicability of their find-ings. But we also have to ask how the effort advanced psychology in the study of its subject matter. Deese, a prominent researcher in the field of rote verbal learning, after a review of the area wrote that "In the study of the higher mental processes, despite nearly a century of investigation, the results have been little more than a long history of doubt, frustration, and trivial generalities" (1969, p. 517). The many studies were never integrat-ed, unified, within an explicit set of theoretical principles, as Deese also noted. "There are very few psychological variables that are linked togeth-er by a well-articulated theory, formal or informal, and most of them were discovered by the early experimentalists in the investigation of perception and the senses" (1969, p. 517). I would like to suggest that the lack of general significance of this experimentalism-directed field was greater even than Deese's statement indicates, for the field of rote verbal learning never linked to any other area of the study of psychology. That is, on face value we would have to expect that the basic study of verbal learning and memory would be intimately related to the way children learn and retain language, reading, number skills, and so on. But the study of rote verbal learning connected minimally, mostly not at all, with the other areas of study with which it should have been unified. As a consequence, rote verbal learning had little significance for psychology, other than for those actively involved in the particular field. Moreover, it did not produce a substantial quantity of information that has been useful to the other areas of psychology that one might think would be relevant to the basic study of verbal learning and memory. The field was scientific in its conduct, and contributed to the appearance of psychology as a science, but somehow its end products were less than science. There was little of a paradigmatic quality to the field, in the sense of providing paths of continuous advancement, or of providing knowledge that would tie into other aspects of the science. The many hundreds of studies conducted in this area could not even constitute a unified body of knowledge within itself. Very few of the studies will have any lasting value.

The example of rote verbal learning has been taken from experimental psychology. Experimentalism has influenced the other areas of psychology as well and has given rise to separatistic and incommensurable bodies of research findings. One additional area will be exemplified, social psychology, in which there has been a growing disenchantment with the sterility that has been produced by the preparadigmatic framework within which the science functions.

Social Psychology and the Separatism of Experimentalism

One can see the products of experimentalism in the following description of United States social psychology made by an Englishman, Michael Argyle, even though he does not analyze what it is that produces the characteristic he criticizes.

> But, I've always tried to keep a bit of distance from American psychology and especially social psychology, because it tends to move in fashions. One year there will be a lot of people working on one or another aspect. Two years later something else. Though I wouldn't want to criticize that particularly, if you try from outside the country to latch onto one of these trends it's hopeless. By the time the stuff starts getting published, probably everybody's given up doing it. So you get in on the act about five years too late and nobody is remotely interested (Evans 1978, p. 7).

Serge Moscovici stated essentially the same thing. "From time to time the interests of the researcher are mobilized by themes or areas which appear new and important at the moment; but sooner or later these prove to be sterile or exhausted and they are abandoned" (Moscovici 1972, p. 32).

These observations may be used to characterize very succinctly the preparadigmatic state of this field. They very clearly indicate the non-building, rather random nature of the enterprise. The characteristic of social psychology is to place a premium on the innovation of a new experimental situation, having to do with some socially relevant behavior, at least on face value. It is newness in some way of generating findings that is considered to define scientific creativity. If the experimental method produces systematic results, and it seems to deal with seemingly significant types of things, a fashion will be established and many studies utilizing the method will be conducted. We have many such examples. A few years back there were many, many studies of cognitive dissonance — for example, that when people write something opposed to their attitudes, their attitudes will be changed less if they are paid more than if they are not paid as much (Brehm and Cohen 1962, pp. 74–78). Another recently popular area of study concerned the "risky shift" phenomenon. Studies have shown that individuals making decisions on their own will do so more conservatively than they will when the decisions are made as a group (Kogan and Wallach 1967), and a plethora of studies was conducted in this framework. Today an area of interest is that referred to as attribution theory and locus of control. This studies the manner in which the individual infers the locus of causation for the behavior of another person or himself. There are studies in this area, for example, that are concerned with the factors that lead one to infer that the situation rather than the person himself has largely determined the behavior, or the opposite (Himmelfarb 1972). None of these areas are related to each other or to other parts of social psychology. No one demands such relatedness.

Social psychology has thus been described as a disorganized area of study in which there are a multitude of idiosyncratic theories, principles, and concepts as well as divergent and unrelated bodies of research literature (Staats, in press). The studies that are published in social psychology each individually meet high standards of scientific method. And various research techniques, along with their typically loose and unarticulated conceptual underpinning, frequently prove to be very heuristic in that many studies will be conducted within the particular constellation. Nevertheless there is the haunting feeling that the individual results as well as the composite findings of all efforts in social psychology do not display the characteristics that we associate with full science. As I indicated in the first chapter, there is a strong opinion in social psychology that the area lacks direction. Social psychologists have "widespread self-doubts about goals, methods, and accomplishments" (Elms 1975, p. 968). In this section like-opinions have suggested that without direction the field is guided by changing fashions of research interest, whose products are soon forgotten. We can see additionally that like the area of rote verbal learning (or experimental psychology and psychology in general) there is no articulation of knowledge in social psychology. Studies in this field deal piecemeal with unrelated phenomena. No organized body of knowledge results in which one can expect to see systematic and long term development. The specific interests in this field do not derive from a paradigm state, and they do not contribute to the development of a paradigm. This circumstance does not provide a basis for continued elaboration of a coherent conceptual framework. This characteristic of social psychology does not provide a framework for a young scientist to select an area of work that will involve continuous development. He has the possibility of jumping from phenomenon to phenomenon, in a patchwork type of development — whether he originates the new experimental procedure or follows in the footsteps of someone else. Rather than seeking organization of knowledge, the impetus is to distinguish one's area or one's findings from others, to find a new experimental technique. The stress is on novelty, not building. We can see dissatisfaction with this state of affairs, as yet muted in the science, in the following remarks, specifically addressed to the area of social psychology concerned with personality, but really generally relevant.

> The substantive problem is . . . that personality research has become variable-centered rather than theory-centered . . . , focusing now on this variable, now on that variable as academic fashion dictates. As a consequence, personality research threatens to become merely an aggregate of empirical findings lacking the theoretical glue necessary for cumulative knowledge building (Weigel 1978, p. 553).

Experimentalism plays a role in providing a framework that justifies the conduct of research in social psychology (as in each subfield of psychology) such that it has these characteristics of preparadigmatic science.

METHODOLOGY-BASED SEPARATISM

In the area of methodology a case could be made that there is considerable paradigmatic unity. By and large new psychologists become familiar with the methods of experimental methodology which are fairly general to the science. For example, it is generally required that students become familiar with experimental design and statistics as they are relevant to psychology.

The fact is, however, that psychology is still rent by methodological divisions. First, there is a very basic methodological schism between be-haviorists and many nonbehaviorists. Behaviorists concentrate their study on behavior and the environmental causes of behavior. Understanding any behavior requires knowledge of the principles of learning—the prin-ciples by which the environment can affect behavior in general.

A quite separate methodological tradition, also important in psychol-ogy, is based upon the conception that the individual's behavior is caused by internal, subjective processes, states, and structures, for example, per-sonality, mind, cognitions, and attitudes. The methodology thus involves the use of observation to gain access to the internal process or state or structure. When the internal personality is known, for example, it is thought, in this tradition, that one can know the reasons for the individual's behavior, predict it, and manipulate conditions to best deal with the indi-vidual. (The difference between these two conceptual orientations, as will be indicated, has separatistic effects on matters other than those of meth-odology.)

The methods of observation devised in this latter tradition of the inter-nal causation of behavior—for example, the construction of personality tests—are ordinarily quite different than those that arise in the behaviorist methodological tradition. This methodological difference has been a basis for a separation between those who follow one or the other tradition. We can see this separation at a much earlier time. Watson rejected the study of internal, inferred, mental processes or entities. And Skinner has contin-ued this tradition with sharp demarcations between what he will consider behavior, and what is to be rejected as mentalistic. This philosophy has prevented most operant behaviorists from the consideration of important parts of psychology (see Staats 1963, 1968a, 1971a, 1975). Skinner has clearly said that the methods employed by personality tests cannot yield knowledge about human behavior (Skinner 1969, pp. 77–78).

On the other hand, the methods for the study of animal learning and its effects on behavior are ordinarily considered trivial by those interested in measuring psychological processes, states, and structures. It may be noted also that although statistical analysis is general to psychology, there tends to be a difference in the statistical methods employed by those who are interested in measuring psychological characteristics and those who are interested in the effects of environmental conditions on behavior. A psychologist can be expert in statistical methods for the one tradition with-out being expert in the other—in fact that is the usual circumstance.

There are other methodological dimensions of separatism, however. Another example involves a narrower schism. In the experimental psy-chology of learning, for example, the group methods of traditional experi-mental psychology were rejected by B. F. Skinner and his followers. And those who espoused group methods rejected the experimental methods of

Skinner's operant conditioning, which was based on experiments employing single subjects. This methodological difference helped inspire a separation into schools concerned with studying the same realm of events. The differences were so sharp that experiments using one methdology were published in one journal and experiments using the other were published in another. While the distinction is no longer quite as strict, it still exists (Bijou, Peterson, Harris, Allen, and Johnston 1969, p. 178). There are various divisions and separations based upon, or partly inspired by, differences in methodology, such that psychologists of one background will be quite different from those with another background — different and quite separate in interests, activities and knowledge.

Moreover, it should be emphasized that there has been a general lack of impetus to consider the various methodologies as constituting a unified body of knowledge. As has been indicated, the leaders in the use of one type of methodology may decry the value of another type. The tendency is to separate, to enhance one method at the cost of the others. Skinner may be taken as a prime example in this area. In contrast, an approach stressing organization within the science would take a different view, as will be indicated later.

AREA-GOVERNED SEPARATISM

It is not uncommon for general sciences to be broken down into smaller specialties. Psychology does not appear to be idiosyncratic, thus, in having subareas like experimental psychology, personality and social psychology, psychological measurement, developmental psychology or child psychology, clinical psychology, physiological psychology, educational psychology, experimental analysis of behavior, and so on. Certainly if these were subspecialties of a major discipline, each with its defined area role, such divisions could be evidence of a systematic paradigmatic development.

However, examination of these area divisions reveals that there is no such systematic development from an integrated general body of the discipline of psychology. There is not a systematic definition of how the areas relate to one another, or how the areas contribute to the field of general psychology, which itself is not systematically defined. In essence, the area divisions of psychology do not constitute a division of labor that has been arrived at through planning or empirical justification for the purpose of systematically developing an organized science of psychology. The divisions, rather, have grown as separate entities.

One can see this separatism clearly by consulting the typical book in general psychology. There is ordinarily no attempt made to tie one area in psychology in with the other—because the science itself does not do this. The ordinary book in general psychology merely summarizes some of the findings in the different areas of psychology, in the most organized manner that is possible. Across the different fields, however, the student must be prepared to learn different concepts and theories and methodologies. It is not a building type of learning. For the most part the student could begin with any chapter in the book, since learning about one area would not provide a basis for learning about the others. Explicit recognition of this state of psychology is given in the following excerpt.

> Moreover, the conceptual ordering devices, technical languages ("paradigms," if you will) open to the various psychological studies are—like all human modes of cognitive organization—perspectival, sensibility-dependent relative to the inquirer, and often noncommensurable. Such conceptual incommensurabilities will often obtain not only between contentually different psychological studies but between alternate but perspectivally "valid" orderings of the "same" domain. . . . [My] analysis . . . shows that the psychological studies must, *in principle*, comprise many communities speaking parochial and largely incommensurable languages, and thus that "paradigms," however general their intent, must remain local to the participating adepts in given, specialized language communities (Koch 1978, p. 638).

Koch, a general psychologist, takes a very explicit and strong position on the separateness of psychology in a very basic and general sense, and his views will be referred to again later. In the present case, however, it can be seen that Koch sees the area separation to occur on the basis of differences in principle. He sees no necessity for striving for continuity between areas, or even of coincidence of views within areas when the differences arise from viewing events from a different perspective. Moreover, Koch's opinion reflects reality. The truth of the area organization of psychology is that areas are largely quite separate fields, with little communication between them. Loyalties attach to one's specialty area.

Crystallization of the specialty area division structure of psychology is enhanced by the publication sources of the field. The pattern of journal publication in part follows the divisional structure of psychology, as well as other more specific interests. We have the following specialty area APA journals: *Journal of Abnormal Psychology, Journal of Personality and Social Psychology* (there are now three specialized journal organizations in this area), *Developmental Psychology, Journal of Educational Psychology, Journal of Clinical and Consulting Psychology,* four separate *Journals of Experimental Psychology, Professional Psychology, Journal of Applied Psychology,* and the *Journal of Counseling Psychology*. There are additional non-APA journals that deal with specialty areas additionally such as

Behavior Therapy (which represents the Association for the Advancement of Behavior Therapy), the *Personality and Social Psychology Bulletin* (put out by the Division of Personality and Social Psychology of the APA), the *Bulletin of the Psychonomic Society* (among four journals published by the Psychonomic Society), *Child Development* (which represents the Society for Research in Child Development), and *Social Psychology* (published by the American Sociological Association). There are a number of other specialty area journals that are not official organs of organizations, but which are directed to the members of such specialties. And there are various journals aiming at special areas or fulfilling other needs like the *Journal of Mental Imagery, Child Behavior Therapy, Behavior Modification*, the *Psychological Record*, and so on.

We may conclude even from this abbreviated summary that psychology is a very productive scientific discipline. More to the point, however, is the fact that the various journals themselves constitute bulwarks against the spread of information across areas. They are implements promulgating separation. Individuals tend to publish in one area of psychology and in one journal, or in the several that are concerned with that area. Moreover, individual psychologists tend to subscribe to the journals that are concerned with their specialty area interests. Even if they receive journals outside their areas, or journals that publish articles from the various areas (like the APA's *Psychological Review* and *Psychological Bulletin*), they tend to read articles that fall within their specialty. As will be indicated later, articles can be published in different specialty journals that involve related topics or principles or concepts that will not be cross-related at all, sometimes because of the separatism occasioned by division and journal barriers.

Delos Wickens captures the present state of affairs, describing the separation by areas, but first referring to the character of bygone general psychologists who, even if they were not concerned with unification, still saw psychology as a single science.

> The point I wish to stress is that we viewed psychology as a wide realm, much of which we ourselves would never explore, but in which we had, because of the broad nature of our science, a vested interest. This view of our science as a whole—the view of the general psychologist—differs markedly from an all-too-prevalent contemporary attitude that seems to consider conceptual psychology a group of principalities, each independent of each other and often feuding (1978, p. 1).

Thus far the description of the specialty division separation has been depicted as largely a passive phenomenon. Because psychologists are not apprised of the knowledge of other areas, they do not utilize that knowledge. However, as Wickens's statement above suggests, there are in psychology separatistic characteristics that are given impetus by the specialty division organization. There has been for years a boiling controversy in psychology that involves the type of separatism that has been described here. With separate organizations, sometimes including separate journal media, the formation of independent political and economic interests and the partisanship that goes with such formations has resulted in internecine struggles within the APA. For example, there have been clinical psychologists who have felt that experimental psychologists have too much power in the APA in comparison to their actual numbers. They feel that too much of the resources of the organization go to the support of the journals devoted to experimental psychology. On the other side experimental psychologists consider that experimental psychology is the core of psychology and should be supported beyond its mere numbers of members, as the following remarks indicate.

> A significant and increasing number of psychologists appears to be growing ever more dissatisfied with the APA. . . . The major sources of dissatisfaction have to do with the current non-representation of the academic-research viewpoint (Thompson 1977, p. 2).

Such dissatisfactions have led to proposals to further separate the parts of which present-day psychology is composed. In my view this occurs in large part because of preparadigmatic factors, that is, that psychology is composed of suborganizations that hardly know of each other's characteristics. Having different interests, and knowing no way of rationalizing the interests of the other suborganizations, it becomes logical that the central society of the science and profession of psychology should be broken up into different societies. This opinion has been expressed variously, both formally and informally. One suggestion has been to increase the separations between the parts of psychology by making the American Psychological Association a federation of constituent societies (Humphreys 1976).

> The members of the American Psychological Association are very heterogeneous in their interests *and* in their needs for a national organization. . . . One of the clearest conflicts is the longstanding one that exists between academicians and clinicians in private practice (Humphreys 1976, p. 2).

A decision to reorganize the large science and profession of psychology along these lines would entail the most central concerns, and the effects would be felt throughout the field, as well as in society at large. This has been recognized. Max Siegel has described such a plan as "divisive, administratively cumbersome, impractical, and above all, absolutely unnecessary" (1976, p. 3). But this opinion (see also Sulzer-Azaroff and Catania 1978, p. 4), while opposed to further fragmentation in the APA structure, did not deal with the root causes of the conflicts described by Humphreys or propose a basis for unity in psychology.

We can see this same expression of the fragmentation within psychology in the competition for influence that presently occurs among the divisions of the science. Each division in the American Psychological Association customarily writes each year to its members requesting that they cast all of their votes (each member has ten) for representatives from that division to the central governing body of the large organization (see, as examples, Mandler 1979, p. 1; Sulzer-Azaroff and Catania 1978, p. 4). This indicates the political maneuvering of the separate entities the divisions represent.

It should be noted that there has already been even further separation of psychology than that which exists in its divisional and publication media structure. For example, in addition to the Psychonomic Society, which now services experimental psychologists, there is the Association for Behavior Analysis, which represents operant behaviorists, as well as the Association for the Advancement of Behavior Therapy, which represents largely clinical psychologists and others directly applying behavioral methods to applied problems. There is the American Educational Research Association that includes many educational psychologists, the Society for Research in Child Development that includes most developmental psychologists, the Society for Experimental Social Psychologists, and so on.

As recognized by Max Siegel, the breakup of the APA would represent a devastating blow to psychology as a science and profession. Recognition of the practical drawbacks to such an occurrence may not be a sufficient measure to prevent it, however. If preparadigmatic disunity is a basic cause of the dissatisfactions and impetus to fragmentation, then the only cure will be the achievement of unity or, actually, the recognition of unity as a goal to be sought, as will be indicated. It is important, thus, to understand the preparadigmatic characteristics of our field, in order to move toward providing a basis for dealing with the problems that arise.

It should be stressed, in summary, that in the present state of psychology, the divisional organization again is in the direction of separation. There has been no discernible effort to decrease competition between the area divisions, to increase integration of the knowledge in the various areas, and thus to effect unification. The major thrust is that of each of the several areas attempting to gain for itself as much influence as it can, for organizational rather than scientific motives.

BROAD CONCEPTUAL OPPOSITIONS THAT
PRODUCE SEPARATISM

In an earlier chapter it was indicated that conceptual elements other than specific theories may be important guides in a science. The concept of the world view refers to a broad conceptual system that may play a role in science, as in other human activities. Zeitgeist is another concept that has been used in a similar way. And some of the definitions of the concept of paradigm can be seen to refer to the same thing. Shapere has indicated that conceptual elements other than formal theories may guide the scientist's behavior. This statement is very much in agreement with the present conception, which is that language in general has the functions of a theory. Everyone acquires language constellations by which we interpret the events of the world in which we live, constellations that serve as a theory for them. This remains true when the individual is a scientist. The more advanced the science, perhaps, the more the scientists' theories deviate from the common language they have learned, and the less likely there will be overlap and interaction between the two — the less likely that individual common conceptual elements will impinge upon scientific decisions. Thus, as an example, it would appear on causal inspection that one's religious beliefs might enter less into the physicist's or chemist's concerns than into the psychologist's or sociologist's concerns.

Be that as it may, the suggestion that is relevant in the present context is that one of the underlying reasons for divisions in psychology resides in competitive variations in conceptual elements of broad import. This topic has been outlined in the context of unifying some of these oppositions (Staats 1975, ch. 13), which are presented in Table 1. The manner in which these conceptual conflicts provide a complex grid for the separatism of psychology will be briefly indicated in the following sections.

The Subjective Versus Objective Schism

Throughout the history of concern with understanding human behavior there have been objective versus subjective approaches. Boring (1950) has indicated that the positions can be differentiated in ancient Greek thought. He goes on to characterize developments in the history of psychology in terms of that schism. "The main line of tradition from Locke and Berkeley to Wundt and Titchener, or, for that matter, to Brentano and Kulpe, was that psychology studies consciousness" (Boring 1950, p. 620). On the other hand, the objectivist tradition was seen in psychology to have been involved in the work of another group.

There have been many more who have argued that it is unprofitable to study consciousness directly and that better data for the same problems

TABLE 1: Characteristics and Concerns Dividing the Humanistic and Behavioristic Approaches to the Study of Man

Humanistic	*Behavioristic (Elemental)*
1. Subjective events	1. Objective events
2. Holistic (man as a whole)	2. Atomistic (elementary principle)
3. Naturalistic observation	3. Laboratory observation
4. Individual (Ideographic)	4. General (Nomethetic)
5. Qualitative description	5. Precision and measurement
6. Understanding	6. Prediction and control
7. Self-determination, freedom, spontaneity in causation	7. Scientific determinism, mechanistic in causation
8. Originality, creativity, and activity	8. Passive respondent, automatonism
9. Self-actualization, personal growth, personality development	9. Conditioning, behavior modification, and behavior therapy
10. Values in science	10. Valueless science
11. Applied, concern with human problems	11. Basic, pure, science; science for science's sake
12. Purpose and goals, future causation	12. Prior and present causation
13. Insight and awareness	13. Conditioning
14. Biological explanation of human behavior	14. Environmentalism

are obtained by limiting research to the study of behavior. This last position has been occupied by the Russian school of Sechenov, Bekhterev and Pavlov, and by the American behaviorists, Watson, Weiss, Holt and the others who came after them (Boring 1950, p. 620).

The specific arguments concerning the important elements of human behavior — whether internal, mental, subjective or external, behavioral, directly observed, objective — vary depending upon the area involved. For example, in the area of the study of language there has recently been a contest between a subjective approach (initiated by the linguist Chomsky) and the objective approach represented by learning theory. The former approach considers language to be largely determined by internal subjective events (Chomsky 1968; Lenneberg 1967). Chomsky, for example, suggests that the human mind predisposes us to language. We need thus only a brief experience with the particular language for our mind to "break the code" and establish the particular categories and rules involved. Learning theory approaches, more objectively oriented, have generally viewed language as a type of behavior and have attempted to specify how it is learned (Mowrer

1954; Osgood 1963; Skinner 1957; Staats 1957, 1963). As another example, take the following statement of a subjective approach, quite in contrast to the behavioristic view. "The humanist psychologist . . . gives primary concern to man's subjective experience and secondary concern to his actions, insisting that this primacy of the subjective is fundamental in any human endeavor" (Bugental 1967, p. 9).

This subjective-objective dichotomous position, however, should not be considered to divide only behaviorists from nonbehaviorists. Within the behavioristic camp, for example, there are conceptual positions that are opposed on this dimension. Thus for such behaviorists as Watson and Skinner there is no concept of personality as an internal, causative process; as Watson indicated, personality consists of the individual's behavior (1930, p. 274). Skinner (1975) has clearly stated that internal, subjective aspects of experience must be rejected as causes in the scientific study of human behavior. On the other hand, behaviorists such as Rotter (1954) and Staats (1963, 1968a, 1971, 1975) have proposed that there are personality processes that must be considered in the explanation of human behavior. As another example, some behavioristic works have rejected such concepts as attitudes as an internal state (Bandura 1969; Bem 1965, 1968; McGinnies and Ferster 1971) while others (Osgood and Tannenbaum 1955; Staats and Staats 1958) have dealt with attitudes as internal states that affect behavior. Staats, in projecting a new generation of behaviorism that considers the matter focally, has stated "verbal reports of subject experiences can index subjective states, and . . . subjective states are causes, not epiphenomena" (1975, p. 463). The point, however, is that this polarity, the subjective-objective dimension, is the basis for separatism in various areas of psychology. Those who are of one position typically reject the work of the other.

The Holistic Versus Atomistic Schism

In the natural sciences one of the methods for gaining knowledge about the world has involved analysis, separating things into their constituent parts to be able to see their basic characteristics, rather than examining them in the complexity in which they are naturally found. The philosophy of the British associationists included a similar approach. In the concept of mental chemistry there was the idea that the complex consciousness of humans was built up on the basis of elements, the sensations. The early experimental psychologists, beginning with Wundt, attempted to establish the principles involved, in the laboratory. The major point is that the strategy was that of employing an analytic approach that would break down the complexity of naturalistic human consciousness into the elements of which it is composed.

The school of Gestalt psychology was formed in large part as a rebellion against this view of psychology. Gestalt psychology said that the way to understand human consciousness was not through analysis. Gestalt psychology said, rather, that psychology must deal with wholes and not with parts. Gestalt psychology said that there are properties that emerge with the whole act that cannot be predicted from knowledge of the parts. Combination of elements, even in chemistry, yields properties in the compound not seen in the constituents.

Thus, one of the sharp schisms in psychology was formed around the issue of whether human behavior, or human character, was to be successfully studied through analysis or through dealing with its complex manifestations. This schism has current, not only historical, significance, as the following statement indicates.

> The customary scientific technique of dissection and reductive analysis that has worked so well in the inorganic world and not too badly even in the infra-human world of living organisms, is just a nuisance when I seek knowledge of a person, and it has real deficiencies even for studying people in general (Maslow 1966, p. 11).

Such views, and they are held by a substantial proportion of psychologists, say that much of psychology is irrelevant. The psychologist with such views will not look into certain fields of psychology for information; will not read certain journals; and will not attend to theories of certain types, because they employ basic principles established through analysis, including sometimes the employment of subhuman subjects. On the other hand, there are many psychologists who will pay no attention to knowledge of humans that has been based upon less analytic observation of human functioning.

The holistic-versus-atomistic schism, it should be stressed, is not a division between behaviorists and nonbehaviorists. Blumenthal (1977) has noted that there are cognitive psychologists who analyze cognition into components and those who resist analysis, illustrating the point by quoting a statement of Von Foerster.

> In other words, by separating these functions [memory, learning, perception] from the totality of cognitive processes one has abandoned the original problem and now searches for mechanisms that implement entirely different functions that may or may not have any resemblance with some processes that are . . . subservient to the maintenance of the integrity of the organism as a functioning unit (Blumenthal 1977, pp. 8–9).

The Individual (Ideographic) Versus General (Nomothetic) Schism

One of the basic assumptions of many psychologists is that there are general laws that underlie all human characteristics. The workings of the general laws in varied circumstances yield diverse individual differences.

The strategy, then, is to attempt to find the general laws, and this is considered to be the task of psychology. In his criticism of this approach Maslow characterizes it as follows.

> First of all, we should be aware that [knowledge] about *a* person is ruled out by many scientists as trivial or "unscientific." Practically all scientists (of the impersonal) proceed on the tacit or explicit assumption that one studies classes of things (1966a, p. 8).

The issue is whether to search for general principles, or to be concerned with individuals only. There is a tendency for those who are dealing with individual problems to be concerned about the ideographic, the individual. But many psychologists take an even stronger position: that there are basic differences between individuals which do not involve the working of general laws. Many psychologists assume, for example, that each child is different and must be treated differently, and that studies seeking to find general laws of behavior will not be productive. Psychologists who study groups of subjects by which to obtain general laws of behavior take an opposite view. Within a particular field of study we may find that psychologists are separated on the basis of this conceptual schism. Watson and Skinner, on the nomothetic side, restricted their approaches more to the concern with general principles in the consideration of human behavior. In the area of animal learning, however, Skinner was on the other side of the schism. Here Skinner proposed that the only way to study general laws was through the study of individual animals, whereas others stated that group data should be used to establish general laws, as has been indicated. We can see in this example the manner in which the basic conceptual schisms can combine in various ways to produce multidimensional differences.

The Biological Versus Environmental Schism

One of the longest standing schisms in contemporary psychology concerns whether the child's development of various abilities comes about through development of biological structures and processes or through learning. There have been many studies whose aim has been to show the importance of biological factors in the ability development of the young, and the negligible impact of experience. For example, Carmichael (1926) showed that tadpoles prevented from gaining any experience in swimming, through the use of immobilizing drugs, nevertheless immediately swam as well as their more experienced brethren as soon as the drugs had worn off. On the human level Gesell and Thompson (1929) gave only one of two identical twin children training in stair-climbing over a period of six weeks. At the end of training this twin could climb stairs somewhat better than the nontrained twin could. However, within two weeks after the training had ceased, the nontrained twin had caught up to the trained twin in skill in this task. In both cases the conclusion was that learning was relatively insignificant in comparison to internal biological maturation factors in development.

In contrast to this, the other side of the schism has aimed at showing the importance of environment in the development of the child. For example, Watson said that he could make a child into anything that was desired, butcher, baker, or candlestick maker. An early study was that of Newman, Freeman, and Holzinger (1937) who found that in identical twins reared apart there were IQ differences as much as 24 points. Woodworth (1941) tabulated data from different environmentalist studies and found a correlation of 0.79 between differences in amount of education and differences in IQ scores. There have also been various studies that have enriched children's environments, usually with preschool experience, and have obtained increases in intelligence scores (Dawe 1942; McCandless 1940; Peters and McElwee 1944).

On the other side have been psychologists attempting to show that human characteristics are inherited. Recent hereditarians are Arthur Jensen (1969) and William Shockley (1971), and a host of others, who maintain that intelligence is largely inherited and is biologically determined. Leon Kamin (1974) and Staats (1963, 1968a, 1971), in opposition, have in contemporary times reasserted the importance of the environment. This schism runs through many types of separations in psychology, involving adults as well as children. There are those who are convinced that the answers to the problems of establishing the science of psychology lie in findings concerning humans as biological organisms. They want to see biologically oriented research supported, they are accepting of theories with a biological flavor, and so on. Individual psychologists with this orientation exist in various fields of psychology ranging from physiological psychology through clinical psychology and including developmental psychology, educational psychology, experimental psychology, abnormal psychology, and so on. Likewise, there are those whose emphasis is upon how humans come to be as they are through experience, and they too may be specialists in the various areas of psychology.

The Experimental Observation Versus Naturalistic Observation Schism

One of the basic conceptual divisions that separates psychologists involves the view of what are important facts in psychology. For many experimentalists the data of psychology are to be drawn from the tightly controlled experimental situation. The more scientific the study is in terms of the apparatus employed, the statistical analyses that are made, the smallness and exactness of the phenomena studied, and so on, the more appropriate the study is for the science. This value has been described to some extent already in the discussion concerning experimentalism, and it is related to the holistic-atomism separation and the ideographic-nomothetic schism.

From the standpoint of this view, as studies deviate from the characteristics of laboratory experimentation, they have less status and value. Thus, the longitudinal methods of child developmentalists, where the behavior of infants and children is simply observed over time, would have less status than tightly controlled laboratory studies. The same would be true of work to construct personality tests, clinical studies and educational psychology studies that deal with more naturalistic observations of behavior, but have less of a laboratory flavor. It should be noted that this point of view does not include a rationale or method by which to move from basic laboratory study to the understanding of actual, functional human behavior.

On the other side, of course, there are psychologists who look at laboratory studies in psychology as having no relevance for understanding the human condition. There is no acceptance in this view of the possibility that there are basic principles that affect human actions, that to isolate these basic principles in their stark, unconfounded simplicity, it may be necessary to simplify the naturalistic situation so that confounding variables do not create perturbations. When a study is done of a laboratory type, these psychologists consider the study to have lost the spark of humanity, and to be in a separate, and irrelevant, realm of concern. We can see some of the conflicting points of view in the following statement, in the context of considering a work on punishment.

> There is a growing disenchantment with many of the traditional methods used by experimental psychologists. Such old standards as the memory drum, the T-maze, and the operant chamber are among the more popular targets of such criticism. Neisser in his recent book, *Cognition and Reality*, suggests that these techniques lack *ecological validity*, which is to say that such methods produce results that are irrelevant to the phenomena one would really like to explain. Like Neisser, Walters and Grusec have offered an eloquent plea for a little more ecological validity in the context of punishment research. A request is made that some of the more sterile, esoteric procedures of the animal laboratory move in the direction of the real world of punishment practices . . . (italics added) (Dunham 1978, p. 552).

The Awareness Versus Conditioning Schism

As will be indicated later, the various dimensions that are being indicated here work in concert in separating psychologists into different subgroups. Thus, within the ranks of those who would follow an analytic, nomothetic, experimentalist tradition, there are still other differences regarding basic conceptions. One that has come to the fore in recent years is that regarding whether or not humans function according to conditioning in an automatic way, or whether the environment only affects the individual through some cognitive process of awareness.

To elaborate, in recent years there have been experiments conducted to study the possibility that humans learn through the same principles of classical and instrumental conditioning that had been isolated originally in the basic laboratory work with lower animals. Joel Greenspoon (1950) attempted to study the possibility that human subjects would follow the laws of instrumental conditioning in their speech behavior. And Staats and Staats (1957, 1958) studied the possibility that attitudes and word meaning could be learned according to classical conditioning. In both cases there were psychologists in opposition who argued that humans are not conditioned in such experimental situations, and in general do not function according to conditioning principles. This view states that the environment affects the individual through his *awareness* of the conditions of the environment and through his *decision* to behave in a certain manner (see Page 1969, as an example). This view states that the subjects in the conditioning studies became aware of what was going on in the experiment, and of the wishes of the experimenter, and that they responded accordingly, in a way that looked as though it was conditioning, but which involved, rather, a cognitive awareness and decision to perform a certain way.

There have generally been, thus, two views of human behavior involved. And psychologists of the two views pursue different courses. They design different types of studies. They read and consult different types of past studies and theories. They interpret studies in a different manner. They accept and reject different studies as being important — in their personal reading and, importantly, in evaluating manuscripts for a journal. I have seen two editorial reviews of the same article on conditioning in humans, one by a behaviorist who recommended publication and the other by an awareness advocate who denied the results showed a conditioning effect and recommended the article not be published. More will be said of such dynamics later.

The Freedom Versus Determination Schism

The schism concerning awareness versus conditioning may be considered to be a specific manifestation of a more general conceptual schism, at least in part. The more general schism involves, on the one hand, the conception that humans have free will. On the other hand, there have been those who have considered man as a machine who responds to certain environmental occurrences.

In ancient times it was said that each person had a little man, an homunculus, within his head that directed what he did. The theological concept has been that humans have a soul that provides them with a free will. In the history of psychology, various theorists have posited various concepts to imbue humans with an internal process by which they exert their self-determination. William McDougall, for example, emphasized the purposive nature of behavior in humans and animals. In the human mind he found "volition and freedom everywhere" (Boring 1950, p. 467).

As has been implicitly suggested in this presentation, the conceptual schisms that create incommensurability may be of ancient vintage and appear to be unresolvable. The same schism may recur in a contemporary form successively and repeatedly. In fact, it is suggested that this is typical, in any case where the schism is not resolved. In the present case we can see the continuation of the freedom-determinism schism in modern clothes. For example, contemporary, humanistically oriented psychologists — and that would include a larger group than those identified as humanists — do not wish to treat humans as an object of study, to assume that human behavior is caused by specifiable events. They hold out for spontaneity, for freedom, for self-direction, for active and purposive behavior. They reject a deterministic conception.

> The various behaviorisms all seem to generate inexorably such a passive image of a helpless man, one who (or should I say "which"?) has little to say about his (its?) own fate, who doesn't decide anything. . . . My crucially important experience of being an active subject is . . . either denied altogether . . . or is simply pushed aside as "unscientific," i.e., beyond respectable scientific treatment (Maslow 1966a, p. 55).

The other position in the schism is the view that human behavior is lawfully determined as are other aspects of the world in which we live. An early form of this view can be found in the position of the French materialists such as Etienne Condillac, Julien La Mettrie, and Pierre Cabanis. Each of these men in his own way said that human actions are strictly determined, either by one's sensations or by the physiology of the brain, or by some combination (Boring 1950).

The behaviorists have generally carried on this half of the schism, and the contemporary position has been stated many times within this orientation. According to this view psychology concerns behavior, which is a function primarily of the environmental conditions the organism encounters. It should be noted, however, that the schism cuts across the theoretical division of behaviorism versus nonbehaviorism. For example, the behaviorist Tolman (1932) was interested in cognitive concepts whereby the organism actively and purposively guides his own behavior. Tolman was interested in behavior, but also in inner mental determinants of that behavior. In varying ways this is true also of Rotter (1954), and of Staats (1963, 1968a, 1971, 1975).

The Special Qualities Versus Quantitative Difference Schism

Another conceptual split that is related to several of the other dimensions should be made explicit. There is a strong belief among many people, including psychologists, that man is more than a physical object, more than a high-class animal. Certainly this position is part of the traditional theology, in which man is considered to have a soul that is a special property over and above his material being. While this conception may not appear explicitly in the technical literature of psychology — where definitions appropriate to an empirical science are usually demanded — it plays a role in various forms.

On the other hand there is a strong view in psychology that the human is an animal. We behave according to the same principles as do other animals. For the biologically oriented scientist of this position, humans are to be understood within the context of considering their nature as biological organisms. The principles involved in type are considered to be the same as those that apply to other animals. For the environmentally oriented, the human is thought to follow the same principles of learning as lower animals, differing only quantitatively in having greater capacity for gaining and storing learned materials. In both cases this view leads one to study lower animals when it is appropriate, with the idea of establishing knowledge about the human, since they are on a continuous scale.

In the present view, however, there is a strong position in psychology that will not accept this characterization of the human. Theoretical or empirical work that gains its justification from the assumption that humans are biological animals, in a continuous line with other animals, following the same principles as other animals, is rejected as a viable approach to understanding humans. We can see that schism today in various areas of psychology. Thus, for example, linguists such as Chomsky have imbued humans with a special mental mechanism that gives them language. This is considered to be an emergent characteristic that other animals do not possess. This orientation, it is suggested, is influential in the rejection of the contemporary work suggesting that chimpanzees can be taught language. We can see this orientation, in its general sense, enunciated by the humanistic psychologists, as the following shows.

> The humanistic psychologist . . . disavows as inadequate and even misleading descriptions of human functioning and experience based wholly or in large part on subhuman species (Bugental 1967, p. 9).

Criss-Crossing Schisms

Some of the positions that have been described thus far tend to be related. Thus, the subjectivist orientation is likely to be related to the ideographic position, the biological explanation of human actions, to the awareness position, to a view of freedom in human actions, to the belief that humans are special. However, the schisms also constitute dimensions that can cut across each other to yield smaller intellectual enclaves. Thus, Rotter's (1954) approach, although behavioristic and objective, could be described as adhering to the awareness position, and including a purposive component that implies freedom. This is also true of *social behaviorism*, in more elaborated form (Staats 1975).

The major point to be made is that there are conceptual positions in conflict with respect to what is important to study in psychology (for example general laws or individual cases), what the explanations are for human actions (for example biological or environmental), what the nature of humanness is (for example special, emergent properties that can only be seen in the whole, versus properties displayed by other animals), where the locus for causation of human actions resides (outside the individual or within the individual), whether there are volitional aspects to human actions or whether behavior is strictly caused, whether psychology can be a laboratory science or whether it must deal with humans naturalistically and holistically, and so on. Centrally, these are examples of schisms that have existed historically. They are in opposition to one another. Since the schisms are not addressed in a manner that results in resolution of the oppositional positions, the schisms continue to work their effects on the separatism and incommensurability that continue to exist in the science. Much of the theoretical conflict in psychology, it is suggested, results from the fact that different theories are constituted on the foundations of these conceptual schisms.

But the theories themselves also contribute to the separatism of psychology. In fact the theory differences that contribute to psychology's pre-paradigmatic state play such an important role in the science's disorganization that the topic requires a summary indication here, as well as a more systematic treatment.

THEORIES AND SEPARATISM

Even a casual inventory will reveal that in psychology there is a plethora of theories, a very large number of unrelated theoretical structures. There is no way that it would be possible to present a representative sample of even theories whose introduction has been recent. Moreover, this would not provide a realistic picture since many theories introduced in the past are still currently employed and are viable theories today. On the other hand, theories continue to proliferate, with no concern for how this fact affects the science. A few theories will be named, just to give the reader a feeling for the diversity that is to be found in this realm of the science.

Personality

Any textbook in the field of personality will reveal the large number of theories that exist in this field alone. Some of them currently serve as bases for very active research programs, others are employed by practitioners in clinical, educational, and child psychology. Psychoanalytic theory is an example of the latter. Although not a new theory it is employed widely by practitioners, and aspects of this theory appear in other efforts. Psychoanalytic theory, it should be noted, is not one theory, but several separate theories — Sigmund Freud being the author of psychoanalytic theory with Carl Jung, Otto Rank, Karen Horney, Alfred Adler, Harry Sullivan, and many others having later developed individual variants. It should be noted that in the typical case the variants have been in competition with the original. It may also be mentioned that there are derivations from psychoanalytic theory that are tested in the laboratory (Blum and Barbour 1979) even though the primary relevance of the theory is in clinical practice.

Another type of theory in personality may be categorized as trait theory, since it posits that personality is composed of traits. The different theorists consider that different traits compose personality and employ different findings to support their cases. Theorists of this variety include Gordon Allport, Raymond Cattell, Hans Eysenck, J. P. Guilford, Edward Thurstone, and many others. There are also personality theorists such as Carl Rogers and Abraham Maslow and Donald Snygg and Arthur Combs who give a central role in their theories to the self-actualization force. In addition, there is a category of personality theory called consistency theory, wherein a major force in human behavior is attributed to the individual's striving for consistency. For example, George Kelley, David McClelland, and Festinger consider that the individual seeks to lessen discrepancies between his beliefs and life occurrences (see Maddi 1972).

Currently, as another example, and based upon past theoretical efforts of such men as Fritz Heider (1958) and Rotter (1954), there is a theory formation around the personality concept of the locus of control. This theory and the body of research associated with it treat the attribution of causality concerning behavior, whether causality is attributed to the performers of an action or to the situation in which the performer is acting. Current workers in this theory context include the following: Kelley (1967); Pines (1973); Himmelfarb (1972); Bem (1965); Zanna (1967); Jones and Nisbett (1971); Schopler and Layton (1972); Storms (1973); and many more.

Another current theoretical interest in personality theory has been referred to variously as interactional psychology, behavioral interaction, and reciprocal determinism. The theory concerns the conception that human behavior cannot be understood in terms of response to the environment alone, or to the manner in which the personality exerts effects, but must be considered as a result of a continuing interaction between the environment and personality. The new statement contains references to principles of behavior (learning). Psychologists who have offered separate theories that centrally include this position include the following: Rotter (1954); Staats (1963, 1968a, 1971, 1975); Bandura (1969, 1977a, 1977b, 1978); Mischel (1973); Endler and Magnusson (1976); among many others.

Then there are a number of theorists associated with a more strictly behavioristic theory of personality, considered as the total behavior the individual has learned (Watson 1930; Keller and Schoenfeld 1950; Skinner 1953; Bandura and Walters 1963; Bandura 1969; Mischel 1968, 1971). This approach is in contrast to the traditional conception of personality that considers personality as a causal factor, and in contrast to the above-mentioned behavioral interaction conception of personality that has arisen.

Learning Theory

The area of learning theory is another one where there are various theories introduced in the past that remain as theoretical structures today. And, in addition, there are contemporary theoretical efforts. In the first generation of learning theories the major works were those of Pavlov, Thorndike, and Watson. In the second generation, whose works have greater current usage, the major figures were Tolman, Guthrie, Hull, and Skinner. Books on theories of learning today devote themselves in large part to the conceptualizations of these men.

But there are more recent theoretical developments also. One that is very current centers around an integration of classical and instrumental conditioning, which had been separated in theoretical considerations since Pavlov's discovery of classical conditioning and Thorndike's isolation of instrumental conditioning. The new integratory approach includes the three-function theory of learning (Staats 1968a, 1970, 1975; Staats and Warren 1974), the perceptual-motivational theory of Dalbir Bindra (1978), the hybrid theory of operant conditioning of Frank Logan (1979; Logan and Ferraro 1970), as well as various others: (Boles 1979; Mackintosh 1974, 1978; and Overmeier and Lawry 1979).

Another less general theory in the area of learning, to select randomly, is the frustration theory of Abraham Amsel (1958, 1967, 1972). The kernel of the theory is that removal of reward availability for the animal brings on frustration that affects the way the extinction of learning takes place. Another example of more specialized theory involves the area of limitations on the generality of learning. A recent conceptualization has suggested that there are limits on the generality of learning laws. (This involves, among others, the ideographic-nomothetic dimension of the previous section.) For example, it has been said that learning principles are not the same over various species (Breland and Breland 1961). Martin Seligman (1970), as another example, has said that species are differently prepared to learn different responses to different stimuli. Others (Garcia, Ervin, and Koelling 1966) state that rats can easily learn to associate being sick to the stomach with novel tastes or odors but not with novel sights or sounds. This theoretical approach gets impetus from its opposition to the behavioral assumption that the laws of learning are general.

In another area of learning there are theories concerning the biological basis by which learning takes place. One theory of learning and memory has been that greater efficiency of conduction from one neuron to another occurs as a result of experience. Another is that biochemical changes take place in the neuron with differently coded RNA molecules being formed. Another theory is that learning takes place in the alteration of the probability of firing a neuron through some metabolic change (see Pfaff 1969). Several learning theorists have treated the relationship of learning and evolution (Skinner 1966; Staats 1963, 1971, 1975). There are thus various theoretical structures in this area, both large and small. This account does not scratch the surface of the variety that is present. There will be additional references to theory separatism in the learning theory area in the next chapter, however, and the examples that have been given here will suffice at this point.

Developmental Theories

There are various theoretical efforts in the area of developmental psychology, so numerous in fact that again only a flavor can be attempted. To begin with one from history that still has contemporary functions, psychoanalytic theory may be mentioned. Freud took a deterministic view of child development, conceptually imbuing the child with internal, biologically based forces that develop in stages and shape the child's personality development, as affected also by parental treatment. The child was viewed as having primitive biological forces at different periods that dictate the child's needs and, depending how these needs were met, the child's character development. Freud's theory gave impetus to various studies to test its expectations. One recent study deals with his theory of psychological defenses and how understanding of such defenses is related to cognitive development (Chandler, Paget, and Koch 1978).

Another approach to child development has arisen in the context of research on children, and has biologically based concepts. Such individuals as Gesell (Gesell, Halverson, Thompson, Ilg, Castner, Ames, and Amatruda 1940; Gesell and Thompson 1938) studied the different behaviors displayed by children of different ages and inferred that the changes were due to biological maturation. We see various examples of this theoretical orientation today. For example, Flanery and Balling (1979) studied the ability of subjects of different ages to make tactile discriminations of objects from right to left hand, or only using one hand. Their conception based on the results was that brain hemispheric asymmetry for some spatial abilities develops during middle childhood, as opposed to earlier ages. As another example, Douglas (1975) proposed that the human hippocampus cortical structure in the brain reaches functional maturity at four-and-a-half to five years of age. Wertlieb and Rose (1979) thus conducted a study over different ages of children based on the assumption that maze learning in children was a function of hippocampal development, and considered the results to support the theory.

A very influential contemporary theory is Piaget's general theory of development, which involves various concepts. It is also a stage theory of development, and it depends upon observing the behavioral skills of children over different ages. The theory states that children of certain ages will have certain skills, while younger children will not, because the child's cognitive structures develop over time. Siegler and Richards (1979) have conducted studies that confirm Piaget's (1969, 1970) theory of the development of the concepts of time, speed, and distance. This is but one aspect of the theory and one experimental test, and there are many of each.

Another current theory is that of learned helplessness, that is, the perception that one does not control the outcome of experienced situations (see Maier and Seligman 1976), a perception that then governs passive behavior. Weisz (1979) has conducted one of the many studies on this theory, finding that when children were subjected to failure they can learn to behave in a helpless manner.

Kohlberg (1969) has a theory that there is a stage progression in moral development in children and that the sequence of the stages is invariant. Anderson and Butzin (1978) have proposed an integration theory of children's judgments of equity in the distribution of rewards. Hoffman (1975) has formulated the theory that physical disciplinary measures lead to external moral orientations of fear of detection and punishment, whereas discipline through reasoning leads to internal moral orientations such as guilt.

In another area, Underwood (1969) has suggested that, as the child develops, different features of encoding are important in semantic encoding tasks. Keller, Ford, and Meacham (1978) have theorized that in self-concept formation perceived motor competencies develop prior to body-image concepts.

Again, in terms of broad theories of development there have been behavioristically or learning-theory oriented efforts. Thus, Watson proposed that the child learned everything and that he could make a child into any type of person through instruction (1930). Skinner has seemingly followed Watson's approach in this respect, although he has not specifically been concerned with child development through learning. Bandura has based an approach largely upon behavior development through imitation (Bandura and Walters 1963), otherwise following a standard behavioral approach (Bandura 1969). These theories have not attempted specifically to deal with the principles and facts of child development. Another learning theory has attempted to treat the traditional concerns of the sequential development of behavior, positing the cumulative-hierarchical learning of basic behavioral repertoires that constitute personality on the basis of which later personality developments are made (Staats 1968a, 1971, 1975). An entirely separate theory (Gagne 1968) also includes a cumulative-hierarchical theory of children's academic skill development.

These are but a few of the theories that reside in developmental psychology.

Social Psychology Theories

Again, it would be impossible to provide a representative picture of the various theories that exist in social psychology. Only a flavor of the variety and heterogeneity of the theories can be given. Carver (1979) presents a cybernetic theory of self-attention processes. This theory includes concepts concerning objects of conscious attention, self-directed attention, behavioral standard salients, behavior-standard discrepancy, and so on. Keller and Schoenfeld (1950) described the manner in which self-awareness is learned. Staats (1963) analyzed the self and self-concept in terms of learning also, adding the concept of behavioral standards (see also 1968a, 1975) and explaining in terms of learning principles how the individual's expressed self-concept affects his own behavior and the behavior of others. Bandura (1977) elaborated the concept that the individual's expectancy of success affects his behavior. Almost none of these treatments of the self and self-concept have been interrelated. There are also many other theoretical analyses of the self and self-concept that remain as separate conceptual entities.

There has been a recent concern with the effects of population density upon human behavior. Schopler and Stockdale (1977) have theorized that the various effects of density may be accounted for under the principle that interference with goal-directed behavior is the stress inductor involved. In the area of how political decisionmaking is influenced by psychological events there have been various theories, as has been indicated by Tetlock (1979), including unresolved psychodynamic conflicts (Glad 1973); the needs for achievement, affiliation, and power (Winter 1973); cognitive maps of the political world (Abelson 1973; Axelrod 1976; Holsti 1976; Jervis 1976); pressures toward cognitive consistency (Jervis 1976); the effects of stress on information-processing complexity (Hermann 1972; Suedfeld and Tetlock 1977); and social pressures towards groupthink (Janis, 1972; Tetlock 1979).

Robert Zajonc (1976) has proposed a confluence theory to account for the facts relating family size and birth order to intelligence. The theory of overjustification (Lepper and Greene 1976) states that a decrement in performance is produced by having extrinsic rewards. This occurs when the rewards do not result in the acquisition of new skills or provide new information about the individual's ability in the task. Conflict theory (Janis and Mann 1968) states that attitude change is enhanced when the subject is stimulated to consider arguments only on one side of the argument (O'Neill and Levings 1979). Robert Cialdini (Cialdini, Darby and Vincent 1973; Cialdini and Kendrick 1976) proposed a negative state relief theory of altruism. The motivation for altruistic behavior is seen as self-gratifying, through mitigating negative mood states.

In the area of attitude theory Anthony Greenwald (1968) describes theorists of a behavioral type as Staats, Bernice Lott and Albert Lott, Ralph Rosnow, and Robert Weiss (and it may be added Leonard Berkowitz 1970, 1973, as well as Donn Byrne and Gerald Clore 1970); learning theorists of an eclectic type as Greenwald, William McGuire, and Daryl Bem; cognitive integration theorists as Thomas Ostrom and Harry Upshaw, Timothy Brock, Jack Brehm and Reuban Baron, and Irving Janis and Leon Mann. And these were only the theorists included in one symposium (Greenwald, Brock, and Ostrom 1968); there are many others.

Another area of concern in social psychology is that of social interaction, the manner in which humans interact, and in this area there are many theories. For example, J.C. Goffman (1959) has theorized that in social interaction persons are concerned with how they will present themselves to others because the impression they create will determine if others will support the goals they have for themselves. Stacy Adams and Rimball Romney (1959) made an analysis of authority interactions in terms of each person constituting a stimulus for the other, each being capable of rewarding the other. George Homans posited that social behavior involves an exchange of goods, which can be nonmaterial such as the symbols of approval or prestige as well as material goods (1961). The focus in exchange theory is on how the rewards and costs that one person gives and takes from the other person, and the reverse, affects the behavior of each and thus the interaction. Another type of theory in social psychology has been called game theory. The interaction between people is considered in terms of the characteristics of winning and losing in the situation. One type of game situation occurs when the fact that one person wins means the other loses. This characteristic of the game situation will produce different modes of interaction than the situation where the participants either win or lose together. There are various possibilities between these two types of interaction, that is, of competition and cooperation (see Vinacke 1969). Another area of theory in social interaction has focused on attraction. Lindzey and Borgatta (1954) have suggested that people are attracted to one another when they share attitudes, values, and interests. Byrne and his associates have elaborated on this theory (see Byrne 1971). Walster (1965) has said that how the other person makes us feel about ourselves is an important element in attraction. Murstein (1971) has said that attraction is based both on having compatible needs as well as on fulfilling the other's role expectations. Much work in social psychology has also been concerned with the manner in which one person's impression of another is important in interaction. Heider advanced a theory of interpersonal perception that has had great influence on later theory and experimentation in social psychology (see Heider 1958). His theory may be summarized by saying that perception of the attributes of one person by another controls the actions and expectations of the second with respect to the first.

Although only mentioning a few of the theories in social psychology, this account will serve to indicate that they are many and diverse. Moreover, it should be stressed that these theories are not articulated with one another, even though they are in the same area of study and even though they overlap.

Cognitive Theory

In this section illustrating the great plethora of theories in psychology a few examples of areas have been indicated, but also one type of theory — learning theory — was also touched upon. Although learning theory represents a class, it is not restricted to a particular area. Another class of theory is that of cognitive theory, which is frequently considered to be in a competitive relationship with learning theory. Frequently, in various areas of psychology, there will be opposing theories, one of a learning orientation, the other of a cognitive orientation. A brief example will be given of some cognitive theories, although some of the examples already given in the different areas are actually cognitive theories, just as others are learning theories.

Memory and retrieval have been important topics in cognitive theories in experimental psychology. As one example, Warren (1977) has proposed that presentation of verbal material to a subject activates other units in the subject's memory that share common semantic features, making these other units more available for processing. Paivio (1975) has a dual-code theory of memory which states that an item may be stored either in the image system or in the verbal system or in both systems. According to late-selection theory (Deutsch and Deutsch 1963; Shiffrin and Schneider 1977) perceptual processing is automatic and irrepressible while, on the other hand, according to multiple-loci theory (see Broadbent 1970; Erdelyi 1974; Treisman 1969) perceptual processing is malleable and can be repressed and changed. Tulving proposed that memory is of two kinds, episodic and semantic. The first stores information that is temporal and personal, and the second stores general knowledge of the world (1972).

An area that has developed in recent years that employs some concepts of cognitive theory deals with reading, as the following excerpt indicates.

> What are some potential sources of individual differences in reading that are based on central processes? . . . A basic claim of many information-processing models of reading [e.g., Estes 1975; LaBerge & Samuels 1974; Massaro 1975] is that reading depends on a hierarchical organization of subprocesses. In constructing a conceptual representation of the material read, it is often suggested that information is first analyzed for visual features and then passed successively to letter, word, semantic-syntactic, and conceptual levels of analysis. Several researchers have suggested a phonological encoding level prior to accessing word meanings [Rubenstein, Lewis, & Rubenstein 1971; Rubenstein, Richter, & Kay 1975], although the role of obligatory verbal coding in accessing the meaning of words is in doubt [Baron 1973; Frederiksen & Kroll 1976; Kleiman 1975] (Jackson and McClelland 1979, p. 153).

As will be indicated further on, this example is interesting in that there are learning theories that are very similar to the cognitive theory analysis of reading, but the theory difference creates separatism so the theories remain isolated. To continue, however, frequency theory states that in a recognition task discriminations between old and new units occur on the basis of a subjective frequency difference with the old units having a frequency of 1 and the new units of 0 (Ekstrand, Wallace, and Underwood 1966). Broadbent, Cooper, and Broadbent (1978) hypothesize that the internal representation of knowledge can have different types of structures, one of which is a hierarchical structure. Hypothesis theory (Levine 1975), in the realm of problem solving, states that subjects solve problems by making a series of hypotheses. Subjects thus sample from a hypothesis domain. If the solution is not in that domain, the subject may first have to exhaust the solutions in that domain before attempting solutions from another domain. As indicated by Sweller and Gee (1978) this theory explains why subjects given a series of similar problems to solve have a more difficult time than ordinary in using a different but more simple solution to a later problem (see Adamson

1959; Luchins 1942). In the processing of information Craik and Lockhart (1972) proposed that information is processed into hierarchically ordered categories or levels. Increases in storage can be increased by the depth of the levels employed. Craik and Tulving (1975) and Lockhart, Craik, and Jacoby (1976) have theorized that increased storage can also be attained by *"elaboration* of encoding operations conducted within one distinct level or domain" (Kunen, Green, and Waterman 1979, p. 574). There are many theoretical structures in cognitive theory, again without articulation. The result, as with the others, is the proliferation of a disorganized body of knowledge.

Separatism by Theory

The material in the above sections does not begin to indicate the diversity that exists in the theories of psychology. Only a few areas in psychology were treated. Such areas as educational psychology, industrial, abnormal, clinical psychology, and many others, were not considered. For example, the state of theory and practice in the field of clinical psychology has been described in the following terms.

> [R]esponsible reviewers have guessed that there may be 100 to 140 schools of psychotherapy — all of them in the mainstream . . . .
> It is difficult to generalize beyond that, Glass agrees, and it is particularly hard to compare the results of one study with another because there are so few common standards. Research on psychotherapy, according to Glass, is an "enormously widespread, unorganized cottage industry. Every university runs its own type in its own way. They don't listen to anybody else. They don't read anybody else's literature. It's quite an odd mish-mash of things" (Marshall 1980, pp. 506-7).

This author, apparently without recognizing its general significance, has provided a specific characterization of a preparadigmatic field of study; moreover, the same description applies to every other area of psychology. The present account can only select a few examples of the variety and diversity of theories in psychology. Nevertheless, even from this brief survey the reader can get the flavor of the chaotic condition of psychology with respect to theory. Even though the summaries that have been given were put as much as possible into common-sense terms, and the summaries were too shallow to deal with the technological details involved, it can be seen that it would be difficult for the student, scholar, or researcher to become even slightly conversant with the various theories. This, of course, makes for separatism. It is not possible for one to learn each theoretical language, even within one of the categories. The fact is, becoming expert in one theory language to the exclusion of the others, which is typical, means that the scientist of psychology is cut off from contact with the products of his colleagues in other areas. As an example, in the section on cognitive theories it was indicated that there were information-processing models of reading that include a theoretical conception of a "hierarchical organization of subprocesses." These theories have been entirely separate from a learning theory of reading that also includes a closely related conception of a hierarchical organization of subprocesses (see Staats 1968a, 1975; Staats, Brewer, and Gross 1970). Although there is much that would be accomplished by interrelating the work of these two separate theoretical and experimental endeavors, the separatism of the theories is an obstacle to that cross-relating. There are other areas in which a schism between theoretical approaches — as in cognitive theory versus learning theory — results in the disadvantageous separation of relevant materials. New and separated theories of intelligence fall into this category also (see Estes 1974, 1976; Staats 1963, 1968a, 1971, 1975; Sternberg 1977; Whimbey and Whimbey 1975). These are but two examples. A later chapter will deal specifically with the philosophy and practice of separatism between theories in psychology. It is important here to indicate, however, that the field of psychology is divided along theoretical lines. There are large divisions, such as that between behavioristic or learning theories and cognitive theories. And within the major divisions there are smaller divisions. The result is the existence of many, many theories in psychology. Each of these constitutes in some sense an island that is isolated from the rest of the knowledge in the science. There are no psychologists who are familiar with the various theories. It would be impossible to do so. Certainly, no attempt is being made to establish what commonalities exist. The most usual circumstance is that the scientist or practitioner in psychology will know one theory well, and perhaps its close relatives, and be only vaguely aware of the character and existence of some of the other theories. Frequently the psychologist will be opposed to theories other than the one he knows and accepts. The central point is that the plethora of theories in and of itself makes it very difficult to attain unity in the science of psychology. The theories, isolated and competitive, strongly contribute to the disorganized, chaotic state of knowledge in psychology.

COMPETITIVE ISLANDS OF KNOWLEDGE

In describing these several dimensions of the preparadigmatic nature of psychology several things should be noted. For one thing, the dimensions may work in conjunction to produce separatism. Thus, a particular theory that is separated from other areas of knowledge by virtue of its theoretical character may also have a characteristic experimental procedure that brings it into contact with special events to study, and it may have methodological developments and a methodological philosophy all of which provide it with distinctive features contributing to its separation from other aspects of psychology. The manner in which the approach deals with the various intellectual schisms may also separate it from other approaches, even when there is much commonality.

A particular approach can then be the basis for a social organization of psychologists with similar views. Depending upon the number of members involved, the organization may be more or less formal in nature. There are approaches that have attained a sufficient number of members to publish their own journals. Others issue newsletters. And, as will be indicated, there are many approaches that provide training specializations that are very different from those of other approaches.

The number of combinations that can result from the types of differences that have been described is so large that the science of psychology is broken into a multitude of islands of knowledge. The diversity is such that it is impossible for a psychologist to incorporate any but a small proportion of those islands that are available — at least as the islands are presently constituted.

TRAINING BASED SEPARATISM

Finally, it is suggested in this section that separatism occurs in psychology based on the way that students are trained. Student training is one of the processes by which preparadigmatic science is promulgated. Training is actually related to the other separations that are being discussed, those based upon methodological and theoretical and organizational separations, and so on. But it is relevant to note the role that student training plays in perpetuating the preparadigmatic state of the science.

To begin, it is usual in psychology today for students to specialize very early in their graduate career. When a student goes into a program in clinical psychology, developmental psychology, social psychology, or experimental psychology, except for some common courses in statistics, there is a tendency to concentrate on one area knowledge to the exclusion of knowledge of other areas or a general knowledge of the science. Since any contact students have had, or now have, with other areas is presented in a manner that is largely unrelated to the knowledge in their specialty, what little exposure is obtained is ordinarily not incorporated, retained, and kept current. The student ends up with little appreciation of the other areas, and little belief that the knowledge of the other areas can be productive. Thus, as an example, clinical psychologists may be interested in the perceptions of their clients' reasoning and problem solving, or verbal and communication skills. However, study of and contact with experimental psychologists or experimental psychology will have given the student little in the way of basic principles that can help in understanding such functional human behaviors. Moreover, it is likely that contact with experimental psychologists will have revealed that they think little of the student's concerns as valid topics of study, or indeed of clinical psychology as a profession. The same is true in general. When the students study animal learning, locus of control, physiological psychology, among others, for the most part they will learn materials unrelated to their interests in clinical psychology. The same general condition applies whether the student is in developmental, experimental, social or some other area of psychology.

The emphasis upon area division of the field of psychology has led to the areas becoming the primary organizations of the field, beginning when the psychologist is still a student. Students gain their identity as scientists or professionals from their area of study. When they receive the doctoral degree they ordinarily become a member in the appropriate division of the American Psychological Association (APA). Advancement to prominence in the field of psychology will be through recognition by specialty area organizations. Status in psychology will be obtained in this way, except in a few unusual cases.

But the separatism that is produced through training is not limited to being trained in one of the divisions of the field of psychology. Students may receive training that will separate their orientation from that of other students on the basis of methodology. The student in child development, for example, may learn methods of longitudinal observation, versus methods that manipulate learning variables. The student in personality may learn multivariate statistical methods, versus the analysis of variance statistical analyses of the experimental psychologist, and also versus the single organism methods of the operant behaviorist.

Moreover, as the last example implies, students may receive training that separate them from other students on the basis of theory differences. Different departments of psychology, or different areas within a department, may follow particular broad conceptual orientations — for example, subjectivist, humanist, holistic, or clinical theories. Or the department or area in a department may follow particular theoretical orientations — for example, cognitive theory, or learning theory, or even more specific theories. The following passage is descriptive of the manner in which a student receives training in a particular paradigm (rather, preparadigm) in psychology. Since other students receive training in other preparadigms, this is a description of separatism produced in training. While the following authors' remarks are addressed to science in general, as psychologists what they describe are the conditions in preparadigmatic science.

> . . . [G]raduate research training gives a considerable element of indoctrination in the prevailing paradigm.

. . . Since the *unselected* data base of any science will encompass a collection that is enormous in size, the facets to which the student is exposed in the course of graduate training represent a process of considerable selectivity and omission. Facts that do not fit the prevailing paradigm are more susceptible to forgetting, not to say conscious omission, and appear with considerably lower probabilities in graduate lectures and publications than those which support it. Selective forgetting, of course, is not the sole exit route for facts that do not fit the prevailing conceptualizations. It is not uncommon for such facts to be attributed to the work of incompetents, to be dismissed as uninteresting and unimportant, or even to be hidden in the files of the researcher who discovered them. Thus, a selective data base is transmitted from one generation of researchers to the next (italics added) (Segal and Lachman 1976, pp. 46–47).

Evidence that students can be systematically trained in one theoretical orientation to the exclusion of others has also been suggested (see Staats 1978). It is part of the present thesis that, although training-produced separatism may be general to science, since the student cannot be exposed to everything in the science, this type of separatism, as the others, is much more emphasized in the preparadigmatic science than in the paradigmatic science.

PSYCHOLOGY: A MODERN PREPARADIGMATIC SCIENCE

It should be noted that psychology came into being as a science after the various foundations of general science had been worked out. As a consequence psychology had (1) a firmly established confidence in the success of specialized observing apparatus to achieve objectivity and reliability, (2) an orientation toward seeking experimental methods and designs to help specify when things are related and when they are not, (3) an empirical logic and a belief in the power of theories, (4) the knowledge of publication media and the need for dissemination of scientific findings, (5) the organization of society to support science, for example, in the university, as well as a host of other things important to the conduct of science, and (6) the knowledge of the success of applying science to worldly problems.

Psychology thus had the basis for a rapid accumulation of empirical, methodological, and theoretical knowledge. In this sense it soon faced conditions that were different than those in the history of the earlier developed, natural sciences. That is, the natural sciences, it is suggested, remained small, sparsely populated, socially unsupported endeavors for a much longer time than has psychology. Because of the earlier developments of natural science, very soon psychology had all the accoutrements of science before it had developed all of the characteristics of the natural sciences. Thus, psychology has had the membership of a large science, has had the support of the university system, has had the journals of a large science, and it thus has had the means for producing an explosion of knowledge. But this occurred before it developed the characteristics by which to organize that productivity. In the natural sciences, the period of preparadigmaticism occurred when each was still small, unsupported, and sparsely populated. As a consequence, paradigmatization occurred before there was the tremendous explosion of knowledge that a modern preparadigmatic science can produce. Organization took place in the natural sciences before the disorganization of the knowledge explosion itself made it difficult to establish paradigms or a paradigmatic science.

Even then we can see from the description of the natural sciences, when still preparadigmatic, that there was a chaos of information. Kuhn describes the knowledge of the preparadigmatic science in terms such as "inchoate pool of information" (1962, p. 17), "facts collected with so little guidance" (p. 16), "random activity" (p. 15), "as many views . . . as . . . important . . . experimenters" (p. 13), "Yet anyone examining a survey of physical optics before Newton may well conclude that, though the field's practitioners were scientists, the net result of their activity was something less than science" (p. 13).

Psychology, it is suggested, because it has all of the accoutrements of a developed science — with huge numbers of scientists and resources — faces the problem of becoming an organized science in much greater degree than was faced in the example above. Psychology has a much greater confusion of elements than Kuhn has described for physics in its preparadigmatic stage of development. What must be recognized and studied are the characteristics that make psychology even more of a preparadigmatic science than were the natural sciences in their preparadigmatic periods. It is the present thesis, as will be indicated, that the preparadigmatic science, because of its disorganization, develops characteristics that are obstacles to paradigmatic development, obstacles over and above the inherent problems of creating united knowledge.

In the present view it is important to study systematically the characteristics of the modern preparadigmatic science, for this is a first step toward improvement of these characteristics. The philosophy of science has not been systematically concerned with the nature of the modern preparadigmatic sciences. There are brief and casual opinions, however, with respect to whether psychology is or is not a full, paradigmatic science, as has been indicated. It is relevant here to note an example of this type of opinion.

> The different men attempting to co-operate in launching a new science (say) may not merely disagree about their particular observations and interpretations, concepts and hypotheses: they may even lack common standards for deciding what constitutes a genuine problem, a valid expla-

nation, or a sound theory. . . . The immediate result of this lack is that theoretical debate in the field concerned becomes largely — and unintentionally — methodological or philosophical; inevitably, it is directed less at interpreting particular empirical findings than at debating the general acceptability (or unacceptability) of rival approaches, patterns of explanation, and standards of judgment. . . . So long as a *would-be discipline* remains in this preliminary, inchoate condition, no agreed family of fundamental concepts or constellation of basic presuppositions — no "paradigm," in Lichtenberg's sense — can establish itself with authority. . . .

The characteristic features of *"would-be disciplines"* can best be illustrated, at the present time, by contrasting the state of the behavioural sciences with that of the physical sciences. Throughout the history of modern science, rival schools of physicists have seen their problems in different proportions, have evaluated their basic concepts somewhat differently, and have interpreted certain crucial phenomena in distinctively different ways; even in physics, that is to say, there has never been unanimity. Nevertheless, by disciplinary standards, these disagreements have remained marginal, and have commonly been limited to alternative intellectual strategies for promoting certain generally agreed goals. The current position in the behavioural sciences is very different. Whether we turn to professional psychologists for explanations of the behaviour of individual human beings, or to professional sociologists and anthropologists to account for the collective behaviour of groups, societies, or cultures, in each case we find a diversity of approaches of a kind unparalleled in physics. Instead of their being united by agreed conceptions of what a "human science" should aim at, or can ideally hope to achieve, we find behavioural scientists split into parties, factions, or sects, which have not managed to hammer out a common set of disciplinary goals (italics added) (Toulmin 1972, pp. 380–82).

This evaluation of psychology must surely come as a bitter pill to anyone who has an interest in establishing psychology as a science. The words "would-be discipline" particularly strike home, because they reflect the fact that prominent scientists and philosophers of science look upon psychology as a pretender to science, but not a science. Since psychology has had full recognition as a science as a central goal, Toulmin's statement, and others like it, must give us pause. Perhaps we must question whether our guiding framework is correct. Perhaps we need a new view of what psychology consists of as a science and what it must develop to be a full science. The central point, in the present opinion, is that scientific status is not to be achieved solely by developing apparatus and experimental methods that are objective and that produce systematic and precise data. As has been indicated, a chaos of competing experimental facts and principles can be produced — and has been in psychology — that evidences none of the organized unity of the scientific discipline. Many psychologists have hoped to create a science by remaining close to the laboratory and demonstrating the productivity of experimental methods in producing objective data. *It must be clear that this is not the road to the science of behavior, for what is produced is still an unorganized assemblage, not recognized to be full science.* There are experimentalists, as will be further indicated, who feel that the answer to becoming a science is to separate scientific psychology from other parts of psychology that are concerned with aspects of behavior other than those typically studied in the laboratory. However, if the experimental parts of psychology have not produced a paradigmatic state, and they have not, such separation will not solve the problem. We must face the possibility that the strategy of generating experimental data is not by itself what we need to advance our field to the level of an advanced science discipline. Experimental data may be necessary, but clearly are not sufficient.

On the other hand, the generation of individualistic theories does not appear to be the answer either. The mélange of different and competing theories that exist in psychology has not advanced us toward the characteristics of organized knowledge that are displayed by the advanced scientific disciplines, and this fact is clearly seen by scholars of science, with only a glance, which is all that has been given. As will be indicated, the guiding methodology of the preparadigmatic science predisposes the scientist in the field to individualistically and separately compose his own theory, concept, or principle, and this methodology contributes to the disorganization of knowledge our field displays. The present chapter has attempted to characterize, as a beginning effort, the disorganization of knowledge that is endemic to our field, since that is the first step toward achieving a solution to the problem. Toulmin does not believe that our field is ready to become a science, as the following statement indicates.

> In the behavioural field, no generally agreed criteria yet exist for deciding when a human action is intelligible or unintelligible, or what types of conduct constitute genuine "phenomena," and so pose theoretical problems for psychology or sociology at all. Still less do behavioural scientists with different orientations share agreed standards for recognizing when a new theory of human behaviour has provided a "complete explanation" of the relevant modes of conduct; or for recognizing what kinds of regularity or mechanism will make human behaviour intelligible; or for judging when a novel conceptual variant has the merits needed for incorporation into an established body of general theory. All this being so, the preconditions do not yet apparently exist, in the fields of individual and collective human behaviour, for establishing a "compact" scientific discipline, possessing a definite strategy and an authoritative body of current theory (Toulmin 1972, pp. 382–83).

In the present view, however, the philosophy of science has not made a systematic study of the behavioral sciences. Toulmin's conclusions have, I believe, been made on the basis of a less than profound contact with psychology. He has been able to gauge the science's chaotic state, but not its potential for unification, a more difficult task. It will be the psychologists' task to systematically consider the science with an eye to whether the field is ready now to begin to advance toward the paradigmatic state, and to consider also what paths to take to achieve that advancement. For the task will require an intimate understanding of psychology, across a broad framework, not the casual glance provided by the philosophers of science. The paradigmatic revolution, as will be indicated, is a gigantic theoretical task, one that will require the work of many members of the science. But we should not be misled to believe that because our science is not now paradigmatic it does not have the preconditions to be paradigmatic. Those preconditions will not announce themselves. They may be there now, (it is the present view that they are), but lie unutilized and unrecognized.

In the present view psychology is a science in its many characteristics. And the scientists in this field do scientific work. They employ sophisticated apparatus, sophisticated methodology in experimental design and analysis. Their understanding of theory construction and the logic of science is sophisticated, for practicing scientists. Yet these very science characteristics provide the profusion of development and knowledge that in part constitute an obstacle to attaining the necessary characteristic that will make the field of psychology a science in the complete sense. That missing part is the organization, unification, that is characteristic of the paradigmatic science. It is the thesis of this book that while psychology is a science in its many characteristics, it has not begun to attain the paradigmatic level of development. Moreover, the unification characteristic of paradigmatic science is a necessary development in *any* science's attainment of the stature of a complete science.

Psychology can continue to proliferate its diverse, chaotic knowledge. It can improve its methods of research in this task, and gain more precise data. But the profusion of knowledge produced in its present disorganized way will never make psychology a complete science. Unlike the view of Toulmin indicated above, the present position is that the preparadigmatic efforts of psychology have produced a great many of the preconditions that are requisite for the paradigmatic revolution. Not all the pieces are there, and there are included erroneous pieces in abundance that contribute to the chaos and disguise the solution that will lead to establishing the paradigmatic science. Nevertheless, the preconditions do exist for establishing a compact scientific discipline. Utilizing the preconditions in the task depends upon a philosophy and methodology that can serve to guide the very large effort that is necessary. But this position requires further elaboration, as the following chapters will indicate.

Chapter 5

Disunity and the Sociology of Science

Early in the present work it was said that consideration of the logic of scientific theories and their empirical correlates did not cover all of the topics of interest to the scholar of science. Aspects of the history and philosophy of science were indicated that pertained to additional topics. While once scholars generally considered science to be a pure and objective search for empirical truth, in contemporary times interest has broadened to include social as well as intellectual concerns of science. We can see this change in the following excerpt.

> Until recently, of course, scientists have cultivated a public image of disinterestedness: and this has carried with it a pretence that the institutional activities of scientists — forming as they do, the professional face of a "rational" enterprise — are somehow exempt from the general principles of political and social action. Happily and more realistically, we are no longer obliged today to suppose that the conduct of scholars and scientists, when assembled into professional bodies, is emancipated from the general laws governing the collective actions of other institutions. Individuals and organizations in fact exercise as real a power and influence over the development of science as they do in any other sphere of human life. Correspondingly, the roles, offices, and positions of influence within a scientific profession are worth fighting for — and are, in practice, fought for — as singlemindedly, methodically, and even deviously, as in any other sphere (Toulmin 1972, p. 267).

Toulmin has clearly indicated that in understanding what science is, it is necessary to consider the intellectual factors involved, the institutional factors, and the personal factors. Very basic in this shift in the philosophy of science to an interest in the social aspects of science has been the work of the sociologists of science. There are some aspects of this work that are germane in the present context.

THE REWARD SYSTEM OF SCIENCE

In his classic work in the sociology of science Robert Merton (1945, 1957) has analyzed the reward system of science, saying, for example, "Like other institutions, the institution of science has developed an elaborate system for allocating rewards to those who variously live up to its norms" (Merton 1973, p. 297). Merton, in his description of the scientific reward system, introduced topics that are important in understanding motivation in science. He cites honorific recognition as primary in the rewards for scientists. This, as he notes, may take various forms. For example, there is eponymy — having some scientific achievement named after the discovering scientist — and this type of recognition can have differing levels. Prizes such as the Nobel constitute another type of reward. There are memberships in honorary and invited societies. There are titles, as given in England for scientific contribution. There are honorary degrees conferred by universities. More generally effective, it may be suggested, is the esteem of one's colleagues, the respect it engenders, and the reward of having an important position in one's science.

It may be added that there are also additional rewards in the system that affect scientists. For one thing the scientist may gain a living on the basis of his scientific work, and this living depends upon the excellence of his work, or upon the degree to which it is recognized. As will be discussed further on, the scientist may also gain power through the recognition of his work. He may influence others, he may direct the course the field takes, he may receive special privileges in his university, he may be invited to travel and speak and be honored and so on, all of which may function as rewards.

The rewards that the science bestows are given for originality, for producing new knowledge. "Recognition for originality becomes socially validated testimony that one has successfully lived up to the most exacting requirements of one's role as scientist" (Merton 1973, p. 293).

> This means that long before we know anything about the distinctive personality of this or that scientist, we know that he will be under pressure to make his contributions to knowledge known to other scientists and that they, in turn, will be under pressure to acknowledge his rights to his intellectual property. To be sure, some scientists are more vulnerable to these pressures than others—some are self-effacing, others self-assertive; some generous in granting recognition, others stingy (Merton 1973, p. 294).

Priority practices of publication are identified by Merton to be a special culprit in promoting competition in science. He indicates that there have been many disputes over priority of origination in the history of science. "The peerless Newton fought several battles with Robert Hooke over priority in optics and celestial mechanics and entered into a long and painful controversy with Leibnitz over the invention of the calculus" (Merton 1973, p. 287). The personal rewards that science offers, thus, being based upon originality, are concerned with priority. "Only original research is regarded as a contribution, and a publication that does not have priority over other publications concerning the same problem is of secondary value" (Gaston 1973, p. 74). "The system of incentives in science does not encourage workers to devote their efforts to repeating past accomplishments when the record of such accomplishments is available in libraries" (Hagstrom 1965, p. 69).

A competitive situation may be said to exist when the behavior of two individuals may each result in obtaining the same reward — obtaining the reward by one precluding the same result for the other (see Homans 1961; Staats 1963). Hagstrom defines competition in science to exist "when scientific research is likely to lead to the same discovery. When scientists are likely to be anticipated, competition is prevalent" (Gaston 1973, p. 75). This is a description of the natural sciences, it may be emphasized, and more will be said of competition further on. To continue, explicit in the writing of Merton and others has been a dissatisfaction with the reward system of science which so heavily involves the personal rewards of recognition, based on originality, as will be further indicated. At this point, however, it is sufficient to note that important rewards affect the scientist.

DEVIANT BEHAVIOR IN SCIENCE

In this context it is relevant to ask what are the behaviors of the scientist that are affected by these rewards. There are various such behaviors (Staats 1963), some positive and some negative. Merton identifies a class of behaviors that are relevant to consider in the present context. He describes what he considers to be deviations in the behavior of scientists; behaviors that abrogate the normal practices of science. The first of these is fraud. Merton suggests that such cases are rare in science. A contemporary and famous case has arisen in psychology concerning some of the data of Sir Cyril Burt. It appears that some of his results may have been fraudulent. Statistics in several of his papers remained exactly the same notwithstanding the fact that there were different numbers of subjects in the several studies involved. Moreover, some of the articles he published in a journal he edited, written in support of his position supposedly by other authors, may have been written by Burt himself. Both of these practices, if they occurred as described, would have had the effect of erroneously strengthening his theoretical approach (Dorfman 1978; Wade 1976). A recent issue of *Science*, moreover, reports the faking of data in a few clinical investigations of drugs. "Kennedy was told of two doctors who had falsified data on new drug testing" (Holden 1979, p. 432). Recent occurrences (see Silberner 1982) have shown that systematic fraudulent practices in science are not as infrequent as Merton has suggested. Moreover, "The great cultural emphasis upon recognition for original discovery can lead by gradations from these rare practices of outright fraud to more frequent practices just beyond the edge of acceptability, sometimes without the scientist's being aware that he has exceeded allowable limits" (Merton 1973, p. 311).

"Deviant behavior most often takes the form of occasional plagiaries and many slanderous charges or insinuations of plagiary" (Merton 1973, p. 312). Merton proceeds to refer to various historical cases in which there is specification, and which are famous in involving famous scientists. One of the best known and substantiated appears to involve the scientist Laplace. In recounting the classic and influential work of Laplace, entitled *Mecanique celeste*, Merton uses a statement of the historian Agnes May Clerke from the eleventh edition of the *Encyclopedia Brittanica*. She states that in Laplace's work "theorems and formulae are appropriated wholesale without acknowledgement." Then Merton continues.

> Some of Clerke's further observations are much in point: "In the delicate task of apportioning to his own large share of merit, he certainly does not err on the side of modesty. . . . Far more serious blame attaches to his all but total suppression in the body of the work — and the fault pervades the whole of his writings — of the names of his predecessors and contemporaries . . . a production which may be described as the organized result of a century of patient toil presents itself to the world as the offspring of a single brain" (*Encyclopedia Brittanica* vol. 16, pp. 201–02) (Merton 1973, p. 312).

Thus, the example suggests that very renowned scientists may display such deviant scientific behavior, extensively using a systematic methodology of noncitation of others' work. Other cases in the history of science are described by Ravetz (1971), as exemplified in the following:

> The distinguished physicist J. B. Biot, who might be called the world's first career scientist, was involved in a number of unpleasant disputes over property. These usually did not involve the priority of the first discovery itself; but Biot's technique, apparently, was to learn of a discovery informally from a colleague or friend, and then with his experimental skill and the superior material resources at his disposal to exploit the dis-

covery and report on his own series of experiments, before his informant had the opportunity to develop the work. The case of the great mathematician Cauchy was even more notorious. On receiving a paper for refereeing, he could not resist the temptation of recasting the proof, improving the result, developing and generalizing it in all sorts of ways, and finally publishing it in a journal to which he had rapid access. When the paper which had originally stimulated him finally appeared in print, it would seem singularly crude and pointless in comparison to the results already published by the master (Ravetz 1971, p. 256).

It appears that the incidence of such deviant behavior in the history of science has not been restricted to small, specific cases. It may also be noted that renowned scientists have displayed such behavior, not only in single cases of deviance but in a systematic way that must have been heavily involved in helping them attain their status in the science. It is important to note that in each case the deviance did not prevent the scientist from gaining a prominent place in the science of his time. In this respect it is interesting to ask about the conditions that existed such that the individual was not called to account for abrogating the practices of normal science. Such deviant practices are not limited to history, and they continue to detract from science, although in the paradigmatic sciences, cases as extensive as those famous in history may no longer occur.

> The theft of ideas is a more serious form of deviation since the reaction to it, secrecy, harms science. . . . Most scientists are familiar with anecdotal accounts of the theft of ideas, and the conditions for suspicion are often present. . . . An organic chemist . . . presented the following episode. X has been known to wipe you out if he finds the direction of your research. He will quickly get into the area and publish the most important results. . . .
>
> What is stolen in such cases are ideas, general information about the goal sought and the means to be used. Usually the thief must do considerable research himself. A mathematician may learn about a theorem someone else has proved and the general techniques used, but to steal the idea he must still produce detailed results (Hagstrom 1965, p. 86).

Another form of taking ideas involves the practices of citation. Depending on characteristics of science that will be discussed later, it is possible in some sciences to use ideas expressed in the work of others in later publications without referring to the earlier work. The example of Laplace briefly described such practices under the heading of plagiarism. But plagiarism is a legal term reserved for cases that are very clear and that are brought to court, something most scientists would avoid. In some science areas concepts and principles can be restated, employing different terms and combined with different materials, so that it may not be so easy to substantiate a charge of plagiarism. Moreover, the imitating theorist may add new materials to that which existed before, so that it is not a case of straightforward copying. Gaston has cited various opinions of scientists that support the occurrence of this type of illicit apportioning of credit.

> I suspect whatever they published and actually made a large part of their publication was stuff that we had developed and published. If they had given our reference it would have appeared very obvious that what they had done something that had already been done (Gaston 1973, p. 112).

The failure to refer to the prior work of someone else may also be a tactic to gain the whole of the recognition for an original contribution, rather than only a portion. When asked to explain why scientists have not referred to his work, a theorist replied, "Possibly a reference to my work would distract from the importance of their work, because what I've done so far in my field has always been new" (Gaston 1973, p. 111).

The mechanics of taking ideas apparently has different forms also. Sometimes it occurs through personal conversation, and other times in other ways.

> There are many people who are not very much aware of who they get ideas from, and six months after they hear the idea they forget who suggested it. Talking to those people about your ideas can get yourself into trouble (Gaston 1973, p. 123).

> One person came to me and asked me for advice on a particular project in which he was engaged, and I spent quite a lot of time with this person and discussed various things with him. I was also engaged in similar projects, and I told him what I was doing—how far I'd got. And the next thing I knew he had published essentially my work. He had memorized enough of it and gone off and written something quickly (Gaston 1973, p. 109).

> We sent a preprint to ––– and in a matter of weeks received a preprint from them showing the same effect, but in a different reaction that didn't give a reference to ours. They also had sent the letter to *Physical Review Letters*. Ours had been delayed at preprint stage before being sent to *Physical Review Letters*, so they arrived about the same time. It was very complicated. We phoned the editor in New York and in the end got ––– to make a reference to our work (Gaston 1973, p. 113).

The practices of the science itself may provide opportunity for deviant behaviors involving usurpation of ideas and the recognition that accrues to the ideas, as was indicated in the previous example involving the mathematician Cauchy. The following explicates a mechanism by which the usurpation can occur in modern science.

> Referees of scientific papers are exposed to the temptation to steal ideas from the manuscripts they review. A referee may be placed in a very embarrassing position when the paper to be reviewed is closely related to his own research. He may be about to submit a paper for publication himself, on an almost identical subject. If he learns, as a referee, that a rival has anticipated him, and if he judges the work to be valid, it is his obvious obligation to return the paper promptly to the editor and recommend its publication. The referee may, however, have valid criticisms of his rival's work, which would call for revision by the author and perhaps for more experiments. What should he do about reporting his own work — rush it in quickly for publication, proceed as if nothing had happened, or quietly bury his own work on the ground that reporting it would now be superfluous? Some highly scrupulous, perhaps overscrupulous will follow the latter course; some who are unscrupulous will seek to delay publication of a rival's work and get their own work out first. . . .
>
> Similar problems face members of panels who review applications for research grants. It is very easy, while reading an application for a grant, to pick up an idea from it and subsequently to think of it as one's own (Edsall 1975, pp. 9–10).

RULES AND SANCTIONS GOVERNING SCIENTIFIC BEHAVIOR

The account thus far has directed itself only toward some of the aspects of motivation that have been described in negative terms, in that deviant behavior is produced. It should be noted that science also has characteristics intended to prevent the occurrence of deviations in scientific behavior, and some of these are motivational in nature. Stated simply, included in the reward system of science is a set of negative rewards (punishments), or sanctions, that are presented to its members who do not display acceptable scientific behaviors in the areas that have been discussed.

Thus, the individual who takes ideas that have been originated by someone else may be punished by the members of the science. As with recognition, a positive reward, the motivational conditions frequently occur on an informal as well as formal basis. Gaston cites a case where one scientist is guilty of not making a citation that would have been appropriate. This case is interesting because it also includes reference to reasons, or rationalizations, for noncitation.

> The first paper I published was remarkably similar in nature to one some-one else had done. He wrote to me pointing out that he had already pub-

lished it. The technique we used was the same, but he had hidden it in ---, which you usually don't take a look at. Furthermore, he had put it in the middle of a very long article. Consequently, two other people [journal referees] and I overlooked it. He [the injured theorist] continues to publish without reference to my article because he can refer to his, although they're not exactly the same (brackets are the original author's) (Gaston 1973, p. 114).

Thus, the injured theorist evened the account by not referring to the transgressor in later papers. The result is thus a change from the usual nature of scientific communication, a topic of interest further on. This account is also significant because it illustrates that journal editors and referees share with the individual scientist the responsibility of insuring that the relevant work of predecessors is appropriately acknowledged, that ideas and findings previously made are not usurped by a later scientist, as the following analysis also indicates.

There are formal and informal sanctions for failure to refer to other research. The informal sanctions involve those scientists who earn a reputation for non-reference, a reputation that travels by word of mouth. . . . References to previous work assist to allocate recognition, so the most important sanction, in addition to spreading the word about scientists who habitually refuse to refer to previous research, is to treat them in the same way. . . .

The formal sanction was also previously illustrated. If referees, editors, or the injured party know a paper has not referred to the relevant research, the first two may require it before publication while the latter may lodge a complaint to the editor and cause the publication to carry proper citation (Gaston 1973, p. 114).

When the case involved is of sufficient scope and importance it may be handled accordingly.

On more than one occasion the AAAS [American Association for the Advancement of Science] has received an appeal from a scientist who considers himself to be the victim of such injustice. He may present extensive documentation to back up his claim. These are grave matters; but it is generally extremely difficult to see that justice is done in such a case. Often no documents exist that could establish what really happened; the crucial events may have involved informal conversations of which no record exists. On rare occasions, when the discovery involved is a truly major one and the evidence of injustice is strong, the AAAS might well decide to publicize such a controversy, permitting both parties in the dispute to state their cases briefly, with suitable references to documentary evidence for those who wish to inquire further into the dispute (Edsall 1975, p. 9).

Reward Sharing Rules in Science

As has been indicated, Merton originally indicated that the scientist's ideas are his intellectual property. These ideas as expressed in published reports are his product and they result in the reward of recognition which the scientist obtains thereby. It should be added that there are other sources of reward for the scientist; there are positive aspects to the reward system of science that were not fully described in Merton's treatment. That is, Merton describes the competitive nature of reward in science. If one person obtains an original finding it means that someone else cannot. Merton suggests that the stress on priority reflects this competition. Moreover, he suggests that the competition is responsible for producing the deviant behaviors exhibited by scientists. While he does also indicate that recognition as a reward can serve to motivate the scientist to achieve, the emphasis in his analysis is on the manner in which the focus on recognition and priority for one's intellectual property produces misbehavior. A few words are justified here in indicating that the reward system for science, while it contains competitive elements, also contains elements for cooperative, shared rewards. There is a built-in exchange system on the basis of equity, as indicated by Hagstrom, who describes science as "an exchange of social recognition for information" (1965, p. 13). This rule works in several ways, it may be suggested in extending the principle.

We can see this rule readily in any project that involves more than one individual in a cooperative effort. In such a circumstance there are expectations concerning the allocation of recognition. Thus, the person who has contributed most to the project expects to receive first authorship on publications that result. Each participant should receive recognition to the extent of his contribution. Equity may not always pertain in such cases; one individual may take more or less than his just portion. One case that comes to mind is that of the author of a book who in the preface expressed appreciation to his wife for efforts he considered worthy of coauthorship, but the book is singly authored. On the other hand, another author reveals that someone has contributed a very small percentage to his book and yet is listed as a second author, when a much lesser appreciation would have been appropriate. Thus, as Merton has indicated, there are individual differences in giving others recognition, or in more general terms in how the rules of sharing are applied. The important point here, however, is that appropriate (equitable) sharing of the rewards of recognition would be expected to lead to mutually satisfying relationships. The reward system includes this possibility, and it apparently works in this manner as a general rule. For there are many more multiple authored publications than there are disputes in science. In addition, however, there are additional cooperative reward possibilities in science.

Let us take the practices of citation as another example of the rule of exchanging recognition for information, a part of a social organization of sharing and cooperation. In this case the author of the later publication receives a contribution from the earlier scientist in the form of knowledge. In acknowledging this gift of intellectual property by citing the earlier work, the later author gives payment in the form of recognition for a valued contribution.

> [T]his is the function of dividing the property in the published report, and providing an "income" to the owner of the property which is used, by showing that his work was fruitful. . . . The material may be crucial, or merely incidental in the argument; it may have been central to the first formulation of the problem, or merely a late addition; and it may have been used as it was published or required extensive re-working. In all these dimensions, there is a continuous and complex scale from complete dependence to near independence. By appropriate nuance of mention, one can under-cite without actually stealing results, or over-cite with the effect of inflating the value of the property of a colleague. Thus the simple system as it stands permits a considerable range of "sharp practice" with scientific property, which if not controlled by an etiquette, can be more corrosive in its eventual effects than outright theft (Ravetz 1971, p. 257).

While this particular excerpt is stated in the negative, it indicates that the practices of citation are employed for sharing recognition, and that there are informal rules for doing so in a mutually rewarding manner. There are, however, various techniques possible for obscuring who has been the originator of a scientific work. Strangely enough, citations of earlier work can be used to hide as well as to reveal the value of the predecessor's contribution. Thus, for example, an author may cite various studies that while related to his work do not show it to be closely similar to an earlier idea which occurs in a work he does not cite. By citing many other publications he thereby shows himself to be generous in citation, while at the same time he obfuscates the real intellectual antecedent to his work. More elaborate ways of hiding preceding contributions have already been implied in some of the examples. There are also cases where the principle (or conception) of a previous theory is used as the basis for a series of experiments. Then the principle is later re-derived as an interpretation of the experiments and it reemerges in a new theory, without citation. Without citation the parallel developments appear to be independent.

An implicit point that is made here, as in the other cases, however, is that the system of rewards does not determine solely the scientific behavior that results. Citation presents a means for sharing the rewards of recognition. The reward system thus provides for sharing and cooperation. The author of the original work can receive recompense. The later scientist who employs and adapts the original can also receive recompense for his further development of the original idea or whatever. The problem comes when the individual scientist does not settle for an appropriate share of the rewards of recognition. When the person on a group project takes more than his share of the recognition through authorship order, or whatever, then a disequilibrium or inequity results. When the scientist does not cite preceding works that were important in his own work in a manner that equitably apportions recognition, then he has not shared the rewards appropriately. The reward system permits the scientists who work within it to behave in an appropriate manner. This demands the type of honesty and objectivity and truth which is considered to be typical of science. A scientist who is not honest and objective in this sphere, it may be added, may be faulty also in the conduct of science itself. It should be part of the specialized skill of the scientist to allocate rewards according to the objective nature of the contribution made. As will be seen, science involves psychosocial matters that are as much a part of its productivity as are its scientific features, the formal features usually described in the philosophy of science. Moreover, as will be seen, it is the present thesis that preparadigmaticism influences these aspects of a science.

EFFECTS OF DEVIANT BEHAVIORS ON SCIENCE

It is not suggested that the concept of the reward system introduced by Merton to account for deviant behaviors of scientists is a complete or sufficient theory of this type of deviant behavior. In the view of the present author this sociological concept of the reward system is not sufficient by which to account for deviant behavior; for one thing individual differences, or personality must also be addressed (see Staats 1975, especially ch. 8). However, the sociological account has indicated some of the important effects of the competitive system of science on some of the behaviors of scientists. Although other necessary elaborations cannot be made herein, within the topics treated, several lines of elaboration will be touched upon. For one, the analysis of science must be elaborated to explore systematically how the psychological-sociological aspects of science affect its formal aspects — influencing such things as the generality and parsimony, communication, and objective evaluation of the science. At present, there appears to be a custom of separating sociological analysis of science and formal analysis, whereas the two interact, as will be briefly suggested.

Generality and Parsimony

Generality in a science occurs in various ways and on various levels. The examples usually employed refer to physical science. Thus, citing a previously used example, generality was achieved by Newton when he formulated a set of higher-level principles that would account for lower-order principles pertaining to separate empirical events (such as tidal action and the orbit of the moon). The mathematical statement of gravitational force has great generality in that it applies to many formerly discretely considered phenomena, and Newton's theory thus served the purpose of better organizing existing knowledge.

Although this is not understood well, this kind of generality and simplicity can occur in scientific theory that is less classic than those couched in mathematical terms — and the value of such formulations in producing generality also involves the extent of the generality. The present author has shown that such theory — which integrates within one set of principles what were formerly considered separate phenomena — can be characteristic of psychology as well as the natural sciences (Staats 1968b, 1970b, 1975). As will be indicated later, however, the search for general and parsimonious theory in psychology conflicts with the preparadigmatic impetus for the psychologist to begin anew, to establish his own, independent work.

Anything that detracts from generality and parsimony detracts from the achievement of the products of these formal goals of science. It is important to note that the deviant behaviors described in the past section can have an effect on these formal goals. Let us take the deviant behaviors with respect to citation. When an idea — principle, concept, analysis, or method — is similar to one previously published by someone else, and this is not noted in the later publication, the goal of generality has been obstructed. The noncitation makes it more difficult for the student, scholar, theorist, or scientist to see the findings reported in the two publications within a common framework. The science is thus more complicated, less integrated.

The sociologists of science have described the deviant practices of science in the context of competition among scientists. The deviant practices are considered only to affect the recognition that the individual scientists obtain, and thus to be unimportant to the science itself. "[B]e it noted that scientific *knowledge* is not the richer or the poorer for having credit given where credit is due" (Merton 1973, p. 307). This statement contrasts with the present view that the deviant practices Merton describes actually do have an effect upon the central, substantive goals of science. One cannot consider these matters simply as a deviant aspect of human competitiveness, relevant only to the consideration of the social aspects of science. For these matters have effects at the heart of science, and should be treated as aspects of methodology of substantive concern to science. The sanctions that were previously discussed that were a response to noncitation have the effect of adding to the breakdown of the search for generality and parsimony. The example previously cited showed how one scientist, because his work had not been cited by another, in turn never cited the other in his later work. In both cases science has suffered because two lines of work that should be closely integrated with one another have been left as disparate. The science is needlessly complicated; it is less organized than that which could be achieved. For the student, scholar, and scientist such practices of noncitation — whether warranted morally or not — contribute to the breakdown of science's goals of presenting an organized body of knowledge.

It may be added that there are various ways of contributing to this breakdown. One way is through simple noncitation, as has been indicated. A more active deed occurs when an idea is taken from the work of one individual and is developed in a different context, as a separate formulation. This is more apt to happen in theory. When this occurs and the derivation is developed as a second and independent theory — perhaps by changing terminology, or by addressing somewhat different empirical illustrations or by conducting and then referring to different experiments — the goal of generality has been set back. The science has become more complicated, less parsimonious, less general, less organized. The sociology of science cannot restrict its considerations of psycho-social events to their effects on the reward circumstances for scientists. The effects on the science itself must be considered and, among such effects, is the efficacy of the science in terms of the extent of organized, integrated knowledge that it produces versus disorganized, chaotic knowledge.

Communication

Communication is closely related to the topics that have just been discussed. That is, the creation of larger bodies of unified knowledge across the demarcation of separated areas of research demands communication.

Gaining knowledge of the world, it should be realized, is a gigantic task and it necessitates the involvement of many people, each of whom contributes to the growing information. If the knowledge is to be functional in the social institution of science it must be communicated to other scientists. That is, science is not only a repository of knowledge, it is an institution to produce knowledge, in an organized way, and to disseminate knowledge. Successful production of knowledge depends upon knowing what has already been found. Otherwise one might duplicate what is already known. Moreover, gaining new knowledge takes place more effectively by building on what has gone before. Theories guide new scientific ventures, but methods of research and apparatus are also important. For these various products of science to have their heuristic function they must be communicated. Science also depends on ideas that indicate fruitful problems. Some scientists have theoretical and research ideas in greater abundance than they themselves can develop. When communicated to others these ideas may contribute to the development of the science. Finally, creativity frequently means bringing things together that have not yet been associated, and which the individual will not be taught in relationship because the relationship has not yet been discovered or indicated. Sometimes theoretically inclined scientists are successful because they acquaint themselves widely with various things, and are consequently able to see relationships not yet noted. Scientists who are not so widely versed may have a part of a solution, but the part is not productive until it has been fitted to the other necessary parts. J. D. Watson's novel, the *Double Helix*, chronicles a scientific discovery that involved such a fitting together of parts, via various forms of communication, the result being a Nobel Prize for several individuals. Functions of communication have been listed elsewhere to include providing documentation of the reliability of an effect, broadening scientists' area of attention, helping scientists to locate and assess the importance of a topic in the current research, and providing scientists with an evaluative response to their own efforts and statements (Sills, Gloch, Mengel, Glaser, and Somers 1958).

There are various ways that communication is implemented in science and it is pertinent in this account to indicate briefly some of them. First, in the beginnings of science there were few involved and they communicated with each other personally, orally, or in writing. Other means of communication were formed later but face-to-face communication remains an important one. It is usual, for example, to have scientists in a university department in communication. Frequently they bring different types of knowledge together in this way to compose a whole that is productive. In communication, by sharing knowledge the individuals may be productive in a way they would not be in isolation. "[I]t is only the unusual scientist who can continue producing in social isolation" (Hagstrom 1965, p. 48). Social communication can also take place at meetings that sciences hold, conferences, and visits. Many scientists gain impetus, ideas, or techniques from direct communication with colleagues at such meetings.

For some scientists, however, a more important type of communication takes place through the formal channels of the science. Within each science there are journals that publish scientific articles and books. In addition, scientists may circulate duplicated preprints of their work before it reaches formal publication. Becoming informed about the advances in ones science through these media is a central concern. "Scientists, as individuals, spend great portions of their time and prodigious amounts of effort at 'keeping up.' The scientific community, through its organizations and institutes, comes to the aid of the individual with an equally prodigious offering of formal media of communication" (Sills, Glock, Menzel, Glaser, and Somers 1958, p. 27). Communication serves a variety of functions; it takes place in a variety of ways. Great efforts have been made to improve methods and means of communication in science. It has been said that "The lifeblood of science is communication" (Edsall 1975, p. 9), because science could not function without it. Moreover, anything that lessens the efficacy of communication lessens the successful conduct of science. It follows that the science must be concerned about any aspect or characteristic of the science that acts as an obstacle to communication.

Ravetz (1971) has considered the scientists' creations to be their property, their intellectual property. He also states that "the social protection of that personal property is necessary if each individual is to embark on his tasks in confidence that he will receive the rewards appropriate to his endeavours" (Ravetz 1971, p. 245). Various writers have described the efforts of the early scientists to protect their intellectual property. For example, one method was to state one's idea in a form that could not be understood, as in an anagram. The scientist would circulate the puzzle to the interested people of science and they would attempt to solve it and thereby learn about the finding. Having gotten the attention of the scientific community all at once, and thus having established ownership of the finding, scientists could then announce their finding without fear that it would be stolen.

> Galileo used this method, and Kepler tried unsuccessfully to decipher his anagrammatic announcement of the discovery of the non-spherical appearance of Saturn. Other users included Hooke, Huygens, and Newton himself. . . . From the difficulties they had, we can see that a significant proportion of the great "scientists" of that age were even more concerned for the protection of their intellectual property, than for an immediate realization of its value through the prestige resulting from publication, to say nothing of contributing to the co-operative endeavour (Ravetz 1971, p. 249).

Imagine how cumbersome this method was in the conduct of science, how it represented an obstacle to communication. It may be noted that Merton's approach was to consider secretiveness as a deviant behavior, an orientation followed in the sociology of science by Hagstrom (1965; 1967) and Gaston (1973). But secrecy detracts from the efficacy of science. Secretiveness as a deviant behavior in science was considered to come about because of the competitive nature of the rewards of originality, and hence the concern of scientists that their creation would be anticipated. "Secrecy is the most prevalent type of deviancy that scientists employ as a response to competition" (Gaston 1973, p. 116). "The scientist in a competitive situation will tend not to disclose his ideas to his colleagues until he is ready to publish an article that will assure him of recognition. He may fear that others will use his ideas to solve his research problems before he does so himself" (Hagstrom 1967, p. 14). The research of these sociologists is informative in showing that a large percentage of scientists are secretive. Hagstrom (1967) found that 42 percent of theorists in physics and 51 percent of experimentalists would conceal the details of their work from others prior to publication.

Gaston (1973) indicates that his research does not support the principle that it is concern for competition that makes the scientist secretive. He shows, for example, that the possibility of being anticipated by competition is negatively correlated with secretiveness in theoreticians. In the present view there is an error in the conceptual view taken by the sociologists of science. The reward system of science is an important item, but it is not the only variable. The individual scientist will also have learned a personal reward system – a set of values. The individual values operate in conjunction with the reward system of the science community to determine the individual's behavior with respect to deviations such as plagiarism, stealing ideas, noncitation, equitable sharing of recognition, and the like. The reward system of science is the same for all. But some scientists' behavior conforms with the stated standards and some scientists' behavior does not. Such differences occur because the different personality systems of scientists yield different outcomes although the situation is the same for all.

Secretiveness, it should be emphasized, is not a direct function of the competitive nature of the reward system of science. It occurs because of the individual scientist's experience that there are other scientists who will use ideas if they are expressed openly. They will take away intellectual property rights. The sociologists of science have collected statements from many scientists that illustrate the process clearly, some of which were quoted in the preceding parts of this chapter.

Secretiveness as a Social Interaction and Personality Effect

Some of these examples show clearly that secretiveness as a behavior can be seen to emerge as an outcome of a *social interaction* process. The example previously given of the scientist who described new work to a person only to find that this person then published the ideas is a case in point. The scientist spoke openly in giving knowledge only to suffer a loss in intellectual property and rewards. In general, such an occurrence constitutes a punishment for candid communication. It is the absence of candid communication which is secrecy. Our knowledge of behavior principles tells us that this scientist will be less likely to be open in the future.

The analysis of the behavior of scientists must include the processes of social interaction in which the scientist participant rewards and punishes the behavior of other scientists, as in the above case. The sharing practices of one scientist will act as a reward or punishment for the communication behavior of others – determining whether the communication behavior will be open or secretive. A scientist who shares an idea with another scientist and in turn receives appropriate recognition for the ideas has been rewarded for the idea and for sharing it. Openness will be strengthened and contributions to the science thereby increased. When an idea is not recognized, when the scientist receives no share of the reward, the opposite effect occurs and science suffers the loss. The problem resides in the nonsharing of the other scientist — who finds the idea valuable, who uses it, but who will not share the recognition.

It should also be noted in this context that the scientist who has the largest number of original ideas has the greatest opportunity to express them to others, and thus has the greatest opportunity to receive reward in the form of recognition. But such scientists also have the greatest opportunity to be punished for openness by losing their intellectual property to others. They may thus directly learn more than others to be secretive, at least in certain circumstances, and to express themselves only in certain circumstances. It is also the case that such scientists have the most to give to science, so their secrecy is the greatest loss.

Carrying the analysis a bit further, it would also be expected that some members of science would learn to seek out scientists who were most likely to be dispensers of valuable ideas. This is seen readily in the way that some scientists are sought as teachers and associates, and in the way that the products of such scientists are imitated or serve as directives for others. When the influence of the scientist is acknowledged by the scientist who elaborates the idea, the social interaction is mutually rewarding, as has been noted. The point here, however, is that deviant behavior can also be learned in the social interaction. The deviant individual who profits from contact with someone, but who does not share the recognition of the product, receives reward for his actions, if no retribution results. He also will have his behavior strengthened by the reward. He will learn to be deviant. This may become a general character of his behavior, to take ideas but not to acknowledge. Some of the cases in the history of science already listed appear to have involved the learning of these types of skills. The term brainpicker has been coined to refer to individuals who have skill in interrogating others to draw out their ideas so that they can be put to use by the interrogator. The case of the physicist Biot, already described, suggests that he developed such techniques to a high level of skill, to the point where they became his modus operandi. For someone in a university post this technique can be used in conjunction with organizational abilities that allow the collector of ideas to then generously give them to his students and associates to develop, thereby gaining also the rewards for being a generous scientist. The following example cited by Hagstrom involves such possibilities.

> I avoided talking to this fellow from [another university] about my work
> on X compounds. This fellow has a whole group of students, I have only

one student working with me. If he wanted to, and if he knew what I was doing, he could get into the area I was working in, clean up the problems, and wipe me out. There is no sense in directing him to the things I plan to do, while it's O.K. to tell him what I've done. After you get to know people you might be able to trust them, and then you can talk freely about your plans (Hagstrom 1965, p. 87).

The point is that both the primary deviant behavior of taking others' ideas, which may involve various skills, and the secondary deviant behavior of secrecy can be learned in direct social interaction processes. It may be added that secretiveness can be learned second hand on the basis of communication — one can hear of others' experiences. Gaston provides an example from one of the respondents in his study, who says the following. "I've been advised — this was when I was doing the Ph.D. — not to speak too much about the idea of doing an experiment in case somebody else gets the idea" (1973, p. 128).

Understanding scientific behavior, like any type of behavior, involves the use of as full a set of principles as can be obtained. It is not the purpose of the present essay to provide these principles of human behavior here, but I would suggest that they are available (see Staats 1975, as one example). The important point here is that communication is basic to science and that there are psycho-social factors in science that affect the quality of communication. As such these psycho-social events must be understood in order to understand the workings of science. It is not enough to know only the formal aspects of science, because the psycho-social factors affect the formal ones. Additional ways that psycho-social processes affect communication and the formal aspects of science will be given in the next section.

Objective Evaluation

Communication has been called the lifeblood of science. But the objectivity of science concerns its basic nature. Rather generally, scientists and philosophers of science would agree that it is important in science to assess science materials in an objective manner, to the degree this is possible. If someone says that the world is such and such, in science this is objectively evaluated by having other scientists impartially observe if this is actually so. If one theory states one thing and another theory states another, then science has a task of objectively seeing which theory makes the better predictions, which theory serves the most useful heuristic purposes, and so on, at least as much as possible within the types of limitations already recognized. The purpose of the present section is to suggest that the psycho-social processes that have been described also affect the formal aspects of science, in ways that can deviate from objectivity. For example, Merton considered another type of deviant behavior, that of retreatism, examples of which he lists as follows.

> The nineteenth-century physicist Waterston, his classic paper on molecular velocity having been rejected by the Royal Society as "nothing but nonsense," becomes hopelessly discouraged and leaves science altogether. Deeply disappointed by the lack of response to his historic papers on heredity, Mendel refuses to publish the now permanently lost results of his further research and, after becoming abbot of his monastery, gives up his research on heredity. Robert Mayer, tormented by refusals to grant him priority for the principle of conservation of energy, tries a suicide leap from a third-story window and succeeds only in breaking his legs and being straitjacketed, for a time, in an insane asylum (Merton 1973, p. 318).

These are all cases that involve the lack of reward for the behavior of scientists who had produced works of the highest merit in science, but the science did not acknowledge the contributions. In one case the problem involved the priority of originality. As has been seen nonobjective conditions may pertain in such cases. One individual may be recognized for a contribution that really was another's. Such nonobjective occurrences in science affect the behaviors of the scientists involved, and they thus affect the objectivity of the science.

In the other two cases the science did not acknowledge the works of the scientists at all. The science did not accept the findings as important. Since the works later were accepted as valuable contributions to our knowledge of our world, the science erred terribly in not recognizing their worth originally. How do such errors occur? For one thing, what the science will consider important work is in part determined by the paradigm. A different paradigm than Mendel's directed the attention of the scientists of his time than the one he was presenting. Toulmin has also indicated that what the science considers important depends on social factors that determine which scientists and groups of scientists gain ascendancy and power in the science (1972).

Mendel's case of retreatism, and others like it, have significance for understanding the working of science beyond that of considering it an example of deviant behavior. As will be amplified further on, science involves competition in views, approaches, theories, concepts, methods— as well as a competition of leaders and influential groups in a science (Mitroff 1974b; Toulmin 1972) — at least in the parts of the science in which consensus has not yet been attained. These science elements may be considered to compete for the attention of the members of the science, to compete for the opportunity of influencing the process of the science. Science consists of individuals working, their work is guided by the events of the world they study, by what has been done, but also by the attention value of what has been done. The scientist decides what to study and how, and this depends upon factors other than just the natural world of events that is the concern of the science.

In Mendel's case, as we now know, the natural events of the world coincided with Mendel's theory, which should have been followed, rather than the path other elements in biology then suggested. The fact that Mendel's lead was not influential illustrates that other than scientific reality can gain the attention of scientists and lead them, sometimes, astray. Ideally, the science element or leader most closely attuned to the aspect of the world being studied would be the most influential in affecting the work of other scientists. Then the greatest productivity would occur. But in the competition for the attention of the science, the most accurate theory or leader may not win immediately.

One is thus led to ask what things besides the nature of the events being studied determine which science elements will gain the attention of the members of the science. For example, one may ask how a theory gains its status in a science. The philosophy of science points toward the formal characteristics of theory, for example, the generality of the theory, its parsimony, its heuristic value, its internal consistency, and the productivity of its observational methods. These are objective means of assessing theories, and should be the characteristics that determine the attention value of the theory. But if there are nonobjective variables that help determine the directions science takes then they should be understood in our attempt to make the progress of science as effective as possible.

Objective Evaluation and the Matthew Effect

Merton, based upon the data presented in a work by Zuckerman (1972), proposed a concept called the Matthew effect. The concept is that in cases of a collaborative work the best known author gets a disproportionately greater amount of credit than the lesser known coworkers. Another facet of the effect is indicated by Merton.

> Such misallocation also occurs in the case of independent multiple discoveries. When approximately the same ideas or findings are independently communicated by a scientist of great repute and by one not yet widely known, it is the first, we are told, who ordinarily receives prime recognition (1973, pp. 444–45).

Merton goes on to say that the Matthew effect can affect the communication in a science. His example is that the famous name on a paper can have a functional effect by increasing the rapidity with which a finding will be used by the science. Merton also indicates that the Matthew effect has functional value, by increasing the influence of men who should have that influence. He does recognize that the effect can function negatively. "For although eminent scientists may be more *likely* to make significant contributions, they are obviously not alone in making them. After all, scientists do not begin by being eminent. . . ." (1973, p. 456).

The importance of the psycho-social principles involved in the Matthew effect as they affect the objectivity of science requires more general analysis. Merton treats the deviations in scientific behavior largely as interesting phenomena in and of themselves. In treating the manner in which deviations can affect the workings of science, however, it is relevant to indicate that such deviations can alter the Matthew effect. The Matthew effect represents a variation from objectivity in which a person gets more recognition for a work than the person deserves on objective grounds. It is thus being suggested that deviations in behavior in science can lead to divergence from objective evaluation, and thus be an impediment to the functioning of science.

To begin, what has been called the Matthew effect should be seen as a general process in which the recognition, status, or value accorded a person or product of science will help determine the influence (directive strength) of that person or product. I would call this more generally the status-attitude effect, in elaborating the concept. The psychological principles involved in the effect can be given precise theoretical and experimental specification on the basic level (see Staats 1975, ch. 4 and 7). The more positive the attitude elicited by a stimulus of any kind, the more the stimulus will control approach behaviors, including those of attending to the stimulus and responding appropriately to the message of the stimulus. The scientist who has a name that elicits a positive attitude in other scientists will thereby tend to attract more graduate students, will tend to elicit positive responses to research grant proposals, will tend to get positive reviews of new works, and so on, influenced by the positive attitude elicited. That is, the directive value of a stimulus is given in part by its attitude value.

Moreover, any time the person or product of science, as a stimulus, is paired with another stimulus that has positive attitude value, the person or product will acquire additional positive attitude value. As an example, whenever a work is recognized as valuable (that is, elicits positive attitude value) in a science, those responsible for the work, because they are paired with or identified with the work, acquire increased attitude value for other scientists. Whenever this scientist receives honors or awards or recognition in the science the attitude value increases. If associated with an institution or professor who elicits positive attitudes, the scientist will thereby gain in positive attitude value. There are various ways that a scientist can be paired with positive attitudinal things and thus elicit more positive attitudes. (This is not to say that these effects may not be mediated by or involve cognitive processes.)

It has been said that social scientists have not recognized the relationship between reward value, attitude value, and directive value in their analyses of human behavior (Staats 1975, ch. 14), and the present concern is a case in point. Merton has considered the reward value of recognition in science. It should be understood, however, that the term reward should be specifically defined. Rewards are stimuli that affect the individual's behavior *by strengthening the types of behavior they follow*. This is the sense in which Merton describes recognition in science. In support of this analysis, Cole and Cole (1967) have found that among scientists who were productive in their early years, those who received recognition for their work continued to be productive later in their careers. Recognition in this example has functioned as a reward in that when it has followed the scientist's behavior, the behavior has been strengthened.

But recognition also has another function. The stimuli of recognition, that is, scientific approval of various kinds, also elicit positive attitudes in scientists. An award, a citation, a positive reference in a book, and so on through the lists of types of recognition, are all stimuli that elicit positive attitudes in the person who reads or hears of the recognition. Furthermore any person (more usually by name) that is *paired* with such recognition will come to elicit a positive attitude in other scientists, as has been indicated. That is, recognition produces positive attitudes when it is paired with an individual. The individual takes on some of the positive attitudes elicited by the recognition.

Thirdly, recognition has yet another function. It acts as an incentive, or directive stimulus, to directly elicit behavior. The individual strives for recognition. Any science avenue (person, institution, theory, or whatever) that indicates it has recognition attached to it will tend to elicit striving behavior in the scientist. For example, a problem that is "hot," that is recognized as important in the science, will attract more scientists to work on it than will a less recognized problem. The scientist, as another example, strives to get jobs at recognized institutions.

This description of recognition has been given to indicate that any stimulus that elicits a positive attitude will also have reward value and directive or incentive value. It does not matter what the stimulus is. The stimulus could be a scientific honor. If it elicits positive attitudes in scientists it can serve to elicit behaviors likely to result in obtaining the honor. And, if the honor is obtained, the honor will act as a reward which will strengthen those behaviors that were involved in getting the honor, so that they are more likely to occur in the future. Thus, the stimulus can be seen to have three functions, (1) it elicits a positive attitude in the scientist, (2) it directs behavior such as to obtain the stimulus, and (3) obtaining the reward stimulus will strengthen instrumental behavior for the future. To understand the workings of the reward system of science, or any other activity, it is necessary to understand the three functions of attitudinal stimuli.

With these concepts in mind it is now possible to consider some of the psycho-social aspects of science, and the effects of deviations in science, in a more revealing manner. We will see that recognition in science is not only of importance to the individual in science as a reward, but also that the practices of recognition affect the general workings of science.

Let us take one of the examples that has been given already. Laplace was described as having included many elements in his work that did not provide appropriate citation of the contributions of predecessors. Moreover, he followed the same practice concerning the work of his contemporaries. This must have had the effect of making it appear as though Laplace himself had made the various discoveries. In the process, Laplace would have come to elicit very positive attitudes in other scientists. By pairing himself with positive achievements, he would become very positive himself. As a consequence he and his products would have become strong directive stimuli for other scientists. Other scientists would have followed his lead more than otherwise would have been the case, would have paid more attention to his publications than otherwise would have been the case, and so on. If he unduly took credit and thus unduly became a positive status figure, then he may have become unduly a directing force in the progress of science, in a direction that could have deviated from objectivity.

Taking credit for achievements done by others can produce the following effects upon science. (1) Scientists secure for themselves rewards that have the effect of strengthening their own behavior, but this means less reward for the individuals who have done the work, and thus less strengthening of their scientific behavior. In the usual case this would be expected to have a deleterious effect upon science, at least in comparison to the case where the reward could have been allotted more equitably to those who were creative. (2) By associating the accomplishment of the work with themselves, the scientists make themselves into a more potent directive stimulus, increasing the extent to which other scientists will be influenced by them. They also weaken the extent to which the accomplishment of the work is associated with those who produced the work, and thus decrease the originator's influence upon science. Again, in the usual case this would be expected to contribute toward the nonobjectivity of science. We can see an example of the directive or incentive process as it affects the attention of other scientists in the following statement.

> As a certification of the scientist's accomplishment, it [intellectual property] can bring immediate rewards. And as an implicit guarantee of the quality of his future work, it brings in interest for some time after its pro-

duction. Because of this predictive and fiduciary element in the scientist's intellectual property, it is impossible for it to be "alienated" like ordinary property, without serious damage to the system of the decision and control in science. If for any reason one scientist ascribes to another a larger share in a research report than is correct, he is not merely giving him more credit than he is entitled to. He is also falsifying an important part of the evidence on which the scientific community assesses the potential for future work of the other man, and thereby distorting the operation of its system of government (Ravetz 1971, p. 246).

Thus, Laplace's actions may be considered to have distorted the operation of science — in the present terms, he interfered with the operation of objective assessment in science. To continue, however, it is suggested that the above principles apply to various interpersonal behaviors among scientists, and between scientists and the products of science. The Matthew effect is but one specific effect that these more general principles would predict. For one thing, the principles suggest that the status effect works in an escalating, cumulative manner. Thus, a scientist or theory with high status will be referred to more often than one of low status, other things being equal, in a manner that decreases the objectivity of science, and with a snowballing progression. The high status of a theory leads to citation. But citation increases a theory's status. It is suggested that exploration of cases in science where a theory or a scientist or a particular work has received more attention and attained more influence than it merited will reveal the operation of such cumulative psycho-social factors, as they have affected the objective evaluations of science. There are results already in the sociology of science that support these expectations. For example, Zuckerman and Merton (1971) have shown that the papers of eminent scientists are reviewed more promptly, and more favorably than papers of lesser-known men. The cases of Mendel and Waterston have shown the opposite effect, when the author of an important work is unknown. (It may be suggested that many additional hypotheses concerning the workings of science could be derived from the conception that recognizes the attitude-reward-directive functions of what Merton has called the reward system of science.) Long and McGinnis have also made an analysis that supports the present conception of the cumulative influence of status effects, as indicated below.

Our findings provide additional evidence for the operation of cumulative advantage in the scientific career (cf. Allison and Stewart 1974; Cole and Cole 1973): initial advantages are soon transformed into additional advantages. For example, having a prestigious doctoral department increases the chances of the graduate obtaining a postdoctoral fellowship or a position in a research university. The position in a research university results in increased productivity; the fellowship directly increases

publications over the fellowship period and indirectly increases productivity by increasing the chances of obtaining a faculty position in a research university, thus providing a secondary effect of doctoral prestige.
. . . [I]nitial advantages are accumulated, resulting in the well-known in-
equality among scientists in levels of productivity (Long and McGinnis
1981, p. 441).

The primary point here, however, is that the psycho-social aspects of
science have an effect upon the objective aspects of science. Some analyses of the psycho-social aspects of science have not seen the relationship
and have not taken a clear stand on the need to decrease deviations in science in the allocation of rewards (Merton 1973; Mitroff and Kilman 1978).
However, standards of science, such as those involved in citation methods
and the allocation of recognition, are important not only in the interests of
justice, or in the interests of the well-being of scientists, but in the development and maintenance of the objective conduct of science. This is said,
more particularly, in the context of a focal concern with the preparadigmatic-paradigmatic characteristics of science. It is suggested that the differences in paradigmatic and preparadigmatic sciences also include differences in social characteristics, as will be indicated; this is a major interest of the present chapter.

SOCIAL ORGANIZATION IN PREPARADIGMATIC AND PARADIGMATIC SCIENCES

Although this has not been a focal concern in the philosophy and history of science, it is relevant to ask whether there are differences between
preparadigmatic science and paradigmatic science in terms of the social
factors of science. Thus, for example, the sociology of science has described
the reward (reward-attitude-directive) system of science and some of the
deviant behaviors the reward system produces. The evidence employed
with which to describe deviant behaviors is drawn both from history and
from contemporary times. No differentiation is made in historical perspective. In the present context, however, the question arises whether or not
there have been changes in science over time, as it has developed, in the
rules which govern the social enterprise of science, and in the definition of
deviant scientific behavior. The present treatment of these topics cannot
be considered to be definitive, but only to open the topics for consideration, because the context of the present analysis suggests such consideration. More systematic study of historical and contemporary sciences will
be necessary to confirm the analyses.

Nevertheless, it is suggested that there has been change over time in the rules of scientific behavior and in the expression of deviant behaviors. The next section will consider these possibilities.

Deviance and Rules: Are There Preparadigmatic and Paradigmatic Perspectives?

The previous sections have presented some of the descriptions of deviant behaviors in science provided by the sociology of science. Some of the types of cases were largely of an historical nature, and this is an important aspect of the present considerations. This historical flavor can be seen in the following excerpt of Merton.

> We begin by noting the great frequency with which the history of science is punctuated by disputes, often by sordid disputes, over priority of discovery. During the last three centuries in which modern science developed, numerous scientists, both great and small, have engaged in acrimonious controversy. Recall only these few. Keenly aware of the importance of his inventions and discoveries, Galileo became a seasoned campaigner as he vigorously defended his rights to priority first, in his *Defense Against the Calumnies and Impostures of Baldassar Capra*, where he showed how his invention of the "geometric and military compass" had been taken from him, and then, in *The Assayer*, where he flayed four other would-be rivals: Father Horatio Grassi, who tried "to diminish whatever praise there may be in this [invention of the telescope] which belongs to me"; Christopher Scheiner, who claimed to have been first to observe the sunspots (although, unknown to both Scheiner and Galileo, Johannes Fabricus had published such observations before); an unspecified villain (probably the Frenchman Jean Tarde) who "attempted to rob me of that glory which was mine, pretending not to have seen my writings and trying to represent themselves as the original discoverers of these marvels"; and finally, Simon Mayr (Marius), who "had the gall to claim that he had observed the Medicean planets which revolve about Jupiter before I had [and who used] a sly way of attempting to establish his priority."
>
> The peerless Newton fought several battles with Robert Hooke over priority in optics and celestial mechanics and entered into a long and painful controversy with Leibnitz over the invention of the calculus. Hooke, who has been described as the "universal claimant" because "there was scarcely a discovery in his time which he did not conceive himself to claim" (and, it might be added, often justly so, for he was one of the most inventive men in his century of genius). Hooke, in turn, contested priority not only with Newton but with Huygens over the important invention of the spiral-spring balance for regulating watches to eliminate the effect of gravity.
>
> The calendar of disputes was full also in the eighteenth century. Perhaps the most tedious and sectarian of these was the great "Water Contro-

versy" in which that shy, rich, and noble genius of science, Henry Cavendish, was pushed into a three-way tug-of-war with Watt and Lavoisier over the question of which one had first demonstrated the compound nature of water and thereby removed it from its millennia-long position as one of the elements. Earthly battles raged also over claims to the first discovery of heavenly bodies, as in the case of the most dramatic astronomical discovery of the century in which the Englishman John Couch Adams and the Frenchman Urban Jean LeVerrier inferred the existence and predicted the position of the planet now known as Neptune, which was found where their independent computations showed it would be. Medicine had its share of conflicts over priority; for example, Jenner believed himself first to demonstrate that vaccinations afforded security against smallpox, but the advocates of Pearson and Rabaut believed otherwise.

Throughout the nineteenth century and down to the present, disputes over priority continued to be frequent and intense. Lister knew he had first introduced antisepsis, but others insisted that Lemaire had done so before. The sensitive and modest Faraday was wounded by the claims of others to several of his major discoveries in physics: one among these, the discovery of electro-magnetic rotation, was said to have been made before by Wollaston; Faraday's onetime mentor, Sir Humphrey Davy (who had himself been involved in similar disputes) actually opposed Faraday's election to the Royal Society on the ground that his was not the original discovery. Laplace, several of the Bernoullis, Legendre, Gauss, Cauchy were only a few of the giants among mathematicians embroiled in quarrels over priority (Merton 1957, pp. 635–36).

These disputes constitute important evidence for the position that will be presented here. In the present view, as has been indicated, there is a development in science from the preparadigmatic state to the paradigmatic state, the latter being a more advanced state of science. This dimension of progress includes more than the growth of unified (that is, paradigmatic) theory in the science. It has been suggested herein that science consists of more than its logical-empirical-methodological characteristics, science also has various social-organizational-personal characteristics. The major point, however, is that there are interrelations between the objective and subjective aspects of science. In the present context it is reasonable to expect that there has been development in the social aspects of science as there has been progress in the logical-empirical-methodological aspects. Toulmin has referred to the evolution of publication media in science over time (1972, p. 263) in somewhat more extended form than Kuhn (1962).

The "invisible colleges" of seventeenth-century Europe were initially linked by the circulated correspondence of men like Henry Oldenburg. With the foundation of national academies, emphasis shifted to their

Transactions and to treatises such as Newton's *Principia*, which were published under their auspices.

In subsequent centuries, the balance has again shifted several times: to quarterlies, to twice-monthly periodicals, weeklies, and even shorter-term publications (Toulmin 1972, p. 275).

Although this was not Toulmin's interest, the description of this progression may be used to exemplify a progressive development in organizational aspects of science. Specifically, the example may be used to introduce the main thesis to be presented here — that as science has developed from its preparadigmatic state to the paradigmatic state, there has also been a development in the social aspects of science. The particular example to be developed here concerns some of the rules of behavior which are related to the reward-system of science. The hypothesis in this context is that there has been a change in the rules (or standards) as the natural sciences have moved from their early beginnings to their present state. Merton has said that deviant behavior occurs in science, under the impetus of a competitive reward system. Let us consider the possibility that there has been a change, a development, in this area. That is, it is suggested that there is a change in the nature of science, as science has developed, in aspects of competitiveness and rivalry, and the deviant behavior involving recognition.

To begin, examination shows Merton's examples of deviant behaviors come from the seventeenth, eighteenth, and nineteenth centuries. The impression is given that *early in the history of science conflicts over the property of new ideas and findings were much more frequent than they are today.* Until a thorough historical study is done to verify this point it must remain as an impression in concert with a deduction from the conceptual analysis that is being made in this study. That is, in the present analysis it would be *expected* that the social relations of science would show development also. Science has been considered to have begun with everyday concern with the events of the world. Progressive development has taken place in methods of observation, logic, and theory. In addition, however, social factors have also changed. Science began with the works of individuals and ordinary communication about mutual interests. There are rewards involved in scientific findings and conflicting interests can occur. In the beginning, because science was a new area of human interaction, it would be expected that there would be few rules of conduct; there would not yet be well-worked-out procedures for insuring that individuals in the scientific community interacted in an equitable way. For example, scientists would not at an early time have worked out procedures by which recognition for scientific findings would be fairly apportioned. Without such rules and mechanisms, scientists of an early time would be forced to rely on the values and rules of conduct of the times. Some of the descriptions of the early conflicts concerning discoveries are interesting in this light, as is the following.

> Very often, the principals themselves, the discoverers or inventors, take no part in arguing their claims to priority (or withdraw from the controversy as they find that it places them in the distasteful role of insisting upon their own merits or of deprecating the merits of their rivals). Instead, it is their friends and followers, or other more detached scientists, who commonly see the assignment of priority as a moral issue that must be fought to conclusion. For example, it was Wollaston's friends, rather than the distinguished scientist himself, who insinuated that the young Faraday had usurped credit for the experiments on electro-magnetic rotation. . . . And so on, in one after another of the historic quarrels over priority in science (Merton 1957, pp. 291–92).

This procedure smacks very much of the social practice of dueling, where it was the duelist's seconds who handled the practicalities of the contest. The illusion of the disinterested scientist is better maintained when he personally is not involved in the specifics of the contest for recognition. The conflicts over priorities, however, were none the less sharp and bitter because they were ostensibly conducted by seconds. To continue, the history of science shows that early scientists developed various procedures for protecting their rights to their works. It has already been indicated that one early form was to write a novel finding in anagrammatic form, which dated the finding and brought attention to it, without revealing it such that it might be taken by another. Various other means were employed to achieve the same purpose. These practices suggest very strongly that it was necessary for the creative scientist to protect individually the rights to his findings. Moreover, apparently all early scientists, even the greatest, had to protect themselves in such ways. This says again that rules of conduct with respect to the rights of discovery had not yet been internalized by the science community. Moreover, the social practice of patent laws and copyright laws had not yet been invented and established. Journals were not yet established, managed in such a way as to help guarantee that the findings to be reported in a manuscript would not be purloined. The rules of conduct of contemporary ethical practice had yet to be established and generally accepted and followed.

The frequency of disputes over discovery that occurred in the early history of science — when there were far fewer scientists involved than there are today — suggests that the external and internal standards of conduct were different at an earlier time than they are now. The frequency of dispute among outstanding scientists suggests that the standards of conduct were less strong than today and that it was more likely at that time that scientists would take advantage of one another. The description of Laplace's behavior, for example, is a case in point. He must have openly claimed credit for others' work. But that seemed not to detract from his reputation. As another example, the case of Cauchy was described as notorious. He would take ideas from papers he was refereeing for journals, and this was known. The rules of conduct considered to be appropriate today have already been presented herein (see Edsall 1975, pp. 9–10). It would seem unlikely that a noted mathematician today could be as systematically deviant as these men without being discredited within the paradigmatic science and in popular media as well.

The suggestion is that some of the social aspects of science have also changed in an historical development. This has been indicated because there are social aspects of science that appear to be related to the preparadigmatic or paradigmatic state of the science, relationships that affect the development of the science. Some additional background for considering such matters will be given in the next section. As an introduction, however, it may be said that discoveries that Merton refers to in his sociology of science are those that involve paradigmatic science. These examples do not involve ideas that were taken from an individual who represented one school, as in preparadigmatic science, and that were used to enhance the strength of a different school. As has been indicated earlier, it has been suggested by Kuhn and others that the theories in preparadigmatic science are incommensurable — there is no communication across theories. Yet some of Kuhn's examples reveal that the conflicting theories prior to acceptance of a paradigm are not entirely different and incommensurable in their various parts. Referring to the "many views about the nature of electricity," Kuhn states the following. "All their numerous concepts of electricity had something in common — they were partially derived from one or another version of the mechanico-corpuscular philosophy that guided all scientific research of the day" (1962, pp. 13–14).

Working on a subject matter that was very similar, aware of each other's results and ideas, at least to some extent, it must be expected that the numerous theorist-experimenters of that time would have borrowed ideas, methods, and findings developed by other "electricians," but used to support their own views. At least in a percentage of cases it would be expected that this would have occurred without appropriate recognition of the origin of the scientific materials so used. Yet the sociology of science has not described the nature of preparadigmatic science with respect to practices of sharing recognition for discovery, and has not described whether and how preparadigmatic science compares to paradigmatic science in such characteristics. The present analysis will suggest that the preparadigmatic science differs from the paradigmatic science; that in the early preparadigmatic, natural sciences there were generally no standards for sharing recognition equitably. That is, in the preparadigmatic science, although an idea is taken from someone else it will be employed in the service of a competitive theory, a theory that is considered different and independent. Since competition and rivalry between theories is the essence of the preparadigmatic state, finer rules such as citing and recognizing the value of someone else's work would be inconsistent with the preparadigmatic practices and spirit. *This is said to suggest that in the early preparadigmatic sciences no rules were recognized or followed. Only after unification began the conflicts of priority became focal — when the disputants could be seen to be discovering the same things.* These possibilities will be explored further on.

PREPARADIGMATIC AND PARADIGMATIC COMPETITION

As has been indicated, science is competitive. In discussing the possibility that there are differences in psycho-social characteristics of preparadigmatic and paradigmatic science, it will be helpful to recognize that there are two types of competition in science. One type, inter-theory competition, is more characteristic of preparadigmatic science and the other, intra-theory competition, is more characteristic of paradigmatic science.

Inter-Theory Competition

As has been indicated already to some extent, competition in the preparadigmatic science occurs to a large degree between individuals or groups holding competing views. This can be called inter-theory competition. Kuhn describes this state of affairs in his general description of the preparadigmatic state of science. The contests involve viewpoint against viewpoint. Each viewpoint, or school, pursues its own path. Competition between schools occurs where each vies with the other for precedence. Competing schools each attempt to convince practitioners of the field that it is the guide toward scientific success and should be followed. And each school attempts to demolish the competitive schools.

Kuhn's descriptions, and those of others interested in the early stages of science, have utilized historic materials as source materials. In the present view, however, as has been suggested, the preparadigmatic characteristics can be seen today in sciences such as psychology (and in fact it is of central importance to focus attention in this direction). Much of the competition in psychology occurs among the different viewpoints it contains. As indicated in the preceding chapter there are various breakdowns of theory, method, and apparatus, into enclaves. Some of the theory enclaves are large in generality and in number of individuals involved. Thus, there are many psychologists who consider themselves to be behaviorists, cognitive theorists, humanists, trait theorists, or psychoanalytic theorists, each orientation in competition with others. There are also breakdowns of the science due to subject matter/theory characteristics — as among the fields of experimental, clinical, and social psychology — and these may also be in competition with one another.

In the preceding chapter indication was given of the competition between divisions of the American Psychological Association to obtain political power for themselves. There are also frequent clashes of sufficient significance to attract wide attention in the field. Theorists representing different schools may be involved focally in competitions, for example. One illustration that is noteworthy consisted of the debates between B. F. Skinner, the behaviorist, and Carl Rogers, the humanist-clinician (see Rogers and Skinner, 1956). One of the largest competitions in terms of systematic involvement existed among the schools of the different learning theories — all within the more general classification of behavioristic theories — which extended from the 1930s until the early 1960s. This took the form of various contests that included theory and experiment, and will be referred to more specifically further on. The investment in this competition was considerable in terms of the man-hours involved, work done, and the publications produced for the science — most of which gave no substantive thrust to the progress of the science, having been conducted in the service of a theory competition and having relevance only for that competition.

Such cases are only among the most prominent. It is suggested, however, that psychology as a preparadigmatic science heavily involves such competitions on a day-to-day basis. We can get some of the flavor of the day-to-day competitions by the following description of Stephen Toulmin, although he has provided the description in support of different conceptual goals than those of present concern.

> [W]e shall have to recognize that the coexisting institutions of any profession are in continual competition for "establishment" or "authority." Instead of working together harmoniously at all times within a single "system," the rival institutions of a profession can easily act in ways that frustrate one another's goals. . . . Instead of competing for influential positions within the established institutions, for instance, individual scientists can alternatively increase their influence on their fellow-scientists — and that of their novel ideas — by setting up rival centres of power or establishing professional splinter-groups, which manage their own affairs independently of older-established institutions. Similarly, instead of fighting to control the most respected existing journals, it may be more effective for them to inaugurate a new journal, relying on the merits of their novel approach to win an influence comparable to that of older periodicals. The functions of periodical literature epitomize, in fact, the functions of scientific institu-

tions more generally. . . . In practice, indeed, the editor of an influential periodical acts in his own person as a disciplinary "filter," sifting out those papers which deserve publication in his journal, and so embodying the disciplinary selection of accredited "possibilities" (Toulmin 1972, p. 270).

And, on a smaller scale, a multiplicity of similar tyrannies is continually being exercised "in the name" of science. Papers are refused publication, academic posts are denied, professional honours are withheld — even from an Ohm, a Mayer, or a Helmholtz — not for lack of worthwhile disciplinary arguments, but through professional disagreement with the editor, the research director, or the influential professor (Toulmin 1972, p. 281).

This account is of the personal struggle among paradigmatic scientists. The account also provides descriptions of the inter-theory competitions that occur continually in a science, without attracting any special notice, and in fact without ever being consciously realized by most scientists as a special source of influence on their science. Moreover, Toulmin's statement can be considered to provide a description of some of the mechanisms by which the inter-theory competition in science occurs. That is, inter-theory competition has the goal of defeating the positions of the "opposition." The mechanisms are varied. One can compete by directly showing the weaknesses in the opposing position. The previously mentioned competition between the learning theories of Hull and Tolman, especially, and the other learning theories involved such direct theoretical and experimental confrontation. But there are other methods also, as Toulmin indicates. Denying publication is one avenue. If the editor of a journal is an adherent of one school of thought he may have different criteria for the acceptance of articles of that view than he has for the acceptance of articles from other schools.

There is evidence indicating that the investigator's viewpoint and his degree of orthodoxy, that is, his acceptance of a dominant paradigm, influences the editor's or the referee's decision to accept or reject his article for publication in a scientific journal (Crane 1967; Mahoney 1975). However, very few studies have been conducted pertaining to this kind of paradigm bias in editorial decisions and this is an important area for further research (Barber 1976, p. 9).

The competition, especially in preparadigmatic science, is for the attention of the other members of the science. Each position has the goal of convincing the other members of the science that its way is the best, that it should be followed and supported — by adherents and by material resources. For it is through gaining that attention and support that the goals of the orientation can be carried through, and it is that attention and support itself that constitutes the rewards of the science. Controlling publications is one way of controlling how the attention and support of the science will be directed. Another way is provided by citations. Each citation of an opposing viewpoint actually constitutes the provision of a forum for that viewpoint, a forum by which to obtain attention and support. For among the various members of the sciences who read the piece that carries the citation, some can be expected to read and be influenced by the work that is cited. By not citing the relevant works of a competing school or paradigm, the scientist helps prevent the competition from gaining an audience and possible support. Omitting citation of opposing orientations is thus another means of waging the battle, of preventing the opposition from getting attention and support.

This represents one of the two forms of competition that will be described herein. Although it has been referred to as theory competition, it should be understood that the basis for different schools may lie in nontheory elements as well. Thus, the basis for the competition may be a methodological difference, a difference in problem orientation, or a personal difference that involves the distribution of power of an individual or group.

Intra-Theory Competition

A second important type of competition in science occurs when there is no difference in the theoretical, methodological, or political aims of the rivals. The rivals may accept the same theoretical context, the same apparatus and methodological knowledge, the same problem area, and yet be locked in a contest in which there will be one winner. This type of competition is that which Merton refers to in most of his examples. The competition involves who is going to attain the expected scientific achievement first. The disputes of Newton, of Hooke, of Adams, of LeVerrier, Jenner, Pearson, and Rabaut, already described in the statement of Merton previously quoted, can be seen to be of this type.

A more contemporary example is provided in detail by Watson (1968). In his account of the discovery of the coding and duplicative functions of DNA in genetics — the double helix structure — Watson indicates clearly how there were different teams of researchers who shared the same goal. Moreover, they had roughly the same background, conceptions, apparatus, and methods. They were working within the same context. The contest concerned who would solve the problems that lay in the way toward the common goal. Very much aware of each other's existence, and of the significance of the discovery when it had been made, each group was in a race to be the first. In contemporary times we have in physics a commonly accepted goal of developing a unified theory that will integrate the several basic forms of energy that exist in the universe. Various individuals have and will attempt to reach that goal first. It should be noted that intra-theory competition need not involve problems of the vast scope and significance of these two examples. The more usual cases involve the smaller advances characteristic of normal science. Not in every case is the goal, the conceptual context, or the methodology, so explicit and so common to the competitors as in these two examples, moreover. However, in general, this is an important form of competition in science.

What the competition involves in the intra-theory case should be considered also. In a case of pure intra-theory competition, such as that described in *The Double Helix* (Watson 1968), the competition drives the parties involved to work feverishly for the scientific development. In such a case it would be expected that the participants would be eager to develop, or gain from some other source, ideas, apparatus, methods, or whatever would aid them in solving the problems that are obstacles to the goal. This motivation could inspire deviant behaviors, but it certainly is the source of support for much positive achievement in science and cooperation and shared recognition as well. Intra-theory competition, it is suggested, has more productive effects than inter-theory competition.

COMPETITION TYPE AND SCIENCE CHARACTER

A primary concern here is that of differentiating preparadigmatic and paradigmatic science. Let us thus ask whether there is a relationship between the two types of competition that have been described and the paradigmatic character of the science. To begin, we can see that in Kuhn's historical account of preparadigmatic science, the type of competition described is of the inter-theory type. A multiplicity of schools were each vying with the other to attain precedence with the audience of uncommitted scientists and the general public for a particular point of view. The sociologists of science, on the other hand, describe the manner in which competition takes place in paradigmatic sciences, that is intra-theory competition. There are several implications involved in this analysis that should be made clear.

The central suggestion, which should be emphasized, is that preparadigmatic and paradigmatic sciences differ in certain essential social characteristics. This does not mean that a sharp dichotomy exists, however. There are certainly cases in paradigmatic science where there is a conflict between orientations. For example, let us refer to the manner in which Kuhn describes science, where change occurs when competing paradigms arise and confront each other. At such times in the paradigmatic science the contest between paradigms would be expected to have the characteristics of inter-theory competition. It would be expected that the competing paradigms would demonstrate competitive behaviors such as theoretical and experimental works to directly disprove the opposing paradigm, denying publication to the works of the opposing paradigm, and omitting citation of the works of the opposing paradigm. In such instances it would be expected that the characteristics of the paradigmatic science would be similar to the inter-theory competitions of the preparadigmatic science.

On the other side, within the preparadigmatic science there are still schools, any one of which may include a large number of scientists. Within the particular school it would be expected that there would arise intra-theory competitions. For example, the recent history of psychology has seen the development of the field of behavior modification. It was based upon several principles of behavior — that desirable behavior can be increased by rewarding it, and undesirable behavior can be decreased by not rewarding it (see Staats 1957). When these principles had been set forth and validated for several types of human-behavior problems, a conceptual-methodological context was established within which a number of investigators began to work. The goals of this context were to extend the principles to additional human behaviors and to improve the methods. The intra-theory race was then on to make the most penetrating demonstrations of behavior modification, of the most significant behaviors, employing the best methods. Many winners were possible in this activity, and it had characteristics of intra-theory competition, although the area involved is a preparadigm not a paradigm.

It is suggested that it is in part because of these overlapping characteristics that there has been ambiguity in differentiating preparadigmatic from paradigmatic science, an ambiguity that was indicated in an earlier chapter. In the aspects of science that are being discussed there is not a sharp differentiation between inter-theory competition and intra-theory competition with respect to whether the science is preparadigmatic or paradigmatic. However, the present view is that there is a difference between preparadigmatic and paradigmatic sciences with respect to the frequency and importance of these two forms. Preparadigmatic science is characterized by a great deal of inter-theory competition. Moreover, the intra-theory competition that takes place occurs within groups of scientists (like schools) that are also engaged in inter-theory competitions with other groups. Paradigmatic science, on the other hand, is characterized by a great deal of intra-theory activity. This constitutes what Kuhn has called normal science. Less frequently this type of competition involves problems of great significance, like the search of contemporary physics for a unified theory, and the competition becomes publicly known. In addition, however, paradigmatic science, to a lesser extent than preparadigmatic science, involves inter-theory competitions of large and small scope. These include the paradigm clashes that were the focus of Kuhn's interest.

The significance of this analysis for some of the work of the sociologists of science should be indicated. That is, if there are differences in sciences, depending upon their paradigmatic character, then both preparadigmatic and paradigmatic sciences require study, distinction, and comparison. The type of competition that is characteristic of paradigmatic science may not represent that which exists for preparadigmatic sciences. This would be true also of the types of deviant behaviors that can occur. Thus, for example, the deviant behaviors of suppressing publication of rival theories, omission of citations, and so on, may be more characteristic of the preparadigmatic science than intra-theory deviations, where controversies over priority within the same orientation would be more prevalent. It is noteworthy that there are no cases of priority dispute that have been systematically published in the science of psychology. Comparing psychology to the natural sciences in this respect yields a very sharp contrast demanding consideration.

Competition Type Affects Unity of Science

Finally, analysis of the two types of competition suggests that different outcomes result from the two types, at least with respect to the advancement toward unity of the science. That is, although there may be competition between scientists in intra-theory rivalry, the product of the competition lends itself to the unity of the science. As an example, there was competition between the Watson-Crick group and other groups regarding the discovery of the double helix structure (Watson 1968). However the discovery emerged from a unified science and when the competition and its solution occurred they gave impetus to further unified research and knowledge acqustion. Inter-theory competition, on the other hand, has the opposite effect. Emerging from disunity, competitive efforts are devoted to further separating the positions that are involved. Differences are purposely sharpened when the positions are compared. Moreover, such actions as denying publication to opposing views and omitting citation are activities that diminish communication across views, and help produce islands of knowledge rather than a unified body. In the paradigmatic science the inter-theory rifts caused by the paradigm clashes described by Kuhn are only temporary. One or the other paradigm is victorious and the other is displaced from the science, and the science then continues on in its unified strivings. The competition between orientations in the preparadigmatic science never ends, however. So the competition is instrumental in adding to the separation of knowledge, producing a growing disunity. The next chapter will explore one aspect of preparadigmatic, separatistic competition — the manner in which theories are separated. It will be suggested that the preparadigmatic science does not have the same methods of citation as does the paradigmatic science, and this methodology contributes to the disunification of its knowledge.

SCIENCE REQUIRES COOPERATION: THIS MUST DETERMINE ITS STANDARDS

In summary, it has been suggested that there has been development of the rules that regulate the behaviors of scientists with respect to the works of one another. Today there are well codified rules for recognizing the work of others, for citing that work, and for sharing recognition on jointly conducted projects. These rules have been worked out in the paradigmatic sciences. At an earlier time in these sciences rules had not yet been established and generally internalized. As a consequence there were many disputes, even among very prominent men of science, for the ownership of scientific discoveries. While there were commonly expected standards, they were not yet explicit and generally accepted, and there were only weak sanctions for breaking the rules. The many controversies that resulted probably were instrumental in the development of today's rules and etiquettes.

There appears also to have been an earlier period than this, which would have corresponded to the preparadigmatic stage of a field of science. In this period scientists did not work within a common paradigm, accepting the same goals and methods. Competition in this period thus involved less the race for obtaining a commonly accepted goal, and more a head on competition whose goal was the defeat of another competitive orientation in the eyes of the scientific community. In this preparadigmatic circumstance there was no basis for cooperation. Thus there were no strongly accepted rules of conduct with respect to the work of others. It was more apt to be accepted that each scientist would do whatever was in his power to enhance his own view and to diminish the power of the other view. Rules for sharing recognition would be inconsistent with the framework of preparadigmatic science, since the essence of such science endeavors is opposition and separation. The thesis, in summary form, is that science's quest for knowledge gives impetus to the development of cooperation. That is, knowledge accrual occurs better when knowledge is shared amongst those who labor to obtain it. It is the demand for sharing that in turn demands cooperation; rules of working together are needed to insure equitable exchange. Without such rules science functions less effectively. These are hypotheses, again, that should be considered in historical studies of sciences that have undergone the transition from the preparadigmatic to the paradigmatic state. These are hypotheses also for the consideration of contemporary preparadigmatic sciences by themselves and in comparison to paradigmatic sciences. The next chapter will consider some of the sociological characteristics of the preparadigmatic science of psychology.

Chapter 6

Separatism: Methodology of Disunity

There has been a change over time, as science has developed, in the rules by which science is conducted as well as in the expression of deviant behavior with respect to how scientists treat each others' work. The present chapter will attempt to show this by dealing with one facet of what is taken to be a characteristic of preparadigmatic science — its abundance of disorganized, unrelated knowledge and the manner in which the rules of citation and general referencing are related to this characteristic. More particular to the previously described development of science, it will be suggested that the rules of citation and referencing are different in the preparadigmatic science than they are in the paradigmatic science. Without consideration it is assumed that all sciences follow the same rules. In contrast it is being suggested that paradigmatic and preparadigmatic sciences are different in character: the former having much greater unification, the latter being relatively disorganized. A central part of this disorganization involves practices and standards of citation that neglect relating similar elements in science to one another. Organization of scientific knowledge depends on the cross-relating of common elements.

These expectations can be derived from the analysis that has already been made. That is, it has been suggested that the character of the preparadigmatic science — the fact that there are no common goals, that different theory languages are used, that the purpose of each school is to defeat the other, and that there is little attempt to join schools toward a common goal — provides a social context in which the cooperative rules of conduct of paradigmatic science make little sense. To elaborate, the rules of conduct of science are by and large cooperative rules. Take, for example, the ethic of the open science — that the scientist is supposed to divulge openly his findings. We can see the rule in the following example of its abrogation. "Upton and

Edison thus violated another of the norms of scientific conduct that . . . had been established in America since the 1850's: 'a full and free exchange of knowledge, without regard to personal considerations'" (Hounshell 1980, p. 157). Like most descriptions regarding science, this one refers to paradigmatic sciences (and a somewhat idealized version at that). But the rule is clear. In the present view, it should be stressed, such rules of conduct can pertain only in a cooperative social atmosphere, where the scientist who divulges his knowledge to another can count on being treated equitably, where those whom his knowledge helps will share in any recognition the knowledge helps them achieve.

When the social atmosphere is such that the scientist cannot count upon just attribution for his contribution, through shared recognition, he does not engage as freely in the open exchange of knowledge. He may resort to various devices to protect his knowledge against depredations from other scientists, as earlier examples have illustrated. The present hypothesis is that the preparadigmatic science does not provide the same social atmosphere as that of the paradigmatic science. In the preparadigmatic science competition is largely of the inter-theory type, where there are no common goals; and the attempt is rather to destroy the other position. In this situation it does not make sense to follow rules that will provide support for a competitive theory.

The foregoing has referred to preparadigmatic sciences of the past. However, a central thesis being developed is that psychology is a preparadigmatic science in the present. We must ask in this context whether these considerations might pertain to a contemporary preparadigmatic science. The question is a large one indeed, and cannot be addressed in full. The present chapter, however, will deal with some materials that suggest that psychology does display characteristics in this area that are coincident with its present description as a preparadigmatic science. Illustration of such characteristics of psychology is important to the development of the thesis of the present book. In addition, analysis of the preparadigmatic methodological characteristics is instrumental in working towards their improvement.

In essence the present chapter will suggest that psychology, with its chaos of information, is in the preparadigmatic state of emphasizing inter-theory competition. As a consequence of this state, the rules of interrelating science findings (and showing commonality) through citation and referencing practices — rules that are promulgated by paradigmatic sciences — appear not to be followed. Rather, practices and a philosophy of citation that are labeled as *separatism* appear to be characteristic of psychology. Separatism occurs when the concept or principle of one theory, as an example, is presented in a different terminology, within a different theory that includes other elements, and is then considered as a separate, independent, and original element. It is the present thesis, moreover, that the practice of introducing conceptual elements in psychology without relating those elements to highly similar, prior elements is so widespread it cannot be considered deviant within the science, at least in its normal manifestations. It is only deviant in extreme cases and when evaluated by the standards of paradigmatic science. The practices and standards of citation of priority in psychology generally deviate from the practices and standards followed in paradigmatic sciences. This is one of the important ways that preparadigmatic and paradigmatic sciences differ.

The present chapter by no means provides a definitive account of the practices and standards in the preparadigmatic science, only an introductory statement. The consideration to be made is large and will require the systematic work of various scholars. A number of questions arise in this context. For example, do parallel elements exist in the science without appropriate cross-citation? Do individuals introduce science elements similar to prior elements, without indicating the original source? Are such elements accepted in the science as separate and independent and as independently created? Do psychological scientists openly accept these practices? Is the science as a consequence seen as less organized, less unified than it actually is? The present account opens this area for consideration.

Since the rules and practices of paradigmatic science are the ostensible norm, even for the preparadigmatic sciences, the characteristics of separatism have not been explicitly recognized. Because psychologists, as other scientists, are nurtured in the philosophy and standards of paradigmatic science, it would be expected, for example, that questioning psychologists openly concerning the rules of science would elicit the same replies that would be made by scientists in a paradigmatic science. The sociology of science has sometimes employed the opinions of correspondents to characterize the practices of scientists. In the present case this type of data might be used if the instruments were constructed to elicit information concerning practices, rather than an idealized version of paradigmatic science standards. However, the basis for the present description of the separatistic character of psychology comes not from indirect sources such as surveys or questionnaires. Rather the evidence involves the direct actions of practicing scientists, direct actions of several different types. First, some cases will be described in psychology in which similar concepts have been presented in different works without adequately relating the concepts to one another through citation. Both past and contemporary works will be exemplified. Secondly, the responses of psychologists that reveal their philosophy of citation practices will be described. These responses were made within the everyday work operations of the individuals involved, rather than through solicited opinions. For example, some of the responses were given as part of editorial duties, in the act of reviewing papers for publication. The evidence thus refers to practices and standards as they occur in daily actions of skilled psychological scientists.

The focus of consideration here will be on the contention that there is a philosophy — separatism — that rationalizes the practices involved, and thereby provides a conceptual basis for the practices. This philosophy operates to allow the breakdown of the priority and citation methods that are considered to be general to science, the result being the separation of realms of knowledge that actually should be intimately related because of their commonality.

SEPARATISM: DISCOVERY AND EARLY DEFINITION

Very early in my studies in psychology, even as a graduate student, I had occasion to note that there were similar conceptual elements in theories, similarities that were overlooked in the effort to distinguish and separate the theories as independent bodies of knowledge. My own work became focally concerned with creating a general, unified theory in psychology. This involved the consideration of various phenomena, concepts, and methods from the standpoint of the same basic set of principles. This mission is one that disposes one to see similarities, cutting through surface characteristics of terminology, methodology, and the specifics of experimental findings. The mission also leads one to see similarities across different areas of psychology. The experience obtained within that quest indicated to me clearly that there were many highly similar concepts, principles, methods, and findings in psychology that were nevertheless considered to be separate, independent, and different in origin. There appeared to be no set of standards that required that commonalities be cross referenced; the methods of citation expected in science generally were not being followed.

I also had occasion to note that the process that generally appeared to be characteristic of psychology also pertained to my own theory. Motivated in part by self-interest, I traced some rather clear individual cases and, as will be indicated later in the present chapter, I witnessed a more extensive, systematic development of this kind. If unified theory and organized knowledge are to be central goals of our science, like other sciences, the separatistic practices that I observed would be severe obstacles, for various reasons. This interest in the matter led me to more generally consider the practices of establishing originality and priority in science and the allocation of recognition for contributions. It was apparent that essential aspects of science were involved in ways that affect the efficacy of science. For these several reasons I began to write on the topic, using materials that were close at hand. It was an entirely new area and just how to deal with the topic was not too clear to me. The topic was a touchy one. Having described psychology's general separatism several times (Staats 1967, 1968a), my first paper focusing on the problem addressed a specific case of separatism between two theories having conceptual elements that actually were very similar. One of the theories was my own. I explained the process as an example of "preparadigmatic separatism" (Staats 1978a). In the first draft of that paper submitted to the *Personality and Social Psychology Bulletin* the following statement of the purpose of the paper was made, a statement deleted in writing this paper for final publication.

> The present paper is written to exemplify the existence in social psychology of a separatism that is an obstacle to unified reporting and unified theory construction in psychology. It is written also to effect such unification in the particular case, as well as to suggest that the separatistic zeitgeist be changed. The case to be described herein concerns the "social psychology of sexual behavior" (Byrne, 1977). It is suggested that the thesis contained in Byrne's article was previously advanced within the social behaviorism paradigm (Staats 1968a, 1970a) and later developed in detail especially in a book by Annon (1975). Byrne's article, which does not mention this work, thus illustrates the preparadigmatic separatism.

The reviewers who read the draft of this article agreed that the two theories indeed did overlap, and the editor accepted for publiction the brief paper written on the topic of separatism (Staats 1978a). The specifics of the overlapping elements of the two theories are not significant here. The case was not unusual in psychology; as will be indicated there are many cases of overlapping elements between theories without citation to indicate the commonality. In introducing the present topic, the important points are those that can be abstracted from the responses that were made to the paper I had written. In response Byrne made explicit the standard that is of concern here. Byrne suggested that *relating the similar parts of two theories was not demanded*, that "parallelism within an identifiable research tradition is to be expected" (1978, p. 498). In the context within which this was written it states that the fact that a later theory develops conceptual characteristics like that of an earlier one does not necessarily demand that the later theory refer to the earlier one.

But the philosophy was made even more clear by one of the journal reviewers involved, who made the following comment on the paper the present author had written on the topic. This anonymous reviewer refers to the uncited similarities between the two theories, in the following terms.

> That is, both [theories] make use of general learning principles including instrumental and classical conditioning and apply them to social and specifically sexual behavior. It would be surprising if there were not sub-

stantial similarity. That there is relatively little cross-citation [actually there was none] may be due to imperfect scientific communication or stylistic preferences as well as to "separatism" or less politely, attempts at personal aggrandizement.

What I want to stress here is that the example being referred to is not an example of deviant behavior in science such as those described by the sociologists of science. As both above statements of the philosophy of theory construction clearly reveal, the fact that a later theory has developed features that are very similar to an earlier theory was considered acceptable and to be expected. Priority was not of concern; the times involved in the introduction of the common elements to the two theories were not considered important, although there was a difference of nine years. The similarity was not important. Moreover, it was not considered necessary to cite the earlier theory. Stylistic preferences were a sufficient reason for the absence of citation. Errors of communication were also sufficient reason; although such errors did not call for correction as shown by the fact that nothing was done to correct the absence of citations involved or to suggest a change in citation methodology.

What was being said was that two theories could progressively develop very similar elements — perhaps original to the prior theory and secondary in the later theory — and there did not have to be indication of priority, or any citation. The methodology of citation suggested, and the general philosophy, are in marked disagreement with the methodology and philosophy that are held generally in the paradigmatic sciences. Nowhere in paradigmatic science is there a philosophy that says that because of stylistic preference it is unnecessary to cite prior theoretical innovations. Nor is imperfect scientific communication an excuse. Errors in science — especially easy in the diverse preparadigmatic science — are to be corrected, not rationalized. As Ravetz has said about the standards of paradigmatic science, the criteria of independence of origin of a science element are extremely strict (1971, p. 253). It is suggested that the separatism of the preparadigmatic science deviates markedly from the practices of our model, paradigmatic science. Yet, the individual case of overlap involved in the present case does not constitute a deviation within psychology, but is the normal state of affairs.

Psychology is a science and large parts of psychology, in the past and in the present, have been devoted to demonstrating that the field is indeed scientific. Assuming that the philosophy of separatism is widespread in the field, one must ask how can there be such a marked difference in fundamental methodology between psychology and those sciences usually used as the models of science? How can the difference have escaped notice? I would suggest two answers. One is that the basic nature of preparadigmatic sciences is different than that of paradigmatic sciences along the lines that have been described already — above — with great heterogeneity and competitiveness and individualism involving every aspect of the preparadigmatic science. This heterogeneity provides the context for the development of the practices and the philosophy of separatism, which themselves deviate from the practices of our model sciences. Secondly, I would suggest that the methods and philosophy of separatism have remained implicit, not public. If they were formally stated they would clash with those held in paradigmatic science, and they would have to be rejected. As will be seen, however, the members of the science are sensitive about the deviance from paradigmatic practices, and generally oppose publication of issues involving citation practices and philosophy. Separatism remains an implicit philosophy that is only made explicit under the circumstances I have described, where the psychologist is called upon to justify his actions and methods. Additional evidence that this is the case will be presented further on.

This is the suggestion. Although the account cannot be exhaustive, and the present analysis must be considered to be an introduction to the concepts that are being outlined, it is pertinent to turn to some examples that can provide us with a basis for considering these important matters of methodology and philosophy.

EXAMPLES OF SEPARATISM

The present thesis is that there are implicit standards within psychology that are not the same as the standards that are operative in paradigmatic sciences. The psychological scientist, it is suggested, does not have to relate his work to the work of others in the same manner as that expected in paradigmatic sciences. He does not have to indicate precisely the origin of the ideas in his work, and he does not have to cite priority with the same diligence and specification. Although the methodological standards that are operative are not stated explicitly or precisely, they are followed. Moreover, there is also a philosophical context for the standards. Again, the philosophy is not stated explicitly, but it is held generally in the science, and it will be expressed in suitable circumstances, especially those involving the need to justify the practices.

In the context of this thesis it is important to assess our field to see the extent to which there are science products — concepts, principles, findings — that are really highly similar but that remain separated from each other in the science through lack of citation that would indicate the close relationship. This cannot be done in a complete way herein, or even in a way that would provide a representative sample — the task is too large. It is suggested that there are many, many examples where individual elements overlap greatly, where there is no indication of relationship between the theories involved, and the science is given to understand that they are independent, separate, even antagonistic theories (Staats 1978a; 1979). A few examples will now be described.

Learning Theories: Similar, but Separate and Competing

As a background for considering what follows, it is germane to briefly discuss something of historical context — although a full treatment of the preparadigmatic characteristics of psychology in historical perspective would take a concentrated effort. As an example, however, let us glance at the field of learning. One might suspect that this area of study would show some unification inasmuch as this field represents a general school that is in competition with other schools of psychology. One might expect, moreover, that scientists accepting the same general approach would share a common goal, and be involved in mutually supportive efforts to further the approach. Even more so, the field has been singular in its adoption of the philosophy derived from natural science, logical positivism, with its emphasis on generalizing scientific principles. One would thus expect such generalization to be important in this field, often called a paradigm.

This has not been the case historically. In brief perspective, the experimental psychology of learning may be considered to have commenced with the discovery of classical conditioning by Ivan Pavlov and of instrumental conditioning by Edward Thorndike. The specification of the principles of learning in experiments accumulated progressively following 1900 and the second generation of the field became preoccupied with assembling the facts into the systematically stated theories. This effort did not involve the systematic assembly of the various aspects of the experimental findings that everyone accepted — representing a unified body of knowledge — with the areas of uncertainty marked out as points of disagreement and exploration. *Rather, the major theorists each composed his own separate and seemingly independent theory.* Sharp lines of cleavage were drawn. For example, one controversy centered around whether there was only one type of learning — either classical conditioning or instrumental conditioning — or two types. And of those who felt there was only one type of learning, there was disagreement concerning whether the one type was classical conditioning (learning through simply pairing things together) or instrumental conditioning (learning through reinforcement or reward). The differences taken by the theorists on this issue were then considered to be the basis for characterizing theories that were in all their other parts also different. Even though these other parts might be highly similar, as will as indicated, this fact was lost in the consideration of the theories as competitive and different.

We can pick up the separatism in views of learning as it occurred very early in behaviorism by comparing some of the accounts of Thorndike and Watson. Thorndike, it will be remembered, isolated experimentally the principles of instrumental conditioning using as the apparatus a "problem" box. The Thorndike problem box was a cage within which there was some trigger mechanism which if moved opened a door in the cage, allowing the animal exit and access to a piece of food. Thorndike observed that animals repeatedly put in the box would progressively be conditioned to move the trigger mechanism more and more quickly.

> When put into the box the cat would show evident signs of discomfort and of an impulse to escape from confinement. It tries to squeeze through any opening; it claws and bites at the bars or wire; it thrusts its paws out through any opening and claws at everything it reaches; it continues its effort when it strikes anything loose and shaky; it may claw at things within the box. . . . The cat . . . will probably claw the string or loop or button [the trigger mechanism] so as to open the door. And gradually [over repeated trials in the box] all the other nonsuccessful impulses will be stamped out and the particular impulse leading to the successful act will be stamped in by the resulting pleasure, until, after many trials, the cat will, when put in the box, immediately claw the button or loop in a definite way (Thorndike 1911, pp. 35–36).

It is interesting that Watson later describes the "growth of a habit" in very similar terms. But, as will be indicated, the similarity is not indicated, rather a difference in interpretation is emphasized.

> To make the whole process a little more concrete, let us put in front of the three-year-old child, whose habits of manipulation are well established, a problem box — a box that can be opened only after a certain thing has been done; for example, he has to press inward a small wooden button. Before we hand it to him, we show him the open box containing several small pieces of candy and then we close it and tell him that if he opens it he may have a piece of candy. If well organized by previous handling of toys, he goes at the problem at once — (1) he picks the box up, (2) he pounds it on the floor, (3) he drags it round and round, (4) he pushes it up against the base-board, (5) he turns it over, (6) he strikes it with his fist. In other words, he does everything he has learned to do in the past in similar situations. . . . Let us suppose that he has 50 learned and unlearned separate responses at his command. At one time or another during his first attempt to open the box, let us assume that he displays, as he will, nearly all of them before he pushes the button hard enough to release the catch. The time the whole process takes, we will say is about twenty minutes. When he opens it, we give him his bit of candy, close up the box and hand it to him again. The next time he makes fewer movements; the third time fewer still. In ten trials or less he can open the box without making a use-

less movement and he can open it in two seconds (Watson 1930, pp. 204–05).

As can be seen the two accounts are very similar. The differences are of specifics — a child not a cat, a problem box to get into instead of to escape from, a difference in the responses, and a difference of theories and theory names as will be seen — but the basic principles are the same, with some new elements in the later account. (This is important to indicate, for changes in specifics are considered in psychology to constitute different positions.) Watson, however, does not indicate the similarity. He elaborates the same principles, actually, but he continues on to interpret the instrumental conditioning in a different way from Thorndike's earlier account.

> Why is the time cut down, and why do movements not necessary to the solution gradually drop out of the series? This has been a hard problem to solve because no one has ever simplified the problem enough really to bring experimental technique to bear on it. I have tried to explain on what we may call a frequency and recency basis, why the one movement finally persists whereas all the rest die away. . . . Only a few psychologists have been interested in the problem. Most of the psychologists, it is to be regretted, have even failed to see that there is a problem. They believe habit formulation is implanted by kind fairies. For example, Thorndike speaks of pleasure stamping in the successful movement and displeasure stamping out the unsuccessful movements. Most of the psychologists talk, too, quite volubly about the formation of new pathways in the brain, as though there were a group of tiny servants of Vulcan there who run through the nervous system with hammer and chisel digging new trenches and deepening old ones (Watson 1930, pp. 205–06).

Thus, despite the great overlap in the elements that compose these theories of learning, the reader is not led to focus on the commonality in theory elements. Rather, the conceptual difference is the focus. Instead of building on the earlier theory, the earlier theory is criticized and separated from the later formulation. The result, notwithstanding the large overlap in elements of principle involved, ends up as two separate, independent, competitive theories. The essential sameness of the two theories was not dealt with by the science by collapsing across similarities to reduce the complexity of the science. The differences were emphasized and these became the focal characteristics, an outcome that was distinctive in continuing the preparadigmatic nature of the field.

To continue, however, even those later considering the principle of reinforcement (reward) to be important in learning did not present a unified theoretical front. Each criticized the others' view of reinforcement.

Thorndike's view (1911, 1932) was considered by some other theorists to be too subjective in flavor. Hull (1943), in separating his position from the others, posited that the reinforcement properties of a stimulus were due to the stimulus reducing the internal drive state of the organism. Skinner (see 1950), as part of distinguishing his theory, rejected this type of theorizing. He stated that reinforcing stimuli should be defined solely by their ability to strengthen the motor responses the stimuli followed (1938). We can see that the preparadigmatic separatism that was followed by Watson with respect to Thorndike was followed by the second generation behaviorists with respect to Thorndike and Watson, not only on the question of the operation of reward but also on other principles.

Reinforcement

Let us further examine the basic principle of reinforcement; called the Law of Effect by Thorndike (1911). Thorndike must be considered to be the originator of the experimental specification of this very central principle in the experimental field of psychology. (The concept of learning through reward [reinforcement] had existed previously on a philosophical level.) When we examine Skinner's theory of learning, however, which is built around his elaboration of the principle of reinforcement, we see scant reference to the work of Thorndike. Actually, at the point where the basic principle is advanced in Skinner's first book there is no reference (Skinner 1938, pp. 65–66). Only much later in this book, where this type of conditioning is compared to Pavlov's classical conditioning, is Thorndike's work cited and then only a mention is made (Skinner 1938, p. 111). For a building process to have occurred in this central theoretical-experimental development, utilizing paradigmatic methods of citation, a much more complete presentation would have been necessary. The two experimental bodies of fact would have had to be related, as well as the two theoretical bodies. The manner in which the later account grew out of and utilized the earlier account would have required description, as well as the ways in which the later account deviated from the earlier account, in discarding certain features, in adding others, and so on. (It should be noted here that although the present examples concern individuals, they are not being singled out for criticism, since their methods are representative of the field in general.)

To continue with this example concerning the principle of reinforcement, let us turn to another of the theories. Hull (1943) later presented a theory of learning that was also based upon reinforcement. In this account the principle of reinforcement is stated in the terms that were special to Hull's theory. Then in a footnote he adds "Actually, of course, this formulation has only the status of an hypothesis. The term *law* is here used in much the same loose way that Thorndike has used it in his famous expression, 'law of effect,' to which the above formulation is closely related (Thorndike p. 176)" (Hull 1943, p. 72). Again, the account does not attempt to build systematically the later theoretical statement on the work that has preceded it. Moreover, there is no mention of Skinner's prior, but more contemporary, theory of learning that also systematically elaborated the principle of reinforcement — with differences in statement from that of Hull. Let us consider an additional example.

Sequences of Responses

It should be remembered that the principle of reinforcement was considered major, central, in the field of learning and in psychology and was widely known to everyone in the field. It is relevant to consider other examples involving less basic elements as well. The present example is that of the response sequence. To begin, it may be said that the basic principles of learning are usually established in the situation where the subject (usually an animal) learns a simple response to a simple stimulus. The concern is with the conditions that affect the learning and with the nature of the process. Functional behavior in everyday life, however, usually includes more than a single stimulus and a single response. For example, frequently series, sequences, or chains of behavior are learned, and in fact many skilled performances consist of such sequences. Let us pick up this concept, in the context of a theory experimentally specifying learning, with the following statement of Thorndike. The term Thorndike employed was that of the "series of associations, where one sense-impression [stimulus] . . . leads to another act [response] which in its turn leads to a new sense-impression" (Thorndike 1911, p. 132).

> Of the formation of such *series* animals are capable to a very high degree. Chicks from 10 to 25 days old learned to go directly through a sort of big labyrinth [maze] requiring a series of 23 distinct and in some cases fairly difficult associations, of which 11 involved choices between two paths. By this power of acquiring a long series animals find their way to distant feeding grounds and back again. But all such cases are examples of the number, not of the complexity, of animal associations (Thorndike 1911, p. 132).

When we turn to Watson's theory we see the same concept of the response sequence. Watson elaborated the concept a good deal. But central principles are the same as Thorndike's. In Watson's terms, a series of responses (reflexes) could be formed through learning. One reflex could bring the individual into contact with a new environmental stimulus, and another response could be learned to this stimulus. He also indicated that the source of stimuli that functioned in the sequence could be internal.

> In the early stages of the learning process, each time the visual stimulus is given us we make a muscular response (primarily with our striped muscles) to that visual stimulus. In a very short time the muscular response itself can serve as a stimulus to set off the next motor response in order, and then the next motor response can set off the succeeding motor response, so that thereafter complicated mazes can be run, complicated acts of various kinds can be accomplished without the presence of visual, auditory, olfactory and tactual stimuli. The muscular [proprioceptive] stimuli coming from the movements of the muscles themselves are all we need to keep our manual responses occurring in proper sequence (Watson 1930, p. 219).

Watson makes no reference to Thorndike's preceding analysis in his account. And his own analysis is treated similarly in the second generation behaviorisms, as will be indicated. That is, later developments of the concept of the response series, response sequences, or response chains do not refer to either Thorndike or Watson. Hull, for example, elaborates the concept of the response sequence to indicate how *knowledge* of worldly events, as indicated by behavioral anticipation, and how *purpose*, behavior that appears motivated to take account of future events, can be explained by the response-sequence concept. He states, in brief, that a series of environmental events can elicit a series of responses, and the series of responses can become learned as a chain. Later, the response chain can occur without the elicitation of the original environmental events. Without referring to it, Hull uses as the explanation the mechanism of internal stimulation also espoused in Watson's statement.

> Now a high-grade organism possesses internal receptors which are stimulated by its own movements. Accordingly each response (R) produces at once a characteristic stimulus complex and stimuli thus originated make up to a large extent the internal component of the organism's stimuli complexes [that can come to elicit a following response].
>
> [T]he organismic reactions (R's) which at the outset were joined only by virtue of the energies operating in the outer world sequence of S's [stimuli], are now possessed of a genuine dynamic relationship lying within the organism itself. The newly acquired excitatory tendencies [learning] . . . should continue the organismic sequence of responses very much as when they were first called forth as the result of the stimulation by the world sequence. . . . The imprint has been made in such a way that a functional parallel of this action segment of the physical world has become a part of the organism (Hull 1930, pp. 512–13).

Although the language is different, the basic principles are the same as in the preceding two accounts. Skinner later develops the same concept as a central element of his learning theory, without reference to any of the preceding accounts, and with a change of terminology.

> The LAW OF CHAINING. *The response of one reflex may constitute or produce the eliciting or discriminative stimulus of another.* The stimuli may be proprioceptive [kinesthetic] (as in the serial reaction of throwing a ball) or produced externally by a change in the position of receptors (as when the organism looks to the right and then responds to a resulting visual stimulus or reaches out and then seizes the object which touches its hand) (Skinner 1938, p. 32).

Serial Verbal Learning and Intraverbals

The examples employed thus far have involved relatively basic principles in the several learning theories treated. A few additional examples will be given that indicate that uncited overlap occurs also in extensions of the basic principles to the consideration of more complex behavioral events.

The first additional case to be considered is that involving paired associate and serial learning, Skinner's concept of intraverbals in language, and Watson's earlier analysis. As has already been indicated herein, there has been a long and varied study of the manner in which humans learn sequences of *word* responses. Watson's analysis may be summarized in his own words.

> It is clear now that word habits are built up like manual habits. You will recall . . . that once a series of responses (manual habits) is organized around a series of objects, we can run through the whole series of responses without having the original series of objects present [this is the same concept as in Hull's later account of knowledge and purpose]. . . .
>
> Now exactly the same thing happens in word behavior. Suppose you read from your little book (your mother usually sets an auditory pattern), "Now — I — lay — me — down — to — sleep." The sight of "now" brings the saying of "now" (response 1), the sight of "I," response of saying "I" (response 2) and so on throughout the series. Soon the mere saying of "now" becomes the motor (kinaesthetic) stimulus for saying "I." This explains why we can shut off the world of stimuli and talk glibly about sights and sounds in distant places or about things that happened years ago (Watson 1930, p. 235).

The analysis of Skinner that is relevant here is that of intraverbal behavior, part of his analysis of language.

[Let us take] the case when the response *four* is made to the verbal stimulus *two plus two*, or *to the flag* to *I pledge allegiance*, or *Paris* to *the capital of France*, or *ten sixty-six* to *William the Conqueror*. We may call behavior controlled by such stimuli intraverbal. . . .

Many intraverbal responses are relatively trivial. . . . More important examples are found in the determination of grammatical and syntactical sequences. . . . When a long poem is recited, we can often account for the greater part of it only by supposing that one part controls another in the intraverbal manner. . . .

One effect of this extensive conditioning of intraverbal operants is the train of responses generated in "free association" — or, as we say in the case of a train very different from our own, a "flight of ideas." One verbal response supplies the stimulus for another in a long series (Skinner 1957, pp. 71–73).

It is interesting to note the differences in terminology as well as the fact that neither Watson nor Skinner makes reference to the extensive work done in the area of rote verbal learning. This work provides the experimental specification of how verbal responses are learned in series. By the time Skinner wrote his analysis there were many experimental results in this area that could have been drawn upon — but it would have meant referring to experiments employing a methodology he did not accept.

Concept Formation and Abstraction

The next example refers to a behavioristic theory of concepts, that is, the manner in which the individual comes to respond in the same way to different stimulus objects or events that have some common feature, suggesting that the individual abstracts that common feature. The theory of concepts was a concern early in the history of psychology, and Hull was the first to provide a behavioristic analysis of what is involved, publishing a lengthy monograph on the subject (Hull 1920). This monograph included the innovation of procedures and materials for experimentation as well as experiments to specify the principles involved. The following outlines in common sense terms Hull's conception.

[T]his is believed to be the method by which the great majority of actual concepts are evolved. . . . A young child finds himself in a certain situation, reacts to it by approach say, and hears it called "dog." After an indeterminate intervening period he finds himself in a somewhat different situation, and hears that called "dog." Later he finds himself in a somewhat different situation still, and hears that called "dog" also. Thus the process continues. The "dog" experiences appear at irregular intervals. . . . Meantime the intervals between the "dog" experiences are filled with all sorts of other absorbing experiences which are contributing to the formation of other concepts. At length the time arrives when the child has a "meaning" for the word dog. Upon examination this meaning is found to be actually a characteristic more or less common to all dogs and not common to cats, dolls and "teddy-bears" (Hull, 1920, pp. 5–6).

Hull proceeded then to experimentally demonstrate the learning process. He employed classes of Chinese characters as the stimuli — each stimulus of a class being different but containing a common, embedded element. The subject had to learn to apply the correct name to all stimuli with the same common element, across the different classes. When the subject had learned to respond to the common element he would correctly name instances of a new character that contained the imbedded element. Hull made the analysis in the context of learning through reward (reinforcement). He also emphasized the importance of language in concept formation, and he further analyzed the process of abstraction or concept formation in more elementary terms. Centrally, Hull indicated that the process of learning involved the presentation of trials that enabled the concept naming response to be associated with (under the control of) the common stimulus element which was embedded in the Chinese character. At the same time "incorrect" associations that would be learned to the other, noncommon elements had to be unlearned (extinguished). That is, a stimulus object involves a host of stimulus characteristics. When the child is told the concept name he learns it to all of the noncommon characteristics as well as to the common-characteristic that constitutes the concept stimulus. The process of concept formation involves additional trials that maintain the concept response to the common-characteristic of the set of objects that will be experienced, while the child learns *not* to respond to the nonessential and incorrect characteristics. Skinner later elaborates the same theoretical analysis as follows.

Behavior may be brought under the control of a single property or a special combination of properties of a stimulus while being freed from the control of all other properties. The characteristic result is known as abstraction. The relation to discrimination may be shown by an example. By reinforcing responses to a circular red spot while extinguishing responses to circular spots of all other colors, we may give the red spot exclusive control over the behavior. This is discrimination. Since spots of other colors apparently have no effect, it would appear that the other dimensions which they possess — for example, size, shape, and location — are unimportant. But this is not quite true, since it is less likely that the response will be made to a red object of another size and shape. We have, in other words, brought the response under the control of circular red spots but not of the "property of redness" alone. To achieve the latter, we must reinforce responses to many objects, all of which are red, but which differ widely in their other properties. Eventually, the organism responds only to the property of redness. The case is exemplified by the verbal response "red" (Skinner 1953, pp. 134–35).

Hull had previously made a more detailed analysis of concept formation or abstraction in terms of the learning involved. He had conducted experimentation that demonstrated the learning principles involved, methods that had potential for the further conduct of experimentation. Skinner had added additional specifications and references to language that were productive. Notwithstanding the commonality of the two theories, the separatism of the methodology of psychology led to two separate, independent bodies of knowledge. The same principles and processes were called concepts by Hull and abstractions by Skinner. This commonality was never cross referenced. The science never recognized, apparently, that there was really only one conceptual framework for the science, rather than two, and that separatism was involved.

Images

Sense perception has been one of the classic areas of concern in psychology, and the concept of images has appeared as prominent in this study. Behavioristic types of analyses of images began to emerge in the experimental literature in the early 1940s and it is interesting to consider the concept in the present context. As the originator, Leuba (1940) conducted an experiment where, using hypnotized subjects, he paired a neutral stimulus (a buzzer) with a sensory stimulus (a pinprick), in a classical conditioning procedure. Later when the subject was brought out of the hypnotized state, the presentation of the buzzer elicited an image of the pinprick, the sensation of a slight tingling at the former point of contact. Leuba found a similar process with visual and olfactory images. Leuba described the formation of images in very straightforward terms as classical conditioning.

> The experiments described in this paper were designed to discover whether sensations could be conditioned to objective stimuli in the same automatic, mechanical, and unconscious fashion that objective responses have been conditioned in numerous experiments since Pavlov's classic ones almost a half century ago (Leuba 1940, p. 345).

> Our experiments indicate that after an inadequate stimulus has been present a number of times, while an individual is experiencing certain sensations, it will by itself automatically, and without the intervention of any conscious processes, produce those sensations. An image can, therefore, be considered as a conditioned sensation (Leuba 1940, p. 351).

It is relevant in this context to compare Leuba's work and theoretical analysis with that of Skinner (1953). Rather than the terms conditioned sensations or images, Skinner uses the label of conditioned seeing.

A man may see or hear "stimuli which are not present" on the pattern of the conditioned reflex: he may see X, not only when X is present, but when any stimulus which has frequently accompanied X is present. The dinner bell not only makes our mouth water, it makes us see food. In the Pavlovian formula we simply substitute "seeing food" for salivating. Originally both of these responses were made to food, but through a process of conditioning they are eventually made in response to the bell (Skinner 1953, p. 266).

Again, the two theories of images are the same in principle. Leuba (1940) provided the earlier analysis, along with experimental data that verify the analysis and suggest other experiments. Skinner employed the principles in a new context, without citing the prior theory or experimental findings. Thus the two bodies of knowledge were separated, with no cross referencing that would aid in unification. For the science they remained separate bodies of knowledge. Since Leuba and others (Ellson 1941, for example) provided experimental evidence and methodological possibilities for research, the absence of citation meant that Skinner's followers did not have access to potentially important materials by which to stimulate additional experimentation.

With respect to the era that has been described, the methodology of separatism has, perhaps, been epitomized in the following excerpt, in the personalized manner that will be quoted, although the present analysis has no evidence that the case was unusual in the context of the competitions of the second-generation behaviorists. The following is written in review of B. F. Skinner's autobiography, part two.

Skinner describes in detail the various recognitions he received in those early years from more established workers in his area. But their work and their ideas are not described, nor are they related to his own efforts. Students of Skinner's 1938 book are aware that he was at that time on top of all the relevant literature, but here, it appears, nothing that anyone else was doing was relevant. . . .

Most scholars delight in a meeting of minds, but not Skinner. The historically inclined reader is going to be distressed that Skinner is so reluctant to acknowledge the existence of kindred souls. Indeed, he goes to some pains to prove the insularity of his work and his ideas. There was Tolman, who once taught at Harvard when Skinner was there and who had already arrived at a nonphysiological behaviorism. All we learn about Tolman was that he stole an idea (a trivial notation, actually) without acknowledgment. The really important ideas that Tolman and Skinner shared are lost in the petulant account of the theft. Then there was Skinner's colleague at Indiana, J. R. Kantor, who is treated cordially enough but very briefly. Are we really supposed to believe that Skinner learned nothing or gained nothing from this man who shared so many of his views about a purely behavioral behaviorism?

The depth of Skinner's "I did it all by myself" attitude is revealed . . . (Bolles 1979, p. 1073).

Whether Skinner's practices of citing others and recognizing their contributions were different from those employed by his contemporaries is an open question. Many other examples could be taken from the first and second generation of learning theories (or behaviorism) to demonstrate the practices of separatism that were involved. The present analysis is meant to pertain to all the classic learning theories. The cases cited, and the many more that exist, may be taken to reflect the generally accepted methodology of theory construction involved and that still exists. The principles and concepts of one theory were not related to like elements in other theories. Moreover, each theory constructed its own language in a manner that distinguished it and made commonality difficult to see. The present investigation reveals no attempt at organization and unification, but only to separate and make independent. It should be noted that learning theory has been taken by many as the model of scientific theory construction in psychology, so the practices of its theorists must have been influential in psychology in affecting the methodology of citation in psychology generally. As will be indicated further on, the several learning theories, as a consequence of their separatistic practices, were not considered to constitute an integrated body of knowledge. The theories were considered to be independent and so different that they were antagonistic. In fact a great deal of time, effort, and scientific publication was devoted to crucial experiments that were aimed to "defeat" one theory and to "prove" the other. This theory competition, characteristic of preparadigmatic science, occurred even though the various theories were actually very similar except for a few areas of dispute. This was not seen, it is suggested, in large part because of the practices of separatism and the preparadigmatic state of the science generally. As a result a generation of researchers essentially wasted their efforts trying to defeat "opposing" theories, while largely remaining in ignorance of those theories. They were unable to use potentially productive methods, apparatus, and concepts associated with the other theories.

The New, "Social" Behaviorisms

Let us leave the first and second generations of behaviorism and advance to contemporary practices in psychology. In the present view the practices and philosophy of separatism continue to be widespread in our field — perhaps more so than in the previous period, as will be described. An example will be given that describes a new, parallel development that is occurring in several of the different, modern behavioristic (or learning) theories. The example will consist of five quotations. The reader may note the high degree of commonality that occurs among the different analyses. Yet the cross referencing is poor, in some cases there is no citation of central, earlier conceptions. There is no concern with priority. Rather, the same principles and concepts are advanced in the cause of independent theories that are considered to be different. The first excerpt is from a theory called the behavioral interaction approach, a part of social behaviorism.

[1] One of the major, unresolved schisms in psychology has separated learning theory (behavior modification or behavioristic) approaches from the personality oriented (psychodynamic, cognitive, developmental . . .) approaches. Until this time the major modern conceptions of human behavior have been those of the latter type that consider the primary determinants of human behavior to reside within the individual. Psychoanalytic theory, for example, has inferred inner needs and personality processes and structures to account for human behavior. . . . Other theorists have inferred inner processes such as the self, self-concept, perceptual field, cognitive states, personality traits, and so on to account for human behavior.

In contrast, a primary characteristic of behavioristic approaches has been to look for the determinants of human behavior in the directly observable principles of learning and in presently acting environmental conditions. This has meant an overt or implied rejection of the various concepts of inner determination of the personality theorists. . . .

The present resolution of the behaviorist versus personality theory schism involves various points (Staats 1971a, p. 6).

In the present case, a central point of the approach has been to resolve the conflict of determinism that haunts psychology as well as other social and behavioral sciences. . . . This basic schism can be resolved by realizing that what the individual is at the beginning depends upon what has happened to him. But what he *is* then determines what will happen to him, and therefore what he will further become. The individual's behavior is determined. But his behavior determines what he becomes. The interaction even at an early point becomes so involved, and continues in such a complex, cyclical and reoccurring way, that in a very real sense there is self-determination [and through personality and subjective states of experience] (Staats 1971a, pp. 335–36).

A general conception of human behavior, according to this theory, must thus show how human behavior is caused by the conditions the individual experiences, but at the same time also indicate how the "nature" of the individual contributes to his behavior (Staats 1971a, p. 253). The second excerpt is from social learning theory.

[2] Many theories have been proposed over the years to explain human behavior. Until recently, some theorists held that motivational forces in the form of needs, drives, and impulses, frequently operating below the level of consciousness, were the major determinants. Since the proponents of this school of thought consider the principal causes of behavior to be forces within the individual, that is where they look for the explanations of why people behave as they do. . . . In the social learning view, people are neither driven by inner forces nor buffeted by environmental stimuli. Rather, psychological functioning is explained in terms of . . . personal and environmental determinants (Bandura 1977, pp. 2–11).

Explanations of human behavior have generally been couched in terms of a limited set of determinants. . . . Exponents of environmental determinism study and theorize about how behavior is controlled by situational influences. Those favoring personal determinism seek the causes of human behavior in dispositional sources in the form of instincts, drives, traits, and other motivational forces within the individual (Bandura 1978, p. 344).

Behavioristic theories addressed themselves to performance but deemphasized internal determinants, whereas the cognitive approaches remain immersed in thought but divorced from conduct. . . . Social learning includes within its framework both the processes internal to the organism as well as performance-related determinants (Bandura 1974, p. 865).

The third excerpt is from the approach that has been called interactional psychology.

[3] *Trait and psychodynamic models.* The trait model and the psychodynamic model propose that actual behavior is primarily determined by latent, stable dispositions. Both assume that the sources for the initiation and direction of behavior come primarily from within the organism. . . .
Situationism. The situational model assumes that the sources for the initiation and direction of behavior come primarily from factors external to the organism. Stimuli are the prime determinants of behavioral variance. . . .
Interactionism. The interactional model assumes that the sources for the initiation and direction of behavior come primarily from . . . the person and the situations that he or she encounters (Endler and Magnusson 1976, p. 960).

To help indicate the nature of the conceptual development involved, it is relevant to indicate that the form situationism was coined to describe the behavioral modification approach as presented by Mischel (1968), which was actually a systematic statement of a radical behavioristic view. The excerpt presented below represents a change in view in the new direction of rapprochement, taken from Mischel's article entitled "Toward a cognitive social learning reconceptualization of personality." The revised theory is called the cognitive social learning approach.

[4] The study of persons may be construed alternatively from three complementary perspectives. Construed from the viewpoint of the psychologist seeking procedures or operations necessary to produce changes in performance, it may be most useful to focus on the environmental *conditions* necessary to modify the subject's behavior. . . . Construed from the viewpoint of the theorist concerned with how these operations produce their effects in the subject who undergoes them, it may be more useful to speak of . . . *person variables* that mediate the effects of conditions upon behavior. Construed from the viewpoint of the experiencing subject, it may be more useful to speak of the same events in terms of their phenomenological impact as thoughts, feelings, wishes, and other subjective (but communicable) internal states of experience. . . . Ultimately, conceptualizations of the field of personality will have to be large enough to encompass the phenomena seen from all three perspectives. The present cognitive social learning approach to persons hopefully is a step in that direction (Mischel 1973, p. 279).

We can see the framework of concepts in yet another theoretical effort, called cognitive learning, one that is directed toward the consideration of psychotherapy.

[5] Clinical psychologists appear to be assimilating two formerly divergent approaches to psychotherapy — the one emphasizing behavioral techniques and the other focusing on cognitive and affective intrapersonal processes. This contemporary integration represents an intriguing interface between two very distinct psychological traditions. The first might be called "internalism". . . . The core assumption of internalism is that the critical determinants of human behavior lie *within* the individual. . . .

It was in the mid-1960s that applied clinical behavior therapy really became established as a serious competitor to traditional intrapersonal therapies. And — at least from first appearances — two competitors could hardly be more incompatible. Their most fundamental assumptions seemed to encourage antagonism and bitter dispute. . . . The one emphasized internal determinism — feelings, memories, psychic energies, and the mysterious workings of poorly understood mechanisms that could only be imperfectly observed by the therapist. The behavioral perspective, on the other hand, emphasized external determinism — stimuli, responses, and contingencies that were clearly articulated in a mechanistic input-output analysis of human behavior. The bitterness of their rivalry was often intense. . . .

[W]e see the emergence of a potential for complementarity between behavioral and traditional perspectives—each bringing its unique strengths and undeniable weaknesses to the courtship. . . . On the other hand, this hybrid recognizes the important role of private events and intrapersonal factors in adjustment, and on the other, it emphasizes the role of environmental variables in influencing personal phenomenology and performance. . . .

For the sake of exposition, I shall refer to this ideological hybrid as a cognitive-learning perspective (italics added) (Mahoney 1977, pp. 5–7).

In these examples we see the same principles and concepts expressed as important parts of five different theories: behavioral interaction (social behaviorism), social learning theory, interactional psychology, cognitive social learning, and cognitive-learning. There is not an adequate indication across these theories concerning the commonality and overlap among them, an indication that would allow the science to collapse the different theories into one, at least with reference to the commonality. Bandura (1979), it may be noted, has stated explicitly that two of the theories involved are distinctly different from each other, in just the concepts presented in the above quotations. It should be noted that the conception involved in this example is considered to be an important, new development that represents a novel direction in the field.

This thus represents a contemporary case of separatism, involving multiple, independent theoretical statements. These cases have only been presented as examples, a sparse sampling. They could be multiplied almost without limit, since there is great lack of cross-referencing of modern learning theories. A very extensive verification of major uncited overlap in central common elements of current antagonistic theories is available in recent papers (Staats 1978b, 1980a).

Societal Adaptation

It is beyond the scope of the present account to extensively document the occurrence of separatism in the various preparadigmatic sciences. The present conception would hypothesize that the same characteristics would be shown in the other preparadigmatic sciences as those that characterize psychology. One brief example that appears to be explicit will be cited, as indicated in the following excerpt.

The four levels of [theoretical] structure postulated and the discussions of flows of energy and control among them are strikingly similar to what the sociologist Talcott Parsons and his interdisciplinary collaborators at Harvard—among them the sociologist Edward Shils, the anthropologist Clyde Kluckhohn, and the psychologists Henry Murray and Gordon Allport—formulated as "the functionalist paradigm" almost 30 years ago in such works as *Toward a General Theory of Action*. The functionalists are not cited, and indeed Laughlin and Brady's approach to the problem of the adaptive process is independent of and different from it in a number of important theoretical respects. Yet there are . . . crucial reasons for wishing that Laughlin and Brady had paid far more attention to avoiding the pitfalls of the Parsonian model.

One of these is stylistic: Laughlin and Brady have unwittingly reinvented the painful prose style of the functionalists . . . (Howell 1979, pp. 1235–36).

While one example cannot be employed with which to characterize the social sciences other than psychology, the above does illustrate that separatism through noncitation does occur in other preparadigmatic fields than psychology. Moreover, the above author's response to the case of separatism contains interesting points that will be addressed further on.

SEPARATISM: AN ASPECT OF THE METHODOLOGY OF THEORY CONSTRUCTION

The sociologists of science have provided us with the historical examples of noncitation and nonreference. These have been considered to be cases of individual, deviant behavior within science, and have been labeled in some cases as stealing. It should be emphasized that the present view considers both the historical cases and the cases that have been described herein differently than they have been considered in the sociology of science (Merton 1973). Let me explain.

The standards and philosophy that the sociologists of science have used in their interpretation of deviant behavior in science have been the standards and philosophy of modern paradigmatic science. Because of the unity of paradigmatic sciences and the integrated nature of the work that is done in those sciences they have evolved a set of standards and a philosophy concerning the nature of science. The standards and philosophy prescribe strict practices of citation and recognition of priority, as has been indicated.

It should be noted, however, that these standards and philosophy did not always exist. They did not pertain when the present paradigmatic sciences were in their infant paradigmatic or earlier preparadigmatic states. At that time what are now called deviant behaviors in scientists were not the exception, they were the rule. Scientists in the early days of the development of the presently paradigmatic sciences clearly recognized the rules, or lack of rules, that pertained in their sciences. They recognized them and they guided their behavior accordingly. That is, knowing there was an absence of citation rules, they used various devices to guard against the unacknowledged use of their ideas by others, one example being the use of anagrams with which to announce a finding. Such practices reveal the standards and philosophy that must have been functioning when those sciences were still preparadigmatic. Such methods would not have been devised and laboriously used unless they were necessary for the protection of intellectual property.

Today a scientist who published his innovation in anagram form would be ridiculed. It would be ludicrous because paradigmatic science has arrived at standards that make the noncitation of others' work unacceptable and has set up procedures and facilities for fixing the source of the discovery or innovation. The fact that there is unity in a science also makes it easier to recognize when materials have commonality and thus easier to see when a similar innovation has been put forth at a later time, a prime deterrent for such actions. Recognition of similarity is not easily provided when knowledge is diverse and there are many different theory languages involved. Scientists of one approach or school might not even know of or understand the knowledge base of the other. Finally, what constitutes an innovative element is more clear in the paradigmatic sciences.

The important point to note in the present context, however, is that practices must have changed in the presently paradigmatic sciences as they moved from the preparadigmatic to paradigmatic state. Moreover, the standards and the philosophy concerning the nature of science with respect to related matters must also have changed. What is considered deviant today, from the perspective of contemporary paradigmatic science, would not have been considered deviant at some time in the past, from the perspective of preparadigmatic science. Although the sociologists of science use the terminology of abnormal psychology in describing deviant behavior in science, it should be noted that deviant behavior is usually defined by the customs of the community. A behavior that is deviant in one society is normal and accepted in another society — as is recognized generally in sociology as well as in abnormal psychology. When behaviors are widely practiced and accepted in a society they are by definition not deviant.

Let us employ another example here. Kuhn has said that "Being able to take no common body of belief for granted, each writer in physical optics felt forced to build his field anew from its foundation" (Kuhn 1962, pp. 12–13). This is a perfect capsule description of the separatism of the preparadigmatic science. However, it is not that the writer is forced to build his field anew from its foundation, it is that the separatism of the preparadigmatic science instructs him to do so. It is not that there is nothing that exists in the preparadigmatic science for the later theorist to use. Rather it is the custom not to cite and recognize others' findings, concepts, analyses, or methods. It is the custom to develop one's own terminology for describing these things. Thus, it appears that each theorist is building his field anew from its foundation. That was why the learning theories of the first and second generations of behaviorism were considered to be different and independent from each other. Each theorist was not forced to build his theory anew from its foundation. Actually he did not; each theory was built on knowledge that was common to the field. It only appeared that each theorist had built an independent theory, anew. As has already been indicated there was actually great similarity among the theories, similarity that went unrecognized because of practices of separatism.

How can we evaluate the practices of separatism in terms of these considerations? Is the behavior in the cases that have just been described in psychology to be considered deviant? One of the purposes of the present chapter has been to answer that question in the negative, for the most part. That is, the chapter has attempted to show in summary form that the practices of separatism are widespread and general to the preparadigmatic science. The usual practices of separatism are not examples of personal deviance within a society that considers such behaviors deviant. It is very clear that the psychology society has not considered the cases to be deviant and in fact has not been concerned in any way nor recognized that the practices involved represent a deviation from the rules of paradigmatic science.

Only in extreme cases, where noncitation is systematically and extensively followed for self-serving purposes, and where profound and extensive materials are involved, can separatism be considered a deviation in the preparadigmatic science. Some of the famous cases in the sociology of science (Biot, Laplace, and Cauchy, for example) were deviations in this sense, at this time, with current standards, if not within the mores of the scientific community of that time. But separatism generally must have been the rule in those days, and the less profound everyday cases were not deviations, they were usual. The same would be true for contemporary preparadigmatic sciences; but to say that usual cases of separatism are not deviant should not be taken as a recommendation for the methodology. As will be indicated, the present position is quite the opposite of this, since separatism in any degree is a detrimental characteristic of science.

The Ambiguity of Preparadigmatic Science

The analysis does not end here, however, because the preparadigmatic sciences of today are actually faced with two "societies." That is, today there is the preparadigmatic science itself, with its practices, its standards, and its philosophy. These constitute a set of criteria against which to judge deviance, as has been indicated. However, in addition there are the practices, standards, and philosophy of the paradigmatic sciences. These also provide a backdrop for the scientist in the preparadigmatic science. It has been said herein that these two sets of criteria are different. The preparadigmatic scientist is thus in an ambiguous situation. The criteria he obtains as a general member of the larger scientific community are of one type. The criteria he obtains from his actual working experience as a scientist in a particular preparadigmatic field may provide him with an opposing set of criteria.

How does the preparadigmatic scientist function in this situation of ambiguity and ambivalence? My preliminary consideration suggests that this is done by having one set of criteria on an explicit level, and the other set of criteria on an implicit level. Ordinarily, the philosophy and standards of separatism will not be made explicit. Although the scientist may operate according to these criteria, he would not ordinarily explicize what they are because the criteria do not agree with those of the broader field of science. For example, such a scientist might, as an editor, see a principle, similar to one previously presented in another theory, without any reference to the earlier work. As an editor the preparadigmatic scientist might accept this practice, on the basis of his implicit standards and philosophy of separatism. On the other hand, the same scientist would be aware of the demands of scientific standards for citation of priority. Asked about his standards regarding citation he might in the abstract situation very well voice the standards of a paradigmatic science.

If that is the case, how are these implicit standards and the philosophy that supports them to be isolated and made explicit? It would not be possible, for example, to simply ask a scientist in a preparadigmatic science whether he thought it necessary to cite prior innovations when publishing scientific work. He would say it was necessary because he knows the standards of general science. He would say also that changing terminology, changing the particular research that is referred to, would not justify introducing as original conceptual materials that which was previously innovated by someone else. He would say that the practices of citation have to record priority of innovation. But in practice the scientist behaves quite differently, as the preceding examples have indicated, and as the following section will demonstrate on the philosophy level.

MAKING THE PHILOSOPHY OF SEPARATISM EXPLICIT

It has been suggested that to get at the implicit standards and philosophy of separatism it is necessary that the investigator tap into the actual, functional, implicit standards and philosophy of the preparadigmatic scientist without activating the paradigmatic standards and philosophy the scientist would ordinarily employ on a verbal level. Serendipitously the present author has tapped into the standards and philosophy of separatism in actual dealings with psychologists, but not in soliciting opinions. The circumstances that have, it is suggested, elicited the actual standards and philosophy have been direct. That is, the procedures involved have not asked the individual what his standards and philosophy of citation are. The individual first has been called upon to make decisions that depend upon a set of standards and philosophy, and then to defend those decisions. The sample is not large. But the situations are of real life. And the individuals have been involved in making actual decisions (mostly editorial decisions with respect to article publication), not the indirect measures of simulations, or verbal responses to questionnaire items. Moreover, the individuals involved are those in the position of influence in the science, individuals expected to know and promulgate the characteristics of their science.

Recognition and Treatment of Separatism in Preparadigmatic Science

The statement of the anonymous editorial reviewer of the previously described Byrne case makes explicit important parts of the philosophy of separatism, which are very different from corresponding standards and general philosophy of paradigmatic science. This case, however, only involved a common neglect of citation in terms of the standards of the paradigmatic science, and only two statements (Byrne's and a reviewer's) concerning the methodology of citations and referencing. It would be important to ascertain whether the philosophy involved was more general. It would also be important to know whether the standards and practices of separatism provide a foundation for works in psychology that neglect the standards of citation sufficiently to be considered deviant in the natural sciences. This section will describe such a case, a case that systematic study demonstrates to be of that type (Staats 1978b, 1980b). In the present context, it is not the substance of the case itself that is centrally pertinent, however, but rather that which the case indicates about the nature of the science. Presentation of the manner in which the deviant theory overlapped with conceptual materials from other theories would require a great deal of space that would be unsuitable here. But the manner in which the case was treated and the statements of philosophy that the case elicited from the prominent scientists called upon to review it, illustrate clearly the characteristics of the preparadigmatic science.

Although the deviant theory appeared to have uncited overlap with various theories, the present author traced the uncited overlap with one particular theory. This involved composition of a lengthy documentary paper that presented matched quotations from the prior theory and the deviant theory. (This documentation included some 50 pairs of quotations, each pair of which compared the two theories on central concepts and principles (see Staats 1978b.) The quotations appeared to demonstrate extensive conceptual overlap between the two theories, in central conceptual elements considered very significant by the science. Yet there was no reference to indicate this overlap — to indicate where the conceptual elements had originated. In many cases the wording involved in the paired quotations was astonishingly close. This paper of documentation was sent to a psychology journal to be reviewed, not for publication itself, because it was too long, but as the basis for a shorter paper that would deal with the topic of separatism, using the two overlapping theories as the example. It should be noted that the other theory in this case was the present author's; thus the reviewers were wary in their judgments concerning the claims of overlap since self-interest might be a distorting element in the case. Again it is not the purpose of the following presentation to describe the case of uncited overlap in the two theories, in the process of establishing the existence in psychology of a major example of deviant practice. That is a separate issue. (Readers interested in the specifics of this priority issue may consult the following papers: Staats 1978b, 1979, 1980b.) Rather, the important matter here is the response of the members of the science to this case, since that is revealing of the philosophy of separatism that exists in the science.

One reviewer, in addressing the evidence of extensive overlap between the two theories treated in the paper, said that the "two theories bear some marked similarities." Yet the reviewer's first impulse was to deny publication of the matter. He stated that "Written 30 years hence, Staats' paper might be welcomed in journals of the history of psychology as an important contribution." Yet he also felt the issue to be too touchy for contemporary treatment and he wished to spare the two theories unflattering exposure. That the philosophy of separatism played a role in his decision-making processes can be seen in his statement, as follows, with X standing for the name of the criticized theorist and Z for the name of his theory.

> I would not disagree, however, that ____[X]____ often shows a notable tendency to incorporate ideas from elsewhere and leave consumers with the impression that these ideas have sprung from the festile fountainhead of his ___[Z]___ theory. Students from the West Coast brand of ___[Z]___ theory often display a notable unawareness of the theory's similarities with other approaches. They seem to discover the wheel with some regularity. But, having said this, I do not feel that things can be set straight or justice served by articles such as the present one.

This reviewer thus has recognized that there are two theories that are markedly similar in some important characteristics without appropriate citation. He considers the matter to be important enough such that when looked at in historical perspective it will be considered to be significant. The reviewer also recognizes that one of the theories under consideration has a general characteristic of "incorporating ideas" and treating them as though the ideas were original to the theory. The characteristic is not limited to the overlap with only one other theory. This appears to be a case like that of some of the early cases described by the sociologists of science — for example, the case already described of Laplace, which involved systematic use of others' ideas without citation.

The statement of the reviewer reveals also that he has recognized in the specific case that the standards — standards not in accord with those of paradigmatic science — were involved in the training of young scientists. That is, he is of the opinion that students within that particular theory are not trained appropriately as to the source of the ideas they learn. And they themselves do not cite others' work, but continue to "discover the wheel." They are thus not trained in the scholarly traditions of paradigmatic science and in the methodology of citation and recognition of priority that is assumed by paradigmatic science.

Very central, for the present concerns, however, is what the statement reveals about the philosophy of the reviewer. The editorial reviewer indicates in his statement that he does not think the matter should be published, at least not in a contemporary period. Actually, as he continued to consider the documentation in the paper he was reviewing, and to think about the matter, he finally agreed that the matter should be published. But his statements reveal his reluctance to publicly consider the matter. That reluctance indicates an acceptance of the practices of separatism. One of the characteristics of separatism that is accepted in this reviewer's statement, albeit with misgivings, is that of training students in a particular school or theory in such a manner that they do not know about the relevant contributions of other scientists.

The second reviewer also considered there to be lack of indication of the source of the ideas expressed in the theory that was criticized. The reviewer, simply on the basis of the documentation of uncited overlap, however, did not feel that the issue should be published. The way in which this second reviewer dealt with the problem of citation is interesting. Again the theorist previously referred to as not citing other's work will be referred to as X, and his theory as Z.

> While not without some value as a "revisionist history" of the development of ___[Z]___ theory, I would evaluate the present manuscript, whatever its ultimate length, as inappropriate for publication in the [present journal]. . . . What would be acceptable in my opinion is a paper which (a) lays out the basic properties of a ___[Z]___ approach and (b) traces the historical roots of each of the major concepts. . . . I do believe there would be great merit in someone writing a thorough *Psychological Bulletin* type paper tracing all the roots of ___[Z]___ theory. We

do need to know the intellectual foundations of our current ideas. My own suspicion is that that goes back much further than any of us is willing or able to acknowledge (e.g., to Adler, Sullivan, Tolman, Kantor, etc.).

Finally, just to provide some perspective it is now widely known that the basic roots of Schachter's two-factor theory of emotion can be found in Bertrand Russell. This is completely unacknowledged by Schachter. Regardless of its roots Schachter's modern version has stimulated much original research whereas Russell's ideas did not. The same can be said of ____[X]____ as opposed to Staats. Why this is true would also make an interesting paper. My own guess is that ____[X]____ has been emulated more because he has been able to keep one foot in the __[theory 1]__ camp and one foot in the __[theory 2]__ camp while Staats is only identified with the __[theory 2]__ tradition.

This reviewer thus clearly recognizes that the theory being criticized has generally not cited the sources of its ideas. Moreover, he recognizes that this lack of citation includes the theory of Staats. He recognizes also that one theory has priority and the other has not. He appears to recognize that there is a problem. But he wants to resolve the problem without a priority issue being raised. That is, he feels that a paper should be written to explicate the roots of the second theory, a paper with an historical rather than confrontational character. Finally, the reviewer adds a central point to the present argument. He says, in essence, that the fact that a later theory contains elements of an earlier theory without citing the source of the elements is not so bad. *For one thing the practice is justified if the later theory stimulates research. Centrally, however, he says let us put this into perspective, this occurrence is not unique; there are other cases of well known psychologists that involve the same practices,* and he cites the example. This writer thus makes the practices acceptable because they are described as characteristic of the science. In doing so the philosophy of separatism is explicized and its generality is again indicated.

To continue on with the case history of the publication of the article on separatism, three editorial reviewers evaluated the long documentary paper with respect to the suitability for publication in a shorter paper of the general concept of separatism supported by the evidence of the systematic and extensive overlap of the two theories. One reviewer — who wished the roots of the criticized theory to be traced in a published paper — was opposed to publication of the confrontation depicted in the documentary paper, and recommended instead the historical, roots-type paper. The other two reviewers were in favor of publication of the issue, one of them with some initial hesitation, as has been indicated. The third reviewer said "The discussion that ensues very likely will be acrimonious, but it can have the salutary consequence of a public evaluation. . . . That is a fundamental part of the process of scientific development, and editors have to be wary of substituting for that process their own personal judgment." Based upon the recommendation of two of the three reviewers, the acting editor said that the psychology journal would publish the issue if a suitably written, briefer article was composed that focused on the general points involved in the case of the two theories.

The present author then wrote an article discussing separatism in psychology (said to be due to the preparadigmatic nature of the science), the lack of the usual standards of citation, the importance of the progressive growth of theory in psychology (involving multiple, successsive contributors), and the role of citation practices in such theory developments. The article was illustrated by reference to the two overlapping theories, as well as by some of the reviewers' statements that have been quoted herein that demonstrate the philosophy of separatism. This article was then reviewed by the same three reviewers and unanimously recommended for publication. The editor clearly recognized the controversial nature of the topic but was not deterred from publication. The editor considered the article to be of rather unique importance, sufficient to make it a special issue, that in addition to the article would include four invited commentary articles, plus the rebuttal of Mr. X. Stephen Toulmin, Robert Merton, Reuben Baron, and Robert Woodward accepted invitations to write the four commentary articles.

At this time the author of the criticized theory was informed of the separation article and the plans for publication, and was invited to write a rebuttal. He responded with a letter to the editor opposing publication on the grounds that the procedure that had been followed was not proper. He said that he should have sent the accusatory document *before* reviewers made their judgments, that legal due process allows the accused to respond to evidence prior to the verdict, and added that it was "demoralizing to see how easy an accuser could use the official publication of psychology to undermine someone's reputation."

Science, of course, does not have the aims of the court of law. In science the aim is to make everything public, so it can be examined by the members of the science, who are the ultimate arbiters. Science sponsors the opportunity to criticize, it does not stifle criticism. It has various procedures — such as anonymous review of manuscripts and research grants — that are quite different than legal procedures, all aiming to encourage open criticism. The editor's response was in this tradition, that science does not operate as does a court of law — that the criticized scientist does not have the right to prior restraint — citing cases where criticisms were published in science before the party criticized had a chance to respond.

Nevertheless, other pressures mounted, according to an informant with first-hand contact with the editorial staff of the psychology journal. The editors of the journal received written and telephone complaints from certain influential psychologists, including four colleagues in the department of the author of the criticized theory; the four condemned the decision to publish the article on separatism. The pressure on the editors of the journal was described as intense, unprecedented in editorial experience. In the opinion of the communicant involved, it was likely that this pressure would have an influence on the ultimate decision regarding publication.

At this point a new editor took over the editorial responsibility, replacing the previous editor. The new editor ordered a new review procedure, to involve three new reviewers plus the three original reviewers. This was an unusual procedure, supported by the fact that Mr. X had written a rebuttal paper that said that several facts in the separatism article were incorrect, and that actually he did not cite the other theory because his theory was first and different. The reviewers were given the task of examining the separatism article, the documentation article on which it was based, Mr. X's rebuttal, and a paper I wrote in response to indicate that my original depiction of the overlap in the two theories had indeed been accurate. I was opposed to the new evaluation procedure on the grounds that it was unusual, would appear to be a function of organizational influence rather than scientific considerations, and that the final resolution of the controversy could not be decided by the reviewers beforehand — that decision belonging to the science. The reviewers' job was to reassess the original judgment that appropriate justification had been provided for presenting the issue to the science. It should be remembered that a very thorough job had already been done in that respect, involving the examination of the long documentary paper as well as evaluation of the separatism paper itself, with unanimous agreement to publish.

It is central to note, moreover, that the new, unusual procedure of having the issue reviewed again did not overturn the original decision as far as the reviewers were concerned. That is, the three original reviewers, after reading Mr. X's rebuttal paper and my analysis of what he had said (Staats 1980), held to their original opinion that the issue should be published. The *four* new reviewers were split, two in favor of publication and two opposed. (A fourth new reviewer had been added to the three additional reviewers proposed. The fourth, who may have been the new editor handling the rereview, was opposed to publication.) In any event, even the unusual procedure of selecting new reviewers, by a new editor, did not overturn the support for publication. Two of four of the new reviewers, selected by the editor who was opposed to publication, nevertheless were in favor of publishing the issue. Since all three of the original reviewers, despite the obvious pressures involved, still adhered to their wish to publish, as did the original editor; the final count was five reviewers for publication and two opposed, and the original editor remained in favor of publication. It is noteworthy, moreover, that in rescinding the plans to publish, the new editor did not support the case by denying the validity of the issue that had been raised.

On the contrary, the letter announcing the change in plans to publish agreed with the original evidence of the overlap of the two theories. The editor agreed that Mr. X and his colleagues had not cited the other theory as much as they should have. *There was thus no assertion that the original analysis of separatism concerning the two theories had been in error.* Although the new extraordinary reviewing process had been called to evaluate accuracy, the decision regarding publication was then made on other bases, for example, that the issue was too personally critical and that publication of the issue would not make the editors "proud." The latter reason was similar to the opinion of one of the two new reviewers opposed to publication, who was quoted to the effect that the issue was beneath the dignity of the profession and the journal. Although the present paper had been duly accepted for publication, considered to be of such significance originally that five additional articles on the topic were commissioned, and although it was not possible to show errors in the content of that paper — establishing accuracy having been the reason for the extraordinary additional review — the planned publication was withdrawn. It appeared that the organization involved was not able to publish a controversial priority issue in the face of the pressure, external to the scientific evaluation, to deny publication. These pressure sources included the major figure in the controversy, whose methods were being criticized, as well as his influential supporters. One of the reviewers of the issue, who had favored publication, wrote the following in response to an inquiry from me.

> The real problem for me in the present case is that the decision to exclude your paper cannot be considered an ordinary error of judgment. Rather, it appears to have been an especially egregious error.
>
> The reasons for that judgment are the following: first, because it raises concern about the degree of access to publication that exists for minority or marginal points of view in the major journal of our profession, a journal that should provide open access to all scholarly perspectives; second, it suggests an effort to evade or damp controversy, an effort that reflects a rather conventional orientation about the progress of science and a failure to recognize the thrust that can derive from the clash of opposing positions; third, it carries the *appearance* of having been a response to pressure even though I must accept [the final editor's] convincing rejection of that interpretation; and fourth, it raises the specter that editorial decisions can be shaped in any direction simply by calling up new cadres of reviewers until their decision is the one desired. The latter procedure could well undermine the commitment of reviewers to continue to participate in the review process, and I must say that when my own expenditure of time, thought, and effort in this particular review came to naught for reasons that still seem arbitrary to me, I began to doubt my own future commitment as a reviewer (Richard Jessor, personal communication, August 25, 1980).

One of the reasons the above reviewer was opposed to the final decision to withdraw the previous plan to publish the case of the overlapping theories was that the damping of controversy appeared to be involved. Anything that has this effect upon science is a disadvantage, as the following indicates.

> [In professional social science journals] critical analysis is often shunned, and emphasis is placed on industrious work to extend dominant paradigms. This emphasis reifies a false image of science as removed from discord. The critical, the controversial, the imaginative are not allowed to see the light of day. To the extent that the professional journals do not encourage controversial work, the spirit of science has been diminished (Lindsey 1978, p. 120).

This case was raised in the science to help show in dramatic form the characteristic of psychology that has been called separatism. It was said that the preparadigmatic science has different standards of citation than the paradigmatic science, that theories can occur in the science that heavily overlap in conceptual materials, without this being noted. Superficial differences, a different name for the theory, the utilization of somewhat different evidence to support the theory, and so on, can give the appearance that a totally new, and different, and original theory is involved. This methodology of noncitation can, perhaps, occur to the point of real deviance. This was a central message of the case that has been discussed. The reactions of the members of the science to this case indicate a great deal about the nature of the philosophy of separatism in the preparadigmatic science of psychology. It is important to stress that the case — possibly of large-scale deviance — was not originally noticed by the science, and was actively hidden after the case was revealed, indications of a preparadigmatic science.

ADDITIONAL CONSIDERATIONS OF SEPARATISM

This description of the practices, standards, and philosophy of separatism must be considered to be preliminary, in the same sense that Merton's first discussion of the sociology of science utilized examples of the behavior of scientists that he wished to describe, but his account did not present systematic data of the type that were later obtained (Hagstrom 1965; Gaston 1973; Barber 1976). The present chapter has attempted in this preliminary fashion to provide examples explicating the implicit practices and standards and philosophy of separatism. Several conclusions may be drawn from the materials that have been presented. These conclusions, because of the preliminary nature of the evidence that has been presented, might more appropriately be considered to be hypotheses that demand systematic study. In any event, they suggest the following points that the preceding material appears to illustrate.

Separatism Is a Practice in Psychology

Numerous examples may be pulled from the literature which involve concepts that are basically the same, but which are not related to their theoretical counterparts through citations. As a consequence theories that heavily overlap are considered to be different and independent, sometimes competitive. Ideas very similar to previously originated ideas are presented without citation of the previous sources. There is continuing reinvention in psychology, it appears impossible to avoid; further research is necessary to specify the generality of the practices and some of the other characteristics of separatism. For example, is it the case that similar ideas will be uncited more to the extent to which different fields of psychology are involved, or different theories or schools? These would seem to be likely expectations. Do other psychosocial factors affect the extent to which a prior work will not be cited? For example, does the prestige of the theory or author have an influence, with low status being associated with more errors in citation by others? Also, does the more prestigious in comparison to the less prestigious author tend to cite predecessors less in terms of indicating antecedent sources of major conceptual elements? And are editors less demanding in this respect, of the more prestigious psychologist? Such questions could be answered by systematic investigation of already published articles. The suggestion is that the citation practices of separatism should be subjected to systematic study. Since this is an important aspect of a science's methodology, it should be open to study with the same objectivity extended to other areas of investigation, although at present this does not appear to be the case.

Separatism Is Promulgated in Student Training

The practices of separatism appear, on the basis of this preliminary evidence, to be part of the training of at least some students in psychology. That is, students may be provided with a selective contact with the science of psychology. They may be introduced to certain works in the field and not to others, thereby gaining an incorrect picture of the source of important developments in their field. One can see how such training methods could be employed by theorists to enhance their own influence. The extent to which this occurs in our science should be studied systematically, to ascertain whether there is a bias in what is learned, a bias dictated by the orientation of the faculty with whom the students are closely associated.

It may be added that two reviewers suggested in their statements that

students trained by a scientist who does not follow the standards of paradigmatic science in his citations will themselves do the same. In such cases
the students in the process of graduate training appear to learn the practices and philosophy of separatism. As an important aspect of the methodology of theory construction in a science, it is necessary to consider the manner in which separatism is implicitly taught, as well as the acceptance of
this aspect of separatism. If there are differences in the extent to which the
methods of separatism are taught it would be important to know the conditions that underlie the differences, for example, whether or not the training
is strongly of a "school" orientation.

Separatistic Standards Are Mixed, Unclear

In the process involved in the consideration of the article on separatism for the psychology journal the responses of some of the reviewers indicated there was no clear understanding of how to compare theories in
terms of similarities and differences. Centrally, there was no understanding of how theories should be related to one another by the citation of overlapping elements. The standards for citation of the reviewers were poorly
thought out, not informed, and were in conflict. On the one hand some reviewers of this issue responded with expected standards, that theorists
must cite the conceptual roots of their work. Other reviewers expressed
quite different standards, however. As has been indicated, Byrne suggested
that citation is not necessary between parallel theories if they have arisen
within a like research tradition. Another reviewer echoed and elaborated
this by saying that uncited overlap of theories that are based upon similar
principles is to be expected. He said that since such theories use the same
basic principles "it would be surprising if there were not substantial similarity." One must ask how this standard would fare against the relevant
paradigmatic science standard. There are any number of cases in science
where different scientists have commenced a problem within the same set
of basic principles, but where the first one to reach the innovative solution
is the discoverer. Very strict rules of priority then pertain. Watson's *Double
Helix* (1968) is an account of several competing teams working within similar basic principles on the same problem, with the Nobel prize ultimately
going to the team first innovating the solution. Nowhere in paradigmatic
science is there a standard that says that efforts beginning within the same
set of principles can thereafter discard the priority rules that generally pertain.

On the other hand, one of the authors invited to comment on this issue
says in his first draft, "Social behaviorism has separate roots from [Z-theory].
. . . I do not see why spokesmen for such *divergent positions* owe to each
other or to the practice of normal science to cite each other" (Woodward

1979a, p. 15). It is interesting that these two approaches say exactly the opposite. One says that theories within the same tradition can have uncited similarities. The other says that theories with different roots can have uncited similarities. Together they say that theories *never* have to cite one another when they overlap, because all cases are included — theories arising in the same as well as in different traditions need not cite one another. We can see further the confusion concerning citation standards and the function of citations in the words of one of the two additional reviewers who was against publication of the paper for the psychology journal.

> Staats' piece is based on a giant misunderstanding of the uses of citations, which [this reviewer] believes function only to "muscle one's arguments in favor of one's point of view". . . . One cites to "nail down an argument". If Staats were right, everyone would go crazy, because any idea can be traced to hundreds of historical antecedents. We would all go on trial for failure to cite our forebears.

A similar expression of philosophy was obtained by the present author in conversation with a young but prominent theorist in psychology. I had occasion to ask him why he had not referred to and cited some previous work very closely related to the approach he was espousing. He acknowledged intimate knowledge of the previous work, having used the source as a "bible" in his graduate student days. He justified his lack of citation of that work on the basis that he wanted to start his own theory.

Neither of these statements reveals any understanding of the demands of science that priority of originality is important, that rules regulating acknowledgment of originality are fixed, or that these rules have functional value for science. Moreover, when one examines and considers the literature in psychology in terms of the present context, it can be seen that these are not the expressions of deviant individuals. The science operates in that manner and the above-expressed standards are frank statements of that fact.

One final example will be given to indicate that there has been no clear understanding in psychology of the role of citations in the development of scientific literature. Without such understanding the individual is unlikely to realize what standards of citation should be. Charles Catania has written a paper devoted to the message that citations should refer "not to a person but to a document" (1980, p. 63). He says it is only the researcher's *findings* that are of interest to science, not the researcher. This is based upon Catania's conclusion that "science should not be a matter of personalities" (1980, p. 63). He thus recommends that author's names should not appear in sentences themselves, but only in the parenthesis following the sentence. Catania further states that including the author's name in the sentence itself "encourages questions about which researcher had priority and about who was right and who was wrong" (1980, p. 63). This is not a well-thought out analysis of citation style, or of the standards justifying the style, nor does the analysis make use of relevant knowledge from the literature. As a consequence, Catania in this analysis does not consider the various functions that citations serve. For one thing, a researcher may also have done a number of other works than the specific thing being cited, and name citation in such cases provides an organizational focus for the reader. Similarly, it is functional to the science to establish the reputation of individuals to utilize in evaluating their work in general, not just for the specific finding, as sociologists of science recognize (see Merton 1957). Oddly, moreover, since he is a reinforcement theorist of the Skinnerian school, Catania also neglects to relate his position to the work of the sociologists of science who point out the importance of citations as part of the reward system of science, the sharing of credit for discoveries and contributions. With respect to Catania's rejection of the importance of knowing what scientist has been right and what scientist has been wrong in a particular case, let me say that this is very valuable information and helps us evaluate the scientist's work generally. Let me suggest as an example that it is helpful to know that Catania has written an analysis that has shown ignorance of the sociology of science literature important to his subject matter. This suggests that his approach, his methodology of using relevant literature from other fields, may be generally weak, and that I should keep this in mind when reading other analyses that he may make, as well as analyses made by other psychologists who use the same approach that he does. It is important for the scientific community to establish reputations for the persons of science and for the methods and approaches that these persons espouse, as was indicated by Merton and Ravetz in the preceding chapter.

The major point that I wish to make here, however, is that the methodology of citations has not been considered systematically in psychology, and the purposes and functions of citations in the organization of knowledge are thus not realized. In the present view this is characteristic of pre-paradigmaticism because recognition of the function of citations necessitates understanding of the goal of unity of knowledge in science. Moreover, as will be indicated more fully later, there appears to be a set of standards and a philosophy of science that rationalize the practices of separatism. These preliminary findings suggest that it would be important to compare systematically the standards and philosophy of paradigmatic scientists and preparadigmatic scientists in the present area of concern. The material developed here suggests a difference. In any event, it appears to be quite evident that psychology must develop a systematic set of standards and a philosophy to be used in interrelating the products of its scientific study. There is great uncertainty regarding what is required and why. This confusion leaves open the door for various types of practices, some of which can be expected to affect the science detrimentally, and to be deviant in character.

Sensitivity and the Separatism Taboo

It is suggested that there is in psychology also an ambivalence regarding separatism. On the one hand, psychologists recognize the explicit standards of paradigmatic science with respect to recognition of priority, and citation of origin. But psychologists also are aware that the practices of separatism are general and involve very respected members of the science. The result is conflict and defensivenes which we may see in the words of one reviewer. "We would all go on trial for failure to cite our forebears," if strict standards were applied. In my experience there is an immediate concern with raising the question of cases of noncitation in psychology, because of the anxiety entailed in the issue. This state of affairs amounts to a taboo.

Evidence of the embarrassment involved in bringing cases of separatism into the open can be exemplified. For example, when Howell (1979) in the previously presented quotation refers to the similarity between the Parsons' functionalist paradigm and Laughlin and Brady's approach she is careful to indicate that although the views are "strikingly similar," and there is no citation, that the later account has "unwittingly reinvented" the earlier account. She feels moved to ameliorate the infraction, to ignore the possibility of poor standards in this case.

A similar case has very recently appeared in the psychology literature. Ross Parke (1979) in reviewing Albert Bandura's (1977) book notes a "puzzling" lack of reference to antecedent works. He also indicates that this detracts from the social learning theory approach. But he softens the indictment by stating that Bandura plans a future book in which the lack of citation may be repaired.

Another example is shown by the reviewer already quoted who did not feel that a paper could be published that showed the uncited similarity between two contemporary theories, but rather that a "roots" type of paper could be published that would generally trace the origin of ideas. The focus then would be on historical review, rather than a case of noncitation. This reviewer also "provides perspective" for the cases of separatism with which he had been presented by saying that there are various examples of noncitation in psychology — thereby rationalizing the practices as common and not aberrant, unacceptable. Another reviewer first recognizes the embarrassment associated with questions of separatism practices by indicating that the paper documenting cases of the practices (Staats 1978b) could be published 30 years hence, but by implication not during the lifetime of the theorists involved.

It is important to note that this embarrassment does not appear to occur to the same extent in the paradigmatic sciences, at least that is the hypothesis that is offered. *Science,* in contemporary times, for example, has carried cases of dispute over the sharing of recognition for achievements in the biological sciences (see Marx 1979, p. 341). I would suggest that this is the case because there is less ambivalence about the practices of citation and the importance of recognition in paradigmatic sciences. Paradigmatic scientists more readily accept that originality and priority are goals of scientific effort, and that there are explicit standards involved for insuring equity in these matters, abrogation of which requires rectification. In the preparadigmatic sciences, on the hand, there is general, if implicit, recognition that practices and standards differ from those of paradigmatic sciences, and there is embarrassment about the topic. One of the reasons the psychology journal would not publish the article on separatism was because of the personal element involved — that a prominent member of the science would be criticized for not giving credit to others in his citation practices. In contrast the natural sciences have publicized many such conflicts.

The major point of this section — supported by face-value inspection of scientific publications, but requiring systematic study — is that paradigmatic sciences have strong, formalized standards for indicating origination. In this sense, as sociology has recognized in a general way, the law defines criminality. Thus, when there are strict standards there will be trespassers. This creates disputes concerning origination of science materials. If one looked at the publication count of such disagreements, and took this as the indication of *lack* of standards, one would conclude that the natural sciences are less developed than the social sciences. That is, there are relatively frequently, published disputes over ownership in the natural sciences. There are almost none in psychology. I have never read of any of importance in modern psychology, although there are multitudinal cases of uncited overlaps of scientific knowledge in this science. Moreover, there is evidence, as already indicated, that science media in psychology shy away from publishing such controversy. The present hypothesis recognizes this difference between psychology and the paradigmatic sciences, but the interpretation is reversed. It is suggested (1) that separatism — the nonindication of prior, related science materials — is endemic in psychology, (2) that as a consequence there are no generally accepted citation standards in this science, (3) that raising an issue of disputed origination is, because of the endemic nature of the difficulty, more than a personal dispute, it raises the specter of unacceptable standards for the whole science, (4) that members of the science are thus sensitive about the issue of standards, and (5) that due to these various factors the many cases of inappropriate noncitation are not disputed, disputes of origination are taboo, and they are not likely to be published in the journal media if they do occur. The paradigmatic science, on the other hand, has set standards. As in other spheres there are individuals who abrogate the "law" and when this happens disputes occur. Such disputes are not uncommon. They are not hidden and they are circulated on informal and formal levels of communication very readily. If one judged by the noise of dispute, members of the paradigmatic science would be characterized as more individualistically competitive than psychological scientists. Based on the descriptions of paradigmatic and preparadigmatic science, we can see the formal tranquility of psychology to be, rather, the symptom of lack of development, not the reverse.

ORGANIZED KNOWLEDGE VERSUS ARTIFICIAL DIVERSITY: THE IMPORTANCE OF SEPARATISM

Psychology is a complex science in that it deals with a broad range of phenomena that constitute a complex and subtle subject matter. The range and difficulty of the subject matter are responsible in part for a diversity in theories and methods, as well as for the science's division into fields, the plethora of publications, and the like. The greater the range and complexity of the phenomena with which a science deals, the greater difficulty the science will have in creating the organized, unified body of knowledge that characterizes the paradigmatic science.

Much of the complexity in a science such as psychology, however, arises not because of the complexity of the phenomena. Rather, the complexity arises in operations of the science. This topic will be treated more fully later. At this point it is sufficient to point out that as the information accrual of the science becomes large in scope the scientist has difficulty in apprising himself of all of the information. Without any self interest involved, this circumstance will make it impossible for the scientist to relate his work to all the relevant works already present in the science. As has been indicated, however, the scientist also may knowingly fail to make reference to other related works, in the service of one interest or another.

What has been called separatism refers to the artificial separation of elements in a science that are actually the same and that should be identified as the same. Each time the scientist establishes something as separate and different from things with which it is essentially the same he has made his science more complex and more difficult, and hence more preparadigmatic. This means that the science contains an additional unnecessary element; the result is the opposite of parsimony and generality. Each case of separatism involves that disservice to the science. The widespread occurrence of separatism in a science will thus mean that there is great artificial diversity in the science, great difficulty for the scientist, student, and scholar, and great difficulty in advancing toward the paradigmatic state of science.

Each of the cases that has been described is one that has contributed artificially to the lack of generality and parsimony in the field of psychology, as well as to weaknesses in communication and in objective assessment of scientific products. These are essential concerns of science, and anything that affects them is an important consideration. Let us take as an example the learning theories of Thorndike, Watson, Hull, and Skinner already described. The case is especially pertinent because perhaps more than any other area that of learning theory has been considered to represent the most advanced notions of theory in psychology. One might have expected this area thus to be advanced in its paradigmatic features for the science. This might be expected also since the various learning theorists worked within the same experimental tradition and the same context of findings, using very similar methods and philosophy of science. One might have thus expected a building, constructive, science process leading to unity and parsimony in a field of knowledge; quite the reverse is true. The same preparadigmatic diversity and competition occurred in this area as in the other areas of psychology. Even when the same concepts were involved, in the different learning theories they were typically not indicated to be the same, as has been illustrated. The differences in the theories were emphasized, not their similarities. As a consequence, what was actually a set of heavily overlapping theories that could have been readily unified into an accepted body of knowledge was not constituted in that way. The approach, rather, was to distinguish the theories as much as possible, to separate them, to show that each was different and original. And the theories were put into competition with one another by their proponents. Students were trained to follow one or the other theory rather than to constructively integrate knowledge in the field. They were led to do research and theorizing that would support one theory as opposed to the others, not to support a unified theory development in the field of learning. Students were trained to use the research methods of one theory but not the others. As might be expected, the results of the theory competition came to naught. The separatism produced no resolution that became a paradigm guiding future development. There was a great wasted effort involved in the theory conflict. We can get some feel for the results of this preparadigmatic (and separatistic) development by referring to a concluding statement of a psychologist who had just written a book reviewing and summarizing the various learning theories during their heyday.

> The array of theories we have examined may be thought to present an unfavorable picture of the state of systematic knowledge about learning. *How can psychologists be helpful to other social scientists or to those who wish to apply their findings if they disagree among themselves on these fundamental matters?* . . . There are no laws of learning which can be taught with confidence. Even the most obvious facts of improvement with practice and the regulation of learning under reward and punishment are matters of theoretical dispute (italics added) (Hilgard 1948, pp. 457–58).

It is clear that Hilgard, in examining these theories, as did the science in general, observed the conflicts between these theories, not their similarities. And this was due in part to separatism. That is, the various theories, in separating themselves to the maximum, appeared artificially to be much more different than they really were. Moreover, the theories inspired followers who divided themselves into schools. As such, the several theories constituted a much less productive foundation for scientists and scholars in other areas to build upon. Largely as a consequence of separatism, far from representing a unified body of knowledge—which could provide a basic orientation by which to study human behavior in various areas such as child development, personality, abnormal and clinical psychology, or educational psychology—the field of learning theory represented a hodgepodge of antagonistic theories, methods, apparatuses, and interests. The field of learning did not begin to offer productive principles to other areas of study until the usable, "heavyweight" principles were pulled out of the morass of conflicting theoretical statements and compiled in an integrated way in the consideration of animal behavior (see Kimble 1961) and human behavior (see Staats 1963). It was neccessary for the inter-theory competition to be ignored as an unproductive path, before the later development of a more organized body of knowledge could occur.

The main point here, however, is that there was in the 1930s, 1940s, and 1950s a great fund of knowledge in the field of learning that was common to the various learning theories. There was a heavy overlap in concepts and principles and analyses common to the various learning theories. The potential for generality and parsimony actually existed. Yet the separatism that was involved in the statements of the various theories helped prevent this area from setting forth an integrated body of knowledge. In doing so the separatism, that is, artificial diversity, contributed to the preparadigmatic state of psychology in this important area of study. Let us look also at the effects of separatism on communication within a science, although the above example may also be considered to be relevant to communication, since it is so central in organizing the knowledge of a science.

Communication and Separatism

Science is a cooperative group activity devoted to advancing knowledge in its area of study (Edsall 1975, p. x). Separatism negatively affects communication in a science, interfering with this goal, as will be briefly exemplified by referring to a specific case. A well-known theorist in the area of behavioral assessment had written a classic article helping introduce the area. In this article he referred as a basic element to a theoretical development which he credited to a particular theory (the already indicated Z theory). Actually, the theoretical development had not arisen in that theory but rather in another theory. The Z theory the behavioral assessment theorist *had* referred to had neglected to cite the earlier theory and in fact had labeled the theoretical development as its own. It was a clear case of separatism. We can see this from the behavioral assessment theorist's response, on being informed of the true source of the conceptual elements he had used. After reading the accounts of both theories he responded that (1) he had not known of the origin of the diagnostic system, believing that it had originated with the secondary source (Z theory); (2) he believed in giving credit where it is due, and (3) in the future he would cite the origin correctly.

The negative effect of separatism on communication is clear from this example. We might consider briefly what the breakdown in communication entailed. Because the secondary source had indicated itself as the originator of the conceptual system involved, not referring to the primary source, the behavioral assessment theorist was not aware of the primary source, and the article he wrote on the topic would also leave his readers unaware of the primary source. This meant the primary source had been cut out of the channels of communication. Perhaps there were other elements of the original theory that would have been helpful to the theorist, and to others. Actually, the original source was a much more completely developed system than the secondary source and contained many other elements that might have been of use to the later theorist and others reading his paper. The breakdown of communication, occasioned by separatism, interfered with these possibilities.

Each of the other cases that has been cited as separatism represents that same breakdown in communication. We can see an especially unfortunate example in the case where students are trained in a separatistic tradition. In the example previously quoted they were so handicapped in their communication with works outside of the theory tradition in which they were trained that they were referred to derogatorily as continually "rediscovering the wheel." Rediscovery in science is an inefficient, costly process. Scientific methodology must be concerned with ways to improve its efficacy, and eradicating the efforts of rediscovery through faulty communication is one way.

Objective Assessment

There are various ways that a theory proves its validity. One way is that of empirical substantiation. A theory may lead to empirical hypotheses that are confirmed or negated. Another proof of value is that of providing a foundation for additional theoretical work, for elaboration and extensions. A theory can also lead to use by others in theoretical elaborations that confirm the heuristic value of the theory being evaluated positively. Popper (1959) has said that a theory is valid and useful to the extent to which its propositions can be falsified. The logic is that if negative results cannot provide a basis for disconfirmation of the theoretical hypothesis, then the hypothesis has not been objectively assessed; for if there is no means of disproof, only confirmation can result. The other side of the coin, of course, is that positive heuristic effects of a theory must also be open to demonstration. A central aspect of confirmation is the extent to which the ideas of the theory are later developed by others. If science practices do not allow such confirmation, problems arise. Objective assessment of a theory requires that empirical and theoretical developments that are relevant to the theory, or that derive from the theory, be related back to the theory. If that is not done, then the objective asessment that is usually accorded by science breaks down. Anything that interferes with the process of assessment, positive or negative, strikes at the heart of the objectivity of science.

Each case where an original element in a science is not cited by a later theory that uses that element represents a deviation from objective assessment in several ways. First, the attribution of the original element that should have occurred did not; the theory originating the element is nonobjectively weaker in the science than it should be. Moreover, the secondary theory that includes a previously presented original element, without citing the source of origin, represents a deviation from objective assessment in that the secondary theory receives nonobjective strength which is greater than it should be. The secondary theory is considered to be original when it is not.

It is important to realize that both of these effects are cumulative, in an autonomous manner. That is, once a theory, let us say, inappropriately claims credit for originating an element, through lack of citation of the original source, later writers will enhance the nonobjectivity. When they cite the secondary source as the origin, they artificially and incorrectly enhance the secondary source, and they artificially and incorrectly weaken the original source. If the element is an important one there is a very heavy cumulative effect, since there will be many generations of citations involved, and much spread of the effect in the manner described in the preceding chapter.

One additional point will be made in this context. The fact that science recognizes priority is not only a practice to guide just reward for its members. It is not only a practice to insure that sources of originality be identified so the most productive influences in science become operational. Priority also serves another function. The fact that only the original is recognized tells the members of a science to work on *other* problems once a concept or finding has been worked out. It tells them that originality from that time on must advance past that point, to a higher level. Explicit recognition of priority is an impetus to go on, disallowing rumination over the already discovered, or wasted efforts dressing up the already discovered in new clothes. Science is conducted more effectively when it rules out duplication of effort and the confusion and competition that results. Separatism in theory that does not use citations to relate its work to others, even if the theory has been independently developed, is a drawback to science. The rules of general science have been established, it is suggested, to prevent these practices and their negative results. That is why, at least in part, stringent criteria are involved both for citation and indication of priority.

As has been indicated here in various places, the paradigmatic characteristics of a science affect the productivity and efficiency of the science enterprise. In that sense these characteristics are essential aspects of the methodology of science, and it is important to make them explicit in psychology. Only in this way will it be possible to make improvements.

Chapter 7

The Philosophy of Disunity

It has been said herein that psychology is preparadigmatic, that the methodology of separatism is practiced, that there are historical and contemporary differences in the sociology of preparadigmatic and paradigmatic science. I will suggest in this chapter that there is a philosophy of science that goes with, or grows out of, the characteristics of the preparadigmatic science. The philosophy encompasses the practices of separatism. In addition I will suggest that this philosophy of science, like its paradigmatic counterpart, has prescriptive powers that influence the conduct of the science. Finally, changing from a preparadigmatic to a paradigmatic science will involve changing the philosophy that is held concerning the nature of the science.

THE NATURE OF SCIENCE AND THE
PHILOSOPHY OF SCIENCE

Quotations have been presented in preceding chapters recording statements of philosophers that science is concerned with establishing general laws, in reaching for ever greater generality and unity. Such philosophies of science can describe science as unified, with general laws and methods because they treat sciences that have developed such products. General laws, general theories, and general methodological principles have been found in the physical sciences. Moreover, there is knowledge of the history of these sciences. Areas of study formerly considered to be disparate and unrelated — preparadigmatic, with different theories, concepts, methods of study, and the like — have later on been united within one formulation. This has occurred in a progressively elaborating way, involving the formation of larger and larger unities of knowledge. The result has been to suggest that nature, at least in the areas so dealt with, is unified and the science as it progresses mirrors that characteristic.

It is suggested that when a science is paradigmatic — when it has reached the point of common theory and methods, across many of its areas — its paradigmatic features are evident to those who are conversant with the science. The members of the science see the unity involved. They come to think of the natural world in which they are interested as lawful and unified, and they see their science as reflecting these characteristics. There may be many things in their science that they cannot relate in a unified manner. *Yet they assume, typically, that disparate events which are not yet articulated to the body of the science will be when enough information has been obtained.* The scientists in a paradigmatic science, thus, assume paradigmatic unity. These assumptions, in the present view, constitute their paradigmaticism — their philosophy or theory that the nature of their science, and the events the science studies, have a unified characteristic.

The scientist in the paradigmatic science sees the specialty divisions of his science to be formed on the basis of convenience and practicality, not as divisions on the basis of a difference in basic principle, divisions made because of inherent incompatibility. The member of the paradigmatic science does not see a chaos of competing theories, philosophies, methods, and unrelated experimental finding. He sees a unified and powerful knowledge system that has a building, advancing structure that involves progressively larger interrelationships. By contrast, when he looks at the preparadigmatic sciences and sees their disorganized, competing knowledge structure he sees the preparadigmatic science as puerile.

The member of the paradigmatic science does not make the types of statements of basic and endemic divisions and incommensurabilities of his science in the manner exemplified by Kuhn in describing preparadigmatic science, or indeed like the already quoted statements concerning the separatism of the social sciences. A major point to be made is that part of the character of paradigmatic science is the belief in the unity of its endeavors. This belief — which I call paradigmaticism — arises from the scientist's experience with his paradigmatic science. Since his science is paradigmatic in nature, as he experiences the science he forms an acceptance of, a belief in, this characteristic as natural to his science. The member of the same science at its earlier preparadigmatic stage, it should be noted, would not have had such a belief. Scientists in physics when the area was a preparadigmatic science would not have had a belief in the unity of their science; they would not have held a philosophy of paradigmaticism. Philosophers of science, also, would have made contrary statements about their preparadigmatic science. This must be said as an hypothesis, of course. However, I would expect that historians of science would be able to find statements of what will here be called preparadigmaticism among physical scientists of the past, when the physical sciences were not yet paradigmatic.

In contrast to the member of a paradigmatic science, the preparadigmatic scientist has a different experience, of a science that has the characteristics described in the preceding chapter. He sees a chaos of theory statements. Different terms are employed, there are differently stated principles, different theory construction methods — even when the theories pertain to the same realm of events, and even when the principles are very similar. He sees a morass of experimental methods and experimental findings that are unrelated. The proponents of the different experimental areas are convinced of the importance of their experimental methods and know little about the methods of others and tend to consider them less than important. He sees different basic methodologies, again in competition with each other. The essential characteristic of the preparadigmatic science is the competition to improve the position of one's own approach and to weaken and defeat other approaches. The preparadigmatic scientist sees the practice of separatism, where each scientist tries to separate and distinguish his work from that of others, and there is little attempt to integrate and organize knowledge. Finally, the field is broken down into various organizational parts that are unrelated and in competition. The knowledge base is a morass, inconsistent and conflicting.

These are the characteristics of the science as experienced by its members. Moreover, these are the characteristics that have always existed in his field. When one is restricted to such experiences it is easy to conclude that these are the basic, inherent characteristics of the science. The scientist whose experience is limited to these preparadigmatic characteristics will form a philosophy of his science that reflects this experience. His belief will be that of preparadigmaticism, the belief that the science is inherently disparate. It is probably the case that this belief becomes stronger as one has a wider experience with the various conflicting products of the science, when one cannot provide a paradigmatic integration. We will see evidence that this may be the case in the statements of Sigmund Koch, editor of a voluminous treatment of general psychology. He has had very close contact with the various parts of psychology, presented in preparadigmatic separatism. What his views are of the paradigmatic potentialities of psychology will thus be interesting to examine.

The following sections will indicate that an important aspect of the philosophy of science of psychology, not generally recognized as such, differs from the philosophy of science of the natural sciences. This philosophy is preparadigmatic and it constitutes a basic feature of the science. This philosophy denies that psychology can be paradigmatic (1) in its theory, (2) in its experimental study, (3) in its methodology, and (4) in its organization. There has not been a philosophy of science in psychology that provides for development along a dimension that would yield paradigmatic unity, and that treats of a methodology for doing so. This is a dimension that should be abstracted for consideration, if movement along this dimension is essential to the advancement of the science, as later discussions will further stress. The next section will characterize the implicit, nonsystematic, but influential philosophy of the preparadigmatic character of psychology.

THE PHILOSOPHY OF PREPARADIGMATICISM
IN PSYCHOLOGY

Psychology has been described as a preparadigmatic science, and it will be said that it has a preparadigmatic philosophy of science. Yet, as has been indicated earlier, psychology has also had a strong proclivity for becoming a science and adopting the characteristics of the natural sciences. Part of these characteristics is the assumption of the unity of science, and that has had an influence upon some members of psychology. As has been indicated, for example, logical positivism had a very strong impact upon psychology at an earlier time, in the work of the second-generation behaviorists. The natural sciences were the object of study of logical positivism, and the second-generation behaviorists took the natural sciences as their model. Spence (1944) clearly described what scientific theory is by reference to Newton's theory, one characteristic of which was its general nature. Newton's theory was seen to have brought together under one set of principles what formerly had been considered as separate phenomena, providing a "theoretical integration of such laws as Kepler's concerning planetary motions, Galileo's law of falling bodies, laws of the tides and so on" (Spence 1944, p. 48).

Creating general theories in this sense was thus integral in the theories of the second-generation behaviorists, although their actual subject matter — the study of animal learning — really constituted only a small part of psychology. Hull, for example, states such a theme in a preface to an early book. Although the contents of the book concern only the experimental psychology of animal learning, Hull states the book "has been written on the assumption that all behavior, individual and social, moral and immoral, normal and psychopathic, is generated from the same primary laws; that the differences in the objective behavioral manifestations are due to the differing conditions under which habits are set up and function" (1943, p. v). This was in agreement with the first-generation work of Watson, and other second-generation learning theorists, such as Tolman, who felt that their learning theories also had the potential for such generality.

The first- and second-generation behaviorists, especially the second, were attempting to structure their theories in psychology according to the characteristics of natural science. Nevertheless, they could not escape from their experience as members of a preparadigmatic science, which prevented them from producing unified works individually, or as a group, as has been indicated. To elaborate, these learning theories, like that of Skinner already described, were derived within the framework of the preparadigmatic state of psychology. They were formulated as theories to compete with other like-minded theories, not to unite to form a truly general theory. Moreover, they were not general in the sense of entering the various areas of psychology and attempting to construct theories in those areas in a manner that would unite the knowledge in the area, as well as unite the various areas under one conceptual framework. In fact the efforts in this generation of learning theory development came to be focused on a competition between these general theories, in a manner that contributed to psychology's preparadigmaticism. Furthermore, general theorists such as Watson (1930), and later Skinner (1953) quite clearly showed preparadigmatic characteristics in actively rejecting large areas of knowledge of research, theory, and method. The knowledge in these areas was and is considered of no value by those of this orientation. These theorists did not attempt to unify diverse bodies of knowledge, but instead largely rejected that which did not coincide with their own specific theory, obtained from the study of only a narrow part of psychology. They also rejected, by and large, the methods and experiments and problems, involved in other approaches in the science. These theorists actually had preparadigmatic orientations and they produced preparadigmatic theories. Most importantly, as already described, the preparadigmatic competition between such theories as those of Hull, Tolman, Guthrie, and Skinner stimulated no movement toward paradigmatic general theory or philosophy or methodology. In the present view the goal of general (unifying) theory was simply "aped," copied from the philosophy describing the natural sciences. As a consequence, with no real understanding of the nature of what psychology was, of how the nature of psychology influenced their own orientations, and of what psychology needed in order to develop as a paradigmatic science, the movement could not as so constituted lead to real unified theory. And that was indeed the result. It was ultimately recognized that their limited attempt to construct general theory had fallen short, as we can see in the words of one of the second-generation behaviorists.

> First, I think the days of such grandiose, all-covering systems in psychology as mine attempted to be are, at least for the present, pretty much passé. I feel, therefore, that it might have been more decent and more dignified to let such an instance of the relatively immediate past bury its dead (Tolman 1959, p. 93).

Thus, by 1959 the disenchantment with what was really a very parochial interest in general theory began to be formally stated. This evaluation of the state of science in the field of learning was developed further by later learning theorists, as the following two quotations indicate.

> Psychologists are no longer content with comfortable generalities that allow labels to be tacked on to results after they occur; they want theories or systems to say what is going to happen and to say it clearly and exactly. . . . It follows from these demands that any contemporary system that fulfills them must be a miniature system, covering only a small range of behavior, perhaps only for a single kind of organism and a single simple situation. We still have too few facts to build full-scale systems (Marx and Hillix 1973, p. 83).

> While there was a time—in the 1930s, 1940s, and 1950s during the era of the great systems of behavior associated with names like Hull and Tolman —when argument raged about the relative value of one or another approach to things, psychologists no longer find it productive or meaningful to pit one theory against another in the form of some "crucial" experiment or the like.
>
> Today, the psychology of learning seems to have passed from an era of the grand, broad theory into an era of the microtheory. Behavior is much too complicated, and far too little is yet known and understood about it, to make the development of general theories of learning a fruitful undertaking at this time. Instead the modern theorist attacks a rather specific bit of behavior, collects a lot of data about it, teases it apart, and then attempts to put it back together in the form of some necessarily limited, theoretical structure (Hulse, Deese, and Egeth 1975, pp. 104–05).

It is interesting that, as the above statement indicates, an interest in general theory is considered to also include competition between such theories. That is what had occurred in psychology. The period of the general theory was not a period of unity, but rather a period of intertheory competition. This development was clearly within the preparadigmatic science framework. It may be added that the assumed connection between general theory and theory competition may be considered detrimental to the development of a paradigmatic psychology, as will be indicated later.

To continue, however, these opinions are not addressed to the question of whether or not psychology is a paradigmatic science or is a preparadigmatic science. These statements merely reflect what these psychologists have noted about the nature of their science. But the statements indicate clearly the characteristics with respect to unity that are being projected. They are stating that the nature of psychology must for a long time continue to be preparadigmatic—to be constituted of microtheories, composed to be relevant to a small, specific, area of study. This plan for psychology does not consider the necessity or possibility of articulation of any microtheory with any larger theoretical framework. This approach actually discourages such interests. That is, when the topic of the possibility of attaining general principles across different areas of psychology is specifically considered, the disbelief in the viability of such a goal is even stronger, as the following shows.

> Finally, *what are the prospects for the eventual development of a single, unifying theory for all of behavior?* As far as I can see, *if this sort of fully integrating principle is ever achieved,* it will almost certainly be basically neurophysiological in nature, with parallel development of inferential theory. But *the prospects of any such development within the foreseeable future are remote indeed,* and for some time in the future we shall need to be satisfied with such less ambitious but more realistic theoretical successes as can be wrung from an ever reluctant, yet exciting, subject matter (italics added) (Marx 1970, p. 40).

This is the statement of a scholar in psychology who has been closely concerned with examining theory in psychology, the philosophy of theory construction, and the nature of our science. His position reflects the zeitgeist and is generally descriptive of psychology. It is an opinion that truly unified, general theory is not possible in psychology now or in a foreseeable future.

To continue, however, perhaps the most celebrated theorist in contemporary psychology, B. F. Skinner, has very systematically structured his approach to be separatistic and nonintegratory, in a manner that very closely provides support for the preparadigmatic paradigm. Skinner's philosophy of science has been in essence that psychology should not be integratory across areas of study. He has criticized theories that refer to another dimensional system, that is, another system of concepts and methods of observation (1950). His view has had implications for separating social science from psychology — since studying the group involves a different dimension than studying individual behavior — as well as for separating various areas of psychology. Importantly, Skinner's approach also has said that principles of behavior were to be separated from the study of physiology of the nervous system. The latter is exemplified in the following excerpt, which elaborates an already presented quotation of Watson.

> We are all familiar with the changes that are supposed to take place in the nervous system when an organism learns. Synaptic connections are made or broken, electrical fields are disrupted or reorganized, concentrations of ions are built up or allowed to diffuse away, and so on. In the science of neurophysiology statements of this sort are not necessarily theories in the present sense. But in a science of behavior, where we are concerned with whether or not an organism secretes saliva when a bell rings, or jumps toward a gray triangle, or say *bik* when a card reads *tuz*, or loves

someone who resembles his mother, all statements about the nervous system are theories in the sense that they are not expressed in the same terms and could not be confirmed with the same methods of observation as the facts for which they are said to account (Skinner 1950, p. 193).

The article in which this excerpt appeared involved a general rejection of theory. Moreover, this article, among the many such statements of Skinner, said that different realms of study should not be unified. One can only get the full impact of this separatistic position by reading other statements of Skinner and by consulting his works. As has been mentioned already, the only methodology that Skinner really accepted was that of his operant conditioning chamber, involving continuous responding with the rate of response being the central and only type of data. Skinner rejected other measurements of learning. Moreover, he clearly rejected other methods of observation such as psychological tests (1969, pp. 77–78). This has been true of the conceptual aspects of his theory. There are almost no references in Skinner's work to concepts or findings outside of his own work or that of a very few other operant workers. There is almost no attempt in his formulations to include concepts, principles, methods, or theories outside of his own. Skinner's major thrust, like Watson before him, was to reject all of psychology except that identified as his, rather than to work for integration, unification, and organization of knowledge in psychology; thus, operant behaviorism has not served as a model for unifying psychology. Moreover, Skinner's statements of philosophy, like those above, promulgate separatism rather than contibute to unification. We can see the same institutionalization of the preparadigmatic state of psychology in the following quotation, written by a theorist in a different area of psychology.

A truism we have come to in our review of personality theory is that the days of hoping to find a single, all-encompassing theory—about anything—are surely past. This plausible assumption of yesteryear was based upon an inaccurate interpretation. . . . In the future, the student of personality must come to know *all* theorists equally well (Rychlak 1968, p. 454).

As will be indicated later, this quotation refers to one of the drawbacks of preparadigmaticism: the need for knowing *all* theorists. In a disparate, chaotic, and hence impossibly complex field such a mission is a major handicap for the student, scholar, and researcher. This mission, moreover, is in conflict with the microtheory approach, which is to know very well and to further develop one restricted set of materials. To continue, however, the generality of the contemporary conviction that a unified, paradigmatic science of psychology is impossible may be seen in a book entitled *Toward Unification in Psychology: The First Banff Conference on*

Theoretical Psychology (Royce 1970). For example, the reviewer of the book (Shaw 1972) devoted a prominent part of his review to emphasizing the disbelief of the conferees in the possibility of unity in psychology. The reviewer, having read the various opinions, records his own belief in what is herein called the preparadigmatic state of psychology by referring to "naive or jaded theorists who in their delusion or disillusion are tempted by simplistic theoretical approaches to unification" (Shaw 1972, p. 75). Perhaps the best characterization of psychology, as treated at this conference examining the possibility of unification of the science, was made in the following statement. It was written by Krech as an epilogue reviewing the conference.

> Unification was, I think, the initial hope and the sustained aim. But it soon became apparent — indeed on the first evening when MacLeod and others commented on Royce's paper — that this aim might remain unfulfilled. As MacLeod said, "If the unity we seek is something that is common to all people who call themselves psychologists, then it is a silly quest" (MacLeod 1970, p. 38). Having delivered this observation, which I think is sound, MacLeod went on to suggest his own guide-line for unification of psychology. Even von Bertalanffy, who subscribed to the thesis behind the Conference, was moved to issue a personal disclaimer, "Of course, there is not and probably never will be a 'unified' psychology, but only a number of different fields subsumed under this name" (Bertalanffy 1970, p. 40). Not all is lost, however, for von Bertalanffy proceeds to assure us, in the very next paragraph, that "there are unifying concepts and principles in science . . ." and while these may not lead to a total unification "they do help to bring different phenomena and more special theories into a general framework" (Bertalanffy 1970, p. 41). My own position — which I have already indicated — was more unyielding than that of either MacLeod or von Bertalanffy: "there is not, and perhaps cannot be, a 'science of psychology.' What we have is a melange of sciences, technologies, professions, arts, epistemologies, and philosophies — many of them but distantly related to each other — all called 'Psychology.' . . . What, then, does it mean when we say that we seek to 'unify' *psychology*? Why seek to unify the potpourri now called 'psychology'?" (Krech 1970, p. 43). My answer to MacLeod who would seek for "the essential unity of any science . . . in the questions it asks" would be this: the various enterprises dubbed psychological share only the most trivial of questions. I am tempted to make a similar answer to von Bertalanffy's suggestion that, abandoning hopes of total unification, we may still find some general concepts and principles that would unify psychology. This is possible but these unifying concepts and principles — when stretched to envelop the entire range of the psychologist's activities — would prove to be a flimsy cover, knit together with trivia.
>
> The reader can imagine how lively and interesting the proceedings became after such a beginning. Unification reared its noble head again

and again, now this man, now that, rose to affirm his faith and hope in psychology unified, meaningful, and integrated. But as each private plan for Psychology Fulfilled was unrolled, it became increasingly clear that these were men who would build not a mansion of many chambers, but a street of semi-detached, and in many instances of completely detached, houses in which physiological psychologists, humanists, and perceptionists, clinicians, existentialists, and animal psychologists would live—in comity, *perhaps*—but in separate though equal houses.

And now for my Charge Direct! It was after the Conference, after analysing what happened there, that Professor Royce rethought its original objectives and lowered its sights. Read again his Prologue. Not only (he tells us) was this Conference designed to make but the merest hint of a beginning *toward* a possible unification, but "The point is that theoretical unification is where you find it, and if it results in fragmentation, then so be it, for our primary concern is to understand behaviour rather than perpetuate a historical chapter heading for political or historical reasons" (Royce 1970, p. 4) (Krech 1970, pp. 300–01).

This statement contains a number of interesting points, some of which will be addressed in later discussions. It may be mentioned here, however, that Krech includes a description of the current state of those in psychology who place a value on unified theory. Contact with the philosophy of science of the natural sciences tells the philosophically oriented psychologist that a primary goal of science is general, unified theory. But he does not know how this is to be accomplished, what the philosophical basis for this goal is to be, what the general methodology might consist of, or what the problems are that have to be solved in attaining the goal. He can only suggest that his particular interest in psychology in some way can be extended to the whole of psychology. But that is not a convincing argument in a preparadigmatic science where almost every other psychologist has his pet interest and approach also. Without the necessary constituents, those arguing for unity in psychology via separate and divergent paths fall beneath the onslaught of those arguing—with abundant, visible justification—that psychology is simply not that way and never can be.

I have saved the next statement for last for several reasons. First, it is the opinion of one of our most eminent general psychologists. Sigmund Koch was involved in planning a seven volume work, a project of the American Psychological Association, entitled *Psychology: A Study of a Science*, which he edited (see Koch, 1959). In this work Koch certainly had contact with the various areas in psychology, and part of the mission of the work was to indicate the interrelationships of the various areas. As his statements show, his experience as a general psychologist resulted in a belief that unity in psychology as a science is not possible. Moreover, the quotation is presented because Koch expresses his philosophy in a manner that institutionalizes psychology's preparadigmatic state. He suggests that we further organize our science to make it even more preparadigmatic — in a projection that is diametrically opposed to the present position, as a later chapter will indicate. Koch's statement epitomizes, succinctly, the preparadigmatic philosophy.

One of the movements toward sanity that has taken place in psychology since the early 1950s has been a growing tendency to recognize that the large integrations that characterized the neobehaviorist interval were merely empty emulations of a misconstrued notion of the character of physical science; in general, one of the happiest things in recent decades has been a tendency to become rather modest — and sometimes even playful — about the range of application of theoretical suggestions or "paradigms." But we have been modest, now, for 20 years or so. Clearly psychology must progress, and so why not have large theories again? This is beautiful documentation of the sense in which this has been — this funny field — largely a role-playing enterprise rather than an intellectually responsible commitment to discover differentiated and meaningful, perhaps illuminating, knowledge about the human condition.

In a more positive vein, my position suggests that the noncohesiveness of psychology finally be acknowledged by replacing it with some such locution as "the psychological studies." *Students should no longer be tricked by a terminological rhetoric into the belief that they are studying a single discipline or any set of specialties rendered coherent by any actual or potential principle of coherence.* The current "Departments of Psychology" should be called "Departments of Psychological Studies." The change of name, which of course is a minor thing, should mark a corresponding change in pedagogical rationale. The psychological studies, if they are really to address the historically constituted objectives of psychological thought, must range over an immense and disorderly spectrum of human activity and experience. If significant knowledge is the desideratum, problems must be approached with humility, methods must be contextual and flexible, and anticipations of synoptic breakthroughs must be held in check.

Moreover, the conceptual ordering devices, technical languages ("paradigms," if you will) open to the various psychological studies are — like all human modes of cognitive organization — perspectival, sensibility-dependent relative to the inquirer, *and often noncommensurable. Such conceptual incommensurabilities will often obtain not only between contentually different psychological studies but between alternate but perspectively "valid" orderings of the "same" domain* (italics added) (Koch 1978, pp. 637–38).

Preparadigmaticism as a Philosophy of Science

The above statements, expressing what is herein called preparadigmaticism, should be contrasted with the statements presented in an earlier chapter of the several philosophers of science who described the importance of achieving general, unified theory in science. The statements employed, referring to the natural sciences, were from philosophers such as Reichenbach, Braithwaite, Feigl, and Shapere. What was said with respect to the natural sciences was diametrically opposed to the statements of the presently described preparadigmaticism, which denies the possible achievement of the generality of unified theory in psychology.

In the generation of psychologists of Edward Tolman, Clark Hull, S. S. Stevens, and Kenneth Spence the philosophy of science based upon the natural sciences was taken as pertinent to psychology. There was a period when the concept of general, unified theory was taken as a goal for psychological theory. As has been indicated, the attempt was simply to append the philosophical unity on to what was really a preparadigmatic science — without understanding what a preparadigmatic science was, and thus what the task of unification involved, as will be further discussed later on. The result was the development of competitive schools each attempting to find a different unified theory based upon contact with a limited part of psychology. The endeavor thus resulted in contributing to the preparadigmatic character of the science. With that failure, as evidenced in the statements that have been presented above, rejection of the philosophy of unified theory for psychology was given strong support.

The important point to stress in this context, however, is that the statements of preparadigmaticism — such as those quoted above — constitute a philosophy of science. In its extreme form this philosophy says that the nature of the phenomena studied in psychology are disparate in fundamental nature. As such, general and unified theory cannot be achieved, because nature itself does not display this characteristic in the area of study involved. Koch's statement says that the idea that psychology can constitute a coherent, organized area of knowledge is a chimera. Incommensurability between and within areas is to be expected. This implies a strict relativism; that there is no way of attaining unity through resolving such incommensurability. Different theories in the same domain can be equally valid.

It should be noted that the philosophy of preparadigmaticism has not been presented and accepted in the systematic way that has been the case for the philosophy of science that has been formulated in the natural sciences. In the present opinion the lack of systematic presentation is due to the fact that preparadigmaticism conflicts with natural science philosophy of science. In a systematic confrontation of preparadigmaticsm with a paradigmatic philosophy, the latter has the more fundamentally sound basis. It would be productive to assemble systematically the various related conceptual statements to fully understand what the philosophy of preparadigmaticsm consists of in its entirety. This should be done in a manner that represents the various preparadigmatic sciences, not just psychology. The statements that have been presented here constitute only a very small sample. Perhaps the present work will provide an impetus for that systematic treatment.

Philosophies Are Prescriptive as Well as Descriptive

When we read philosophies of science we see continual recourse to examples of natural science that are used to illustrate the general principles of the philosophy. The example of Spence (1944) suggesting that Newton's theory could be the model for psychology has already been presented. Shapere, as indicated in an earlier chapter, describes unified theory in physics by referring to the originally separated investigations of electricity and magnetism, and how the various very diverse phenomena involved were unified within a common theoretical context.

Philosophies of science are in this sense descriptive. When the philosopher of science says that generality is at the heart of explanation, with many productive consequences, as does Reichenbach, he is not making an assumption, arrived at solely on a rational basis. He makes that statement as a description of what has occurred successfully in the past. And that is the source of the philosophy of preparadigmaticism also. It is based upon observation of the state of psychology. When psychological scientists say that the quest for unity in psychology is a chimera, they are saying that psychology has not and does not display characteristics of unity and unified theory. Ample evidence has been given in earlier chapters of preparadigmatic disorganization in psychology's knowledge pool. Frequently when we observe things, however, we also tend to conclude that what has happened involves fundamental, inherent circumstances. Thus, the preparadigmatic philosophy may also add that not only is there no unity in psychology, but none can be expected, because disunity is the fundamental nature of psychological phenomena. It is thus important to understand, however, that the philosophical statements concerning the impossibility of unification in psychology rest only upon the fact that psychology has not as yet demonstrated unified knowledge achievements.

This analysis refers to the descriptive quality of a philosophy of science. In this sense a philosophy is an effect or a dependent variable — it depends upon the characteristics the science has exhibited. But, as we saw to be the case with the concept of paradigms, something can be an effect and a cause as well. Although the philosophy of science may depend upon description of the nature of the science, once stated, the philosophy of science also comes to be an independent variable. Scientists will guide what they do in accordance with the instructions they receive from the philosophy. Thus, the philosophy of science of the natural sciences prescribes in part what natural scientists should do. In the present context, the philosophy of science that is generally held in the paradigmatic science tells the practicing scientist to look for underlying unity of theory even before it has been found. Unified theory is set up as a goal and scientists undertake the quest for unity with dedicated effort — pursuing tasks individually and as a group that are difficult and time consuming, all aiming toward that goal. Without this effort they would not achieve unified theory in the manner that they do. We have an interesting case before us in contemporary physics. A very central theoretical and experimental quest currently being pursued is the search for a unified theory that will integrate in one theoretical structure the four basic types of physical force (strong and weak nuclear force, gravitational force, and electromagnetic force), thereby indicating the relatedness of the several types of force (Glashow 1980). In Braithwaite's words science places great value on finding "more knowledge of the interconnectedness of Nature" (1955, p. 349). The scientist with that philosophy is moved to expend his efforts seeking that knowledge. Contemporary theoretical physicists seek that unified theory in part because they are paradigmatic scientists with that philosophy.

And therein lies one of the powerful reasons why preparadigmaticism must be a subject of important inquiry. For as a philosophy of science — albeit largely informal — it has a prescriptive, causative property. A philosophy can set the goals of the science. When Koch asks with heavy irony "Clearly psychology must progress, and so why not have large theories again?" (1978, p. 637), referring to the failures of the self-proclaimed general theories of the 1950s, this constitutes a restrictive guide to other psychologists telling them not to expend effort in trying to formulate such general theories. When he says that "Students should no longer be tricked . . . that they are studying a single discipline or any set of specialties rendered coherent by any actual or potential principle of coherence" (p. 638), this is an injunction against the search for unification. When Krech says "unifying concepts and principles . . . would prove to be a flimsy cover, knit together with trivia" (1970, p. 301), this provides no guide or impetus for a great investment of time and effort in the search for a unity which can only be trivial. In sum, such statements do not compose a philosophy that leads one in experimental, methodological, and theoretical works to effect unified knowledge, or to develop methods by which to conduct such activities and to attain such ends. If the search for unification is as difficult and elusive a quest in the study of behavior as it has been in the study of physical phenomena such as electricity, and later electricity and magnetism, in the study of gravitational phenomena, and currently the four basic physical forces, and many more, we must ask whether such a philosophy will serve well to guide and to energize us for the task of unification in psychology (and the social sciences). Perhaps we need a philosophy that will provide that incentive and perhaps we need the methodological guides that will be requisite in that very large task.

It is true that psychology is completely heterogeneous and this is an obvious, continuing characteristic. The diversity and competitiveness and incommensurability of psychology give a deep and general characteristic to the science. Psychology has produced a mishmash of disorganized knowledge, which typically is handled by individual scientists with a simplifying retreat to a delimited specialty field of knowledge. This has been the state of psychology. It is presently the state. It is difficult to see how this state will change to one that is characteristic of the unification of paradigmatic science. Can we conclude on this basis that this is the fixed nature of our science? Should we continue to avoid the truly gigantic effort of unifying knowledge in our science? Or are we experiencing the preparadigmatic night before the paradigmatic dawn? The stakes are too high to answer the questions without systematic effort, for the answer dictates the path we should take in developing our science.

THE INTERACTION OF PREPARADIGMATICISM AND SEPARATISM

A word should be said about the interaction of the philosophical statements of preparadigmaticism and the methodological statements of separatism. To begin, there are different types of originality in science. Discovery or origination may involve the first observation of a natural occurrence, such as a star, the production of a new substance, such as penicillin, the experimental demonstration of a principle, such as Thorndike's demonstration that reward strengthens behavior it follows, or the discovery of a new method of making observations, such as the telescope or intelligence test. As has already been indicated, and as will be further discussed later, another type of scientific originality of great importance involves new integratory theory that shows the interconnectedness of phenomena previously considered as different. This type of originality does not so much involve discovery of new phenomena and concepts as it does the conceptual tying together of already existent phenomena and concepts, frequently through use of a deeper theoretical statement. Newton's theory is an example in physical science. In this sense the integratory theory is a building operation, rather than a discovery operation, a building of interconnectedness and unification. The science must be attuned to see the originality that is involved in such scientific works.

In the paradigmatic science, the importance of integratory theory is clearly seen, and referred to in the philosophy of science that is followed. The philosophy of the preparadigmatic science — which we have just seen describes the preparadigmatic science — does not sufficiently include an exposition of integratory theory, the methods of integratory theory, or the value of integratory theory. That leaves such theory out as a type of originality for the preparadigmatic scientist. Thus, preparadigmatic scientists do not realize how they can be creative in their science by formulating theoretical integrations. In the present view the preparadigmatic scientist thus must look for originality elsewhere: find a new observational method, demonstrate experimentally phenomena and principles not before shown, devise new methods and observational devices, and so on. While these may be valuable, they do not derive from an integrated conceptual body, and they do not contribute to a unified, organized body of knowledge.

Moreover, as has been suggested, the preparadigmatic context, rather than providing a framework for building-type theoretical endeavors, asks the scientist to find something new, and original, in the discovery sense. He is thus moved to see things as different rather than to find relationships. He looks for the new and different, and ways to make things appear new and different. What was described as separatism in the preceding chapter frequently involved the type of seeking of originality through differentiating one's own conceptual works from others.

In return these practices of separatism help make the science preparadigmatic. Each time a scientist artificially differentiates his work from a work that is actually closely related the scientist adds another disparate element to the disorganized knowledge of the field. Each time a new terminology is introduced for phenomena that may appear slightly different, but which are actually in principle the same, the complexity and disorganization of the field has been increased. The practices of separatism are the opposite of the search for generality and unity that is central to the paradigmatic science and that has been glorified in the philosophy of science of the natural sciences. The point is that what originality is considered to be will differ on the basis of whether the science is paradigmatic or preparadigmatic.

In summary, the preparadigmatic state of science leads to a preparadigmatic philosophy of science that espouses the goals of the preparadigmatic science. The latter, in its prescriptive role, provides a basis for the methodology of separatism. And separatism contributes to the preparadigmatic state of the science. It is hypothesized that there is a relationship between the philosophy of preparadigmaticism and the methodological philosophy of separatism. Belief in the underlying disparateness of the phenomena of study in psychology, it is suggested, is compatible with a methodological belief that knowledge does not have to be organized through citations, and so on, as is expected in the paradigmatic sciences. This is a topic requiring systemic research, toward gaining a knowledge of the differences between preparadigmatic and paradigmatic science and toward solving the special problems of the former.

PREPARADIGMATICISM: AN ESSENTIAL INGREDIENT
OF PREPARADIGMATIC SCIENCE

In elaborating the concept of the paradigmatic science it was said that paradigmatic sciences have (1) paradigms, (2) in good proportion relative to preparadigmatic features, and (3) an overriding, umbrella structure of theory, philosophy, and method that serve to unify the various paradigms within the science, or a good proportion of them. One other essential ingredient has been added in the present chapter. (4) It has been stated that the members of the paradigmatic science have a belief or philosophy that assumes unity in those aspects of nature studied, assumes the potential unity of their science, leads them to expend effort in searching for unity, and tells them that unified theory is a prized form of originality in science.

In my view psychology is not potentially different from the more advanced sciences in all respects, and in many of its scientifc achievements. I will add here that I think that psychology is basically different than the more advanced, paradigmatic sciences. It does not have the four developments listed in the above paragraph. Moreover, these are central elements that help determine the level of advancement of any science. This has not been understood, it is suggested, by those who are most concerned with developing psychology as a science. The emphasis upon experimentation of science-oriented psychologists has been described earlier. There have been many experimental psychologists who have worked under the belief that the advancement of psychology as a science primarily rested on the demonstration of its potentiality for experimentation, and in developing sophisticated apparatus, experimental designs, and methods of data analysis. They have equated the level of advancement of the science with its experimental advancement. It is possible to realize the importance of experimental advancement, but also to realize that by itself experimental achievement will not yield progress toward paradigmatic science, and in fact, may detract from that goal. Experimentalists who have focused on experimentation without regard to the paradigmatic characteristics of their science, I would suggest, have missed a central dimension of potential advancement of their science. A neglected feature in consideration of advanced sciences is their paradigmatic nature and their paradigmaticism. Psychology will never be viewed as an advanced science as long as its contents are preparadigmatic, as long as its methodology for producing unified, organized knowledge is weak, as will be indicated further on and, especially, as long as its philosophy is that of preparadigmaticism. Psychologists who are concerned about advancing psychology as a science must become concerned with advancing its paradigmatic characteristics, in the present view.

The major point to be made in this context, however, is that a preparadigmatic to paradigmatic dimension exists in the development of science fields, and this can be employed to gauge the advancement of the science (or at least some sciences). A science may be said to advance as it acquires paradigms. Past a certain point, ordinarily, it becomes evident that there is considerable paradigmatic development. Moreover, at a later point it becomes clear that various paradigms can be considered within the same general framework and that there is considerable unity in the field. The works within the field lose their competitive quality and begin to be complementary in treating those aspects of the world relevant to the science. Recognition of this nature of the science provides a basis for the emergence of paradigmaticism, the philosophy that values the unity of the science and of nature. Such paradigmaticism further guides the scientist to look for unity, to seek relationships, and to develop a methodology for doing so.

Movement along this preparadigmatic-paradigmatic dimension is a gradual one, in the present view. Advancement does not ordinarily take place in a revolutionary way, although as will be indicated this would be possible in psychology and the other social sciences. Ordinarily, advancement awaits the gradual accrual of paradigms. Then developments have to occur that further unite the paradigms. The science ordinarily becomes paradigmatic from below, so to speak, being built up as unity occurs between formerly preparadigmatic separates. And ordinarily the philosophy of paradigmaticism awaits these lower developments.

NATURE, SCIENCE, AND PARADIGMATICISM

It is useful in considering these matters to break down the several realms of science that are involved. To begin, there is the realm of nature. Nature does not occur in compartmentalized segments. A man, for example, is not solely a psychological entity. He involves materials that are of a physical kind, like the rest of nature. He involves chemical events, physiological events, behavioral events, sociological events, and political events. He is all of these things. The world is not broken into categories.

When it comes to the study of the events of the world, however, there is categorization. Natural events are very complex and difficult to understand. Moreover, they cannot be studied in one fell swoop. We simplify, and this means breaking things into smaller areas because this diminishes the task and allows us to obtain a grasp on it. Following the above example, a man could be studied for chemical processes, physiological processes, behavioral processes, and sociological, political, and economic processes. Sometimes in our divisive strategy — employed because of practicalities, not necessarily in coincidence with reality — we get diversity, disparity in our constructions of the categories of natural events. It is at this level of scientific study that we reach the level of unity or disunity that makes our field of study either preparadigmatic or paradigmatic. Unity or disunity does not lie in the realm of natural events itself, but in the study of those events.

In addition to these two realms there is a third. There is the realm involved in describing the first and the second realms, especially the second. This realm is the philosophy-of-science level. In this realm, we are concerned with the characteristics of science; for example, with whether or not it is unified and paradigmatic. This is the level of our present considerations, the concern with preparadigmaticism versus paradigmaticism.

The important point is that these realms of concern are independent, although ordinarily related. Nature may not show discontinuities or categories; yet the sciences that describe nature may categorize and in other ways separate nature. Similarly, the science might be paradigmatic, or potentially so, but its philosophy of science could conceivably display preparadigmaticism. This would be unlikely if the science was actually paradigmatic in a clear way, since the philosophy of science is ordinarily descriptive and would describe this characteristic. But to exemplify the point, let us look at the opposite case. Let us say the science is preparadigmatic; it still has not found unification in major proportions. Notwithstanding, it could nevertheless develop a paradigmatic philosophy of the science. This could be done through the knowledge that other sciences had beginnings in preparadigmatic conflict and later attained paradigmatic unity. It could be projected that sciences generally move progressively toward the paradigmatic state. Realizing the importance of the paradigmatic state, and realizing that preparadigmaticism is an obstacle to this advancement, a philosophy of paradigmaticism for the science could be developed — even though the science had not yet built from below to achieve paradigmatic qualities. Essentially that is the type of projection that is involved in hypothesizing unity in nature before it has been found — for example, contemporary physicists looking for a unified theory. Because other unifying theoretical efforts have been productive in physics in the past, it is assumed that unity exists where it has not yet been found.

It is suggested that development of the philosophy of paradigmaticism in psychology could aid in the development of the science toward the paradigmatic state, by providing impetus for the necessary time and effort expenditure. Until there is a systematic search for unity it will not be found. This possibility is the concern of the present work, as it applies to psychology (and to the other social sciences). Ordinarily, psychology would have to gradually evolve to be a paradigmatic science before its members would have paradigmatic beliefs. But if paradigmatic beliefs are productively dynamic, it would be unfortunate to have to wait until the science changes before the belief changes.

The fact is that beliefs can be changed on a philosophy-of-science level.

Paradigmatic beliefs do not have to await the development of the paradigmatic science. If we have those beliefs we can attempt to establish a paradigmatic science before it would arise in its ordinary, trial-and-error development. One of the purposes of the present essay is to raise the possibility that paradigmaticism can be established conceptually, rather than through after-the-fact-experience with the unified knowledge of a paradigmatic science. Another purpose is to suggest that this paradigmaticism can serve as a foundation for hastening progress toward the attainment of paradigmatic science in psychology and in the social sciences more generally. More will be said of these possibilities in later chapters.

But, one might say, granted that psychology is preparadigmatic and that it has a philosophy of preparadigmaticism, so what? What is the importance of preparadigmaticism? The answer is that preparadigmaticism is an obstacle to progress toward the more advanced paradigmatic state of psychology. In addition, however, it has other dynamic characteristics that interfere with central characteristics of the science. It is in part the intent of the next chapter to outline additional drawbacks of preparadigmaticism in scientific theory construction. In my opinion there is no more important way of advancing psychology as a science than there is through developing an understanding of preparadigmaticism and the preparadigmatic nature of the science.

The president of the Division of Experimental Psychology expressed the following opinion in referring to the general science, in requesting that members of the APA (American Psychological Association) give their votes to having members of the Division elected as representatives to the APA.

> I have become increasingly concerned with how little the field of psychology is perceived as a scientific discipline — by the lay public in general, and by scientific administrators and by legislators in Washington in particular. It seems to me that the future status and vitality of psychology as a science depends in a significant way on the representation of Division 3 [Experimental Psychology] within APA (Shepard 1980, p. 1).

The suggestion when stripped to its essence is that the path to creating a true scientific discipline is through support of the experimental works of experimental psychology. As indicated in chapter 4, however, the experimentalism of experimental psychology is a contributor to the preparadigmatic state of psychology. Moreover, it is the preparadigmatic confusion of the knowledge of psychology that is a major reason why psychology is not widely considered to be a science. If that is the case then increased support of additional experimentation will not result in advancement toward the scientific status desired by experimental psychologists. That advancement will require the systematic development of a philosophy of paradigmaticism as well as the development of methods for creating the unity of knowledge that is evidenced by paradigmatic sciences. The next part of the book will deal, at least on an incipient level, with a discussion of this methodology for creating unity in the science.

Part III
Methodology for Unification

Chapter 8

Constructing Unity in the Disorganized Science

In Chapter 2 it was said at some length that logical positivism took the example of the advanced theories of the physical sciences to be the model by which scientific theory was to be judged generally. There was great emphasis upon the axiomatic-mathematical form of such theory. The other realm of interest was with the formal empirical definition of the empirical terms of such theory. We saw how some of the behaviorists, such as Hull, attempted to follow the guides of logical positivism rather completely, down to the axiomatic form of theory, the use of mathematics, and the emphasis upon precise experimental measurement and the establishment of exact mathematical functions. Skinner, on the other hand, chose to emphasize the nature of the construction of theory strictly through induction of more general principles, on the basis of empirical data (see Bayes 1980; Sidman 1960).

But the conception of theory set forth by logical positivism and operationism did not result in the production of theory in psychology that has been successful in the sense achieved by the paradigmatic sciences. The major theories constructed under the aegis of logical positivism, as we have seen, have been rejected by the body of psychology. Certainly they did not succeed in establishing a paradigmatic revolution in any area of the science. Moreover, these theories have played no role in reducing the pre-paradigmatic chaos of psychology, or in promoting unification. During the period when logical positivism was in sway psychology continued in its pre-paradigmatic development, becoming ever more complex, diverse, and disorganized.

Logical positivism, and psychological philosophies and theories based upon logical positivism, have not provided methods or a program for creating unity of knowledge in the preparadigmatic sciences. Logical positivism provided no understanding of preparadigmaticism, of the special need for organizing knowledge in the preparadigmatic science. With the failure of the learning theories based on logical positivism, in terms of producing a paradigm for psychology, there was a turn away from concern with general theory and from concern with philosophy of science and with theory construction methodology, and a turn towards strictly empirical activities with little theory development.

The latter orientation, however, has not solved the problems of the preparadigmatic science, nor provided a program by which to do so. The disenchantment with logical positivism (see Weimer 1979) has not provided a conceptual foundation for progress in that respect either. Moreover, the field of the philosophy of science has not really dealt with the contemporary preparadigmatic science and its special problems. In the present view, understanding the special characteristics of the preparadigmatic science is basic to understanding theory construction needs in the preparadigmatic science. That is why, as will be seen further on, it was important to describe the characteristics of separatism and the citation methodology involved, for these characteristics have contributed to the artificial diversity of knowledge in psychology. A philosophy of science for psychology must recognize such characteristics as well as the deleterious effects they have upon the science. This knowledge of the preparadigmatic science can provide a basis for considering the special problems of theory construction faced by such a science, as well as for considering methods by which these special problems can be solved.

The point is that a paradigmatic philosophy for psychology is not the same as a philosophy of science derived from the study of paradigmatic sciences. While the latter may be useful in part, it cannot completely serve as a guide. There are special conditions in the preparadigmatic science that the traditional philosopher of paradigmatic science can no longer experience in studying the natural sciences. In short, we need a philosophy of preparadigmatic science that includes a methodology for advancing to the paradigmatic state of science. What is needed is a program for unifying, organizing, and making general the knowledge of psychology, a program that will decrease the separatism practices and the confusion of knowledge in the science. It is the purpose of this chapter, in the context of the present discussions, to make a beginning in this very formidable task. It must be realized that the beginning of any undertaking of scope is incipient and puerile, bound to be bumbling and incomplete. But such beginnings are necessary to open the way for the decisiveness, clarity, and sophistication that can later develop through systematic study.

CITATION METHODOLOGY AND THE SPECIAL CHARACTERISTICS OF THEORY CONSTRUCTION IN THE PREPARADIGMATIC SCIENCE

The importance of the organization of knowledge in science has been indicated, for such things as (1) communication, (2) parsimony, and (3) objective assessment. We can see references to the importance of the organization of knowledge in science. For example, a recent analysis of Thomas A. Edison's effect on science in the United States indicated that a significant segment of the scientific community did not consider Edison to be a scientist, in part because he did not always conduct his work within the systematic knowledge base of science and he did not always publish his findings so they would contribute to the organized store of scientific knowledge (Hounshell 1980, p. 613). The scholar's and the researcher's work is made tremendously more effective by virtue of organized knowledge in contrast to disorganized knowledge. Yet we have seen that the contemporary preparadigmatic science does not have organization of knowledge as an important goal. An essential part of the organization of scientific knowledge resides in relating the works of science to each other, as closely and compactly as possible. Citations play an important role in this task. We cannot see the importance of citations until we consider the preparadigmatic science and we have the opportunity to realize what occurs in the absence of appropriate and necessary citation methodology.

It was for this reason that the examples of separatism were given in detail in Chapter 6. In the present view, systematic study should be made of the weaknesses in citation that occur endemically in psychology, in cases small and insignificant and in cases extensive and of central meaning to the science. As members of a preparadigmatic, separatistic science it behooves us to become fully aware of this area of methodological weakness. It will only be when members of the science have become cognizant of the nature of the problem, and have begun to actively look for deficits in citation, that our science will develop the standards of the natural sciences, the standards that it needs. The lack of citation occurs so customarily in our science because psychological scientists do not have standards that demand otherwise. We do not recognize cases of noncitation. And when we do recognize things that are similar but that are not cross-referenced we do not label this occurrence as an abrogation of standards, as something that is harmful to the science and that should be discouraged. The practices of noncitation are too widespread. Dealt with on a piecemeal basis we would have to make the issue of noncitation continuously.

So our preparadigmatic science needs to realize the extensive deviation from the standards of science that occurs in this area and the enormous and detrimental effect that the deviation has on our science. The systematic study of this area, however, must do more than establish the existence and significance of the lack of an adequate citation methodology in psychology. We must study the other practices related to noncitation that have the same effect, that is, the separation of knowledge that should be integrated. These practices are part of what we might call anti-unity methods and skills. As an example, the author of a work who wishes to separate it from other works and establish the work as an independent element in the science can employ a terminology that is different than the other works. A colleague, Hamid Hekmat, called to my attention an interesting historical case that I can use as an example. The words are by one of the two very famous individuals involved.

> At this time a foreign physician, Dr. S. Freud of Vienna, came to Salpetriere and became interested in these studies [traumatic memories in hysteria]. He granted the truth and published some new observations of the same kind. In these publications he changed first of all the terms that I was using; what I called psychological analysis he called psychoanalysis, what I called psychological system, in order to designate that totality of facts of consciousness and movement, whether of members or of viscera, whose association constitutes the traumatic memory, he called complex; he considered repression what I considered a restriction of consciousness; what I referred to as a psychological dissociation, or as moral fumigation, he baptized with the name of catharsis (Janet 1924, p. 41).

What Janet is claiming is Freud's practice of utilizing previously formulated theoretical elements, without citation, while actually obscuring whatever similarities are involved by changing the names of the elements. This practice appears to occur innumerably within the multitudinous elements of psychology and the result is enormous artificial complexity and disorganization. Theorists should, rather, feel it to be necessary to simplify and organize the science as much as possible through terminology and citations. Standards should be set up and practices introduced that discourage the introduction of new terms for concepts or principles that already exist under another name. New terms should only be introduced for new elements. Moreover, discovery and identification of cases involving the same or similar concepts existing in two theories, under different names, should be considered a productive finding in our science — a finding that is worthy of publication when the elements involved are important to the science, or when the resulting simplification to the science merits publication.

Another example of anti-unity methods can refer to the case of separatism described in Chapter 6 that involved extensive overlap between two theories. The theorist, whose theory was said to lack the many citations that would have indicated its intellectual roots, defended his lack of reference to one closely related theory in a way that revealed additional aspects of his separatistic methodology. As an example, this theorist substantiated the priority of his introduction of an important concept by saying that as of a particular date the competitive theorist had written a book that had not even mentioned the particular concept in the subject index. That was true, but entirely misleading. While the concept was not listed in the subject index of that book, the concept was explicitly introduced into the basic principles of the theory involved, and the concept's applications were spelled out in detail in another section of the book. And that book, with its original materials, was read by the criticized theorist prior to his own introduction of the concept. The criticized theorist also rationalized his noncitation of the earlier work by suggesting that his own theory was different, and thus the overlapping of certain parts did not call for citation. This has been described to indicate that separatism is a methodology with distinct skills.

It is thus proposed, contrary to the methodology of separatism, that two similar elements must be cross-referenced regardless of what the authors of the elements think regarding the differences in their theories. There should be no excuse for the absence of citation if the theories have begun in the same tradition. If one of the theorists has originated new elements that are later added to the other theory, than the later theorist should acknowledge the source of those innovations. It is important to the science to know from whence the originality has come, and to know that the two theories are the same in this element. It is also important that the recognition of the value of the innovation be appropriately credited to the proper theorist, to supply his rewards and to maintain his productive efforts, as well as to give the status to his theory that will objectively assess its rightful influence in the science.

The same is true if the theories have begun in different traditions, regardless of the fact that one has different underpinnings, a different terminology, or that the theory takes different positions in basic and schismatic areas. If that theory has an element that is the same as some competitive theory, then the theory should cite that competitive theory and indicate the overlap. The goal here is not the maximal separation of the theories, to show as much originality for the particular theorist as possible. The goal must not be to exclude one's competitors from the enhancement that citations bring. *The goal must be the organization of knowledge in the science and the proper apportioning of value that constitutes objective evaluation.* We cannot continue to accept preparadigmatic standards that allow the abrogation of the need for organization and objective evaluation. When a theory has not cited a prior, related work then the theory is in error.

Whether there has been a scholarly oversight, a deliberate omission, or an inability to see relationships in the face of superficial differences, the error should be corrected.

Very importantly, the science must accept the correction of such errors as a valuable addition to the science. Because the separatism in our science is so great there are innumerable cases of noncitation and nonrelating of similar elements in our science. We thus should devote space in our journals to notes that perform cross-referencing when this has not been done adequately by the theorist who has published a paper. This practice would do wonders for immediately improving the organization of our science. Not only would the notes providing the cross-referencing do a service in their own right, the practice of publishing such notes would have the immediate effect of getting authors to be more searching and analytic in composing their works. While it might be said with good reason that it would be impossible to trace every antecedent to some conceptual element, it is nevertheless the case that there should not be glaring omissions and egregious errors. The point is that these types of errors occur endemically today, and have occurred in this manner in the past. It is time that our standards be raised so this is no longer continued. More will be said of the other concerns that arise in the context of achieving organized knowledge.

To continue, however, there are other skills that make up the methodology of separatism. The author of a conceptual work, for example, may use citations to cloak the fact that he has not cited the materials most relevant to his conception — materials that are sources of origination for his work. That is, the author may abundantly cite works that are tangentially related and omit reference to a central predecessor. When such a case has been seen, it should be the occasion for an analysis that would indicate what has happened, even if the analysis is by the author whose work has been omitted. Again, adoption of a policy of publication of important works of this kind would have an immediate effect on curbing the practices involved. It might be said that self-interest might motivate authors to complain of noncitation and result in a superabundance of such notes submitted for publication. I would think not. For one thing, if this occurred, editorial standards would form such that only the most deserving cases would be published, and this would quickly be conveyed to those who otherwise might write up undeserving cases of citation breakdown. As in any other type of publication, potential authors would begin to weigh the reward-cost factors in spending their time on this type of article versus another type. It is important, however, that such an avenue be opened.

Another way of taking conceptual materials from someone else without citation is to develop the materials in a different field or in a different way. Sometimes the original conceptual material may at first be presented in an undeveloped way. Although the material has much heuristic value even in that presentation, development in full panoply could be done in a manner more impressive than the original work. Credit for the full originality of the conception could accrue to the secondary effort, by its ability to outshine the original work. The case of Cauchy described by Ravetz (1971, p. 256) can be used as illustration here. He would take the idea of a paper, which as an original would be presented in relatively undeveloped form, and elaborate the idea, generalize it in various ways, and then publish it without reference to the original. His masterpiece of work would make the original seem jejune, and he would thus snare the credit for his own work. The point is that there are a number of such cases in psychology, and these have the pernicious effects upon the science that have been described. Again, presentations of such cases to correct the errors that have been made should be considered as of publishable merit, when they have been well-done and when their content is significant to the science. The fact that concepts and principles are developed with different subjects, different apparatus, or different types of behavior, should not mean that the researcher or theorist does not have to cite the original work involved.

Thus, what is called for here is a change in our citation methodology. This should include a systematic study of what our citation methodology is at the present time and what it should be to promote the organization of knowledge that is a primary characteristic of advanced sciences. This should include developing our standards of citation. And it should include introduction of procedures that will correct current errors and that will insure the diminution of such errors in the future. "It is vital to maintain the continuity of the scientific enterprise: hence great stress is laid on the requirement that scientific investigators give due credit to their predecessors by proper citation of their work" (Edsall 1975, p. 10). That standard of paradigmatic science should be extended to the contemporary preparadigmatic sciences. Articles that cross-reference and thus integrate formerly separate, but similar, science elements would contribute more to our science than most published articles or novel findings and theories.

Historical Citation

In the chapter on separatism in psychology an editorial reviewer, remarking on the case of the theory that had not adequately cited its relationships to other theories, said that there would be "great merit in someone writing a thorough . . . paper tracing all the roots . . . of the theory involved. We need to know the intellectual foundations of our current ideas." This need is not clearly understood in psychology, as is attested by the opinion of another reviewer who said that "everyone would go crazy [attempting to trace the roots of a theory], because any idea can be traced to hundreds of historical antecedents." Both of these psychologists, with such opposite opinions, are prominent in the science, and presumably sophisticated in the ways of the science. Their disagreement, however, is in a fundamental aspect of methodology. The science is obviously confused on the topic, yet it is not one that has been given systematic consideration. This suggests that this important aspect of methodology be given the study that is necessary to indicate why standards of citation are necessary that indicate the historical derivations of theoretical principles and concepts.

One of the reasons that separatism exists, as has been indicated, is because there is an unclear conception of what constitutes originality in psychology. It is felt that for a theory or concept or principle to be original it must be novel, rather completely. A very general view is that if derivations are indicated from previous theoretical statements, then the contribution is correspondingly devalued. Because there is an imprecision in what psychology considers as originality in theory construction, the science does not provide good guides concerning how to relate one's work to the work of predecessors.

This requires elaboration. That is, we must consider that scientists in a preparadigmatic science like psychology are torn when they introduce a theoretical work. On the one hand the scientist knows his or her theory includes originality. Yet, the theory has roots in previously published works, let us say. As a consequence we would expect the theorist to be moved by personal ambitions to maximize the originality. Minimization of the contributions of predecessors to the ideas in the theory, moreover, will accomplish that goal. That constitutes strong motivation for neglecting to relate one's work to that of preceding works.

This is given impetus in a science that does not have a good idea of how originality occurs in science. In the science that understands the manner in which conceptual materials grow, with various contributions to originality in a building process, there is greater understanding of shared recognition. The individual can indicate what it is that has been derived from the past, and thus indicate that which is an original contribution. An equitable sharing is possible. However, if the science is confused by its chaos of knowledge and does not have rules and standards for assigning originality to progressively developing science materials, then there is not a good guide for the scientist in the task of attributing originality. There is pressure on the scientist to maximize originality and to minimize that which came before. When this is a general aspect of the theory construction methods of science, then occurs what Kuhn has described for the preparadigmatic scientist, where each scientist "feels" that each theory must be built from scratch. I would state this differently. It is not that preparadigmatic scientists have nothing upon which to draw in setting up their own theory. It is more that the preparadigmatic science says that only the pristinely new is original. This conception of the science tells the scientist to differentiate the theory as much as possible from predecessors and the theory construction task is approached in that manner. This process has been exemplified earlier. Thus, the second-generation learning theorists, in constructing their learning theories, did not systematically trace the development through the preceding first-generation learning theorists, and beyond. Each formulated his own theory, which was then to be considered as an independent theory. With that methodology as a model, the next generation of theorists is moved to continue with the same type of development. The result for the field of learning is much less organization and simplicity than the science could provide.

It was in part to correct the preparadigmatic conception of originality that the concept of the career of a theory was introduced, along with the concept that ideas develop in a progressive manner. This may be elaborated by saying that ideas first arise in a vague statement, typically. The vagueness may be the result of the fact that the idea is mixed in with an unorganized, inconsistent set of conceptual materials. For example, one can find the roots of well-formulated contemporary concepts in ancient writings. But examination of those writings will reveal that the ideas were included along with others that were later discarded because they had no scientific value. The ancient scholar consulting those writings would thus have had a very confused conceptual system that did not at all indicate in a special, clear way the value of the idea. Only when the conceptual chaff had been removed could the good idea be joined with other good ideas to represent a clear, systematic, and heuristic conception.

In other cases the idea has been advanced at an early time, but the idea is stated in a very undeveloped form. For example, Aristotle stated at a very early time the empiricist position that the mind at first is a blank tablet, later filled in by the individual's experience. Aristotle thus anticipated the later British empiricists. But the British empiricists added specifications and clarity and observational examples to the original statement. That conceptual framework then provided a background for later developments that in contemporary times have culminated in scientific works in learning theory and cognitive theory in psychology. Another contemporary example has been described as follows.

> For example, Lewin did indeed introduce a concept of interaction, as did Rotter, and these may be considered as antecedents to the social behaviorism theory. The central point, however, is that Rotter's account of interaction is not simply a repetition of Lewin, Rotter added original elements. And the social behaviorism account is not simply a repetition of the previous two. Much was new in social behaviorism's theory of interac-

tion. And its heuristic value may be considered to be shown by social learning theory's later development of similar elements (Staats 1979, p. 10)

It would be efficacious for our science to become clear on its theory construction methodology. Knowing about the historical, sequential development of original theory is important in our science. For this knowledge can tell us that conceptions typically arise historically and part of the theorist's task is to indicate this, and share the credit. This will also remove the necessity of attempting to create distinctive theory, of dressing up theoretical ideas with new terminology and other idiosyncratic paraphernalia. The theorist can realize that his task is not to disguise (consciously or unconsciously) what has been created before, but is to show originality in terms of clarifying, organizing, integrating, deleting, and adding original elements to previously existing elements. The result of such theory construction can be an original theory, without involving denial of what went before. But for that to be the case the science must have clear standards of the progressive development of theory, and of the extent to which originality involves improving previous ideas. We need systematic consideration of these aspects of theory construction in achieving a unified science. It should be noted, moreover, that the lack of tracing, as assiduously as is practicable, the step-by-step development of ideas detracts from our ability to understand the actual dynamics of theory development. When historical and contemporary citation is missing we are given an inflated idea of theory emerging by only saltations rather than by the actually occurring building process, with steps as well as jumps.

THE INTEGRATIVE RESEARCH REVIEW: RECOGNITION OF NEED FOR UNIFICATION

One of the characteristics of psychology described here is its chaotic state of knowledge and the lack of effort to correct this characteristic. Various methods are needed to organize the knowledge of the preparadigmatic science. We can see support for this, at least in part, in the statement, "The most common challenge of integrative reviews of modern social science is finding order in apparent chaos" (Jackson 1980, p. 444). There are frequent reviews of areas of research findings in the social sciences and it might be thought on this basis that a major investment has been made in this area and in the methodology of organizing our knowledge. It is thus interesting to consider the state of development of the integrative review of the literature, for it is a rather singular attempt at organization in the preparadigmatic science. Jackson has recently described the purpose of such reviews as follows.

Reviews of research are a fundamental activity in the behavioral sciences; they usually precede any major new research study and also are done as independent scholarly works. The focuses and purposes of such reviews vary substantially. Some investigators are primarily interested in sizing up new substantive and/or methodological developments in a given field. Some are primarily interested in verifying existing theories or developing new ones. Some are interested in synthesizing knowledge from different lines or fields of research, and still others are primarily interested in inferring generalizations about substantive issues from a set of studies directly bearing on those issues (Jackson 1980, p. 438).

Although the words employed in this summary seem to involve some of the goals of the types of integatory theory that will be discussed in a later section, in actuality there are very few reviews of research that attain anything in the way of unified theory. The interest in synthesizing knowledge from different lines or fields of research, moreover, is very poorly developed, and there is little in the way of such integration. The point has been made here that the psychologist lacks the methodological tools, the orientation, and the motivation to attempt the task of unifying knowledge across the superficial differences that are considered important in the pre-paradigmatic science. Jackson's article is proof itself of this assessment. His major point is that there is no methodology even for the integrative research review and that this area of interest has been totally ignored.

Given the importance and widespread conduct of integrative reviews, one might expect a fairly well-developed literature on methods, techniques, and procedures for conducting such reviews, but this is not the case. An earlier examination by this author of a convenience sample of 39 books on general methodology in sociological, psychological, and educational research revealed very little explanation of matters other than the use of card catalogs, indexes to periodicals, and note taking. Only four of these books discussed how to define or sample the universe of sources to be reviewed, three discussed criteria by which to judge the adequacy of each study, and only two discussed how to synthesize validly the results of different studies. None of the discussions exceeded two pages in length.

Similarly, a preliminary examination of journal article titles in *Sociological Abstracts* . . . , *Psychological Abstracts* . . . , and *Current Index to Journals in Education* . . . revealed a dearth of work on integrative review methods. Entries under the following subject headings were examined: literature reviews, methods, methodology, research methods, and research reviews. Only five of the titles from approximately 2,050 entries appeared directly relevant. Upon examination, one of the sources proved to be inappropriate and another could not be located. . . .

Additional evidence that there are few explicated methods, techniques, and procedures for integrative reviews is that few published integrative reviews adequately describe the methods used (Jackson 1980, pp. 438-39).

It should be remembered, moreover, that Jackson's concern is with the integrative review of research, in rather well-defined problem areas, and not with the unified-theory orientation seen to be so necessary in the present analysis. Nevertheless, Jackson's evaluation reveals that even such a first step in organizing knowledge as represented by the integrative research review receives little attention in psychology and the social sciences. Further support of this suggestion is given by Feldman, whom Jackson also quotes. Feldman stated there is "little formal or systematic analysis of either the methodology or the *importance* of . . . reviewing and integrating . . . the 'literature' " (1971, p. 86, italics added) and, further, that "half-hearted commitment in this area might account in part for the relatively unimpressive degree of cumulative knowledge in many fields of the behavioral sciences" (p. 86).

These observations coincide with and substantiate the view that has been described here in the chapter on separatism; that is, that theories with heavily overlapping elements do not indicate the commonality involved, through appropriate use of references and citations. It has already been suggested that editorial reviewers in the preparadigmatic sciences are not sure of the standards that apply, and thus cannot perform their role of guaranteeing the citation of relevant literature. We see the same processes referred to in the discussion of the integrative research review. "The failure of almost all integrative review articles to give information indicating the thoroughness of the search for appropriate primary sources does, however, suggest that neither the reviewers nor their editors attach a great deal of importance to such thoroughness" (Jackson 1980, p. 444). Moreover, there is recognition that the reviewer may function according to unspecified, perhaps personally selective, methods. "Despite the lack of explicit methodology for doing integrative reviews, each review is the result of implicit methods, consciously or unconsciously selected by the reviewer" (Jackson 1980, p. 440). Even in the integrative review of research, a methodology is important to insure that selective factors have not biased the results. The following corroborates some of the points made in discussing separatistic lack of citation in theory construction where, in the present view, the methodology is even worse than it is in the integrative research review.

There are . . . reasons for carefully reporting the literature-search process in an integrative review article. First, it helps the reader to judge the comprehensiveness and representativeness of the sources that are the subject of the review. Just as the sample in a primary study can critically influence the findings of the study, the selection of the primary and secondary studies that are included in a review can seriously affect the results of the review. The bibliography of a review article indicates what individual studies were included in the review, *but it does not indicate what broad classes of possibly relevant studies were excluded*. A person with a thorough knowledge of the research on the topic will be able to infer such omissions by carefully examining the bibliography, but persons with less-thorough knowledge of the topic will not be able to do so (italics added) (Jackson 1980, p. 457).

It is thus an important development that the topic of methodology of integrative research reviews is becoming of interest in psychology and the social sciences (see also Rosenthal and Rubin 1978; and Schmidt, Hunter, Pearlman, and Shane 1979). There is an incipient recognition in this work that our science has not given an appropriate attention to the necessity for organizing the chaotic fund of knowledge that it has produced. This area of concern has not gotten to the heart of the problem, however, to the preparadigmatic nature of social science and the need for a broad development toward paradigmaticism and the paradigmatic state of science. Nevertheless, this concern with the research review has isolated one symptom of the preparadigmatic state of social science. And systematic study of the integrative research review is important in the same way that systematic consideration of integrative theory, citation methodology, and related topics are important.

INTEGRATORY THEORY

When we talk about omissions of citation of related materials we are talking about errors. The same is true when studies are omitted from an integrative research review, when those studies should have been included. That is, we are saying that there are materials that are recognizably similar that are not being cited in that manner. We are not dealing with making an original discovery of similarity of things that have formerly been considered in the science to be distinctly different. It should be noted, however, that there is not a strict dichotomy involved here. A fact that should be recognized, especially in the preparadigmatic science, is that the detection of sameness, on the basic level, cutting through the haze of superficial differences, can be creative insight of immense value to science. This type of insight can occur on various levels of significance, involving various degrees of difficulty in recognizing the sameness; and different people have differing abilities to see relationships.

The central point in the present discussion is that there is a continuum of the closeness of similarity between knowledge elements of a science.

There are cases where there are elements in two theories, for example, that are clearly the same. If there is an absence of citation in such a case, this is clearly an error. No special insight is necessary to see the similarity when the materials are compared. Only when the principle or concept is developed in the context of different subjects, different apparatus, or different experimental procedures does it require some analysis to see underlying similarity. Then there are cases where there is similarity on the basis of underlying, basic principle but where the differences are of such an extent that it is very difficult to see the similarity. The task will be more difficult, even requiring an original insight, if one does not clearly know the principles. Thus, the task may be a theoretical task of formulating, as a discovery, just what those principles are, so that one can see similarity where no one could see it before.

The citation-methodology section dealt with the lower end of the continuum where the similarity in materials is clear, where the similarity has not been cited, and where this is an outright error. The present section, and the next section, will deal with the parts of the continuum involving relationships in scientific knowledge that are not so apparent, where an act of originality may be involved in detecting similarity.

Let us begin with an example in learning and motivational theory. As was mentioned in an earlier chapter, following Pavlov's discovery of classical conditioning and Thorndike's discovery of instrumental conditioning, theorists took different positions concerning the basic principles of learning. There were those (for example, Hull) who thought that both types of conditioning involved strengthening responses to stimuli through the responses being followed by reinforcement, as occurs in instrumental conditioning of motor responses. Then there were theorists (for example, Guthrie) who posited that both types of conditioning occurred through contiguity of stimuli, as occurs in classical conditioning of emotional responses. Finally, there were theorists (like Skinner) who considered there to be two types of conditioning, but the two types were entirely separate. In addition, there were various two-process theories that suggested that classically conditioned emotional responses could serve in some manner to bring about instrumental behavior (see Kimble 1961; Miller 1948; Mowrer 1950; Overmier and Lawry 1979; Rescorla and Solomon 1967; Staats 1963).

In contemporary times there have emerged several different, unrelated theories, based upon previous two-process conceptions, that have elaborated and emphasized the interactions between the classical conditioning of emotional responses and the instrumental conditioning of motor responses. The theories state that emotional responses are conditioned to stimuli via classical conditioning, that as a consequence the stimuli gain incentive (motivational) properties in the sense that motor responses not previously learned to the stimuli will then be elicited by the stimuli. The several theories state that the manner in which a stimulus will elicit approach behaviors or avoidance behaviors from the organism will depend upon whether the stimulus has been paired previously with positive or negative emotional stimuli. Bindra (1978) states this theory in the context of animal learning theory, animal motivation theory, physiological psychology, and ethology. Overmier and Lawry (1979) state this theory in the context of animal learning and the mediation of behavior in the type of experiment referred to as "transfer of control," in which it is shown in a specific type of apparatus that a stimulus previously paired with an emotional stimulus will, with no other training, have tendencies to elicit approach or avoidance motor behaviors. Byrne and his associates (Byrne and Clore 1970; Byrne 1971) have briefly elaborated like principles in the context of attraction experiments in social psychology. The present author has developed the principles as basic in a theory that deals with various aspects of psychology ranging from animal learning to complex social behaviors (Staats 1963, 1964, 1968a, 1968b, 1975).

It should be indicated that each of these theories has its own concepts and analyses and empirical findings that are different from the other theories. Moreover, the terminology is largely different from one to another theory. These theories arose in independent work, are considered as separate and independent, and the phenomena to which they address themselves are considered as separate and independent. There has been a minimum of integration of the knowledge bounded by these theories. There is no mention of relationship of the theories across the interest areas of human and animal learning, for example. To illustrate, the fact that the theories of Byrne and Staats utilize and verify the principles on the human level is not integrated into the animal learning theories, and the reverse is also true, for the most part. This separation is not a question of weak citation methodology, however. The science itself imposes the separation. The areas of research are considered to be different and independent. An act of originality is necessary to bring together what today are considered to be these quite different theories, to show their points of overlap, to organize these aspects of knowledge of the science.

The point is, thus, that the preparadigmatic science of psychology needs integratory articles that will establish the relationships between its related knowledge elements. In the above example, it would be very important for the animal-learning theories and human-learning theories to be related to one another. There is important commonality, and the implications are very significant for the science. We have today in psychology articles whose purpose is to review the literature — usually experimental literature — in a particular area. However, these reviews deal with elements that are already clearly demarcated as being in the same area of concern. The type of integratory article that is proposed here as a theoretical task concerns the unification of theoretical efforts that are similar, without the similarity being apparent. The divisive nature of the science has erected barriers to unification across the areas involved, yielding multiple, competing theories. Moreover, the science has not set — as an important, creative task — the formulation of integrations of theories that have overlapping common elements.

We need integratory theorists, and works that pull together the chaos of such materials that exist in psychology. Following the above example, it is important to know that a set of principles is heuristic in the context of animal studies involving "transfer of control," and so on, in the context of ethnological and physiological considerations, in dealing with the topic of interpersonal attraction and other interests of social psychology, and in other areas such as personality, abnormal psychology, and psychological testing. One of the most important characteristics of scientific principles concerns generality. How can psychologists know the value of the principles of the new two-process theories unless the relevance of the principles for *various* phenomena is known? The inability to provide such integration leaves us in ignorance of the generality of the principles involved in each of these theories. This means psychologists cannot experience the fact of unity and simplicity that the science knowledge actually contains in this area. This is but one case. Psychology is full of such cases; they are endemic. An earlier chapter showed that the classic learning theories of the 1940s compose such a case. Today there is an unrecognized confluence of theories of intelligence that consider intelligence to be learned, at least in part. There is another unrecognized confluence of similar principles in theories of child development based upon hierarchical learning of repertoires of skills. Another case involves the new theories of personality that include behavioral principles and environmental-personality interaction. Another case involves theories combining both cognitive theory and behavior theory principles. There are many, many more. Because there are theories in each case with overlapping principles whose similarity goes unrecognized, the science is more complex, less organized, less unified than it could be. In other terms, our science is more preparadigmatic, or less paradigmatic, than it could be. This need for integratory theory and integratory theorists is great, for the unrecognized commonality in psychology is great.

Collapsing Theories

The present topic has been that of integration of theoretical elements that are actually overlapping. It should be noted that the proportion of overlap that exists between two or more theories may vary in amount. There may be a small proportion of overlap (which it may be noted is still important for the science to know). Or, the overlap may be a very considerable proportion. Cases described in the last chapter of theories that overlapped extensively in central principles are examples.

The present message is that when the amount of similarity in basic principles is large enough — when the overlap involves a good proportion of the basic elements of the theories — then the integratory theory should actually constitute a collapsing of the theories, rather than an indication of the overlap between the several theories involved. There is a point where the science would be better served by having one theory rather than several. The one theory would then present all the commonalities — the overlapping elements — of the several theories. The differences that exist between the several theories would then be indicated as the areas of unsettled knowledge that were still in dispute.

The learning theories of the second-generation theorists such as Tolman, Hull, and Skinner could have been collapsed in this manner. The common elements these theories shared were greater in importance and amount than those that were disputed. Ultimately, the field of learning theory arrived at the point of ignoring the differences in the learning theories by attending only to experimenting on the specifics of the field of learning. It was said that the task was to do detailed work on specific principles rather than to be concerned with grand, general theories. That is an unsatisfactory resolution, however. For one thing that resolution does not realize that there are various fields in psychology that need a general learning theory as a basis for dealing with their problems. In such a case the scientist in that field can only meet his need by selecting one of the existing learning theories. When several such scientists select different basic learning theories, this insures that the things they develop will continue the separatism of the basic theories. If the basic theories were collapsed in an integratory theoretical effort, however, there would be no impetus to separatism. For this and other reasons, collapsing theory of an integratory nature would be very important. There are, moreover, many divided areas in psychology that could be unified by constituting such integratory theories.

INTEGRATORY SKILLS: ANALYSIS BY PRINCIPLE

It has been said that we need conceptual works that strip away obfuscatory distinctions to reveal simplifying commonality. It is the central weakness of the preparadigmatic science that it cannot recognize commonality. For to recognize the forest of commonality in the complexity of all of the trees takes skill. The integratory theorist must be able to go into different areas of the science and cut across the fact that the relevant similarities may be embedded in theories that have differences in addition to the similarities. The scientist must be able to cut across differences in methods, apparatus, terminology, and subjects. As will be indicated, the integratory theorist must have skills of theory construction that are not presently taught in the preparadigmatic science, and also have goals that are not presently a part of the preparadigmatic science.

Let me elaborate; take the example that was developed in the earlier section concerning the overlapping theories that have emphasized the interactions between classical conditioning and instrumental conditioning. For one thing, the principles regarding the interactions of conditioning — the part on which the theories overlap — are basic. The rest of the theoretical structures of the theories involved, their less basic parts, are quite different. Bindra (1978) includes in his theory concepts like pexgo, contingency organization, and pexgo priming. The terminology of Overmier and Lawry (1979) deals with the concepts of AvCSs (aversive Pavlovian CSs), ApCSs (apetitive Pavlovian CSs), r_p-s_p (detachable components of shock-elicited pain, R_p, and its feedback, S_p), and so on. Staats (see 1968b, 1975) employs terms like CS, DS, and RS (standing for conditioned stimulus, directive stimulus, and reinforcing stimulus), and extends the principles in a variety of ways. And Byrne and Clore (1970) describe their model very briefly, not indicating a foundation for the principles in basic animal study, but extending the model to attraction research. In each case, thus, the overlapping principles are only a part — albeit a central part — of a complicated theoretical structure that deals with complex experimental findings, in different research areas, using different methods. The science would be simpler and more useful if the principles common to all of these theories were abstracted as one theory. Then theorists could pursue their individualistic tasks on the basis of a common foundation. But seeing the common principles is not easy.

Seeing similarities requires skill. Before one can perform analyses that abstract similarities from among a bewildering assortment of differences, one must have intimate knowledge of the materials involved. Gaining that intimate knowledge is a big task. One must also have the goal of finding similarity, and tools by which to recognize it. If psychology is to have that skill in some of its members, it must begin to train students as theorists, with the appropriate background and purpose. We can see what is needed by contrast with paradigmatic science, as the following indicates.

> Lacking time to multiply examples, I suggest that an acquired ability to see resemblances between apparently disparate problems plays in the sciences a significant . . . role. . . . That ability to recognize group-licensed resemblances is, I think, the main thing students acquire by doing problems, whether with pencil and paper or in a well-designed laboratory.

In the course of their training a vast number of such exercises are set for them, and students entering the same specialty regularly do very nearly the same ones, for example, the inclined plane, the conical pendulum, Kepler ellipses, and so on. These concrete problems with their solutions are what I previously referred to as exemplars, a community's standard examples (Kuhn 1977, p. 471).

Weimer describes this concept succinctly in saying that "What the scientist learns in working with exemplars is how to see disparate phenomena as manifestations of common underlying principles" (1979, p. 54). Psychology students, as has been indicated, have no training in abstracting common underlying principles from disparate phenomena or from theories with disparate characteristics. That training will only be provided after psychological theorists engage in the type of unifying works that are being described here. These works will then serve as the exemplars for students in their training to use to recognize commonality in their science as well as to recognize the importance of discovering common principles within the obfuscation of disparate appearances. The ability to see common underlying principles is essential to each of the types of unification that is being discussed here. That ability is learned, and the preparadigmatic science of psychology does not teach it presently.

SCHISM UNIFICATION

In Chapter 4 some of the schismatic issues were described that divide psychologists. The issues involved broad conceptual elements rather than specific theories. Various schisms were exemplified such as the subjectivist-objectivist (phenomenological-behaviorist) schism, the nature-nurture schism, the holistic-versus-atomistic schism, the individual-versus-the-general schism, the freedom-versus-determinism schism, the basic-applied schism, and so on. The important point in the present context is that these schisms each underlie multiple divisions in psychology. For example, the experimental-observation-versus-naturalistic-observation schism occurs in various areas of psychology. There are clinical psychologists whose knowledge is based upon clinical (naturalistic) observations and who have no confidence whatsoever that anything that takes place in the experimental laboratory will have significance for psychotherapy. And there are experimental psychologists who entirely eschew naturalistic observations such as those that occur in the clinic. Such experimental psychologists may be developmental psychologists, social psychologists, or educational psychologists. Thus, various theories may be constructed in opposition to one another because they take different sides on schisms of this and other kinds.

The point is that these schisms represent obstacles to the attainment of unified theory and unified knowledge in psychology. Such schisms are the basis for separating theories completely even when they contain commonality. But there have been few attempts to resolve the schisms within a framework that is constructive on the one hand, and scientifically productive on the other, attempts that deal with the particular issue on a basic level of resolution.

In the present view an important aspect of theory construction for a paradigmatic psychology must include consideration of the types of schisms under discussion. From my own work, within the theoretical approach that is to be mentioned in the next chapter, I can make some suggestions concerning the objectives of such consideration, and a few points concerning a methodological orientation. To begin, in the present view the theorist who wishes to resolve one of the conceptual schisms must consider each side and clarify the objectives of each side and the knowledge that each has accrued in the development of its position. This is part of formulating the goal of unification. Presumably, if able individuals have been concerned with an orientation over a long period of time and have developed scientific materials in the process, there will be productive elements involved. However, also presumably, if two positions having productive elements are nevertheless in direct opposition to each other, then there are elements involved in the positions and in the statement of the conflict that are unproductive. It should be noted that the schisms include not only the knowledge base and the position of each side, but also a particular characteristic involving the way the battle is enjoined, the way the disagreement is stated.

Ordinarily it will not be sufficient that one merely attempts to patch up a disagreement by recognizing that each position has value. We have an example of such an attempt in the "interaction" approach to the nature-nurture schism. That is, after psychologists had argued over a long period the relative contribution of biology and environment in determining intelligence, without resolution of the schism, it was suggested in the interaction approach that intelligence was a function of both heredity and environment. The suggestion was to stop fighting, for both sides were important. This served the purpose of temporarily quieting the argument — which had more or less worn itself out for the time being — but the interaction position provided no real resolution of the conflicting opinions. Something more is required than merely saying that both positions have merit. In the specific case each approach has continued to strive to indicate its own importance in contrast to the other, as shown in the work of Jensen and others (Jensen 1969; Shockley 1971), on the hereditarian side, and Kamin and others (see Heber, Garber, and Hoffman 1971; Hirsch 1981; Kamin 1974), on the environmentalistic side.

The nature-nurture schism has broken out anew and today is as intense as it ever was. The concerns of each side have not been met within a common framework that is generally accepted and that can serve a heuristic purpose for each side. (A general framework for the resolution has been provided — see Staats 1968b, 1971a, 1975 — and works specifically treating the topic have been formulated, see Staats 1981; Staats and Burns 1981.) In the present view there is no question that, on the biological side, there is a powerful fund of knowledge. We know a great deal about things biological in terms of anatomy, physiology, and genetics. Investigators today are delving into the secrets of heredity on the very basic level of microbiology, and new potentialities for affecting hereditary traits are being investigated. And in psychology many observations have been made and much conceptual development has occurred that has stemmed from the conception that very central human characteristics are inherited and develop in the child through biological maturation. It is undeniable, on the other hand, that organisms have great ability to adjust to the environment through behavioral alterations, that is, through learning. In humankind this ability is so great it constitutes a quantum jump over the learning ability of the lower animals. There is also a fund of knowledge in this sphere ranging from the basic principles of conditioning to applications in clinical, child, social, and educational psychology of recent vintage. These are thus two imposing bodies of knowledge locked in opposition. The point is that any general theory of human behavior must deal with the facts of inheritance, and the various types of knowledge in psychology, based on the assumption of inherited human characteristics, in a manner that interlocks productively with the consideration that important human characteristics are heavily determined by learning. When two empirically sound bodies of knowledge exist, our grasp of the history and character of paradigmatic science justifies considerable confidence that the bodies of knowledge will not fundamentally be inconsistent — that one will not demolish the other as erroneous or insignificant.

In resolving such schisms it must be assumed that there are important bodies of knowledge on both sides, as well as elements on each side that are not productive. The resolution of a schism then must be a task of the true theoretician, for what is demanded is the formulation of a set of principles that will allow one to consider in basic terms the productive information on each side, in a way that unites the two bodies of knowledge. This will demand seeing also that not all of the elements of one or both sides contribute to this solution, and in fact the task may necessitate rejection of central elements, or relegation of them to a body of knowledge that is irrelevant or nonessential to the building of the general theory. While the resolution of such schisms is a task for special and detailed consideration, perhaps it will be possible to exemplify what is being suggested.

Let us refer to the schism regarding whether human behavior is determined by external forces (the environment) or internal personal forces. The latter view is the traditional view. It is that humans have an internal personality, free will, soul, mind, or what have you, that acts as a determinant of his behavior. It may be recognized also in this view that individuals are affected by their environment. But nevertheless it is emphasized that the individual's personal forces are the specially potent sources of causation. Not everyone will respond the same in the same environment, according to this view, and there is much naturalistic evidence that supports this. This conception has various implications for the study of human behavior. For example, if it is true that humans have personal characteristics (a personality) that determine how they behave, independently of other causal circumstances such as the environment, then it is reasonable to construct instruments to measure personality. In psychology a very important segment of the efforts of the science has gone into developing these possibilities. Many psychological test instruments have been constructed that follow that conception. To elaborate, different ways of responding are observed that appear to be a function of an internal personal characteristic, and a test is systematically constructed to measure that aspect of personality. Intelligence tests constitute one type of personality test. Such tests have proved their ability to predict future performance, and to serve practical purposes by means of this predictive value. There is a great deal of substantive and methodological knowledge concerning human behavior that is given by such tests.

Theorists of personality and of personality measurement, however, have also tended to downplay, or to pretty completely reject, the importance of learning as a determinant of personality. Although they might admit that humans have an ability to learn that is very great in comparison to other species, their concern is not with how humans learn their complex human characteristics. Rather generally they assume the characteristics are inherited. Their conception, centrally, orients them in the direction of establishing the personality characteristics that determine human behavior. Moreover, their methodology never studies the way human behavior is learned, and in this state of ignorance concerning learning—and from the standpoint of their special knowledge of personality—such psychologists continually interpret aspects of human behavior in terms of inherited personality, not in terms of learning, and this constitutes a rejection of learning, even when it does not occur in an overt oppositional action.

Let us consider the other side of the schism. A primary tenet of behaviorism from its inception has been that the existence of internal processes and structures having a determining effect upon humans' behavior should not be inferred unless there are observations on which to base such inferences. For example, at one time it was popular to infer the existence of an instinct by which to explain every type of behavior that was observed. The behavioristic position was that the concept of instinct was circular, being inferred as a cause of a particular type of behavior, when in fact the only observation that had been made was of the behavior itself. Behaviorism said we can observe the organism's behavior. That is an objective fact. We can observe the environment, also objectively. We can establish the principles by which the environment affects behavior. These are the types of principles that have explanatory value, that can lead to the control of behavior (as in the treatment of problems of behavior). But instincts are never directly observed.

Furthermore, the behavioristic position in its actions rejected the concept of personality (among other subjective concepts). It said that personality was another circular term; personality theorists had observed that there were different types of behavior and then had inferred that there were personality traits that determine individual differences in that type of behavior. But, behaviorists said, no one ever observes a personality trait, such as intelligence. One only observes behavior. Some people demonstrate better problem solving, academic performance, and so on. People behave in certain characteristic ways. That is actually what constitutes their personalities in this view. People have simply learned to behave differently. It is thus a waste of time trying to measure personality. There is no personality, only the way individuals behave. The task is to study the principles of learning. Behaviorists thus ignored any individual differences in their study. Tolman introduced a theoretical term in his learning theory to be concerned with individual differences in learning. But the term was never developed. The field of personality was entirely ignored and rejected by behaviorists such as B.F. Skinner and his followers in continuing the Watsonian orientation.

As is general in such schisms, the statement of the confrontation, the framework of the positions, does not provide a means by which each side can employ to any advantage the very great time and effort expended and the productive findings that have been established by the other position. Personality theorists traditionally make no use whatever of the vast amount of knowledge that is to be found in the study of learning. And behaviorists traditionally make no use of the vast knowledge that is to be found in the field of personality and personality testing. The theoretical framework that can unify these knowledge domains has the potentiality for unleashing great productivity (see also Staats 1971a, 1975; Staats and Burns 1981). In brief it has been suggested that it is necessary to recognize the fact that the individual has personality characteristics that determine his behavior and what happens to the individual. But it is necessary to do so in a way that is not circular. This means that personality must be objectively defined. Moreover, the way that learning affects personality must be indicated. The conditions and principles of learning must be specifically stated as well as the specific effects upon personality. But that is not enough. In addition, the principles by which personality affects behavior must be made explicit and specific.

The theory that resolves the schism is that personality consists of repertoires of behavioral "skills." When the measures of personality are examined, they are seen to be standardized observations of the manner in which individuals differ in these repertoires of skills. Intelligence tests, when examined in that way, are seen to be composed of items that assess the presence or absence of various language-cognitive skills (Staats 1968b, 1971a, 1973, 1975; Staats and Burns 1981), for example. Moreover, when the skills are analyzed in terms of their components it can be seen how they are learned. Other theorists have in recent years presented analyses that are very coincident with this view (Resnick 1976; Estes 1974, 1976; Sternberg 1977).

The important point in terms of the resolution of the schism, however, is that the theory utilizes both domains of knowledge. The theoretical resolution states that the knowledge of personality tests provides the basis for the stipulation of the repertoires of skills that compose the personality trait of intelligence. Moreover, the knowledge of how intelligence affects school and job performance, and so on, is incorporated into the theory. However, the great knowledge of the field of learning theory is also tapped by the unifying theory. The principles of learning are employed to analyze the repertoires of skills. This analysis stipulates conditions that are responsible for the individual acquiring his intelligence repertoires, and the analysis implies thereby that research can be conducted to discover how intelligence is learned. Staats and Burns (1981) have conducted three experiments that show the heuristic value of the unified theory, that intelligence can indeed be learned and hence taught. The findings suggest much additional research, with significance both for the personality theory as well as for behavioral psychology. The unifying theory has heuristic implications also for the construction of intelligence tests and for the use of intelligence tests in dealing with human problems (Staats 1975, chapter 12; Staats and Burns 1981). The fruits of this unifying theory have not yet been exploited in their full measure, but the possibilities of unifying theory can be seen in this illustration. This type of theory can be expected to have all the heuristic potentialities that true unifying theory has. In fact this should be one of the criteria for judging the success of efforts to resolve the schism treated, as will be indicated.

One other example will be examined here, in greater detail to bring out some additional points. The example is very general because it involves a schism that cuts across a number of divisions in psychology, and is related to other schisms as well. The topic thus deserves a very general treatment, which has been given to some extent (Staats 1975, chapters 13 and 15). The schism is that which has been widely recognized between a subjective versus an objective approach. The schism has also been named by referring to behaviorists, on the objective side, and phenomenologists, on the subjective side. Subjectivists have felt that the matter of study in psychology is individual consciousness, the mind. In this view it is the experience of the individual, as given in consciousness, that determines how the individual behaves; thus subjective experience is the key to understanding behavior as well as the mind. Strict behaviorists such as Watson and Skinner rejected the concepts involved in this approach, saying that there was no objective way to study the mind, consciousness, feelings, or other subjective experiential states.

Yet we all have experience with our conscious thoughts in planning and deciding. We all experience emotional states such as anger and joy and love. We talk about our states to others and they to us. And we are better able to deal appropriately with each other as a consequence. The patient refers to and describes subjective states and thoughts and interpretations of life events to the therapist. And the therapist is better able to deal with the patient for having those descriptions. And the patient also appears to profit. It would be a chimera to tell clinical psychologists that they could not use the patient's reports of subjective experience as a source of information about the patient. Telling the therapist that subjective experience was not valid would be foolish, since therapists generally have found in practice that the verbal reports of subjective experience have value, if not perfect reliability or validity. Moreover, as individuals very few of us would want to say that our thoughts, plans, decison-making analyses, and feelings and emotions played no role in influencing what we do. Importantly, psychologists who accept the subjectivist approach do research and conduct psychotherapy, in ways that are highly productive.

This is to say that there is a large fund of knowledge that has been accrued in the service of the subjectivist approach. The methodology of unification would suggest that this body of knowledge should not be ignored, rejected without consideration, or opposed on doctrinaire grounds — as has been the practice of standard behaviorism. (Although this is not relevant to the present discussion, as indicated in chapter 4, subjectivist orientations in turn reject the behavioristic body of knowledge as a means of understanding human behavior.) It is true that there are real problems involved in accepting the subjectivist position as is. The fact is that we cannot observe the mind, or consciousness, or feelings in the sense that has been demanded by standard behaviorism. When a person has said that he has had an experience of a certain sort, or reports an activity of consciousness of a certain sort, there is no way that we can directly observe the internal events involved. Moreover, reports of subjective states do not explain those states. We have ample proof from the history of psychology (Boring 1950) that the methods formulated for the direct study of consciousness and the character of the mind — the methods of introspection — came to naught, because there was no way of using introspection to establish an objective consensus concerning another person's subjective experience.

We must thus ask how we can resolve the schism in such a way that we can include subjectivist interests and subjective events in a psychology that attempts to meet the standards of objective observation. The schism unification was achieved in an earlier analysis (see Staats 1975, ch. 1 and 13) in both a methodological and theoretical manner, the former being the present focus. To begin, the idea of direct and indirect observations in psychology was introduced. Edward Tolman had earlier attempted to incorporate concepts of mental events into a behavioristic approach by saying that such events could become known as they act as a "set of intermediating functional processes which interconnect between the initiating causes of behavior, on the one hand, and the final resulting behavior itself, on the other" (Tolman 1951, p. 88). Tolman called the internal process an intervening variable. Clark Hull employed this methodology also in treating of internal concepts. An example of such intervening variables that Hull (1943) elaborates from Carnap (1935) is that of a man's inferred anger. Hull suggests that anger "lies between 1) the antecedent conditions of frustration and what not which precipitated the state, and 2) the observable consequences of the state, i.e., anger is an unobserved intervening variable" (Hull 1943, p. 277).

For Hull, however, there was to be no other meaning to the intervening variable term than the meaning given by observing the antecedent situation and the consequent behavior (Spence 1944). An intervening variable was considered to be only a logical term. In the present view that was not the correct solution to the problem. In the first place the concept of the intervening variable did not satisfy subjectivists and, furthermore, the approach did not instruct us very much concerning how to integrate knowledge based on subjective experience with objective behavioral knowledge. Observing that (1) in a certain situation (2) a person displays angry behavior does not tell us (3) what went on inside the individual. Nor does the intervening variable, anger, answer the questions of individual differences. There are many situations that will produce angry thoughts in one person and not in another, and the thoughts then affect the behavior displayed. Centrally, the methodology of the intervening variable has not resolved the schism, for the schism between objectivists and subjectivists continues, dividing behaviorism from all of the other approaches that wish to recognize the importance of internal, subjective events in the determination of human behavior.

To elaborate, Hull attempted to sanitize the study of internal events by referring them to external events, to external stimuli on the causative side and to external responses as the end product. This reduced the intervening variable to a mere computational figure in establishing how stimuli cause behavior. But subjectivists are interested in internal events in large part because it is felt these events add something in addition to the external stimulus events, and because we experience the fact that there is indeed something different within us than just the external stimulus situation. We think, we feel, we imagine independently of the external situation. Moreover, there are individual differences in subjective response to the same external situation. The first step in the present summary of the unified position that is involved is to state that something like anger — what we can describe by referring to an anger-producing situation and the angry behavior we see — is not to be considered as an empty logical term but as an actual process. Like subjectivists, we may accept the idea that anger is an internal process that has causative effects on behavior. But, in accord with the demands of science, we have to recognize that we must have some way of specifying the term anger by observational means. And that is where the methodological concept of indirect observation comes in.

When the person is subjected to anger-producing situations and he behaves in an angry fashion, does his heart beat increase in rate, does he perspire more, is there a change in the blood volume of various organs, are glandular secretions, such as adrenalin, increased? These are not direct observations of the subjective experience of anger, that is true; we have not dug into the person's mind to directly observe a mental state. But we may be able to gather much indirect observation and measurement of a subjective state. Moreover, we may be able to characterize the principles that are involved in subjective states such that we can include those principles in our theory of human behavior in a way that gives us a more powerful, comprehensive, unified theory.

Let us elaborate this a bit, using another example. Let us take the concept of pleasure-pain and consider some subjective ideas on the topic. We have much self-observation (introspection) about pleasure that has supplied some of the principles involved, for example, that it has intensity. Based upon such self-examination and other naturalistic evidence the philosophers of the utilitarian hedonism school added other principles. For example, Jeremy Bentham's nineteenth-century principles included stipulation that "each portion of wealth has a corresponding portion of happiness . . . , he who has the most wealth has the most happiness . . . [and the] excess in happiness of the richer will not be so great as the excess in his wealth" (Bentham 1931, p. 103ff). The latter principle is stated in somewhat more modern form in contemporary economics. "According to this law, the *more* an individual has of some given commodity, the less satisfaction (or utility) he would obtain from an additional unit of it" (Ulmer 1959, pp. 319–20). Such principles are based in part upon the self-reports of others as well as introspection of one's own experience. Interestingly, when we come to the study of ethics we see the same concern with the individual's pleasures and happiness. Thomas Hobbes, a seventeenth-century philosopher, wrote in his statements regarding the relativity of ethical principles that "men differ not only in their judgment on the senses of what is pleasant and unpleasant to the taste, smell, hearing, touch, and sight but . . . the same man in diverse times differs from himself, and one time praises — that is, calls good — what another time he dispraises and calls evil" (Hobbes 1969, p. 225). We may widen our scope by reference to the field of aesthetics, that is, the philosophy of art, or taste, or beauty. Santayana, for example, considers that "The philosophy of beauty is a theory of values" (1965, p. 371) and adds, " . . . [W]e must widen our notion . . . to include those judgments of value which are instinctive and immediate, that is to include pleasures and pains; and at the same time we must narrow our notion of aesthetics as to exclude all perceptions which are not appreciations, which do not find value in their objects" (1965, p. 372).

Finally, to complete these types of examples, let us refer to the concept of values in sociology and other social sciences. As the following excerpt will indicate, the concept is based upon expressed judgments of people concerning what they like or dislike, that is, what pleases them or displeases them.

> People cherish certain ideas or beliefs which are often called their "values." These ideas contain or express the judgments which people have of the relative worth or importance of things. . . . In America, for example, we characteristically value highly such things as success, beauty, a high standard of living, and education (Cuber 1955, p. 42).

To anticipate an argument to be developed later, let us realize that none of these theoretical statements are based upon the methodology of standard behaviorism, which would demand direct observations for the concept of pleasure to be objectively defined. To continue, however, let us refer to another body of knowledge based upon a different type of evidence, that obtained from direct study of the biological organism. For example, although we cannot establish directly, in the intact human organism, that subjectively experienced pleasure involves precisely traced neural activities, there are various lines of evidence that are relevant here. For one thing anatomical studies tell us that there are neural mechanisms that correspond to pleasure and pain stimulation. While we cannot know, using a straightforward example, that a person feels pain when presented with a certain stimulus, we do know from other studies that there are pain receptors in the skin, let us say, for that particular stimulus. We also have studies that show that organs associated with emotional responding will be activated when such a painful stimulus is presented, for example, changes in heart rate and perspiration. Moreover, we have studies (Maltzman, Raskin, Gould, and Johnson 1965; Staats, Staats, and Crawford 1962) that show that physiological emotional responding to a stimulus *follows the same principles* as the subjective report of pleasure (as shown on a rating scale indicating pleasantness-unpleasantness), as will be indicated later on. As another example, let us take the serendipitous discovery that there are "pleasure" and "pain" centers in the brain. Olds and Milner (1954) found that there were areas in the lower brain which when stimulated acted as rewards and punishments. This was shown by implanting an electrode in the particular part of the brain and sending a weak electric charge as the stimulus. Animals will learn to make a response for the reward of brain stimulation. Similar techniques have been employed to produce "rage" in cats or the converse. It could be said that electric charge to the particular area of the brain had the same effect as subjective pleasure-pain principles would lead us to expect.

Thus far we have considered in this account two types of knowledge, (1) that involving the conceptions of pleasure-pain stemming from subjectivistic methods, and (2) that involving biological lines of research that are related to the anatomy and physiology of pleasure-pain. Let us consider also in brief terms a third type of knowledge, that based upon the direct observations of the type recommended in behaviorism. To begin, the classical conditioning of physiological emotional responses by Pavlov provide an easy translation to the concepts of pleasure-pain. Pavlov first worked with food as the stimulus to elicit the response of salivation. But food is an important type of stimulus that induces pleasure. Certainly there has been wide recognition that classical conditioning principles and the emotional responses dealt with had some relationship to subjective emotional states. Conditioning studies tell us, in brief resumé, that stimuli paired with other stimuli that are pleasurable will themselves come to elicit pleasurable responses in the individual.

But there were behaviorists who separated (1) emotional states that were classically conditioned from (2) the way the individual behaved. Skinner (1975), for example, has been very clear in this regard, and very clear in saying also that it is a chimera to be concerned with such subjective states, or with conditioned emotional responses, if one is interested in understanding human behavior. This standard behavioristic position is bound to alienate phenomenologists since they are interested precisely in understanding subjective states, in part as a means to knowing about human behavior. One of the problems of Skinner's learning theory, that makes it unsuitable for the purpose at hand, is that it does not indicate the relationship between emotions (and other subjective states) and behavior. But, as earlier examples have shown, there is a close interrelationship between emotional responding and the way the individual behaves, and there are modern theories of conditioning that recognize this (Bindra 1978; Overmier and Lawry 1979; Staats 1961, 1963, 1968a, 1968b, 1970b, 1975). The importance of this type of formulation for the solution of the subjective-objective schism can be indicated in brief.

To begin, there are stimuli that elicit emotional responses which are experienced as pleasant, on the one hand, or unpleasant, on the other. These stimuli vary in the intensity of the emotional responses they elicit. These emotional responses, while originally elicited by certain biologically relevant stimuli, are in humans conditionable to many other stimuli that naturally do not have emotional value. The conditioning takes place in very human types of ways, in social interaction, through language exchanges, in social experiences such as belonging to a particular church, family group, or economic class. While these ways are very human in character, experimental analysis can reveal the basic principles of conditioning involved. A more complete understanding, nevertheless, also demands that the way the conditioning takes place for humans, for example, through language, also be explicitly studied. Such experimental study reveals similarities in principle to that which has been established through more subjective investigation. To illustrate, the quotation of Jeremy Bentham said that as the individual gained in wealth each additional unit acquired brought less pleasure to the individual (which in modern economic terminology is called the law of marginal utility). In the experimental laboratory it has been firmly established that the degree of deprivation or satiation of food affects the extent to which the stimulus that has been associated with food, (as well as food itself) will elicit an emotional response in the organism. Finch (1938) has shown this with animals and Staats and associates with humans (Harms and Staats 1978; Staats and Hammond 1972; Staats, Minke, Martin, and Higa 1972; Staats and Warren 1974). It is rather important that the principles for the subjective concept of pleasure or satisfaction agree with the objectively studied concept of the conditioned emotional response.

To continue, however, how is it that emotions and feelings, that are of such importance in the study of human experience, are important in terms of helping determine the individual's behavior? In the subjectivist's descriptions it is simply understood that things that are pleasurable to the individual will be approached, behaviors that yield pleasure will be performed, and the converse is true for pain and displeasure. For example, Freud, basing his theory on the subjective descriptions of his patients' experiences, first set forth what he called the pleasure principle, which said in essence that people do things that are pleasurable for them. But as is not unusual with the accounts of phenomenologists, or those who employ such evidence, Freud's account did not detail the exact principles involved. We thus might ask how it is that subjective states such as emotions influence the things the individual does, and by what principles. And why do emotions have that effect? Is it built into us, or learned? We must acknowledge that the greater our specification in this sphere the better will be our knowledge and understanding of human nature and behavior.

Drawing upon the basic theory of conditioning, which relates the classical conditioning of emotions to the instrumental conditioning of motor behavior (including speech and language behavior), we can see a relevant body of knowledge. That is, the basic theory states that both learned and unlearned stimuli that elicit emotional responses will affect the individual's acts in two general ways. First, whatever event is pleasurable for the individual will also function as a reward. The technical term for reward is positive reinforcer, as has been indicated. There are many, many studies of the explicit manner in which a reward presented following a particular behavior will strengthen the future occurrence of that behavior in that situation. This principle applies to various types of organisms, including human subjects, in various situations, involving various behaviors. We have a great deal of knowledge of the principles that state that any stimulus that elicits an emotional response in the individual will be capable of affecting the individual in various ways, if the stimulus is applied like a reinforcer — that is, is presented, or occurs, following the behavior in question. Is this knowledge of how pleasures, that is, rewards, affect behavior irrelevant for the individual who bases his understanding of human behavior upon phenomenological knowledge? We will return to this question.

To continue, however, there is another way that the subjective states of emotion affect the individual's behavior. Events that create positive emotions in the individual will serve as incentives for him if he has not yet obtained them. As has been indicated in detail, all of us in an extensive history learn to approach in a variety of ways stimuli that are pleasurable for us. And we learn to avoid stimuli or events that make us feel displeasure or unpleasantness. Ways of approach and avoidance may be cognitive as well as motoric, as in avoiding thinking about a topic that elicits anxiety or unpleasantness in us. The point is, however, that there is a host of experimentation and knowledge of the principles by which events act as incentives to elicit behavior. Moreover, this has been extended into work with humans, involving typically human types of stimulus events. One contemporary experiment presented subjects with a reaction time task of either pulling one type of word towards them or pushing another type away. Various food words constituted the type that had to be approached, that is, pulled inwards in the apparatus. Subjects who were deprived of food learned to respond significantly faster in pulling the food words toward themselves than did subjects who had not been deprived of food (Staats and Warren 1974). The study showed specifically how deprivation increases incentive value of things that are pleasurable for us, providing an objective basis for the subjective principles of the utilitarian hedonist. A very recent study showed that subjects with high religious values, for whom religious events would be pleasurable, better learned an approach response, in the same type of apparatus, to religious words than did subjects whose measured values were not religious (Staats and Burns, 1982). It is thus possible to directly study the incentive value of pleasurable events in typically human areas, where the individual differences in behavior are due to complex personality processes (religious values) rather than basic principles such as food deprivation. The important point, however, is that there is a wealth of knowledge of how pleasurable events can affect behavior according to incentive conditions and principles that are experimentally specified.

Let me add one further point in regard to the question of making objective such subjective experiences as pleasure. The work to be described provides links between (1) the behavioristic interest in the manner in which emotions are conditioned, (2) the subjective experience of pleasure-displeasure, and (3) the biological mechanisms involved. In one study (Staats, Staats, and Crawford 1962) the present author and associates presented a conditioning experience to subjects to study how humans can learn a physiological emotional response (negative) to a word stimulus, by pairing the word with mildly painful stimuli. One way of measuring the negative emotional conditioning was through a self-report that involved rating the pleasantness-unpleasantness of the stimulus. It was found that the subjects acquired the physiological emotional response according to conditioning principles. Moreover, the conditioned subjects reported on the rating scale a stronger subjective unpleasantness to the stimulus than did a control group of subjects. This study showed (1) that subjective pain can develop according to conditioning principles and (2) that objectively created pain can be reliably reported subjectively. Additional verification of the objective quality of the self-report was the fact that physiological measurements of emotional response were in agreement with the self-report. That is, subjects with more intense conditioned emotional responses of a physiological nature also gave more intense self-reports of unpleasantness. An important result of this experiment thus was to show the relationships between the three types of observation, the self-report of subjective experience, the physiological (biological) measurement, and the behavioristic data involving the conditioning principles for emotional learning. (This discussion will also be significant for the next topic of concern that deals with the unification of separated research methods.)

It can be seen, in the way that this has been written, that there are relationships between the three areas of knowledge that have been described. Notwithstanding this, in contemporary psychology the several schisms remain. First, there is a deep and long standing separation between those who cleave to phenomenological knowledge and those who cleave to behavioristic knowledge. Secondly, there is a lesser, but evident, schism between phenomenological knowledge and that involving the study of the biological mechanisms of behavior. And there is a deep schism between standard behaviorists and those who take a biological orientation toward the study of human behavior. Each of these knowledge areas is well developed with a rich literature. Ordinarily, that literature is not brought together in any meaningful way, and proponents of one or the other are ordinarily in an adversarial relationship with the others. In the present view this is an unfortunate circumstance for each body of knowledge. For there is relevant knowledge, for each body, in each of the other bodies. Moreover, these particular schisms contribute centrally to the preparadigmatic confusion of knowledge in the general field of psychology, adding to the various disadvantageous conditions that have been described, while preventing the benefits that the emergence of unity would bring to the science.

Theory that bridges schisms between important types of knowledge can be expected to pay important dividends. For one thing, if two bodies of knowledge are each valuable, and being a devotee of one has precluded access to the other, then bridging theory may be very valuable in removing the obstacle provided by the separatistic characters of the position involved. Of equal value, schism-bridging theory should be heuristic for each position in the schism. Following the present example there is in the human conditioning principles much objective knowledge concerning *how* individuals acquire their distinctive personalities in terms of what will be pleasurable or displeasurable for them. These principles are relevant to values, attitudes, interests, desires, traits, needs, motivations, and other personality theory concerns. While these principles were established via objective methods of study, they are relevant to dealing with individual human concerns and group concerns as well. The principles are also valuable as instruments by which individuals can better understand themselves, as well as other people, topics of importance to subjectivists.

The same is true in the other direction, to give another example. There is a vast amount of knowledge of human experience and human behavior that has been accumulated by individuals who work within what they consider to be a subjectivist approach based upon individual experience given through self-reports. The vast amount of clinical knowledge available in psychology is in good part of this type, gathered by many individuals who consider themselves phenomenologists. Behaviorists who restrict themselves only to the knowledge provided by the objective study conducted in the behavioristic laboratory, either animal or human, have a very small knowledge pool. The individual with only laboratory knowledge of conditioning will be lost in terms of understanding and dealing with people. Most of our knowledge of human behavior has been given by humanists, literary figures, social scientists, clinicians, and others, who are not behaviorists. The behavioristic clinician, child psychologist, or social psychologist, is isolated from a vast amount of knowledge when restricted to behavioristically based information. As the above example is intended to indicate, the three areas of knowledge — phenomenological, biological, and behavioristic — are not so mutually exclusive when their knowledge elements are described in a theoretical framework constructed to incorporate each in a direct, heuristic relationship. While the example could not present in detail the unified theoretical framework involved, it did indicate that the knowledge areas could blend together and be supportive and heuristic rather than conflicting.

The present discussion has not been in the service of promoting a particular theoretical approach, although one is involved. Nor can the present summary claim to have already resolved the subjective-objective schism (although providing a framework for that goal is an important goal of the author, see Staats 1963, 1968b, 1971a, 1975, 1979, 1980b). The present aim, rather, is to say that if we are to find unity in our science we must be prepared to expend a great deal of time and energy and theoretical skill in doing so. And, if we are to accept the goal of unity and make that expenditure we must have an orientation and a method. Perhaps we can only dimly perceive at this point what that method will consist of, for it is only by the dint of much labor that one can arrive at the methods and outcomes that will ensue. Setting the goal for our unified type of theory, however, plays a prominent role in determining the outcome. At this point our analysis tells us that we must begin to confront the theoretical schisms that obstruct our progress in establishing a unified body of knowledge in science. Our methodology, it is suggested, must involve consulting the bodies of knowledge on the two sides of any split. The theorist must be directed to learn about the characteristics of the opposing theories and their supporting facts, to find out what each side yields in terms of positive science products, such as prediction, control, and understanding of the events that are of interest. In this task theorists must think in terms of general principles such that they are not caught up in a partisan position on the basis of nonessential particulars that prevent them from seeing the unified theory. The theorist must then formulate a set of principles that will allow unification of the two or more bodies of knowledge in such a way that potentialities of each other position can be utilized better than is provided for by any of the competitors alone. Moreover, the unified theory should have heuristic potentialities for each domain.

The complete theoretical task would include cutting across different fields of psychology, different methodologies, different apparatuses and technologies, and different bodies of findings. This may be considered to be a large theoretical task. And well it might be in any particular case. But we should also find that when we begin systematically facing such tasks we will develop knowledge and methods by which to be successful, and that the task of unification of schismatic knowledge will become progressively easy. (That has been my personal experience.) In the present view such attempts will yield immensely productive results now, across a wide variety of schismatic approaches problems, areas, and methods. When there are knowledge domains that are relevant enough to each other to be in schismatic conflict, they are likely to contain complementary materials that are capable of being united. What is needed is the philosophy to guide us to make the commitment to the effort. Moreover, theories that claim to be general in scope should be required to demonstrate that they are so by confronting the various issues, the schisms, in psychology with an objective of resolution. That is a central responsibility of the theorist, and this must be recognized.

UNIFICATION OF METHOD AND APPARATUS

It was said in the fourth chapter, in describing the preparadigmatic state of psychology, that one source of the preparadigmatic disorganization of the science lay in the many competitive differences that exist in methods and apparatus. The lines of this cause of preparadigmatic divergence are very complex and can only be briefly described as a means of encouraging the systematic effort necessary for adequate treatment. (Karl A. Minke and the present author are doing a systematic work in this area.) The important point to be made in the present context is that the same type of unification must be made for the methodology of the science as the unification we need for substantive knowledge of a theoretical and empirical type.

It will be helpful in approaching the topic of unification in this area to consider briefly psychology's preparadigmatic separatism, for it exerts its influence in the area of methodology and apparatus, as it does in other areas of the science. The psychological scientist presently has little interest in considering unity among what appear to be disparate methods. Moreover, the skills by which to see methodological unity rest upon a conception of unity in the science, and members of the preparadigmatic science do not have such a conception. As in the other areas, the psychological scientist is oriented towards originality, with originality considered to be that which is different. As a consequence, the psychologist is driven toward the discovery of new methods and new apparatus, of distinguishing one's methods from those of others as much as possible. Thus, we have various different psychological tests, many measuring the same psychological trait, we have various different methods and apparatus for the study of basic learning principles, many different methods and apparatus for studying facts of social psychology, and so on. Psychologists who group themselves around a particular method and apparatus are interested in distinguishing that methodology from others, rather than in seeing similarities or complementarities. In matters of methodology and apparatus the science is again pre-paradigmatic, following the implicit philosophy of preparadigmaticism.

We can see the artificial diversity that occurs, utilizing examples that were referred to in chapter 4. It was said in that chapter that there were (and are) different methods for the study of animal learning principles, differences that helped define opposing approaches. One example was that B. F. Skinner and his followers employed his operant conditioning chamber and the recording of the rate of response of laboratory animals for their study of instrumental conditioning. But they would not use the latency (time) of response in a straight runway, the time to escape from a problem box, or the number of incorrect or correct choices in a T-Maze, as means of studying such conditioning. They would not publish studies using such methods of experimentation. Such separations have been widely characteristic in psychology. Since the same general principles in the field of learning have been studied using different methods-apparatuses, the separation of knowledge because of that difference must be considered artificial and unnecessary. It is important to realize, in any event, that although method-apparatus differences arise in psychology because of the science's preparadigmaticism, the method-apparatus differences in turn contribute to the disorganization of the science.

It should be emphasized that many of the method-apparatus differences that pertain in psychology have theoretical roots. That is, method and apparatus are ordinarily developed in psychology under the press of local, specialized needs, in the study of specific problems. The conceptual relationship of the phenomena studied by one apparatus or method to other phenomena studied by other methods is rarely systematically considered, and the same is true of the methods themselves.

Let us take, as an illustration, the methods of study of the traditional child developmentalists. Psychologists such as Gesell (Gesell and Thompson 1938) systematically and in detail studied the behavior of individual children over time, or observed the behavior of a number of children of a certain age in comparison to the behavior of groups of children of different ages. (This method is specifically called longitudinal study, but in its general form is employed in many types of research.) These longitudinal observations are organized into statements that reveal the behavioral development of the typical child over time. This method of study has provided the norms of child development that have been and are used so widely by child psychologists and pediatricians and by theorists in child and educational psychology.

Since the observations involved are of behavior it might be thought that behaviorists would consider the findings of the child developmentalists to be important sources of knowledge. Not so, however. Behaviorists in general have almost entirely ignored the findings of child developmentalists that are relevant to age-graded behaviors. The reasons involve the general separatism of the science, where each approach aims to develop its own methods of study. In addition, however, as indicated already, observational methods are ordinarily intimately tied up with a theoretical orientation. We saw an illustration in the case cited earlier concerning Galileo's observations of the mountains on the moon. "But his 'observations' were not 'observational' in the sense of being observed by the — unaided — senses: their reliability depended on the reliability of his telescope — *and of the optical theory of the telescope* — which was violently questioned by his contemporaries" (italics added) (Lakatos 1970, p. 98). Philosophers of science have employed the understanding of the role that theory plays in observations as a means of showing that observations are not the citadels of objectivity they were once thought to be. I would suggest, however, that this understanding has additional significance. It helps explain also the separatism of the preparadigmatic science. Employing the present example we can see more clearly why the methods (and the observations) of the child developmentalists are not accepted and employed by behaviorists. That is, centrally, the child developmentalists' methods of study involve the conception that behavior develops in the child as a function of the child's biological maturation. Observations of the behavior development of children over time were considered by child developmentalists to show that the processes of biological maturation and development are systematic and take place in a defined order and that this process is generally the same for all children. This has generally been the conclusion even though the effects of learning on the child's behavior development have not been controlled or taken account of. The theoretical concept implicit in this methodology is that learning processes play a relatively small role in human behavior development and can be largely ignored.

Behaviorists, of course, are diametrically opposed to the conception of the child developmentalists that excludes the importance of learning in behavior development. As a consequence, the methods as well as the findings of the child developmentalists are not considered, incorporated, and utilized in the work of behaviorists. Rejecting the conceptual basis of the child developmentalists brings about rejection of the methods of study as well as of the findings. A work based on such methods would not be published in a behaviorists' journal or book. The *Journal of Applied Behavior Analysis*, as an example, demands that environmental circumstances affecting behavior be experimentally manipulated over time in each study. No behavior change without such manipulation is accepted.

This dynamic of methodological conflict in this one case has a very widespread effect in promoting separatism in psychology. As another ex-

ample, behaviorists have not made use of the methods of intelligence testing — methods and findings based upon the same type of rationale as the
age-defined behavioral observations of the child developmentalists. The
huge fund of knowledge that is contained in the field of psychological testing is largely ignored by behaviorists even today. The same rejection holds,
for the same reasons, for the methods and findings of various cognitive psychologists, who study many types of behavior — problem solving, thinking,
perception, linguistic rules, information processing. There are various important methods of study employed in these investigations. Ordinarily,
however, these methods are constituents, along with their findings, of a
certain conceptual view of psychology. That view involves a concept of the
human mind. In general, the aim of cognitive psychologies is the stipulation of the characteristics and structures of the mind. That conceptual system is anathema to behaviorists. Again, the methodology of cognitive research ignores the stipulation of the manner in which learning may affect
the behavioral measurements made to index the mental processes. As a consequence the findings and methods that are involved are rejected or ignored
by behaviorists.

As one might imagine the same is true in the other direction. Child developmentalists typically do not concern themselves with the findings within the fields of animal and human learning. The psychology of learning assumes that there are basic learning principles that are the same across various species besides man. The approach is to isolate those basic principles,
the assumption being that human characteristics are learned via those principles. Child developmentalists, personality testers, and cognitive psychologists generally do not accept that position. The methodology, thus, of
studying animal learning, as a basis for understanding and studying human
activity, is rejected by psychologists of these orientations. As one example,
although child developmentalists are concerned with the way in which behavior develops over time (age), they do not generally employ the methodology developed within behavioristic approaches which would allow them
to study or to produce behavior development in children through learning.
Thus we see a child developmentalist such as Jean Piaget study with great
detail and ingenuity the cognitive development of children (Piaget and Inhelder 1964). His methods consist of employing problem situations to reveal children's abilities, the problems being presented to children of various
ages. The method is very much in the tradition of the early child developmentalists and intelligence testers. Like these others, Piaget's work has revealed characteristics of children at different ages. But, like the others in
this approach, Piaget never joined to his own methods the fund of methodological knowledge established by learning theorists and behaviorists. For
example, Piaget never reductively analyzed the nature of the tasks with
which he dealt into the components by which they are learned. And he never

studied how the child could learn those components according to basic learning principles, that is, he never studied how the child learns cognitive skills. Piaget did not employ such methods of learning research, established for the study of children's skill acquisition (see Staats 1968a; Staats, Brewer, and Gross 1970; Staats and Burns 1981). The same is true of other cognitive psychologists.

To continue, in general the longitudinal method of study, which systematically observes and records children's behavioral development over long periods of time, has been separated from the behavioral methods which demand that learning variables be manipulated — presenting reward for behavior acquisition, for example, for a period, followed by a period of no reward. The latter method may be termed experimental (or manipulative), in contrast to the nonmanipulative longitudinal methods. In my view there have been important findings made by both methods and for this reason they should be unified. But, also, there are important phenomena that cannot be studied with each method alone. Thus, for example, longitudinal methods do not indicate what the causes are for the behavior development of children; perhaps much development is due to learning. On the other hand, the methods of experimental manipulation have a characteristic of dealing with subjects only for a short time, using repeated measurements of the same simple behavior under different learning conditions, and this precludes the analytic study of long-term development of complex skills. In examining these methods the author saw that elements from each must be combined to contribute to a new method that studies behavioral development over long periods, dealing with complex skills, but that does so in an analytic, experimental manner where learning procedures and outcomes are explicitly recorded (see Naitoh and Staats 1980; Staats 1968b, 1977; Staats, Brewer, and Gross 1970; Staats and Burns, 1981). The method is called experimental-longitudinal research and it combines different methods of the study of behavior so that the causes of behavior can be studied longitudinally. The point is that when one examines different methods of study with a paradigmatic attitude, trying to establish what each method can and cannot contribute to a study of the various phenomena important to psychology, it is possible to begin to obtain a general picture, and to devise methods relevant to that picture. Besides organizing this area of knowledge in our science, the suggestion is that a general paradigmatic view provides the basis for seeing methodological areas that need development.

Primarily, thus, it has been suggested that the unifying task demands an open, positive approach — one that considers each method-theory to be potentially valuable as a source of knowledge. This may be expanded by saying that such a position may call for setting aside theoretical considerations, actually the theoretical considerations both of the area within which the method-apparatus developed, as well as the theoretical considerations of the areas that are opposed to the method-apparatus area. This may be elaborated using the example already given. Let us take the methods of the traditional child developmentalists in observing children's behavior development over time. The theory of these child developmentalists was that they were observing the development of behavior as a function of the child's development as a biological organism. They saw the behavior change to reflect internal maturational processes. But it should be understood that their observations have their potential value whether or not the theory itself is valuable. Accurate, detailed observations of the changing behavior of children, advancing over time, are important pieces of knowledge, without any assumptions concerning how the changes come about, whether through maturation or through learning. The observations constitute important facts to be accounted for, in and of themselves. Moreover, these facts may be important as they can be related to other observations, perhaps in a cause and effect way. The development of behavior over time may be related to biological changes in structure and function in the child. The development of behavior over time may be related to the child's experience and learning. The important point, however, is that it may help us in accepting the value of the method of research, and the empirical findings thereby established, by realizing that these elements have importance that is independent of the theory body within which the method and findings arose. Rejecting the method and its findings because we reject its associated theory amounts to throwing out the baby with the bath water.

Bridging Structures in Method-Theory Interactions

Thus, a unifying effort in the area of methodology may involve considering the types of data provided by the different methods-apparatus types, in a relatively theory-free way. On the other hand, as has been indicated, much of psychology's method-apparatus separatism is related to theory separatism and to more general schismatic issues of theoretical orientations. When that is the case, establishing bridging, unified theory bodies can result in unifying methodologies. The task of method unification can commence with theoretical unification. As an example, let us take the separatism between the methodology of psychology testing and the methodology of behaviorism that has been described. A short time ago the separation between the methods was rather complete. However, an approach showing the theoretical harmony between personality testing methodology and behavioristic methods of study has been outlined (see Burns 1980; Staats, 1963, 1968b, 1971a, 1975, 1980a, 1981; Staats, Staats, Heard, and Finley 1962). To elaborate, behaviorism which had no theory of personality as a causal process could not accept as valuable personality tests whose aim was to measure personality, considered as a cause of human behavior. By the introduction of a concept of personality into a behavioristic theory — a concept defined according to methodology acceptable to behaviorism, but which also recognized the causative role of personality — a theoretical approach was established that connected the two fields. This connecting theory was applied extensively to the consideration of intelligence (Staats 1968b, 1971a; Staats and Burns 1981). There are now further developments in the consideration of intelligence development that fall within this bridging theoretical endeavor (see Bijou 1976; Estes 1974, 1976; Meichenbaum 1977; Resnick 1976) that also provide the basis for methodological unification. This general development is still in its growth stages, but it provides a useful example, and one that I would expect will undergo marked expansion in the future in a way that will remove one of psychology's important schisms of method and findings and theory. The major suggestion is that the methodology for integrating theories that are considered disparate, the methodology for bridging theoretical schisms, and the methodology for establishing unified theoretical bodies will also include or provide a basis for seeking method-apparatus unification. And method-apparatus unification should be sought conjointly along with the conduct of these other unifying efforts.

One final point to be made is that the method-oriented, nontheoretical approach to method-apparatus unification that has already been described can, in the reverse, provide a basis for theory unification. That is, a position in favor of method-apparatus unification can provide the impetus for finding a connecting theory that will unify the separate theoretical bodies in which the separate method-apparatus developments have occurred. The author has found this to be the case many times. When one rejects the preparadigmatic framework that says two methods are incommensurable, the new view of things that is provided can lead one to consider conceptual ways by which to accept as valuable separate bodies of empirical and methodological knowledge. As one example, the present author was confronted in the early 1960s with the separatism in the study of language between the methods and data of learning theory and those of Chomskian linguistic theory. Behaviorists, interested in language learning, paid no attention to the methods and data of the linguists and psycholinguists, describing language and language development. On the other side linguists and psycholinguists criticized and rejected the methodology of a behaviorist approach. They rejected the idea that language could be learned as well as the methods for studying human learning and the manner in which the child can learn language from the parent. Neither side spoke of the manner by which to consider the value in the methodology and findings of the other position. Consulting the methods and data of the psycholinguists, however, revealed productive elements to the present author and the concepts that arose in these considerations led to bridging theoretical structures (Staats 1963, pp. 177–78, 1968b, 1971b, 1974). Since that time there have been experimental studies that have verified the bridging theory uniting these two formerly separated areas (see Ervin-Tripp 1971; Sailor 1971; Snow 1972). These studies have demonstrated that linguistically described aspects of language development are subject to learning experiences provided to the child. The elaborations made in each case involved use of the bridging theory for the generation of new types of experimental study, producing empirical results relevant to both behavioristic and psycholinguistic bodies of knowledge. Thus, positions that were formerly opposed produced unified knowledge, utilizing their own methods of research.

There are many methods-apparatuses employed in the science: personality testing, clinical observation, behavior modification treatment, psychophysical study, information processing study, memory experimentation study, perception study, child development study, animal and human learning experimentation, social interaction study, reaction time study, computer assisted instruction study, and many others. The goal of a paradigmatic science would be to see how all these methods provide access to phenomena that are related within the unified purview of the science — justifying and making important in the knowledge foundation of the science the various methods and apparatuses.

To conclude, it is clear, again, that the preparadigmatic philosophy presently points psychology in the direction opposite that of unification. The preparadigmatic philosophy directs the psychological scientist to emphasize distinctiveness and difference — considered as creativity — in the area of method-apparatus as in the other areas of the science. The paradigmatic philosophy that is being presented in this book, on the other hand, points out the importance of and the need for unification. In this context it should be indicated, as a qualification, that there is the need in the development of a science for the proliferation of methods and apparatuses, on the one hand, and there is the need for organizing method-apparatus knowledge, on the other, in the same way that there is the need for organizing other types of knowledge. We have to search for new method-apparatus discoveries. But we must also search for the manner in which method-apparatus elements provide a basis for unity of conception and philosophy. In line with the discussions of the temporal dimensions that must be included in a philosophy of science, it is pertinent to indicate that proliferation of method-apparatus elements is very crucial at the proliferation stages of science development — when preparadigmaticism is actually called for. When a great deal of method-apparatus development has occurred, however, as part of the general knowledge development of a science, in such a manner that chaotic and conflicting conditions arise, the career of the science then demands incorporation, organization, unification. In the present view the latter is the state of psychology at this time. It is time that we begin generally to unify and organize our methods and findings, as well as our theories.

ECLECTICISM: MIXING RATHER THAN UNIFYING

Works in general psychology are concerned largely with the teaching of introductory psychology courses. Although less popular today, at one time doctoral students in psychology frequently took their degrees in general psychology, which meant that they had scholarly proficiency in psychology across the various fields of which psychology is composed.

Training in general psychology, however, does not involve the type of approach being discussed, with an understanding of the need for unifying the science, or of methods by which to move toward that goal. General psychology is the label for an eclecticism. We can see this clearly in general psychology textbooks. Such books consist of a potpourri of knowledge in the different fields of psychology. Usually included are chapters on motivation, emotions, learning, sensation and perception, memory, child development, clinical and abnormal psychology, statistics and research design, cognition, language, personality, social psychology, and educational psychology. The chapter names may differ somewhat, but general psychology books attempt to give in summary form an introduction to the knowledge that a number of the parts of psychology has produced. The central point is that general psychology books simply present summaries of the materials in the different fields as the fields exist. Since the different fields of psychology, as has been indicated, are preparadigmatic and lack unification, general psychology books have the same characteristics. The material in such books does not represent in any way a unified theory, nor is there an attempt in this direction. The various chapters in such books are quite independent. They even include concepts and methods that are considered to be in opposition to one another. The student in moving from one chapter (and area) to another must learn different conceptual languages, and it does not matter in which order the chapters are read. That is, the principles learned in one area do not apply to the other, and it does not help in learning about one area to have already learned the material in another. This is the sense in which general psychology textbooks are considered in the present view to be eclectic. They mix the various disparate elements of which psychology is presently composed. This is not a criticism of general psychology textbooks in that their goal is to present a summary picture of the science. They succeed in this in part by showing that psychology's knowledge consists of a constellation of unrelated elements.

There are also theories in psychology that claim a more unified characteristic, but which are eclectic in the sense that they contain parts that have not been unified in principles. Rather the parts are included in the same conceptual schema, but the parts are unrelated and perhaps even inconsistent. For example, in recent years social learning theory has made a point of bringing together terminology from cognitive theory and learning theory. Woll (1978), however, has suggested that social learning theory has mixed the concepts from the two approaches but has not joined them. Rather, he says that only superficial terminology has been employed from cognitive theory, and that the effort in social learning theory, despite protestations to the contrary, is in fact a learning theory. The previously described attempt at resolution of the nature-nurture schism that was called the interactionism approach was also eclectic. It said that both approaches were valuable — one emphasizing inheritance in behavior development and the other emphasizing knowledge of the effects of learning on behavioral development. But the interactionism position did not present a unified set of principles within which both types of knowledge could be considered in order to lessen their oppositional confrontation. The interactionism approach did not present a heuristic theoretical framework for each area of knowledge. Interactionism never resolved the schismatic separation; it constituted an eclectic approach.

The type of unification being proposed here is not eclectic. The proposal is for the development of true unified theory and method. One example given was of the knowledge of psychological testing methods (and concepts such as intelligence) as unified with the knowledge of learning principles. The unification provided a theoretical framework for the heuristic projection of basic and applied research on the learning of intelligence and the measurement of intelligence and the solution of problems involving intelligence (Staats 1968b, 1971a, 1975; Staats and Burns 1981). In general it is to be expected, when there are two or more disparate areas of knowledge, that a unified theory that integrates the two areas will have heuristic projections for each area. If that is not the case then what appears to be a unification may only be a desultory mix (See Staats 1975, ch. 16).

In combining and mixing different, sometimes opposing, conceptual materials the eclectic approach does not pick and choose, at least according to some basic set of principles that underlies the justification for the combination. The task of constructing a unified theory, however, may be expected typically to involve critical selection. Kuhn's description of preparadigmatic areas of scientific knowledge indicated that in the preparadigmatic state there were bodies of knowledge that included bona fide scientific principles, methods, and findings. But these elements in the knowledge base were mixed with elements that involved sheer conjecture, myth, common sense, and worse. Moreover, these two types of elements were not separated, but were equal members of the same knowledge base. Kuhn's description agrees completely with my experience with psychology, as might be expected from the fact that it is a preparadigmatic science. That is why unified theory cannot be the same as eclecticism. When the paradigmatically oriented psychologist faces two bodies of knowledge that he thinks can be unified via a common theoretical structure, he will not do so in the spirit of eclecticism. Rather a true theoretical task is involved in separating the wheat from the chaff. It has been said herein that when psychological scientists have labored for much time in a particular area of study, under the aegis of a certain conceptual formulation, it is reasonable to suppose that there is some value in what they have produced, and in the conceptual system that gave rise to their efforts. At least it would be reasonable to examine the body of knowledge with the expectation that it will include productive parts. But this is not to say that it would be reasonable to accept the body of knowledge entirely. There is much that will prove useless in any area of psychology. The task of the unified theorist is to compose theoretical principles that will utilize essential parts of two bodies of knowledge, but it would be expected that large parts of any preparadigmatic body of knowledge will contain conceptual, theoretical, and empirical elements that will be of no value in the ultimate advancement of the science.

LEVELS OF GENERALITY IN UNIFYING ELEMENTS IN PYSCHOLOGY

To continue, however, in expanding the purview of this programmatic statement, in the present view it is necessary to construct theory with an eye to its integratory potential. When a new set of principles, or a new theoretical concept, is proposed one aspect of its evaluation should be its potential for unification. One avenue of advancement of the new theoretical material should be in attempting to use it in the pursuit of unification. For example, a currently popular concept in psychology is that of the locus of control — that some people consider themselves to be primary causes of their destiny, while others see the control to occur from the outside. One aspect of the theory has involved the demonstration of the concept, that is, the construction of a measuring instrument, a test, that separates people into internal-locus-of-control types and external-locus-of-control types. Experimental studies have also been conducted to specify the characteristics of locus of control. Another aspect of the work in this interest area has been to do experiments that show that internals behave in various situations in a manner different than that of externals.

I would suggest that establishing the range of behavioral phenomena that can be considered and unified within this conception is an important part of the theory construction task that considers the objective of unification in psychology. To elaborate, when a theoretical concept or principle has been introduced, we must ask what are the phenomena in psychology that are accounted for by the concept or principle. For example, Gore and Rotter (1963) found that students in a black college differed in terms of interest in civil rights social action, depending on whether they were internals or externals (the former expressed more interest in social action). Other studies have shown that internals, who feel they personally control the outcome of their experiences, make a greater use of materials given them in a task they have to perform (Crowne and Liverant 1963; Lefcourt 1966; Lefcourt and Ladwig 1965; Rotter 1954). Weiner, Heckhausen, Meyer, and Cook (1972) have found a relationship between self-attribution of effort and the extent that the individual would self-reinforce (reward) himself.

These studies help establish the generality of phenomena to which the concept of locus of control pertains. But the consideration of the unificatory power of a theoretical element, and consideration of its place in a large effort to establish unified theory, must entail additional concerns. It is important to establish the range of behavioral phenomena that can be treated within the theoretical element. The above studies are relevant in this respect. In addition, the task must include also consideration of the limits of the explanatory value of the theoretical element. Does the concept of internal locus of control, for example, explain how the child learns to read? Can we use the principles involved for training the child in toilet skills? Is intelligence to be explained by the principles? Or interests, abnormal behavior, problem solving, and so on? Can we use the principle to account for various phenomena in the experimental psychology of human learning? Can we use the principles to account for animal learning phenomena? Animal and human motivation? Do the principles link to our knowledge of physiological psychology in a mutually explanatory manner?

Perhaps we have a set of theoretical principles with great generality, that can contribute to the unification of knowledge across the breadth of psychology. Perhaps, however, we have a concept or principle of far less generality. For all of our concepts, principles, and theories we must ask what the relationships are to other bodies of empirical and theoretical knowledge in the science. Are the principles very general and basic, or of a more restricted range? In the former case there must be other principles that can be derived from the very general basic principle. In the latter case there must be basic principles that will connect to the specific principle or phenomenon. The point is that these are considerations that the context of striving for unified theory sets for us, considerations that the present structure of preparadigmatic psychology does not. The paradigmatic context provides impetus to look for a framework not just to look for a new phenomenon, new concept, or new experimental procedure. When we consider not only the single element, but how the element relates to other elements we have a basis for introducing organization into our knowledge base. Following the example, when the concepts and principles and observations concerning the locus of control have been examined for unifying power and for their range of explanatory power more will be known about how this development fits into a structural framework — either further related to other principles and phenomena, or still isolated and less general.

As we work through our concepts and phenomena, searching for unity, for the range of explanatory significance, we should begin to see what we have in terms of an ordered (or disordered) structure. We should begin to have some grasp concerning which of our principles are capable of generalization and unification, across other principles, concepts, and phenomena; which principles and theories are capable of organizing and relating and making sense of different methods and apparatus and types of findings. We have today different theories. Most usually those theories arise in a restricted set of experiments or observations of some type. Frequently, nonetheless, the theory is implicitly or explicitly expected to have a more general applicability. But this characteristic is typically not specified systematically. Let us take another example. Freud's psychoanalytic theory was considered by him to apply very generally to human behavior — and there are many psychoanalytically oriented professionals today who would feel similarly. However, the theory arose in the context of a limited type of methodology, primarily that of the psychoanalytic therapist-patient interaction, and limited phenomena of human behavior. It has been assumed that psychoanalytic theory applies generally to human behavior, but we must specifically consider the task involved of unifying psychology through the use of this theory. We must ask in the present context, to what extent has psychoanalytic theory been systematically considered for its relationships to the knowledge base that we have in psychology — and for its ability to organize that knowledge base, of which psychoanalytic theory is only a part? Such considerations are necessary to evaluate a theory that claims to have very general applicability. Moreover, how does psychoanalytic theory relate to other theories in terms of similarity of principles, overlap in the phenomena that are considered, and in terms of methodological characteristics? Can psychoanalytic theory be collapsed into another theory, or the reverse? Can various less general concepts and principles and phenomena that have arisen under the impetus given by nonpsychoanalytic considerations nevertheless be subsumed by psychoanalytic theory and incorporated into psychoanalytic theory? Or is psychoanalytic theory pretty much restricted to the types of phenomena and methods involved in its inception, and not capable of great generality — the implication being that its elements, rather, are likely to be grist for some more general theoretical mill, or are likely to only constitute one part of a more general theory.

Today psychology is not a limited field. It has many, many products in its knowledge base. There is thus a vast potential, of immense value, in the present opinion, for theoretical works that will fulfill the types of unificatory goals being discussed. It is a great oversight, surely, that there is no systematic effort toward organizing those products in the theoretical endeavors of the science. In the present view this has occurred because the science in its preparadigmatic obsession is concerned only with generating the independent, new product — not with what that product means in the science, with what role the product can play in the organization of the science. In the present view we must develop a program for confronting the task of organizing the science. Each phenomenon, theoretical term, and method must be considered in terms of its general characteristics with respect to what it relates to, in terms of its unifying power, and in terms of how it can be unified with other elements of knowledge.

It should be emphasized in this regard that theoretical unification must be sought in varying levels of generality. Each theoretical concept or principle should be considered in terms of its own generality, evaluated accordingly, and placed within a growing framework of organized knowledge. The present chapter has dealt with unification efforts that are not of the most general type, but actually with the innumerable acts of unification that must take place, ranging from the improvement in citation standards by which elements in the science can be related, to reviews of research areas, to integratory theory and integrations of separate phenomena in unified theory, through unifications of schisms, methods, and apparatuses. But there are additional concerns in this area, and the present chapter has not discussed methodological questions involved in the production of large-scale unifying frameworks, that is, with very comprehensive, unified theory. This topic is the focus of the next chapter.

Chapter 9

Interlevel and Multilevel Theory

The preceding chapter has dealt in a preliminary way with the methodological foundation for developing unified knowledge in psychology. The methodology presented, however, pertains to building unity in pieces — by bridging theory that resolves schisms, integrates diverse concepts, principles, phenomena, findings, theories, and methodology. There has not yet been a discussion of a methodology for constructing larger, unified theories in psychology, although this goal is implicit in what has been said thus far. That is, if one accepts that the task of unifying knowledge in psychology is one of building theoretical structures that will bring out the commonality among presently diverse materials then this implies that large, unified theory structures will ultimately be the result. Although we might start with unifications that do not have generality, each one would have greater generality than the separate elements that existed before. Moreover, in the next step, if we unify such previously accomplished unifications, yet greater generality would result. Conceivably, a strategy could be to ultimately attain a very general, unified theoretical structure that was "built from below" in this manner. The logic involved is like that of empirical inductive methods, for example, as in the method of abstracting more and more general principles from experiments on conditioning (Bayes 1980; Dorna and Mendez 1979; Sidman 1960). This logic has not been applied to theoretical as well as empirical generalizations, and not to the problems of preparadigmatic separation that have been the focus of the present approach.

In the present view, however, this strategy of building unity of psychological science from below does not exhaust the possibilities. The attempt of the second generation behaviorists (see Hull 1943) to construct grand theories has already been described. Although this effort failed, it

was not because the goal was improper, as Koch (1981) would have us believe. It was because the second-generation behaviorists did not understand
the nature of their science, and thus what was needed in the construction of
a general, unified theory. This chapter will elaborate the methodology of
the present approach to the construction of general, unified theory in psychology. In addition this chapter will discuss a statement in the philosophy
of science, with respect to developments in the natural sciences, that is very
much in agreement with overlapping interests of the present approach.

BRIDGING (VERSUS REDUCTIONISTIC) THEORY

The reductionism methodology of logical positivism has been outlined
in an earlier chapter. Reductionism pertains to two theoretical bodies that
are stated in axiomatic form, the first theory being more general and capable of incorporating the less general theory. Everything in the less general
theory can be derived from the first theory, which in this sense swallows the
less general theory, making it unnecessary. As has been indicated (Staats
1975, ch. 16), this is not a pleasing methodology for many social scientists.
It implies that one's own field of study is likely to become expendable, when
it is swallowed by some more basic conception that has been formulated in
some more basic area of study. Reductionism as a methodology for unification in psychology cannot be considered to have been a success. In the present view this was the case in good part because it was not pertinent to the
task of theory unification for psychology. As will be seen in a later section,
there are important cases in psychology of knowledge areas in which one
area is more general than the other, in the sense that its principles will be
basic to the other area. But the situation is not one of having well-stated,
axiomatic theories in the two areas; and the task is not one of showing how
the principles of the less basic area can be derived from (swallowed by) the
theory of the more general area.

The task in psychology may be described quite differently. Let me give
an example. Let us say the theorist is interested in uniting the fields of animal learning theory and abnormal psychology. Let me begin by saying that
in psychology there is the field of study of animal learning. This field attempts to establish what the basic, elementary principles are by which organisms' behavior is lawfully changed through learning-types of contacts
with the environment. The principles that are studied in this field are
thought to be general throughout the phylogenetic scale, at least extending
downward from humans a long way. Now in the study of human behavior
there are various fields of special consideration, the study of reading, for example, or of social interaction, personality, psychological measurement,
language acquisition, and so on, as well as the field of abnormal psycholo-

gy. Many of the human behaviors of concern in each of these fields are commonly thought to be learned. The task of establishing unity of knowledge in psychology might be thought to involve, in part, unifying the several fields of study of human behavior with the basic field of the study of animal learning.

But in no case in this task would we be dealing with theories that would fall into the reductionistic methodology. There is no axiomatic theory in the field of animal learning (at least that has general acceptance), and there is no axiomatic theory in any of the fields studying human behavior. The task thus is not to derive, as a task of formal logic, the theory in the less basic fields from the more basic field. Moreover, we should look more closely at the nature of the task of unification, before we can make conclusions about the methodology that would be appropriate to the task. To elaborate, let us accept that there are principles in the field of animal learning that are basic to the fields studying human behavior. However, even though this is the case, this is not to say that the field of animal learning has been constructed in such a way as to be concerned solely, or even focally with what those principles are. It has not been the mission of the field of animal learning to isolate the principles that will be the most valuable for understanding and dealing with human behavior. As part of a preparadigmatic science, the specialty area of the science dealing with animal learning has developed as an independent area, with its own parochial interests. It thus contains myriad elements of knowledge, obtained in the pursuit of a wide variety of interests. Some of these knowledge elements would be relevant to human behavior phenomena studied in other specialty fields, but many of the elements would be irrelevant, even antagonistic to the task. That tells us that if we are to construct a bridging theory between the field of animal learning and, let us say, a field in the study of human behavior we will first have to construct from all the elements in animal learning a new and smaller set of principles that will serve as this part of the theory for the bridging endeavor.

But the same thing pertains in the other field that is to be involved in the bridging task. In each field concerned with the study of human behavior there are myriad elements. Not all of them will deal with phenomena that will be relevant to a general theory that has learning principles as basic elements. In our example we will take the field of abnormal psychology. This field deals with a wide range of human behaviors. There are concepts and findings in this field that may be considered in terms of learning, and others that may not. The important point here, however, is that the field of abnormal psychology itself has not been composed so that it can be linked to a theory constructed of basic learning principles. For the theorist who wishes to perform that linkage, therefore, the field of abnormal psychology is a chaos of knowledge elements, and provides both wheat and chaff in the theory construction task. Again, this area of knowledge must be set into suitable form.

Having made this description, we can see better what the nature of the task is for constructing a theory that will bridge the knowledge in the two fields, following the above example. The theorist has the task of formulating from the chaos of knowledge in the field of animal learning a set of principles that is basic for the field of abnormal psychology. And the theorist also has the task of abstracting from the chaos of knowledge in the field of abnormal psychology those concepts, principles, and phenomena that can be dealt with by the learning principles. This involves a large theoretical task also. Then there is the task of formulating theory to unify the two areas of knowledge. The several theory tasks in concert can yield what I call interlevel theory. None of these is a theoretical task of the precision or logical and mathematical formality that is idiosyncratically characteristic of a few areas of the natural sciences. But that is not to say that the task of constructing this type of bridging theory is any less important than unified theory has been in those areas of the natural sciences. Moreover, the bridging theory task is no less difficult, only different. A background in mathematics may be less important, for example. But the ability to abstract principles from the hodge-podge of disorganized knowledge may be more demanding than occurs in the physical sciences.

As has been indicated earlier, I have been involved in constructing the type of theory exemplified above for several decades. It has been my experience that, when one deals with the general characteristics of this task of unified theory construction in psychology, there is considerable similarity to what is involved in the natural sciences. But the specifics are quite different. If we get hung up on specific characteristics — like whether the theory is mathematical and axiomatic — then it is not possible to see the commonality, and as a result it is not possible to profit from the experience that has been accrued in other sciences. As will be indicated, there are similarities between the sciences in the task of constructing unified theory. But this cannot be seen when one is transfixed by the specific characteristics that are only typical of some of the exact natural sciences. We can see this in other sciences than psychology. Interestingly, recently two philosophers of science appear to have recognized that the methodology of reductionism cannot be applied to some other areas of science, and they have suggested also the need for a bridging type of theory that does not fulfill the characteristics of reductionism.

> Interactions between different areas or branches or fields of science have often been obscured by current emphasis on the relations between different scientific theories. Although some philosophers have indicated that different branches may be related, the actual focus has been on the rela-

tions between theories within the branches. For example, Ernest Nagel has discussed the reduction of one branch of science to another (1961, ch. 11). But the relation that Nagel describes is really nothing more than the derivational reduction of the *theory* or *experimental law* of one branch of science to the theory of another branch.

We, in contrast to Nagel, are interested in the interrelations between the areas of science that we call *fields*. For example, cytology, genetics, and biochemistry are more naturally called fields than theories (Darden and Maull 1977, p. 41).

In this account Darden and Maull are also critical of the previous concentration of the logical positivistic emphasis upon the analysis of the relationships between highly formal theories, to the exclusion of the consideration of other aspects of theory construction. They state that it is necessary to consider also theories that bridge related areas or fields of study.

An interfield theory functions to make explicit and explain relations between fields. Relations between fields may be of several types; among them are the following:

(1) A field may provide a *specification of the physical location* of an entity or process postulated in another field. . . .

(2) A field may provide the *physical nature* of an entity or process postulated in another field. . . .

(3) A field may investigate the *structure* of entities or processes, the *function* of which is investigated in another field. . . .

(4) Fields may be linked *causally*, the entities postulated in one field providing the causes or effects investigated in the other. . . . (Darden and Maull 1977, pp. 48–49).

These authors then ask what the reasons are for generating an interfield theory. "In brief, an interfield theory is likely to be generated when background knowledge indicates that relations already exist between the fields, when the fields share an interest in explaining different aspects of the same phenomenon, and when questions arise about that phenomenon within a field which cannot be answered with the techniques and concepts of that field" (Darden and Maull 1977, p. 49).

Darden and Maull illustrate the manner in which interfield theories function to explain relations between fields referring to such areas as the chromosome theory of Mendelian heredity as an interfield theory that bridged the fields of genetics and cytology. In the present context it is relevant to illustrate some examples of bridging theory in psychology, beginning with the specification of physical location. As will be indicated later, the work of the present author in constructing unified theory in psychology has developed the concept of interlevel theory which, as we will see, is very much the same as Darden and Maull's concept of interfield theory. Let us see how their description of interfield theory can be used to support the interlevel theory conception that arose with psychological phenomena.

> One of the important functions of stimuli . . . is that of reinforcement. Some stimuli have the ability to reward in the sense that they strengthen future occurrences of the responses they follow; and other stimuli punish in the sense that they weaken responses they follow. . . . It is thus of interest to note that the physiological mechanisms involved in the action of reinforcing stimuli have begun to be explored. Although the work began in serendipity (Olds and Milner 1954), the discovery of areas in the lower brain which, when stimulated, provided reinforcement for instrumental responses has led to a great deal of research on the phenomenon. Olds and Milner permanently implanted electrodes in the limbic systems of rats' brains. The rats were then allowed access to a chamber which included a lever. When depressed by the animal, the lever would produce a slight electric charge to the brain. The animal's bar-pressing response was increased in frequency and maintained by the reinforcing action of the light shock to that part of the brain.
>
> Investigations have also found that stimulation of some areas of the brain will serve the same function as a negative reinforcing stimulus (Cohen, Brown, and Brown 1957; Delgado, Roberts, and Miller 1954). The animals would learn to perform responses that would terminate the brain stimulation (Staats 1975, p. 536).

This is a good example of interlevel theory (in which the phenomenon of one area is *positionally* established in another area). This would be more clearly theoretical if the finding had been arrived at in a theoretical manner rather than as a serendipitous experimental finding. That is, prior to Olds and Milner's study, there was a body of knowledge involving the localization of brain function — stipulating which parts of the brain were especially important to certain behavioral functions, for example, brain centers for motor functions and for sensory functions. In the other level, or field, there was a body of knowledge indicating that reinforcement was a very universal and important behavioral process. An interfield theoretical effort could then have bridged these two bodies of knowledge by suggesting that there *should* be a brain center positional site that was responsible for the phenomena of reinforcement. Actually, various aspects of each body of knowledge would have suggested that expectation. However, the serendipitous discovery of a center for positive reinforcement and one for negative reinforcement provided the findings before the development of an interlevel theory that might have predicted a physical location of such a center. But the example stands. The serendipitous discovery provided a bridging interfield theoretical body. This conceptual body then led to a further unification of behavioral research methods with physiological methods, resulting in many new findings. The fact that psychology has not been concerned with interfield theory unifications has meant that this significance of the Olds and Milner discovery has not been emphasized. It is important, however, to see such examples as an important type of *theory* development in psychology, as has been indicated (Staats 1975).

Another of the types of interlevel theory similar to that described by Darden and Maull occurs where one field may indicate the physical nature of a concept employed in another field. As an example, another type of research on the biological bases of learning involves attempts to establish the actual mechanisms by which elementary learning occurs.

> Another strategy for investigating the neurophysiological bases of elementary learning principles has involved the use of organisms with primitive nervous systems. This is done, again, to get the simplicity necessary for experimental control so that elementary principles can be studied. Horridge (1962), for example, has utilized headless cockroaches, with all legs removed but one, to study the possibility that avoidance conditioning of a leg withdrawal could occur. The results were positive. . . .
>
> The processes by which the organism's experience results in a change in behavior that is retained is still not known, however. The mechanisms of learning and retention have been the subject of theoretical consideration nevertheless (Pfaff 1969). One theory of learning and memory has been that greater efficiency of conduction from one neuron to another occurs through changes that take place in the synapse connecting the neurons. . . . Another hypothesis is that biochemical changes occur in the neuron on the amounts of differently coded RNA molecules formed . . . (Staats 1975, pp. 553–54).

This is a clear example of an area of interlevel or interfield theory which involves the attempt to establish the physiological and biochemical nature and structure of the learning process, the functions of which are studied in the field of learning. In this effort the study of learning is linked to the level of the study of neural function. It was the purpose of the account given above to indicate the need for interlevel theory connecting the biological level and the basic conditioning level, in the service of a theory intending to cover the whole range of levels of human behavior study (Staats 1975).

To continue, it is also relevant here to indicate the manner in which interlevel or interfield theory is important in relating different areas or fields within the study of human behavior, as well as to illustrate that interlevel theory may involve causal linking of one field to another, the principles studied in one being causes of the events studied in the other. The example to be given herein involves one of the author's first theoretical analyses, in the field of abnormal psychology. Several psychiatrists had reported the case of a patient with a new type of symptomatology, that of "opposite speech," where the patient would say the opposite of that which was appropriate for the situation (Laffal, Lenkoski, and Ameen 1956). The authors of the report specifically stated that the case could not be accounted for by a learning-theory-based analysis. Their position was an example of the schism between the field of learning theory approaches to human behavior and traditional approaches that utilized psychoanalytic and other theories seeking explanation by concepts of internal personality dynamics. The analysis of the present author (Staats 1957) showed how the opposite speech displays of the patient could have been learned, indicating also that the psychiatrists who were treating the patient were involved in the inadvertent training that produced and maintained the patient's abnormal behavior. That is, the psychiatrists were interested in the patient's abnormal behavior — because they felt it might mean something with respect to the patient's mental dynamics. As a consequence they gave the patient social attention when he evidenced the abnormal behavior, asking him questions about his intentions and so on. His more mundane, but appropriate, behaviors did not get that type of attention. Social attention may be considered to be one type of reward (or reinforcer). When a reward follows a behavior, the behavior increases in frequency. That is to say the behavior is learned, which in this case was the abnormal behavior of opposite speech.

This analysis contradicted the psychiatrists' maintenance of the schism which said the field of learning theory had no relevance for the consideration of the field of abnormal behavior. The analysis provided an interlevel, bridging theoretical structure. The interlevel analysis, by its successful consideration in terms of learning of an actual abnormal behavior in a hospitalized psychotic patient, had a number of implications. The analysis generally said that the field of learning had relevance for actual, functional human behavior. The analysis said that abnormal behavior in general was learned — as had been suggested also by some other behavioral psychologists (e.g., Dollard and Miller 1950) — and the analysis specificed how reinforcement could directly be involved in the development and maintenance of an actual symptom of schizophrenia. The specificity of the interlevel theory made evident other empirical expectations, some of which were assessed in any initial manner by the present author (see Staats 1975, pp. 293–95). For example, the bridging theory stated how the abnormal behavior could be treated by manipulating the conditions of reinforcement for the patient. If the patient was not rewarded for opposite speech it would be expected to disappear. It is important to note that two years following publication of the interlevel learning analysis of the case of opposite speech, the first study was published that showed formally that the abnormal symptoms of psychotic patients could be learned through reinforcement (Allyon and Michael 1959), and another study dealt with the same thing with abnormal behavior of a child (Williams 1959). Both cases involved the treatment of the abnormal behavior by manipulating the conditions of reinforcement in the way suggested in the bridging theory. Within a few years there was a profusion of such empirical studies, and it was no longer possible to maintain the separation, as had the original psychiatrists, of the knowledge of the field of basic learning theory and the knowledge of the field of abnormal behavior.

The analysis dealt with in the case of opposite speech was a very abbreviated version of the various developments that contributed to the appearance of what may be called the interlevel or interfield area of "theory" that is named behavior modification. There were various analyses by various investigators that contributed to the interfield theory involved (see Staats 1963, ch. 11). And the interlevel theory was more elaborated than has been presented here and contributed to a greater number of other developments than have been considered here (see Staats 1963, ch. 11). However, the example holds in the present context. Darden and Maull state, "In brief, an interfield theory is likely to be generated when background knowledge indicates that relations already exist between the fields, when the fields share an interest in explaining different aspects of the same phenomenon, and when questions arise about that phenomenon within a field which cannot be answered with the techniques and concepts of that field" (1977, p. 50). The interfield theory involved in the analysis of opposite speech involved such elements. There was background knowledge, there was an interest sharing between the fields of learning and abnormal psychology, and there were questions arising in the field of abnormal behavior that involved learning, and questions arising in the field of learning that involved abnormal psychology, questions not answered well by concepts that emerged within either field itself. And importantly, the principles of conditioning provided knowledge concerning the causes of the abnormal behavior.

Other Types of Bridging Theory

Several types of theory that bridge one or more fields or areas of psychological study have been illustrated, four of them indicated by Darden and Maull also in the fields with which they are concerned. It should be noted that this does not exhaust the types of bridging theory that will be important to psychology, as can be briefly indicated with other examples. An important type of bridging theory can be achieved when one area has worked out principles in elementary detail and when the other area has the same type of principles, but in a far less developed way. Let us take the study of reading, a large field of interest to both education and psychology. This is a field that has grown largely by dealing with the problems of reading acquisition in children. Dealing with complex events in the naturalistic situation, the field had not had the means for establishing the elementary principles underlying reading or reading acquisition. While it was generally understood that learning was definitely involved in acquiring reading skills, the field itself did not deal with or formulate a detailed theory of elementary learning principles. This is a case where one can see the potentiality for an important bridging theory effort. The field of animal learning has isolated in detail the basic, elementary principles of learning. But this field has not developed the study of complex human learning. The field of reading has isolated and described many of the phenomena involved in the complex learning task of the acquisition of reading, and has devised methods for teaching reading. A bridging theory that would analyze the processes involved in reading acquisition in terms of the detailed, elementary principles of learning would provide something that neither field by itself could produce and that would be valuable to both fields. Such a theory would be expected to yield a much deeper, more detailed understanding of how reading is learned, as well as extend our knowledge of the importance and generality of basic learning principles. (See Staats 1968b, for an example of such a bridging theory.)

Another type of bridging theory can occur when the principles from one field can be employed to show the relationships that exist among phenomena that are considered to be disparate in another field, or fields. As one example, a theory of emotion-motivation has been formulated that pertains to disparate phenomena in the field of social psychology. Attitudes, attraction, social interaction in general, leadership, and values, have been analyzed in terms of the principles of the theory of emotion-motivation (see Berkowitz 1970a, b; Byrne and Clore 1970; Lott and Lott 1968; Staats 1963, 1975; Staats, Gross, Guay, and Carlson 1973; Staats and Burns 1982). Other types of bridging theory already exist in psychology, it is suggested, and will be described when we begin to make a systematic study of this aspect of the methodology of unification.

The Bidirectionality of Interlevel Theory

It should be noted that an important characteristic of interlevel theory is that it has significance in both directions, for each of the fields that is unified by the theory. That is one way that one knows that true interlevel theory has been established.

> . . . In true [interlevel] theory, which includes direct derivation from the elementary level to the more complex level, there is actually mutual influence and relevance from one level to the other. [Cases where one theory serves to influence the other area, but not the reverse, were seen to be cases of pseudo-interlevel theory.] Verification and disconfirmation of elemen-

tary principles with more complex phenomena is relevant to and influences the elementary theory level. Moreover, the source of creative developments can arise in either level. A number of examples have been included herein in which elaborations of the elementary level are suggested by the investigation at the more complex level. Thus, knowledge of behavior principles can suggest research in the physiology of learning. . . . Still another example is the productive relationship which was demonstrated between some of the principles in economics and [the theory of emotion-motivation] (Staats 1963). . . . The interdisciplinary research suggested would have significance both for economics and for behavior [theory] work (Staats 1975, p. 567).

Without such bidirectional heuristic significance what seems to be interlevel theory may just be an eclectic mixture, or what may be involved is the analogical extension of one theory to another field. When one uses the terms of one field of study as an analogy, rather than as a direct, bridging theory there are ordinarily no heuristic implications from the field in which the analogy is used back to the more basic field. Many theories in psychology use other fields — such as biological concepts — as analogies, without creating true bridging theory. Staats (1975, ch. 16) uses some of the concepts of Jean Piaget's theory of child development as an example. That is, Piaget explains the learning of the child in terms of the principles of biological assimilation and accommodation. But this type of usage does not bind to each other two formerly separate levels of study, resulting in close theory-empirical relationships between the two levels. The conception rests on an analogy, that human learning has an appearance like that of biological assimilation and accommodation. If the principle of assimilation is negated in psychology, however, this will have no significance for the importance of the concept in biology, indicating that bridging theory is not involved.

Let us generalize this discussion a bit by saying that there are varying degrees of explicitness and detail and directness with which the knowledge of two fields may be unified. For example, it is one thing to suggest that abnormal psychology and learning theory are mutually relevant fields. There was that type of interest in psychology for a long time (Dollard and Miller 1950; Mowrer 1950; Skinner 1953; Watson 1930). However, the generality of this early interlevel theory was such that little research and few treatment procedures were constructed on the basis of the loosely stated unification. When abnormal symptoms, however, are analyzed in terms of the specific responses and the specific stimuli involved and when the principles of the learning and maintenance of the responses are stipulated, then the interlevel theory reaches a degree of specificity that provides the basis for specific research operations. The above example thus illustrates a dimension of unified theory advancement. When the interlevel theory becomes sufficiently specific it can be enormously heuristic, as occurred in the present case in the interlevel area of behavior modification (Staats 1957, 1963).

Interlevel (Interfield) Theory Has Escaped Notice

Darden and Maull make an additional statement that contains elements very similar to the position that has been taken in the works of the present author with respect to unifying theory methods. Moreover, they also indicate what they mean by reductive theory.

> Let us now suggest why interfield theories have been ignored by philosophers of science. Philosophers have not usually discussed areas or fields of science, much less relations between them; instead they have concentrated on theories and on the relations between those, and thus have tended to view fields as theories. Furthermore, theories were viewed as being of the same type, interpreted axiomatic systems, and the relations between theories also were thought to take a single form, namely derivational reduction. After a derivational reduction had occurred, one theory had been "eliminated," at least in the sense that it had been explained as a deductive consequence of a more general theory. Reduction analyses were taken to provide an interpretation of the unity of science. For example, Oppenheim and Putnam (1958) interpreted the unity of science as the cumulative microreduction of theories. And progress was identified with successful reductions.
>
> Although the above overview of a tradition in philosophy of science may be simplistic in certain respects, it is sufficient to show how a concentration on reduction relations between theories would have obscured the nature of fields of science and relations between them established by interfield theories which are not reductive. An interfield theory, in explaining relations between fields, does not eliminate a theory or field or domain. The fields retain their separate identities, even though new lines of research closely coordinate the fields after the establishment of the interfield theory (Darden and Maull 1977, p. 60).

It is important to note that this has been written by two philosophers of science concerned with fields in the natural sciences. Yet the position and concepts involved are very similar to those that have been developed in the present work, based upon experience with the social science of psychology (see Staats 1975). This is an impressive indication of the generality of the concepts for various sciences. This similarity of principle may be noted while at the same time recognizing that the statement of Darden and Maull is a description of what has happened in the science areas they treat. They thus do not address the special problems of the preparadigmatic science, which must be understood and confronted before it will be possible for the science to accept the goal of interlevel or interfield theory as generally important to the science, and before skill in constructing such theory will be developed and disseminated widely in the science.

HIERARCHICAL, UNIFIED THEORY

In describing their ideas concerning interfield theory Darden and Maull reject the methodology that has been called reductionism. In doing so they seemingly reject the notion of hierarchically arranged theory structures, or at least they do not provide a basis for considering the importance of such theory structures. They do not thus provide a foundation for considering central matters of theory construction for the preparadigmatic science of psychology, and their statements lose generality for other sciences and theories as well. It should be noted that classic theory is of the hierarchical type that involves basic premises with derived laws and yet more specific empirical propositions. We can see this in psychology's description of Newtonian theory, a favorite model of classic theory construction as it derived from logical positivism.

> The physicist is able to isolate, experimentally, elementary situations, i.e., situations in which there are a limited number of variables, and thus finds it possible to infer or discover descriptive, lower-order laws. Theory comes into play for the physicist when he attempts to formulate more abstract principles which will bring these low-order laws into relationship with one another. Examples of such comprehensive theories are Newton's principle of gravitation and the kinetic theory of gases. The former provided a theoretical integration of such laws as Kepler's concerning planetary motions, Galileo's law of falling bodies, laws of the tides and so on (Spence 1944, pp. 47–48).

The learning theorists, it should be stressed, took this as the model of theory, literally. Hull, for example, saw the theory construction task to be that of inferring the more abstract principles that would bring the lower-order laws of learning (conditioning) into relationship with each other. Other specific characteristics of Newton's model were adopted, such as the axiomatic statement of the theory, the incorporation of precise mathematical functions in the theory, and so on.

This was the model of grand theory that failed, that fell into the abyss where discards lie in the practice of the science. This is the model that has been in recent times formally rejected by philosophers in the social sciences such as Koch (1981) and Giddens (1976). Rejection of the particular grand theories is one thing, appropriate because they ceased to inspire positive advancements in psychology. But the rejection has been extended to the general goal as well, the goal of seeking general, unified theory in the social sciences.

It is the present position that the rejection of unified, hierarchical theory in psychology and the social sciences is not justified, because the general characteristics of the methodological formulation are rejected along with the specific characteristics of the theories involved. Hull's theory, to illustrate, failed because it did not use the Newtonian model appropriately. For one thing, the conditioning principles themselves are the "abstract" (that is, basic) principles for a general, unified theory in psychology, rather than some more abstract, inferred principles. For another, mathematical statement of the theory and mathematically precise measurement of learning laws is unimportant. The general form of the laws is important, but it will be a long time before mathematical precision will be important in dealing with the way the environment affects human behavior. The push toward mathematical form to theory was a concern with the specifics of classic theory, constituting just the converse of what is needed for unified theory construction of a comprehensive nature that is to deal with human behavior.

The present view is that the classic theory of Newton has much significance for theory in psychology and the social sciences. Not in its specific characteristics, but in some of its general characteristics. Thus, for example, there is a hierarchical character to classic, axiomatic theory. Some principles are more basic than other principles in that the former explain the latter. As will be exemplified for psychology, conditioning principles are basic to various forms of response in human behavior. (This, it must be emphasized, does not mean that the principles of human behavior are any less independent, or any less important than the more basic principles of conditioning.) It is also the case that some areas of study of human behavior, while less basic than the conditioning principles, themselves have found principles that are basic to some other area of the study of human behavior. For example, the principles of the learning of language in humans is basic to understanding various areas of human behavior, since much human behavior takes place through language interactions.

It is the present view that the extraordinary broad range of phenomena in psychology are generally related to each other in a hierarchical form. Psychology is a science of levels, as will be indicated in depth, levels that are related in a hierarchical manner. Newton's theory is far from a good fitting model for theory construction for psychology. But if one ignores the specifics and directs oneself to the general form of the model, one can derive the characteristics that are important. While the following quotation actually pertains to different things than the construction of hierarchically arranged levels of theory in psychology — for it is specifically a description of classic, Newtonian-type theory — the wording is particularly apt for the concepts that are being developed here.

[A theory is] a set of hypotheses which form a deductive system: that is, which is arranged in such a way that from some of the hypotheses as premises all the other hypotheses logically follow. The propositions in a deductive system may be considered as being arranged in an order of levels, the hypotheses at the highest level being those which occur only as premises in the system, those at the lowest level being those which occur only as conclusions in the system, and those at intermediate levels being those which occur as deductions from higher-level hypotheses and which serve as premises for deductions to lower-level hypotheses (Braithwaite 1955, p. 12).

It will be the purpose of the remainder of this chapter to elaborate a theory construction methodology by which to create general, unified theory in psychology that is of a multilevel, hierarchically-arranged type (Staats 1963, 1968a, 1970b, 1975). Let me exemplify the simple, hierarchical theory construction methodology, before going into the more complex developments of that methodology. The simple form can be exemplified as follows, using the principle of classical conditioning originally isolated by Pavlov. The principle may be stated simply as follows: if a stimulus (called the conditioned stimulus) that does not elicit a response is paired with a stimulus (called the unconditioned stimulus) that does elicit the response, then the first stimulus will gain that eliciting power. This principle pertains to internal physiological responses, for example: glandular responses, such as salivation, sweating, or adrenalin flow and responses of the smooth muscles, such as blood vessel flexion. If a sound (or sight or smell, or most any stimulus) is paired with an electric shock — a stimulus that elicits the response of perspiring, for example — the sound will come to elicit the response. This principle has been found to function with various organisms, with various physiological responses, with various stimuli. When the principle remains in the confines of such laboratory studies, however, it cannot be seen as a principle of overwhelming importance. Who cares what it is that makes an animal sweat a little more, that changes the animal's heart rate briefly, that makes an animal salivate a little, and so on.

But there is another area of study that is concerned with human behavior, the study of what has been called emotional behavior. Sometimes people display fear, for example, or joy, or grief. There are many observations that have systematically described the types of emotions humans display, under what conditions, and the like. Watson and Rayner (1920) showed that a human emotional response could be learned according to classical conditioning. They presented a white rabbit to a child — the conditioned stimulus — and then presented a loud sound that made the child cry. After a few such conditioning trials the child showed a negative emotional response to the white rabbit. This study thus constitutes a conceptual bridging from the field of animal learning to the field of studying emotional behavior in humans. Many other implications can be derived from this bridging effort, and the next area involves one of them.

It has been noted since long ago that language communication has certain functional effects on human behavior. Traditionally it was said that meanings were exchanged via language; that the meaning from one person's mind could be transferred to another person's mind through communication. More objectively it was said by various theorists (Cofer and Foley 1942; Osgood 1953; Mowrer 1954; Staats and Staats 1957) that what was traditionally called word meaning consisted of the individual response that had been conditioned to the word. Mowrer (1954) interpreted the traditional transfer of meaning that takes place through communication in these terms. He suggested that when the sentence "Tom is a thief" is stated to someone, what actually occurs is that the word "thief" elicits a negative response in the listener, and this negative response is conditioned to the name "Tom." Staats, Staats, and Crawford (1962) contributed to this bridging development in a study showing that an emotional response could be conditioned to a word by pairing the word with electric shock. Thus, words can gain their physiological, emotional meaning through classical conditioning. Furthermore, other experiments showed that a word that does not elicit a particular emotional response will come to do so if it is paired with other words that elicit that emotional response (Staats and Staats 1957, 1959). This provided support for the principle that emotional learning could take place through language, bridging the areas concerned with classical conditioning, the conditioning of emotions, and the study of some of the effects of language communication.

But, let us now turn to another level of study, that involving abnormal psychology, which we can consider to be the study of abnormal behavior and the causes of such behavior. There is, of course, a very extensive set of observations and conceptual elements in this area. One subarea of abnormal psychology concerns what are called phobias. The term phobias is applied to irrational fears that are severe, sometimes to the point of incapacitating the individual — as when the individual is so afraid of being outside that he is restricted to remaining in the home, to the detriment of work, recreation, and so on. There is a good deal of information concerning phobias, and they have been considered by different theorists to involve various things and various causes. Freud's theory was stated in the context of the case of a child, Hans, who had an unreasonable fear of horses, which Freud considered to stem from the child's repressed sexual attraction for his mother. "Thus, by fearing horses, Hans was said to have succeeded unconsciously in avoiding the fear of castration by his father . . . " (Davison and Neale 1974, p. 125). Very early the bridging theory connecting phobias to classical conditioning was formulated in outline form (Dollard and Miller 1950; Staats 1963). That bridge suggests that the principles of classical conditioning will apply to the formation of phobias, that if the individual has experiences where the phobic stimulus is paired with other stimuli that elicit a negative emotional response the phobic stimulus will come to elicit the negative emotional response.

This example involves a direct link between the basic principles of conditioning and the field of abnormal psychology. This is not a multilevel extension, level by level, from basic principles through less basic fields and on to a still less basic field. But this does not exhaust the significance of the example in the exemplification of the multilevel model. Let me elaborate, by referring to the genesis of phobias. The fact is that with many phobias there does not appear to be a past history of direct negative conditioning. That is why Freud probably had to concoct his interpretation for little Hans's fear of horses, for the child had never been punished in the presence of horses, had never been injured by a horse, or whatever. As another example, many people have severe phobias for flying in airplanes. Yet few people have ever experienced a severe negative emotional conditioning directly with respect to airplanes. How did they get their phobias? The theory levels that have been described provide a means of answering that question, and exemplify the importance of the multilevel development of the theory. By introducing the additional levels we can see how human learning occurs, since much human learning customarily does not involve primary classical conditioning of the variety to which animals are largely restricted. For one thing, humans learn a great deal of their characteristics from language. People with a phobia for flying for the most part have not learned their fear from having been in an airplane accident. They have acquired their phobia from hearing about airplane crashes, from reading about such crashes, from seeing television coverage of crashes, and from thinking or imagining such crashes. We can understand the development of such phobias by utilizing the level of our theory development that showed how words can come to elicit emotional responses, and that showed how words can transfer those emotional responses to other stimuli with which those words are paired. When a person reads the description of an airplane crash — with phrases such as "mutilated bodies and wreckage" — this can elicit a negative emotional response that is conditioned to flying and to airplanes. The level of theory that develops the principles of language learning — based upon the principles of classical conditioning — provides a basic conceptual foundation for further linking with more advanced fields of study such as abnormal psychology. Moreover, those same principles apply to other types of abnormal behavior such as fetishes, abnormal sexual preferences and sexual behaviors. At this point we have several levels of theory development: (1) the animal level of classical conditioning, (2) the explanation of the emotional characteristics of language communication in terms of classical conditioning, and (3) the explanation of phobia acquisition in terms of the communication of emotions through language.

Let me go on by indicating that the abnormal psychology level of theory development can then provide a conceptual foundation that can be linked with yet other fields. Thus, when we have a theory of phobias, to follow our example above, that includes an understanding of how such irrational fears can be learned through language communication; we have a conceptual body that additional bridging theory can extend into the field of psychotherapy. Such a bridging theory has been proposed (Staats 1972). It states that emotional responses that have been created by language communications can be removed via the same mechanisms. Hekmat and Vanian (1971) have shown this to be the case. Using the original methods of producing emotional conditioning through language (Staats and Staats 1957), Hekmat and Vanian reduced a phobia for snakes by pairing the word "snake" with positive emotional words. Various other studies have shown that the language conditioning methods may be employed to benignly change undesirable emotional responses.

This exemplifies there are four levels of theory, each actually a field basic to the next level. It is important to realize, that what is involved is a case of classic theory development that has the same implications for understanding theory construction methodology as Newton's model has had for theory construction in the natural sciences. Multilevel theory, it is suggested, has great potential power — for explanation as well as unification. The general message is that unity in the disparate knowledge of psychology can be achieved through the type of theory methodology that has been characterized — not in a few isolated cases, but very widely, very extensively. What is only necessary is a commitment to the goal, and the realization of the methodology by which to achieve the goal. Additional points may be made in characterizing the multilevel theory methodology.

MULTILEVEL THEORY

It has been said in several places in this study that the present author has devoted himself to the construction of a general, unified theory in psychology. It is not a goal of the present work to present this theory, even in summary form. However, construction of that theory has involved a methodology that may be further abstracted in indicating how unified theory may be constructed very generally in psychology. This methodology may be summarized by saying that it combines several of the elements that have already been explicated, (1) the concept of classical hierarchical theory in which certain parts of the theory are basic to other parts, (2) the concept of interlevel theory in which the levels are the major fields of psychology, and (3) the understanding of the preparadigmatic nature of psychological knowledge and with it the understanding of the nature of the theoretical task.

Fields of Psychology

There has never been an attempt to construct a unified theory in psychology, of the type that will be described herein (other than the theory that is the basis for the methods to be presented). There have been theories that have intended to be general to psychology, and of a unified nature. Psychoanalytic theory is a good example of the methodology usually involved. Psychoanalytic theory was based primarily upon experience in working with patients in a therapy relationship, on the study of abnormal behavior, and upon observations of human behavior in the naturalistic situation. There were very minor attempts at a later time to relate psychoanalytic theory to other types of knowledge in psychology, but these attempts were incipient and abortive. Ordinarily when theorists consider their theories to be general to the knowledge of psychology they do so in the same sense. Their theory has been established within the confines of a part of psychology — ordinarily less than the concerns of a whole field of psychology. Then the theorist makes some attempt to extend principles of the theory to some examples of human behavior in another field or fields of psychology, usually on an informal basis, lacking the same objective qualities of theory construction employed in the primary theory.

The classic learning theories of the second generation were refinements of that methodology. As has been indicated, their specialized area of study was animal learning. The intention, however, was that their theories of animal learning would extend very generally to human behavior. But the extension of the animal learning theory to human behavior was not of the same methodological quality as that involved in constructing the primary theory. Skinner (1953, 1971) has stated that his theory is general in the sense of applying widely to human behavior. But his extensions to human behavior have been conjectural, based upon informal observations of human behavior, without making use of more systematically accumulated knowledge, and without systematically being addressed to the problems and interests that other psychologists have uncovered in their systematic studies of human behavior.

In essence, this approach is a methodology of exclusion. The theorist attempts to attain his goal of having a general, unified theory by excluding all but his own areas of knowledge. Generality is achieved conjecturally. Psychoanalytic theory does not deal with the major fields of knowledge of psychology, and the same is true of the grand theories of the behaviorists. Watson, and Skinner later, formalized this methodology by explicitly excluding large blocks of knowledge and various fields of psychology from the purview of scientific psychology.

Unified and general theory in psychology cannot be established via the theory construction methodology of exclusion. In the present view that methodology is itself a product of the preparadigmatic mentality of psychologists. Preparadigmaticism leads the theorist to be ignorant of the contents of other fields of study in psychology. Because the theorist cannot make sense of the knowledge of other areas of study that knowledge is defensively devalued and rejected. General, unified theory cannot be established without a positive regard for fields, areas, and products of study other than one's own. It was said in the previous chapter, in discussing the resolution of schisms in psychology, that the theorist had to assume that there were positive contributions to knowledge on both sides of a schism and that the theorist's job was to join those contributions. The same is true in the construction of general, unified theory. It must be assumed (albeit my own experience tells me that this is not just an assumption) that there are contributions to knowledge in most of the fields and areas of psychology. When highly trained individuals work in an area for an extended time and produce a good deal of systematic knowledge, in the absence of proof to the contrary one has to expect that things of value will have been found. Very surely, if the theorist's task is the construction of a general, unified theory, it is not justifiable to cross out some field or area of study on the basis of some superficial rationale obtained via a glancing contact with the field, or whatever. The theorist must take the field or area of study seriously. The theorist must consider what the workers in that field or area of study are concerned with, what they are attempting to find, and what problems they are attempting to resolve. Only through exploring these things, and the progress that has been made in attaining knowledge of them, will the theorist be able to realize something about the importance of the field or area of study.

Fields of psychology like personality, personality measurement, social psychology, abnormal psychology, clinical psychology; areas of study like language acquisition, communication, reading, psychotherapy, cognitive theory; must be examined for what they can contribute to a general, unified theory. The assumption, until proved incorrect, must be that an active field or area will have knowledge to contribute to the whole. If that assumption is to be rejected, it must be done on the basis of an informed evaluation, with adequate justification of how the general, unified theory structure will be constructed without that field or area.

Interlevel (Hierarchical) Theory, over the Fields of Psychology

Classic theory, as we have seen, involves a hierarchical structure — ranging from basic premises to specific experimental hypotheses formally deduced from more basic theoretical constructions. As has been suggested already this theory construction method was applied in psychology in a very stereotyped way. Nevertheless, it is the present contention that the classic hierarchical theoretical structure is relevant to psychology. A specific example has been given of this type of theory development.

But this example does not exhaust the importance of the hierarchical theory exemplar — which cannot be seen until it is combined with the concept of interlevel theory that involves the bridging of the fields and areas of study of psychology. In the example given, of hierarchical theory construction extending from the basic animal learning principles of classical conditioning to the advanced field of clinical psychology practice, what was involved was a narrow set of principles. The phenomena treated in the example were correspondingly limited in range, in each of the levels dealt with. Some of this limitation was due to the fact that only an example was dealt with in the restricted space available in the present work. But some of the limitation was due to the fact that the more complex, general conception was not developed in the example. The general conception is that the classic hierarchical theory exemplar in psychology is relevant to the organization of the whole science, across the various major fields of psychology (and beyond to the social sciences).

Let us develop that more general conception. To begin, the fields of psychology have not been established through a systematic construction of a general theory framework. As a consequence, the character of the various field specialties of psychology might appear to be accidents of history, divisions formed to meet organizational needs of the burgeoning science — rather than to be systematically arrived at products of science. Such a conclusion is bolstered by the fact that the several fields are typically not related to each other, in any meaningful way. In the present view, however, although the science generally has not been able to see this, the nature of the events to be studied may be considered to have played a strong role in the development and differentiation of the various fields and areas of study of psychology. The different fields of psychology have been founded, basically, because groups of psychologists have ascertained that there are phenomena to be studied in the field that they considered important, phenomena that were not being adequately studied in already established fields of the science. This need not mean that every field and every area of study in psychology is needed as a specialty area, or that all of the specialty areas have already been demarcated. It only means that the fields as presently constituted allow for the study of phe-

nomena in psychology that have an objective significance, that the fields
are germane to the general mission of the science, and that the fields generally contribute part knowledge to the whole which is sought.

On the basis of this analysis, by itself, we might expect that there
would be a relationship between the fields of psychology, in that they
should make contributions of knowledge to the whole represented by the
interest of the science. We can see in the natural sciences that there is a
progression from the more basic science fields to the less basic. As was described in an earlier chapter, it has been considered that physics is more
basic than chemistry which is more basic than biochemistry which is more
basic than biology and so on. On the basis of this widely significant circumstance it might be justified to look for a hierarchical relationship between the separate fields of psychology. It is also reasonable to suppose
that establishing this relationship would be one of the important items in
constructing a unified science of psychology.

The present conception is that the various fields of psychology can
only be organized through a recognition of their hierarchical relationship
to one another, and through establishing interlevel theory that bridges the
present separations between the fields. Part of the task of creating bridging theory will depend upon the recognition of the "basic to less-basic" relationship of the various fields — where the principles and analyses of one
field will then provide principles with which to consider and deal with
the principles, analyses, and phenomena of the less basic field. While it
will not be possible to even summarize the multilevel theory that has followed the above rationale and that exemplifies the methodology involved,
a very brief description will be made to characterize the theory. Table 1
can be employed in this exemplification.

In the present view the elementary level of the theory is that of the
Basic Learning Theory. This is a choice that is still of issue, since from the
viewpoint of some psychologists the basic level for the explanation of human behavior lies in the study of biological science. In the present view
such a stand, however, creates insuperable problems in the construction
of the type of general, unified theory being described. This issue cannot
be dealt with here in any depth, however. It can also be said that a schism
is involved that is resolvable at least in one productive way. This resolution
is that the Basic Learning Theory Level of the unified theory be productively and heuristically linked to the biological level of study. An outline
for this linking has already been presented (see Staats 1975, ch. 15). It may
be said here that this bridging theory recognizes that the principles of
learning themselves require explanation in terms of the neurophysiology of
learning. Moreover, the terms of the Basic Learning Theory level must be
capable of objectification on a physiological level — that is that there be
physiological structures that correspond to the basic terms like stimulus,

TABLE 1: The Multilevel Theory of Social Behaviorism

Fields	Areas (Examples)
Biological Mechanisms of Learning	Sensory Psychology Brain and Central Nervous System Response Systems Evolution of Learning Structures
Basic Learning Theory	Conditioning Principles Generalizing Principles, in Stimuli, Response Systems, and Species Treated Motivation Principles
Human Learning Principles	Complex Stimulus-Response Learning Cumulative-Hierarchical Learning Principles and Others Unique to Humans Extending Basic Principles to Human Level
Child Development Principles	Language Development, Intelligence, and Language Mediated Modeling Sensory-Motor Development and Imitation Emotional Development through Learning
Personality	Personality Theory The Personality System — Language-Cognitive, Emotional-Motivational, and Sensory-Motor Personality and Environmental Interaction
Personality Measurement	Theory Relating Behavior Principles and Personality Measurement and Assessment Integrating Tests with Theory (Clinical, etc.) Constructing Tests and Behavior Assessments
Social Psychology	Attitudes and Social Cognition Interpersonal Relations with Group Processes Personality Processes, Individual Differences, and Cross-Cultural Psychology
Abnormal Personality	Deficits in the Personality Systems Inappropriate Aspects of Personality Systems Diagnostic Categories in Terms of Personality Systems Interaction of Personality and Social Systems
Clinical Psychology	Behavior Modification of Simple Problems Personality Change and Personality Measurement Language-Cognitive Methods of Treatment Children's Problems and Treatment
Educational Psychology	Learning Theories of School Subjects Intelligence and Readiness in School Learning

(continued)

TABLE 1: *(continued)*

Fields	Areas (Examples)
	Problems of School Learning
	Motivation and School Learning
Organizational Psychology	Personnel Selection
	Motivation in Organizational Settings
	Behavioral Analysis of Jobs
	Organizational Conditions and Problems

response, and stimulus-response associations (the neurophysiology of learning). Furthermore, it is necessary to establish relationships between the Basic Learning Theory level of the general theory and such biologically important questions as the evolution of learning mechanisms and structures (see Staats 1963, 1968b). Nevertheless, the more advanced levels of the theory derive from the Basic Learning Theory level of the general theory, not directly from biological levels of knowledge.

The grand theorists, such as Hull, Tolman, and Skinner, were primarily animal psychologists — at least in their focus of scientific work. Their context for the formulation of their learning theories was the fund of theory and the experimental findings concerning animal learning. The study of animal learning is the primary context for the present area of the field of the learning. This is said to underline the major point here, which is that theories of learning have ordinarily not been composed to serve as the foundation for general, unified theories of human behavior. Although some of the behaviorists who composed learning theories thought their theories would apply generally to human behavior, they did not take into account the knowledge of human behavior in the rest of psychology when they composed their theories. The Basic Learning Theory level that is being suggested, however, is not one of the existing animal learning theories. Formulated as theories of animal learning, they have features that are inappropriate as the Basic Learning Theory. Hull's concentration upon the axiomatic statement of the laws of learning, and his focus on unnecessary intervening variables is a case in point. Such animal learning theories also are unsuited for the present task because they lack features that are necessary. Skinner's theory, for example, does not indicate how the two major principles of learning — the classical conditioning of emotional responses and the instrumental conditioning of motor responses — interact with each other. Without a basic theory that shows this interaction it is not possible to deal with matters important in the more advanced levels of theory development, such as the way that emotions affect the way the individual behaves. This is a good example showing how the construction of the Basic Learning Theory level must be formulated to utilize the context of knowledge of human behavior as well as of animal conditioning experiments. There is a general message here: that theoretical development is necessary to turn the raw material of each level-field into a component of multilevel theory.

In the already-given example of hierarchical theory possibilities in psychology, where the principle of classical conditioning was extended to types of human behavior, in an advancing way, one of the extensions was to use the principle to account for the emotional meaning of words and the manner in which such words can themselves produce additional emotional conditioning. This was done to illustrate a central point in the theory construction task being summarized, that is, that the elementary principles of the Basic Learning Theory must be subjected to additional theoretical-experimental development before complex human behavior can be dealt with in terms of learning. For one thing, the learning of humans is different from the learning of animals that is studied in the laboratory. The latter is simplified as much as possible to establish the elementary principles with good reliability. So a simple stimulus, a simple response, and so on, are used. Human behavior is rarely so simple. There are usually multiple stimuli acting on the human, who is capable of multiple responses. Moreover, humans have an exceedingly long learning history, where learned skills can build on top of previously learned skills, and the former then can serve the basis for additional skill learning, in a process called cumulative-hierarchical learning. An example has already been given. Humans learn through conditioning to respond emotionally to many words. But language then is a complex mechanism for producing much further emotional learning in the human. The principles of language communication are Human Learning Principles. Cumulative-hierarchical learning and other important principles must be developed at this level, if the theory structure is to be adequate for understanding human behavior. This was not understood by the traditional learning theorists, and their theories were as a consequence not credible to those interested in the study of human behavior.

The Basic Learning Theory and the Human Learning Principles levels of theory must be further developed before they can be generally extended in a productive manner to understanding human behavior. The next level of development needs to establish the general principles of child development. This is an area in which there has been schismatic conflict regarding whether the child develops behaviorally on the basis of physiological maturation and genetic factors, or through learning. The schism requires resolution and the learning principles by which the child develops require presentation. The present theory has introduced the concept of the basic behavioral repertoire, which is central for understanding human development and human behavior. That is, complex human learning depends not only on the basic principles of learning, but also on the skills that the individual brings to the task. A child may be perfectly normal in his ability to be classically and instrumentally conditioned — that is, in his very basic learning ability. But that is not sufficient when the child is presented with the task of learning to read. In order to learn to read the child must have a normally rich language repertoire, for example. Without the various subrepertoires that compose language, which some children have not acquired, the child will fail in the reading task. Therefore, there are basic behavioral repertoires, such as language, that are requisite for many types of human learning tasks. These repertoires must be described, both the manner in which they are learned, as well as the manner in which they affect the child's later learning (see Staats 1968b, 1971a, 1975; Staats and Burns 1981). Thus, the theory introduces the central concept of intelligence (for example) and deals with the fund of knowledge residing in this area of study. Such elaborations exemplify what is meant by the Child Development Principles level of the theory structure, and much of the subject matter in this level comes from the field of child (or developmental) psychology.

The Child Development Principles level provides the basis for the development of the next level of the general, unified theory. The concepts of the basic behavioral repertoires and cumulative-hierarchical learning, provide a basis for the concept of personality. This area is again schismatic, with traditional psychology accepting personality as a process or structure within the individual that determines the characteristics of the individual's behavior. Personality, in this view, is a causative process. Behaviorists say there is no causative process of personality, personality is simply behavior. Behaviorists thus reject the consideration of individual differences in response to the same environmental situation, which is the central concern of the field of personality. The concept of the basic behavioral repertoire provides a basis for resolving the schism and for joining the knowledge of behavioral psychology with that of the traditional field of personality theory. The Personality level of theory develops the basic repertoire concept into the three general areas of personality characteristics, the language-cognitive repertoire, the emotional-motivational repertoire, and the sensory-motor repertoire. The theory calls for specification concerning how the basic behavioral repertoires are learned as well as how they function in helping determine individual differences in behavior and learning. This level of theory demands integration with psychology's traditional knowledge of personality and its effects (see Staats 1971a, 1975;

Staats, Gross, Guay, and Carlson 1973; Staats and Burns 1981; Staats and Burns, 1982). As with the other levels, there are additional developments that cannot even be alluded to here.

The Personality level of the theory development then provides a basis for incorporating the knowledge of the field of personality measurement. The field of personality measurement has remained separate from learning theory or behaviorism formulations — by mutual agreement. An important aspect of developing a unified theory is the task of providing bridging theory here, as in the other cases. The concept of the basic behavioral repertoires as the constituents of personality provides the preliminary basis for that bridge. Additional bridging theory involves the analysis (1) of traditional personality tests in terms of the basic behavioral repertoires, (2) of how traditional personality test characteristics are learned, and (3) of how they function in determining the individual's behavior, and so on (see Staats and Burns 1981, 1982; Staats, Gross, Guay, and Carlson 1973). Later developments will be the use of the Personality Measurement level of the theory as a basis for designing better personality testing instruments. In addition, the integration of the Personality Measurement level of the theory with the more advanced levels of the theory structure open additional heuristic opportunities. Thus, for example, traditional psychological testing has been useful in diagnosing problems, but is typically less useful as a source of knowledge concerning how specifically to treat the problems that are diagnosed. When personality is specifically analyzed and when the way it is learned is indicated, then directives are provided that indicate what should be done to bring about changes in personality for benign effects in the practice of clinical, child, or educational psychology. This example thus indicates clearly the hierarchical nature of the theory structure across the fields with which it deals. The several fields above Personality Measurement allow the knowledge of the field (at least in part) to be considered and organized in a unified, heuristic manner. But in turn the field of Personality Measurement, becomes, because of the unified properties of the theoretical structure, basic to other fields of study in heuristic ways.

The example of this particular general, unified theory will not be further developed here as it applies to the fields of psychology not yet mentioned but that are designated in Table 1. Let it be indicated, however, that there are extensive developments in the Social Psychology, Abnormal Psychology, Clinical Psychology, Educational Psychology, and Organizational Psychology levels that fit into the particular multilevel structure, aside from the works conducted specifically within the multilevel theory. As with the other levels, much of this knowledge comes from traditional psychology. And there are also other theories and findings by learning theory and behavior theory psychologists that provide very direct support. Seeing this support requires only that the principles, concepts, and results be theoretically translated and modified to coincide with the characteristics of the present multilevel theory that are different from the other basic learning theories employed. Thus, as examples, Berkowitz (1962, 1964, 1970a, 1970b, 1973, 1974), Byrne and associates (Byrne and Clore 1970; Byrne and Griffitt 1969; Sachs and Byrne 1970) Lott and Lott (1968, 1972), Weiss (1971; Weiss, Boyer, Lombardo, and Stich 1973), and many more, have contributed important works that lend themselves to the development of the Social Psychology level of the theory (see Staats, in press). The areas of behavior modification and behavior therapy in psychology have produced too many works to even mention that lend extensive support to the multilevel theory structure. The same thing is true in the field of Educational Psychology. As in the preceding level of study, the present theory has done pioneering work in applying learning principles to study central problems of these fields. But a number of other workers have done so also, in a manner that contributes research and analysis that strengthens and elaborates the multilevel structure.

PREPARADIGMATIC PSYCHOLOGY AND THE UNIFIED THEORY TASK

We are thus not talking about a hypothetical projection. When one looks at the range of work produced by learning-oriented psychologists one feels surprised. When one further puts this work into the unified, multilevel structure, removing the misleading divisiveness of the idiosyncratic theories, and incorporates large parts of traditional psychological knowledge into the structure, with heuristic implications, one's surprise becomes astonishment. This is to say that there is no question that proposing a general, unified theory in psychology appears at the outset to be the height of grandiosity, in its unrealistic sense, such that it is difficult to obtain widespread attention for such a project. Yet if one will examine what many have already accomplished as a basis for the effort, one can only be surprised at the substantive development that already exists. Why is there such a discrepancy between achievement and acceptance? The answer is given by the analyses that have been presented herein. Most of the various contributions to the multilevel structure have been completed in the interest of separated and seemingly independent, even competitive, small fractionating theory structures in different fields and areas of study, using different concepts and methods. The various contributions are not considered to contribute to a general, unified theory because of our science's divisiveness. The preparadigmatic nature of the science of psychology prevents the members of the science from taking a good look to see if anything unified is really there. Without something to tear away this preparadigmatic blindfold, the possibilities of general, unified theory in psychology may be unrealized for a period of time like that involving the lag between Mendel's discovery of the principles of inheritance and the recognition of the potentialities his work suggested.

The major task of tearing away the blinders involves realization by the science of what its preparadigmatic nature is. It is the purpose of the present book to provide that realization. When we realize how separatistic, conflicting, and chaotic our science is, it becomes possible to realize how there may be hidden unity and commonality in the science. One of the important things that we can abstract from Kuhn's brief description of preparadigmatic science is that in the divisive conflict of the preparadigmatic science, across the diversity of warring schools, there exists commonality. That commonality, it is suggested, is the basis for the paradigmatic unification that follows. And it is the present premise that there is vast commonality in the fund of knowledge that psychology has already created. In the preparadigmatic science the commonality is hidden by the chaotic nature of that knowledge. And that is the case with psychology. The important point is that the commonality is *not* invisible, impossible to detect. Rather, it cannot be detected because no one looks. The preparadigmatic character of the science prevents the search. It does not provide the search as a goal of the science. And it does not provide the skills by which to conduct the search. When the psychologist has both the goal and the skills, the task becomes manageable. Understanding this, in the present view, will begin the paradigmatic revolution. But other topics of methodology remain.

The Nature of the Task

There are some general characteristics of the task of constructing multilevel, unified theory that may be mentioned. Each field can be expected to be composed of a mixture of "junk" along with the valuable. The theorist must separate the junk from that which can be used productively in the theory construction task. In addition, the theorist must abstract from the hodgepodge of detailed information in a field that which has significance for a general, unified theory. The knowledge of the field will have grown without the guidance of general principles and the goal of unified theory. Thus, much of its content will be superfluous to the unified theory task, or even antithetical to it.

In this task of theory construction — of finding commonality in a field and of organizing it into a structure relevant to the general, unified theory — the methodological points that were made in the preceding chapter will be significant. When the field is made more organized by appropriate citation methods, its knowledge will be more accessible to the detection of commonality. When integratory theory has been constructed to bring to light the common elements in diverse theories, the knowledge of the field will be more accessible to organization for unified theory construction. Each schism resolution in psychology that allows the bridging of separated and conflicting bodies of knowledge will make the knowledge easier to unite within a field, and between the levels of fields. This is said to indicate that the specific unifying methods described in the preceding chapter are part and parcel of the grand task of constructing multilevel, unified theory.

Characteristics of Early Unified Theory

A word should also be said about the characteristics that in general we can expect early unified theory to have. Such theory will not be couched in the mathematical purity of axiomatic theories of the physical sciences that have served as the philosophy of science models for psychology and the other social sciences. Unified theory in psychology will have to be hierarchical and systematic, but in a less formal sense. The derivations of the bridging theories between the levels in the unified theory have to be consistent always with the basic principles and the previous derivations. But these theoretical structures will not be stated in formal logic and mathematics. The material to be handled is too complex. The first theories can be expected to be couched in the common language, refined by the technical concepts and principles that are introduced on the basis of systematic study. The fact that the common language is employed, however, should not mislead one from the realization that such theory is as classic in its unificatory and hierarchical sense as the classic theories in the physical sciences.

It should also be realized that any general, unified theory in its early development will not be detailed throughout its range of extension. It is very clear to me that no one person, during one professional lifetime, will be able to span the range and confusion of knowledge of contemporary psychology in constructing a unified theory, and do it in homogeneous detail throughout. The task is too immense. When one examines the theory that has been employed as the exemplar herein (see Staats 1975), one will see varying degrees of specificity and detail. In no case is one of the fields that composes its levels dealt with in the range of detail that one can find in the standard specialty treatments of the field. But it is important to realize that the simplification of a field, away from the detail of specialization, may be of intrinsic importance to the theory-construction task. Thus, for example, the field of animal learning is a blooming confusion of findings, methods, principles, and theories. In constructing the unified theory this overly complex fund of knowledge had to be boiled down to a skeleton theory composed of animal and human learning principles that have special value as a basis for considering the phenomena of human behavior. The skeleton theory, it is suggested, is a better vehicle for considering those phenomena than any of the specialty theories that are available in the field of animal learning; their greater detail is actually a handicap in the unified-theory task.

One reason it is important that this be realized is that otherwise the general, unified theory may be rejected by the population of psychologists — all of whom are specialists — because the level in the theory that is relevant to any particular specialist will not be as detailed as the standard works in his area. The simplified treatment of the field in the unified theory, nevertheless, can have value that the specialized treatment cannot yield. That is, it can give direction to the way that the specialized field should be developed to be part of the large, unified theory structure. The detail can be added later when co-workers enter into the framework theory of the field and perform the necessary theoretical, empirical, and methodological work necessary to turn the framework into a detailed structure.

I will return to this point. First, however, it should be noted that although the early version of a general-unified theory may not be indicated in detail throughout its range, it should attain that detail at selected points. Only in that way can it demonstrate its heuristic potentiality. The multilevel theory that has been described here has been presented in detail and has proven heuristic for psychologists at various levels of the structure. The development of its basic "three-function learning theory" (Staats 1968a, 1970b, 1975; Staats and Hammond 1972; Staats and Warren 1974; Harms and Staats 1978) for example, has been corroborated by similar developments in animal learning theories (Bindra 1978; Overmier and Lawry 1979). Its analysis of language learning has been the most complete of those of a learning theory framework and it has introduced experimentation in this area (see Staats 1968b). The approach has been one of the pioneering learning theories in the field of social psychology (see Staats 1963, 1968a, 1975, in press). It's development of behavior modification and behavior assessment concepts, methods, and principles (see Staats 1957, 1963, 1968a, 1971a, 1975; Staats and Butterfield 1965; Staats, Finley, Minke, and Wolf 1964; Staats, Staats, Schutz, and Wolf 1962; Staats, Brewer and Gross 1970) have been seminal in these areas of study. It has developed a theory of intelligence (Staats 1971a) with supporting research (Staats, Brewer, and Gross 1970; Staats and Burns 1981) that is certainly the first and most detailed theory that deals with the manner in which intelligence is acquired through learning (a contemporary interest). As another example, it has developed a new theory of personality that is beginning to provide a rapprochement between learning and traditional views (Staats 1963, 1968b, 1971a, 1975; Staats and Burns 1981; Staats, Gross, Guay, and Carlson 1973; Staats and Burns 1982). In each case, moreover, there has been incorporation of materials from traditional psychology and from other learning theory works. The point to stress here, however, is that an important way that a general, unified theory can be expected to prove itself lies in the ways that all theories do, that is by the products the theory stimulates — new analyses, new theory, new research, and so on — that are found to be valuable. The unified theory, however, must do this across a sufficient range of the fields to which it addresses itself to give confidence that it has general heuristic power. The traditional general theory has merely suggested that it is widely applicable, without showing its merit across other fields in a specific and heuristic manner.

Framework-Theory Requirements

All theories are skeletons in the sense to be considered here. That is, the events of the world constitute a vast multitude. Attempting to specifically treat that multitude in totality would be impossibly complex. A theory ordinarily must select from that multitude, dealing in empirical stipulation only with some of the events in a particular realm of nature, with the expectation that the full set could be dealt with should there be reason to do so. A sufficiently large sample of such stipulations must occur before we become confident that the theory would hold in the other cases that are not specifically considered (Reichenbach 1951).

In psychology there have been various theories that have claimed in one or another way to be general. None of them, including the multilevel theory briefly described herein, has been presented in detail throughout the range of psychology's interest. This fact means that the sampling of stipulations for any of these theories has been less than complete. Why is it that the present account evaluates negatively some of the theories that have been mentioned, with respect to their value as general, unified theories of psychology and why has the multilevel theory been evaluated positively? Why can one general theory be called a heuristic theory when it is only a framework, and another rejected? The answer lies in the program and methodology and goal for establishing the generality of the theory, in the detail with which the efforts have been elaborated, in the evidence that the theories do indeed make "reality contact" with a range of areas, at least in a sampling treatment. This notion requires elaboration.

Programmatic-Theoretical-Empirical Requirements

If a theory that has arisen in one field of psychology is to claim generality with respect to other fields of psychology it must have a program by which to advance to that generality. What is the program for Hull's or Skinner's learning theory to become a general, unified theory? Skinner's programmatic statement in actuality was that all types of behavior were to be experimentally analyzed in his conditioning apparatus (see Sidman 1960).

This is not really a program, in the present sense of the term — nor is there such a program in any other orientation in psychology. But a systematic effort to construct general, unified theory will be unlikely to grow through unguided efforts.

In addition to a program, general, unified theory must have exemplary theoretical extensions to a good sample of the areas for which it is said to pertain, and it must have demonstration of its empirical potentialities in a good sample of those areas also. On the one hand, it is recognizable that the first step in formulating a general, unified theory for psychology will not constitute a completed effort. The complexity and variegation and extensiveness of the phenomena, concepts, findings, and methods in psychology preclude that possibility. On the other hand, a theory that aims for generality within a unified set of principles cannot stop at the suggestion that it is general and unified. Beginning the progression toward the attainment of such theory will fall between those poles of the continuum. As an example, for psychoanalytic theory to demonstrate that it is general it would have to show the ability of its principles to extend to important aspects of such fields as reading, intelligence, animal learning principles, language acquisition, problem solving, behavior modification, social interaction, attitude formation, number concept learning, and many more. There is a large literature in each of these areas. How do the principles of psychoanalytic theory fare when asked to derive the phenomena, concepts, and findings in each of these and other areas? Do analyses show that the phenomena, concepts, and findings in a good sample of these areas could have been derived from principles in psychoanalytic theory? Do the analyses taken as a whole show that there is considerable commonality among the phenomena, concepts, and findings across the several areas when couched in psychoanalytic principles? Do the analyses demonstrate psychoanalytic theory to be a productive theoretical structure in the various areas, such that the psychoanalytic analysis in a particular area competes successfully with the specialty theory or theories in that area? Does it provide a basis for the theoretical derivation of new concepts and principles when applied to new areas? These are important questions, and an affirmative answer in each case would raise our confidence in the generality and relevance of psychoanalytic theory.

To continue, however, it would be equally important that the general theory show its heuristic potentiality for producing empirical products in the various areas to which it was applied. Following the above example, when psychoanalytic theory is applied to the analysis of reading does the analysis yield implications for creating a method for teaching reading, for dealing with problems of reading learning, or for experimentation showing the basic nature of reading? These questions pertain as well to the other areas of psychology. And the questions pertain for any theory presuming to be general and unified.

Method Generality Requirements

It may be added that there are methodological considerations in this evaluation also. Following the example, psychoanalytic theory was largely based on clinical and other naturalistic observations, with a primary concern with unconscious mental phenomena. If psychoanalytic theory is to be proposed as a general theory it must show how it is coincident with such major efforts as the laboratory study of animal learning and its various methods, with the child developmentalist's longitudinal observation of children's behavioral development, with the methods of psychometrics, with the methods of sensory psychology, and so on. A general, unified theory would presumably be able to indicate in a unified manner the way in which the different observational and experimental methods contribute in an integrated way to the knowledge of psychology.

At this point it is relevant to indicate that in the senses that have been described, it cannot be said that psychology has ever tried to create general, unified theories (other than in the multilevel theory described here). There are no theories that have had a program for advancing in generality through extending their principles to the major fields of psychology in a systematic and heuristic way, utilizing the sources of knowledge that are already available in those fields. There are no theories that have been developed systematically to incorporate the knowledge of psychology that is based upon different methods of investigation. It cannot be concluded, thus, that grand, unified theory has been tried and has failed.

Fleshing out the Skeleton

We may debate the feasibility of attaining general, unified theory in psychology. But debate, although it may be productive, is not the complete answer. We will only find out how to organize the knowledge of psychology, to attain unified theory, through efforts to effect that result. Since each unified theory will at first be in good part a skeleton, we must realize that progress will involve an immense theoretical and empirical task. The framework of a general, unified, theory will prove itself only through providing a basis for productive theoretical and empirical (basic and applied) efforts in a large number of areas of study in psychology. The work of confirming and developing a skeleton theory cannot be the work of an individual theorist, nor would this take place in one fell swoop but rather in generations of efforts. Such a task must be the work of many minds and many hands — theoretical work, experimental work, and applied work. Applied work is an essential ingredient, for psychology includes many findings and concepts in applied areas that must be unified with basic study. It would be expected that the elaborating and fleshing out of a skeleton theory would be analogous to what Kuhn has called normal science. For a general, unified-theory skeleton in psychology, however, it would be expected that the creation of this "normal science" would be as creative a task as the setting forth of the original skeleton. Much of the work would be theoretical. It would be expected that the theorist working in the paradigm would first become highly skilled in the principles of the skeleton theory. Then he would enter the new area of study into which the skeleton theory was to be projected. He would have to become expert in the knowledge of the special area. This foundation would be the basis for making a full theoretical extension of the skeleton theory projection into that area or, if the area had not yet been dealt with at all in the general, unified-theory effort, the task might begin with the first skeleton theory extension into the area.

Thus, developing any general, unified theory will involve a huge theoretical, methodological, and empirical task. In every major and minor area of psychology there must be the actual theoretical-empirical work necessary to realize the potential of the general, unified skeleton. In the present view when psychology begins being influenced by such unified theories a tremendous power will be released. The presently chaotic state of psychological knowledge will take on an organized character. The theoretical-empirical works in various areas of psychology will contribute to one another and support one another, to create a growing body of integrated knowledge that cuts across the presently arbitrary divisions of the science. In the process of such paradigmatic work the strengths and the weaknesses of the original theoretical structure will become apparent. Changes in the fundamental nature of the general-unified theory may be demanded. As has been indicated, entirely new theoretical structures will emerge that were not treated by the original general-unified theory, as well as new methods of study, and so on.

Importance of Unified Theory as a Framework

It has already been suggested, at least implicitly that a unified theory — in its role as a framework — is also a valuable structure. It has been said that the framework theory for an area can provide a foundation for the specialist to compose a more detailed, heuristic theory in the area.

In addition to this product, framework theories of a multilevel, unified type have other contributions. A unified theory structure can be expected to give specialists in psychology a general meaning to their science. They, by virtue of such a general theory structure, will be able to see the relationship of their work to that of others, across different fields of psychology. This is an important product in and of itself. In addition, the framework theory will allow specialists to make sense of others' works so that they can be utilized in a relevant manner. The extent to which the unified theory encourages this across areas, fields, theories, and methods of psychology is the extent to which the theory will be valuable in this sense. When paradigmatic skills have been accumulated and disseminated to psychologists they will be better able to do the job of crossing fields and to translate diverse knowledge of the science into a form that they can appreciate and use.

THE MULTILEVEL METHOD IS A GENERAL METHOD

The multilevel method of theory construction has been explicated with reference to the theory called paradigmatic behaviorism. But that is not to suggest that this particular theory preempts the use of the method. It is the present position that the theory-construction analysis presented represents a general method of wide scope for developing unified theory in psychology. There are other general theories in psychology — for example, psychoanalytic theory, Hull's theory, Skinner's theory, cognitive theory, and so on — at least on a suggestive or conjectural basis. It is important, in the present view, that such theories make their general nature explicit in the process of attempting to be true general, unified theories. The methodology of multilevel theory construction, it is suggested, may be employed in constructing new general, unified theories, or in reconstructing already existing theories — such as those mentioned above — into actual, general, unified theory structures. We will find out a good deal about these theories, and about the nature of constructing general, unified theory, when we subject these theories to the types of development and evaluation that have been discussed herein.

The fact is that someone must take these theories and see what they can produce as general, unified theories. Can they cover the various levels of knowledge of psychology? Can they do so in a manner that is heuristic theoretically, empirically, and methodologically? What are their limitations in this respect, in terms of coverage and in terms of producing valuable bridging theory?

Why Multiple Editions of Unified Theory
Will Not Enhance Preparadigmaticism

In the present conception there are some very important demands that must be made of any theory that claims to be general and unified. Most centrally, the various major fields and areas of study of psychology must be included in any general theory. That stipulation removes immediately any theory claiming generality that does not provide a meaningful place for one or more of the major areas, without justification. Thus, for example, a theory that considers human behavior to be explained by biological variables, and that makes no meaningful use of the vast knowledge of learning and social-environmental causation, cannot be a general, unified theory. On the other hand, a behavioristic theory that makes no meaningful use of the vast knowledge of areas like personality, personality measurement, social psychology findings, an abnormal psychology, and that does not indicate how the biological level of study relates to the theory, cannot be a general, unified theory. The environment does have powerful effects upon human behavior, and there is a large fund of knowledge concerning the basic principles of learning. We must expect that a general, unified theory in psychology will deal with this knowledge. Likewise, a general theory must show how it links to biological science as well.

This is an important point in considering what the creation of multiple editions of unified theory will do to the preparadigmatic nature of psychology. Would not the creation of several general, unified theories simply lead to the type of preparadigmatic competition that existed between the theories of learning of Tulman, Hull, and Skinner? I do not believe so, if the present conceptual framework is employed. For one thing, the goal of unity of psychology would demand that the several general, unified theories relate to one another in order to achieve the unity of science that is sought. In addition, I would expect that the nature of the task of creating a paradigmatic psychology would impose characteristics on any general, unified theory that was constructed. This would have the effect of making general, unified theories very similar. In the present view, one of the central reasons why present-day theories have such great dissimilarities stems from the fact that they arise in different contexts of findings, methods, preexisting concepts, and philosophies concerning scientific objectives. For example, learning theories deal focally with the findings, concepts, and methods of animal learning and do not consider other bodies of knowledge such as those of cognitive psychology, clinical psychology, or psychometrics. And the same occurs in reverse, with theories that arise in one of these other areas and traditions. It is inevitable that the theories that emerge will be different and, following the nature of preparadigmatic science, compete with one another. The nature and objectives of preparadigmatic science guarantee these outcomes. We cannot see this until we make those characteristics of preparadigmatic science clear, and we will not see the potentialities of paradigmatic science until we begin working within that framework.

When each prospective general, unified-theory aspirant must deal with the same knowledge bases, ranging from the study of basic learning (and the biology of learning and related matters) to the study of complex social events, in a specific and heuristic manner, this will have the effect of imposing certain characteristics on the products of the task. In the present view, it will turn out that there are fewer ways to theoretically organize this range of knowledge than we can presently visualize. The general, unified theories that emerge will have considerable commonality, when they treat the same knowledge bases. We cannot visualize this outcome because of the plethora of small and diverse theories that presently bewilder us, and because the simplicity of unity has not yet emerged. This simplicity is the type of thing that we will only find out about in the doing. We must certainly recognize this possibility, however, in considering whether our science should devote some of its efforts to the task of becoming paradigmatic.

In my mind there is conviction that setting at least part of the efforts of psychology toward the goal of attaining a paradigmatic psychology will commence an undertaking whose products will reveal new knowledge in abundance, in various aspects. The task itself will require new skills of theory development to arise. New standards for evaluating theory will become necessary. The development of research methods will take on new characteristics. The assessment of past efforts and their products will undergo change. These are but examples, for we can be expected to gain knowledge of types that cannot be projected from what we presently know. That expectation adds excitement to the already great possibilities of the path before us.

Chapter 10

Prescription for the Crisis of Disunity

An example has been used elsewhere in this book to describe the search for a unified theory in physics. The time and effort of that search is based upon an assumption that there is unity of principle across diverse phenomena in nature. An assumption is involved in the sense that the time and effort is being expended before the unified theory has been found. In actuality, of course, the search for unity is not an assumption. As has been indicated here, such projections are conclusions that have been derived from past experience. That is, study has repeatedly shown in physics and the other natural sciences that the same principles apply to diverse phenomena.

Psychology is in a similar position of ignorance with respect to whether there is a unified set of principles that applies widely to the diverse phenomena of this very broad field. Perhaps there are principles that generally operate, cutting across psychology's various areas of concern, like problem solving, human motivation, personality, communication, reading, interests, attitudes, educational problems, memory, abnormal behavior, psychological tests, perception, social interaction, and so on. If so, then we would very surely say that our science should be paradigmatic, and seek unity. Since the phenomena involve common basic principles, our scientific treatment of those events would be expected ultimately to reflect that unity. If we knew that to be the case, our science should espouse a philosophy of paradigmaticism, even before unified theory had been worked out.

On the other hand, if we knew for certain that the events of study in psychology and the social sciences were fundamentally, intrinsically diverse in principle — that different laws operated across different areas of concern — then we would be justified in expecting our science to be preparadigmatic. It would be senseless to strive for unity and cohesion — for paradigmatic

337

science — if the nature of the underlying real world of events did not have these characteristics.

At this point in time, let us say, we cannot be sure about either of these possibilities. The fact that psychology is disunified does not mean anything. For there is much evidence in history to indicate that each of the sciences that is now paradigmatic was first preparadigmatic; Kuhn's work and that of others attests to that. Even though the underlying nature of reality was paradigmatic, the sciences began in the same preparadigmatic state that is characteristic of psychology. Moreover, the scientists in these formerly preparadigmatic sciences must have doubted the underlying unity of the events studied in their science. Based upon this historical knowledge, it might be justified to assume that our reality in psychology is actually unified although most cannot see it, and that our science will move to a unified, paradigmatic state eventually, as have other sciences.

But let us ignore the lesson of history, and the various versions of the injunction, those who ignore history are compelled to repeat it. Let us say that we have no idea whether there is underlying unity of principle in our social sciences. Even in that circumstance, it should be stressed, it would be reasonable to take an affirmative position, at least with a part of our resources. For the fact that a science field *is* preparadigmatic — a field characterized by diversity of concepts, principles, findings, problems, methods — does not tell us about the underlying nature of the events being studied. Regardless of the fact that the underlying nature of the events studied involves unified principles, the science will not begin to reflect that unity until it has attained an advanced stage of development. We know this from the history of science. Each science in its inception and for long afterward, (the length of time dependent in part upon the complexity and difficulty of the study) is confined to preparadigmatic characteristics. Paradigmatic theory and paradigmatic science are only built on the basis of unification of preparadigmatically diverse findings and the unification of preparadigmatic diverse conceptual treatment of those findings. Again, we have abundant evidence of this in the history of development of other sciences. There is a progressive movement from specificity and diversity toward generality and unity in the advanced, paradigmatic sciences. But such unity of science must be fought for and worked for relentlessly in the chaos of knowledge the modern preparadigmatic science presents.

Following this rationale, in any event, we must realize that the fact that a science is preparadigmatic does not insure that the realm of events of concern to that science is also preparadigmatic, to be characterized by essential diversity in basic principles across the various phenomena of concern. When the science has labored through its period of preparadigmatic disorganization to establish general principles that apply in a unified way to its phenomena, we can say with some confidence that the underlying nature of reality, indeed, is paradigmatic. But when the events we study appear to be diverse and discrepant, it may be because we have not yet found the unifying theory framework that is there to be found, or that we have not been able to convince others that we have found it. Certainly, it would take a lot longer than the period of the existence of the social sciences to conclude that the underlying nature of the events we study are in principle diverse and discrepant.

In view of this it is not logical to develop our science in a manner that is based solely upon diversity and discrepancy, to organize our science as though its preparadigmatic character reflected the nature of reality. The fact is, nevertheless, that this is the present status of our science. We have made no provision for the possibility that the events with which we are concerned are really paradigmatic. We have made no real effort to support search for that paradigmatic nature. We have not been concerned with developing a methodology or philosophy aimed at creating unified knowledge from its present disorganized state. The philosophy of science — with its fixation on the natural sciences as a model — has not provided an understanding of modern preparadigmatic science, and it has not provided a methodology, a goal, or a program for advancing our modern preparadigmatic sciences to the paradigmatic state.

Moreover, we have accepted a philosophy of, and skills of, preparadigmaticism that smother paradigmatic efforts. I believe that we must change our science in certain ways that provide for the possibility that our reality is paradigmatic in nature, that provide for a philosophy of science and methodology that recognize and support endeavors to study that unified nature. We have an adequate basis from the history of other sciences for us to recognize and act on the possibility that our own science may be paradigmatic in fundamental potential. Nevertheless, this recognition and action must rest upon grounds that are more generally conceptual — or philosophical — rather than precisely theoretical or empirical. There are several points that we can discuss in concluding this work, points to be touched upon in a final "mop up," and points that may add to this conceptual context and lend their weight to the preparadigmatic-paradigmatic decision that our science must make.

WHAT TO DO: GENERAL STEPS IN THE SEARCH FOR UNITY

The preceding chapters have attempted to characterize relevant characteristics of science in demarcating preparadigmatic and paradigmatic science. Psychology has been described as a preparadigmatic science and some of the significant features of the modern preparadigmatic science have been outlined. Finally, in the preceding chapters of this last part of the book, methodological considerations to be employed in creating unified knowledge in the preparadigmatic science have been considered, at least, in initial form. These various treatments have implications for additional general steps we need to take in our science to create the unity that is seen in the full-fledged, paradigmatic science, as will be briefly indicated.

A Standard of Unity

Perhaps the most salient distinguishing mark of the paradigmatic science is its search for unity — even before unity has been found. As has been indicated, the contemporary search for unified theory in physics is one example. This is in marked contrast to the preparadigmatic science that not only does not expect unity, or seek unity, but rather in various ways seeks newness and difference where unity exists already or could readily be shown. The latter is a characteristic that needs to be changed for psychology to realize its potential as a science. Psychologists must seek assiduously to find unity in each of its endeavors, as will be indicated by separate mentions of experimental, theoretical, and methodological unity.

Toward Experimental Unity

The manner in which an area of research can develop, based upon a method of experimentation (without regard to how the findings of the research area relate to other aspects of psychology), has been described herein. It has been suggested that such efforts frequently arise within the context of our preparadigmatic science. When they remain unrelated to the work of other areas they increase the preparadigmatic nature of our science. Moreover, when such research strivings — which may be costly in time and effort — remain in preparadigmatic isolation, they may as a consequence contribute little to the general growth of the science.

In the present view, thus, we should have certain paradigmatic criteria in mind when we evaluate research efforts and experimental procedures. It is not enough that a particular procedure and apparatus produce data that systematically index certain experimental manipulations. Whereas at one time it was important to establish that psychology, like other sciences, was capable of producing systematic experimental data — a possibility that was in doubt — this has already been done many times. Experimentation for its own sake is no longer of central importance. We must now begin to take the building characteristic of paradigmatic sciences seriously. It is not enough that we can produce experimental findings systematically. We have to be concerned with how the product fits into a structure — a building, advancing structure.

When a concept or principle has been developed in the context of a particular phenomenon or method of study—for example, rote verbal learning methods, or attribution study methods, learned helplessness, or the risky shift phenomenon—we should ask how the theory relates to other areas of psychology, and to other concerns. The fact that the phenomenon is new and has common-sense face value and can be used to generate additional experiments, should not be sufficient. We must get away from newness and novelty having such a disproportionate value in evaluating the worth of our science products. We must begin to support and encourage building and unifying endeavors. Does this mean that all experimental work should be evaluated in terms of its paradigmatic value? The answer to that is, "no." It would be stifling to take such a position. For one thing, there may be various works that are important without having paradigmatic significance, or even without being related to other aspects of the paradigm, as has been indicated. But if there is an expectation that an area of work will fit into the paradigmatic aspects of the science, if it is thought the work has some generality, as would ordinarily be the case, then, at some point in the development of the area, it will become relevant to evaluate the extent to which it actually does. Using the extensive work in the area of rote verbal learning as an example, it would seem that there were at least implicit assumptions that it did "fit in." That is, the name of the research area, rote verbal learning, suggests a relationship to language study, and there is face value that in working with the memorization of verbal material one is working with cognitive phenomena in general. In such a case it would be relevant to evaluate the research effort for the extent to which it gives meaning, actually does relate to, other works in the science. Many products develop in a science that are seen later on to be peripheral, to be unrelated, and to be unnecessary in the development of the science. We need to evaluate efforts in psychology—after a suitable period of development—for their contribution to a paradigm as well as for other contributions. And we should be skeptical at the beginning, when the importance of the phenomena studied resides primarily in newness and in the fact that reliable research results can be generated. It is suggested that such considerations will help systematize our approach, adding to a preparadigmatic evaluation that is made solely on the basis of parochial criteria and novelty.

Toward Theoretical Unity

The same pertains to theory in psychology. Let us recall Kuhn's description of the manner in which each preparadigmatic scientist felt constrained to build a theory de novo—as though nothing that preceded it, or was contemporary with it, had any relevance. Moreover, it has been suggested herein that in the preparadigmatic science there is a philosophy and methodology which I called separatism. According to the standards of separatism it is not necessary to cite predecessors when one introduces a theory or theoretical concepts and principles. In fact, in describing the practices of psychology it was said that the methodology of theory construction induces theorists to separate and distinguish their theory as much as possible from other theories. This involves skills of various sorts: the innovation of new and different terminology, the reference to different bodies of research literature, the development of the principles in the context of different phenomena, and so on.

This methodology of separatism and its products must be subjected to scrutiny and evaluation. Psychology must become concerned with how its theoretical structures are constructed in terms of relating those structures to other existing theoretical structures. We must demand that the theorist, in introducing a new structure, state what the basic principles are in the structure. We must also demand that the theorist relate his principles to the principles in other theories indicating how they are the same and how they are different. We must demand that this relating be done across different terminologies, across different approaches (for example, cognitive-theory approaches versus learning-theory approaches), and across different fields of study (child psychology versus abnormal psychology) and different phenomena (reading versus creative problem solving) — wherever it is relevant to do so. We cannot indulge theoreticians in idiosyncratic proliferation, as if past and contemporary knowledge in the science can be ignored. This criticism, moreover, must be extended to include the philosophy of separatism that commands the psychological scientist to build his theory as though it was being built from its foundations, even when those foundations are already available in the work of others.

Toward Methodological Unity

It has been said in an earlier chapter that there are divisions in psychology that are based upon the methods of investigation. One example was that between the single-organism methods of Skinner's operant behaviorism and the more general group methods of research, a separatism that continues until this time (see Gentile 1982; Knapp 1982). It has been said that methodological unification is part of the task in creating a paradigmatic psychology. In this unification one must reject parochialism, avoiding approaches (for example, B. F. Skinner's) that attempt to convince one that a particular method is *the* method and that we should ignore the others. There are many experimental methods that produced what were essentially useless data for the science, that needlessly complicated the science without advancing it. We also must apply paradigmatic standards to methodological contributions. At some point, the value of a method must be considered in terms of whether it produces meaningful findings of lasting and general significance — not just whether the method produces findings. What, one may ask, does the method contribute to the creation of unified knowledge in the science?

The important point is that methodologists must become concerned with paradigmatic concerns. The various diverse methods involved in the study of and practice of psychology need to be considered within a unifying conceptualization. One of the things we have to consider is what the various methods contribute to the understanding of the problems and questions that we face in our field. The objective must not be to demonstrate the singular value of one method. The goal must be to realize the value of each method in producing knowledge about the events that are studied across the range of phenomena of concern. Unified theory is necessary to bring into productive relationship the various types of knowledge available in psychology. And unified methodological development will involve showing the contribution that the various methods make to the unified knowledge pool.

Toward Philosophical Unity

An earlier chapter described the philosophy of the science of psychology to be that of preparadigmaticism, that is, one that considers the chaotic state of the science to be its true nature. It has been said also that a very important development for psychology will be the acceptance of a philosophy of paradigmaticism, a philosophy that guides psychologists to look for unity in their science in the way that is practiced for members of the advanced sciences. It should be noted that there is some incipient opinion in this direction. Thus, for example, the late Jean Piaget, although considered to be a theorist in developmental psychology, recently made the following statement that can be seen to be a call for unified theory construction.

> Psychology, like all other sciences, can live and prosper only in an interdisciplinary atmosphere. Interdisciplinary relationships indeed exist, but they are still insufficient. In the science of human beings, it is clear, for example, that the study of intelligence brings up the problem of the relationship between thought and language — hence a collaboration between psychology and linguistics; and the current work of linguists on transformational grammar and linguistic structure in general is very promising for possible comparisons with the operatory character of intelligence. But this is an immense field to cover, and collaborations are only beginning. Likewise, there exist numerous relationships between data from the science of economics and of "conducts," and game (or decision) theory, which was elaborated by economists, constitutes a very enlightening instrument for the analysis of "strategies" of behavior. But here, too, collaboration is only beginning. The relationship between psychology and sociology is evident but still not sufficiently elaborated, notably in the realm

of development. As far as the biological sciences are concerned, the connections among psychology, physiology, and neurology are close, but many relationships between general biology and the theory of intelligence remain untouched (Piaget and Kamii 1978, p. 651).

Piaget did not present a specific attempt to construct a unified theory on the basis of his own theory nor, as will be indicated, did he indicate a specific program or method by which to create unified theory structures. But it is clear, at least in the very preliminary stage, that he had begun to recognize the importance of such a striving. Royce has also voiced a philosophy regarding the possibilities and need for constructing general theory. He rejects the work of the second generation behaviorists in this regard, and mentions the possibility of a different path toward the goal.

> While the efforts of neo-behaviourists such as Hull and Skinner started out as reasonably modest statements about very simply learning on the part of very simple animals such as rats and pigeons, it is unfortunately true that these authors have published volumes with such questionable titles as *Principles of Behavior* (Hull, 1943) and *The Behavior of Organisms* (Skinner, 1938). In other words, they have tended to overgeneralize in the same way as did their predecessors. . . .
> On the other hand, there are several very significant general theory efforts currently under way with an orientation radically different from the earlier vintage of general theory. In my opinion, the most promising of these efforts are those which have grown out of the concern for the unification of science and the development of scientific generalists along with the usual scientific specialists — namely, the interdisciplinary efforts of Bertalanffy's general systems theory, and the general behaviour theory which is emerging from the inter-disciplinary team . . . under the leadership of James G. Miller (Royce 1970, p. 18).

In this context, it may be added that social learning theory has begun to accept at least in a general way, the notion of the need for unified theory. Operant behaviorism, the leading behavioral approach, has never provided a philosophy supporting unified theory that would encourage incorporation of nonoperant works in psychology. In fact, quite the opposite has been the characteristic of operant behaviorism. However, we now can see incipient interest in accepting some generality. That is, the operant Division of the American Psychological Association (number 25) took a goal of increasing breadth as the theme for its presentations at the 1979 annual convention of the Association, as indicated in the following announcement to its membership.

> This year's Co-Chairs believe strongly that the future vitality of Division 25 within the APA rests in large part on our ability to demonstrate the

functional relevance of behavior analysis to the full range of concerns voiced by American Psychology. The APA convention is the logical forum in which to demonstrate such relevance, but this cannot be accomplished if we talk to ourselves only about matters of interest to ourselves. Hence, the emphasis will be on interdivisional presentations that are likely to attract large, heterogeneous audiences (Goldstein and Pennypacker 1978, p. 1).

This is not exactly a call for unity, of course, but it does represent movement in an approach that has in the past been very parochial. Recent works have placed further emphasis upon the need for unified theory in psychology (Royce 1982; Staats 1975, 1981). It appears to this author that coming years will see this interest increase greatly, given impetus by the recognition of the various issues that are involved in the present study.

Toward Organizing Unity: A Division of Paradigmatic Psychology

One of the primary problems of psychology today is its separatism and its impetus toward organizational fragmentation. While practical reasons have been voiced for holding psychology together, no one has solved the problem that gives rise to the impetus to fragmentation. There has been no amelioration of the differences between the parts of psychology and of the organizational competitions that result from the differences. It is the present position that the organizational conflict in psychology is largely a direct result of the preparadigmatic disunity of the science and profession. There has been no recognition within the science of the types of needs for unification that are the focus of the present work. As a consequence, there has been no systematic concern within psychology for organizational entities that would contribute to the unification. There is a Division of General Psychology in the APA, and a Division of Philosophical and Theoretical Psychology but the missions of these divisions are not like that which has been described herein for advancing psychology to the paradigmatic state of science. To illustrate, the quotations from Koch (1978) that affirmed the incommensurable, fragmented nature of psychology were the opinions of a president of the Division of General Psychology of the APA. One of the steps toward the creation of a unified science of psychology, it is suggested, would lie in the direction of creating a specialty in the divisional structure of psychology whose mission would be unification of knowledge in psychology via the various avenues that have been described herein. The division would be devoted to creating small as well as large unifications in theory, in method, and in experimentation. The division would encourage conceptual formulations that would resolve the many continuing schisms in psychology. The division would attempt to link up the various areas of psychology. The division would have such general aims as examining psychology toward the goal of rationalizing its subdivisions. And, as a later section will indicate, the division would be concerned with the philosophy of preparadigmatic and paradigmatic science and with topics relevant to progression from the early to the more advanced unified state of psychology.

The present work is a call for a very major theoretical and meta-theoretical interest in unification of psychology. The call includes a basis for forming a division organization for this work, the *Division of Paradigmatic Psychology*. And the call includes a basis for establishing a scientific journal to provide a source for the publication of works whose aim is the unification of psychology, as the next section will indicate.

Toward Unity Through Journal Development

As has already been suggested, there is greater difficulty in realizing unity in a modern preparadigmatic science than there was in the cases of the natural sciences. When the natural sciences were preparadigmatic and faced the task of unification there were few scientists, few science areas, few scientific journals. There were few science organizations that institutionalized preparadigmatic separatism. In those days the individual scientist could more easily be conversant with everything that went on in his field, and frequently other fields as well. It was possible to know everyone and to have knowledge of everyone's findings. This made unification relatively easy. Contrast this with just the problem of being conversant with the knowledge that must be unified in the modern preparadigmatic science.

> Initially, psychologists accumulated information at a rate roughly equivalent to the manpower growth in psychology. From 1910 to the present, however, the information production (doubled) . . . every 15–20 years. . . . It would appear . . . that the individual scientist is being overloaded with scientific information. Perhaps the alarm over an "information crisis" arose because sometime in the last information doubling period, the *individual* psychologist became overburdened and could no longer keep up with and assimilate all the information being produced that was related to his primary speciality (Garvey and Griffith 1971, p. 350).

The growth of information that makes it impossible for the scientist to keep up with his own *specialty*, much less the general science, means that the circumstances are set for maintaining preparadigmatic separatism even in the narrow area. The specialist who is so burdened will have very little acquaintanceship with the information in other parts of his speciality let alone other areas of science. On this basis alone there is a necessary separatism of knowledge and a consequent growth of preparadigmaticism. When this is taken into account, one realizes that the forces contributing to preparadigmaticism in psychology are greater than those that pertained prior to the development of paradigmaticism in the classic sciences such as physics — when the information explosion had not yet occurred. The importance of this circumstance for the progress of the science in all its characteristics cannot be overestimated. The following was stated in a report by Dorwin Cartwright and Arthur Melton, the first two Chairmen of the Board of Scientific Affairs of the American Psychological Association, "BSA considers the problem of efficient and effective communication of scientific information to be perhaps the most critical problem faced by scientific psychology today" (Garvey and Griffith 1971, p. 349). Attempts to solve the proliferation of information and the problems it raises have tended to involve the creation of better storage and indexing systems and the like. For example, Doszkocs, Rapp, and Schoolman (1980) have written an analysis of automated information retrieval in science and technology. Like many other scientists they are concerned with ways of establishing retrieval systems for scientific knowledge, using computers. Computers have the capacity for storing huge quantities of information, organized in different categories, such that it may be retrieved to suit varying purposes. As these authors indicate, however, there are aspects of such systems in addition to the grasp of the machines involved. Centrally, the *index* used in storing information will in part determine the utility of the system. And the index used is limited by conceptual factors, for example, what "criteria should be used to determine whether a datum or statement is a valid entry to a data base"? (Doszkocs, Rapps, and Schoolman 1980, p. 30). They further ask what literature should be employed in indexing systems, what expert opinions, and so on.

There are those who believe that the increasing amount of scientific and technical research will create a volume of information so large as to frustrate the very purpose for which it was created. If this prediction is not going to become a reality, then a larger percentage of the resources now expended on generating scientific and technical information must clearly be invested in research on how to handle the mass of information being generated (Doszkocs, Rapp, and Schoolman 1980, p. 30).

As this analysis indicates, the focus on solving the problems of the information explosion and formation utilization by scientists has been on improving systems of storage and retrieval. This effort is certainly to be lauded. However, in the present view this effort does not get at the heart of the problem, at least for the preparadigmatic science. The basic problem in psychology is in the disorganization of its knowledge, and the unnecessary increase in the number of elements of knowledge that results. It is that disorganization that is fundamental in the science, and fundamental in any storage and retrieval system developed to aid in the solution to the problem. There is no way of organizing and simplifying knowledge by computer, when the science itself has not recognized the relatedness of the elements involved. As the science presently exists, theories, concepts, findings, and methods that are highly related to one another will be placed into storage systems in the disparate manner by which they are presently labeled and presently understood. That means that the relationships involved, and the commonality that exists in the science materials, will not be introduced into the storage and retrieval system. If the knowledge is not organized and simplified when it is stored, it cannot be organized and simplified when it is retrieved.

In the present view, the conceptual organization of the knowledge of the preparadigmatic science takes precedence over the system of storage and retrieval that is employed — for the organization of the latter depends in large part on the organization of the former. And that organization is the theoretical task of creating an organized science, not an indexing task. In the present view paradigmatization of the science will do more for the science than will the progress of the science in storage and retrieval systems. This statement is not meant to denigrate the importance of such systems, which is large, but to indicate the primary importance of paradigmatic unification. Moreover, in view of this analysis, it makes no sense to make large expenditures on storage and retrieval systems in the science, without the expenditure of a sufficient amount on the simplifying potential that the paradigmatic avenue would provide.

The possibility raised here, thus, is that the answer to psychology's central problem of communication is the great *simplification of our knowledge through the achievement of paradigmatic conceptual unity.* Each time we unify two or more concepts, theories, findings, methods, or what have you — elements that were distinguished and considered as separate — we will reduce the complexity of knowledge involved. We will have thereby made the field simpler for the student and scientist in the field. And we will have made progress in solving the problems of communication and thus progress toward the other goals of science. We can, in the present opinion, simplify our science remarkably by paradigmatic unification. I believe this is the only possibility we have for avoiding inundation by our own science products.

It has been said herein that psychology needs a divisional organization whose goal is to simplify and organize the knowledge of the science. By the same token our science needs a journal devoted to this task. We have many journals devoted to the production of diversified knowledge, which in its present form — even if it is lastingly valuable — contributes to increased complexity of the knowledge of the science. I would propose establishment of a *Journal of Paradigmatic Psychology* whose aim is to publish works of the unifying type that have been described herein.* The journal would serve

---

*Since this philosophy of psychology was written, a journal has been inaugurated whose publisher describes it as being concerned with the fragmentation of psychology. The stated mission of *New Ideas in Psychology* is the publication of articles aiming to integrate separated conas a means of communicating progress in the advancement toward the paradigmatic state of science. And the journal would help make the work directed toward that end achieve the importance it deserves — the importance that will motivate capable members of our science to devote themselves to this task. In a general sense the journal would be the paradigmatic way of answering the crisis of information storage and retrieval that has been thrust upon our science by its enormous generation of unrelated knowledge. For each article that unifies formerly disparate knowledge in the science will in this manner simplify the science, to extents that may be very large.

There are articles in some of our journals now that review and organize various parts of our literature. But the journals that publish those review articles do not have the type of mission that is being suggested. For the most part, moreover, review articles involve presenting materials that are already recognized to be related to one another, whereas what is being discussed are the many, many elements that could be, but are not now, recognized as related because of psychology's preparadigmatic state.

PHILOSOPHY OF PSYCHOLOGY, PARADIGMATIC CHARACTERISTICS, AND THEORY CONSTRUCTION

Following the advent of the first and second generations of behaviorism there was a resurgence of psychology's identification with the natural sciences. The philosophy of behaviorism was very much in accord with logical positivism, the dominant philosophy of science. For a time, thus, psychology's philosophy — at least its dominant philosophy — marched in accord with the dominant philosophy of science for the natural sciences. During that time the philosophy of science and the methodology of theory construction were very popular topics of concern in psychology. But the theories that were constructed within that framework did not fulfill their promise of providing a general theoretical structure for psychology. Their status as general theories was progressively lost and the philosophy of science within which the theories were constructed came into disrepute (see Koch 1981). (Moreover, logical positivism as has been discussed already has lost its dominant role in the philosophy of science.) No new philosophy of science has had the same impact on psychology as logical positivism had. There are

---

ceptual materials in the science. One of the individuals who founded this journal, John Broughton, read the first two parts of the present manuscript to evaluate the book for publication. To the extent that this journal fulfills the projections made here, it may be said that this part of the book's proposal has already begun to be implemented.

abundant references to Kuhn's concept of paradigm, and there is discussion of whether or not psychology is paradigmatic. But theories are not constructed today that employ this or any other philosophy of science as a guide. Moreover, there is not a deep and resourceful and productive generation of knowledge in the philosophy of psychology that is having an effect upon the work of psychology.

The present work, however, suggests that we return to our concern with the philosophy of our science, and with the philosophy of social science in general. It is a rather well-established fact now that logical positivism has not provided the foundation for the social sciences that has led to continued progress. The present work has attempted to indicate in depth a central area where the science must concentrate its efforts, and a foundation for this concern did not derive from logical positivism or the philosophy of science of the natural sciences, although it does not disagree with a good deal of that philosophy. The suggestion, at any rate, is that psychology must rejuvenate its interest in what it is as a science, and where it must go to continue to progress as a science. Central in this effort must be the consideration of what the preparadigmatic and the paradigmatic sciences are. We must systematically study what the characteristics are of preparadigmatic science toward the goal of improving those characteristics when they need improvement. Within this effort we must become centrally concerned with what the role and nature of theory are in the preparadigmatic science. Implicit in a number of the discussions that have been conducted herein is the idea that the model of the axiomatic type of theory espoused by logical positivism does not pertain to psychology and the other social sciences, at least in major part. Moreover, it has been suggested that very centrally in psychology theory construction must be concerned with unification, with the means for creating organization, relatedness, and simplicity through integrating in a consistent framework principles, concepts, findings, and methods, that are similar to a far greater extent than has been realized. The philosophy of preparadigmaticism occludes the perception of unity; it provides neither the impetus nor the skills needed to obtain unity of presently very diverse but unifiable knowledge.

The present position, thus, is that psychology and the other social sciences cannot look to the philosophy of science that is based upon analysis of the natural sciences to supply the necessary solutions to the crisis of preparadigmaticism. The philosophy of science of the natural sciences does not systematically study preparadigmatic science, and is therefore not prepared to characterize the modern preparadigmatic science. That philosophy of science is not prepared to say what the problems of preparadigmatic science are. Without such knowledge, however, there is no impetus for a change in the preparadigmatic paradigm that directs psychological science. Moreover, philosophy of science based on the natural sciences is not prepared to provide a methodology by which to remedy problems of disorganization, a methodology to provide a program for advancing from the preparadigmatic to paradigmatic state of science.

The present work is thus a call for a systematic study of the topics that have been raised. This is the call of a new philosophy of science in psychology, the present work constituting an opening step in that endeavor.

THE SECOND REVOLUTION

The development that resulted in the establishment of psychology as a science involved a struggle against the restraints imposed on the field because it was part of philosophy. It was a revolutionary development that made it possible for psychology to attack its subject matter with the tools of natural science. A direct result of this development was a tremendous advancement in scientific knowledge. Psychology went through a stage of expansion in terms of the phenomena that were dealt with, and the theories, methods, apparatus, findings, journals, organizations, and so on, by which to confront those phenomena. The guiding framework — that psychology is a science — has been very valuable, taking the field from a state of relatively scant naturalistic or philosophical inquiry to a state of a powerful social institution, science, and profession. This development has also involved a tremendous advancement toward diversity — from a simply developed body of knowledge to an exceedingly complex and variegated corpus.

The proliferation principle has guided the field since its organization as a science. The very success of scientific inquiry, however, produces another problem. The ultimate explosion of knowledge, as it occurs in the modern preparadigmatic science, results in the presentation of a new circumstance — one that was not present in the philosophical stage of inquiry or in the early period following the revolution that produced scientific inquiry. That is, the explosion of diverse knowledge constitutes a demand itself, along with the anomalies of separatism created by the diverse knowledge and by the philosophy and practices of preparadigmaticism. These occurrences provide a new press or tension. There results an impetus to put the diverse, chaotic knowledge together. In the preparadigmatic to paradigmatic progression, this circumstance must lead to the second major stage of science when unification has been accepted consciously as the task. We are now at the brink of that development, in the present opinion. I do believe that the progress of our science in its first stage of growth and expansion has brought us to the point where the elements are there for the second stage of development, the second revolution of psychology. But full entrance to that advanced state of development needs the *paradigmaticism* we have lacked. I became convinced of this dynamic in psychology a long time ago, as the following excerpt will show, in words that help conclude the analysis that has been presented.

> In conclusion it may be stated that . . . present-day . . . psychology in general . . . consists of unorganized striving in large part, and great separatism. It is in a prescientific state in which there is much idiosyncracy, and the individuals still see the "innovation" of minor concepts that deviate from past formulations as a step toward distinction. But the science . . . has great basic constituents. It has the experimental methodology, basic . . . principles, sophistication in the logic of science, and a comprehensive subject matter that goes from the simple to the very complex. It is a fund of knowledge and technique that with the concentration of a guiding framework — and the participation of a large number of the science's members — could enter into the first rank of sciences. It is a science on the verge of making it big. These possibilities are obscured by the elements of separateness and antagonism that characterize the field of psychology, and by the lack of comprehensive theory to unite the separate strivings. A common set of goals within a common theoretical framework could mobilize the immense strengths now hidden in the field. It is suggested that we must strive for a theoretical framework which has those qualities (Staats 1970b, pp. 234–35).

I have written this work not to present a particular theory. My thesis is that psychology is ready for paradigmatic development. I am saying that the new frontier of psychology (and other preparadigmatic sciences as well) concerns the advancement to the philosophy of paradigmaticism and to paradigmatic characteristics in general. Whatever one's orientation, it now becomes important — if this is correct — to work on the unification of methods, concepts, theories, and research areas.

Toulmin (1974) has said that there are decisions in science, made on a rational judgmental basis, that are not matters of logic (which pertain to the internal characteristics of a theory). Such judgmental matters are decisions that may induce major shifts in a science. They arise not from the paradigm clashes and tensions described by Kuhn as leading to revolutions in science, but from contact with a field, its past, its present and a grasp of future extrapolations. Toulmin cites the disagreement between Max Planck and Ernst Mach over the path of physics in whether to pursue metaphysical concerns or stick to observational activities. Another example involved the decision to turn toward the reductionism of molecular biology and away from a descriptive methodology. The latter decision influenced so greatly the development of contemporary biological science, yet it was a judgmental (philosophical) decision, not a theoretical decision. Revolutionary developments can involve such judgmental decisions in a science — it is suggested that the original decision that the study of human behavior (mind) should be a science instead of a philosophical inquiry was such a revolution.

In the present view also psychology must now face a second major decision choice-point. We no longer have to prove that we can do scientific work in psychology. There are many psychological scientists, psychological organizations, research funds, and research journals. As a social institution our science is a going concern. But we do have this problem of chaotic diversity and disorganization — and that characteristic does prevent our science from attaining the full measure of the advanced sciences shown by their impressive order and unity. Can we step back and look at what we are? Can we look back to the history of science, and at science today, and gain a perspective on what we are and what we could be? There will be those quick to say psychology is not ready for unification efforts. But this makes the decision without giving paradigmaticism its due. I have become acquainted with my science, I feel, originally by the serendipitous experience of attempting to construct a general, unified theory, and by the experience of the manner in which the science considers such a theory and responds to such a theory. And for a long period, I have been standing back and more generally considering the science from the vantage of the viewpoint this experience provided. I think we are ready for a paradigmatic psychology; but first we must make that judgmental decision. It is a momentous decision, and we cannot take the task lightly. It behooves psychology to pay its dues in the systematic study of the preparadigmatic nature of our science and its paradigmatic potentiality, so the decision can be made rationally. For the second revolution should have an impact as great as the first, or greater.

Bibliography

Abelson, R. P. The structure of belief systems. In R. C. Schank and K. M. Colby (Eds.), *Computer models of thought and language.* San Francisco: Freeman, 1973.

Achinstein, P. *Concepts of science.* Baltimore, Md.: Johns Hopkins Press, 1968.

Adams, J. S., and Romney, A. K. A functional analysis of authority. *Psychological Review,* 1959, 66, 234–251.

Adamson, R. Inhibitory set in problem solving as related to reinforcement learning. *Journal of Experimental Psychology,* 1959, 58, 280–282.

Albee, G. W. The uncertain future of clinical psychology. *American Psychologist,* 1970, 25, 1071–1080.

Alker, H. A. Is personality situationally specific or intrapsychically consistent? *Journal of Personality,* 1972, 40, 1–16.

Allison, P. D., and Stewart, J. A. Productivity differences among scientists. *American Sociological Review,* 1974, 39, 595–606.

Allport, G. W. Attitudes. In C. A. Murchison (Ed.), *A handbook of social psychology.* Worcester, Mass.: Clark University Press, 1935.

Amsel, A. The role of frustrative non-reward in non-continuous reward situations. *Psychological Bulletin,* 1958, 55, 102–119.

Amsel, A. Partial reinforcement effects on vigor and persistence: Advances in frustration theory derived from a number of within-subjects experiments. In K. W. Spence and J. A. Taylor (Eds.), *The psychology of learning and motivation.* New York: Academic Press, 1967.

Amsel, A. Behavioral habituation, counter-conditioning, and a general theory of persistence. In A. Black and W. Prokasy (Eds.), *Classical conditioning II: Current theory and research.* New York: Appleton-Century-Crofts, 1972.

Anderson, N. H., and Butzin, C. A. Integration theory applied to children's judgments of equity. *Developmental Psychology*, 1978, 14, 607–613.

Annon, J. S. *The behavioral treatment of sexual problems. Vol. 2.* Honolulu, Hi.: Enabling Systems, Inc., 1975.

Axelrod, R. (Ed.). *The structure of decision.* Princeton, N.J.: Princeton University Press, 1976.

Ayllon, T., and Michael, J. The psychiatric nurse as a behavioral engineer. *Journal of the Experimental Analysis of Behavior*, 1959, 2, 323–334.

Bandura, A. A social learning interpretation of psychological dysfunctions. In P. London and D. Rosenhan (Eds.), *Foundations of abnormal psychology.* New York: Holt, Rinehart and Winston, 1968.

Bandura, A. *Principles of behavior modification.* New York: Holt, Rinehart and Winston, 1969.

Bandura, A. Behavior theory and the models of man. *American Psychologist*, 1974, 29, 859–869.

Bandura, A. *Social learning theory.* Englewood Cliffs, N.J.: Prentice-Hall, 1977. (a)

Bandura, A. Self-efficacy: Toward a unifying theory of behavioral change. *Psychological Review*, 1977, 84, 191–215. (b)

Bandura, A. The self system in reciprocal determinism. *American Psychologist*, 1978, 33, 344–358.

Bandura, A. Separatism, dating practices, and the parentage of constructs. Unpublished manuscript, 1979.

Bandura, A., and Walters, R. *Adolescent aggression.* New York: Ronald, 1959.

Bandura, A., and Walters, R. *Social learning and personality.* New York: Holt, Rinehart and Winston, 1963.

Barber, T. X. *Pitfalls in human research: Ten pivotal points.* New York: Pergamon Press, 1976.

Baron, J. Phonemic stage not necessary in reading. *Quarterly Journal of Experimental Psychology*, 1973, 25, 241–246.

Bayés, R. *Una introducción al método científico en psicología.* Barcelona: Editorial Fontanella, 1980.

Bem, D. J. An experimental analysis of self-persuasion. *Journal of Experimental Psychology*, 1965, 1, 199–218.

Bem, D. J. Attitudes as self-descriptions: Another look at the attitude-behavior link. In A. G. Greenwald, T. C. Brock and T. M. Ostrom (Eds.), *Psychological foundations of attitudes.* New York: Academic Press, 1968.

Bentham, J. In C. K. Ogden (Ed.), *The theory of legislation.* New York: Harcourt, Brace, and Co., 1931.

Bergmann, G., and Spence, K. W. Operationism and theory in psychology. *Psychological Review*, 1941, 48, 1–14.

Berkowitz, L. *Aggression: A social psychological analysis.* New York: McGraw-Hill, 1962.

Berkowitz, L. Aggressive cues in aggressive behavior and hostility catharsis. *Psycho-*

logical Review, 1964, 71, 104–122.

Berkowitz, L. Experimental investigations of hostility catharsis. *Journal of Consulting and Clinical Psychology*, 1970, 35, 1–7. (a)

Berkowitz, L. Theoretical and research approaches in experimental social psychology. In A. R. Gilgen (Ed.), *Contemporary scientific psychology*. New York: Academic Press, 1970. (b)

Berkowitz, L. Words and symbols as stimuli to aggressive responses. In J. F. Knutson (Ed.), *Control of aggression*. Chicago: Aldine, 1973.

Berkowitz, L. Some determinants of impulsive aggression: Role of medicated associations with reinforcements for aggression. *Psychological Review*, 1974, 81, 165–176.

Berkowitz, L., and Knurek, D. A. A label mediated hostility generalization. *Journal of Personality and Social Psychology*, 1969, 13, 200–206.

Bernard, C. *Introduction à l'étude de la médicine expérimentale*. Paris: Garnier-Flammerion, 1966.

Bertalanffy, L. von. General systems theory and psychology. In J. R. Royce (Ed.), *Toward unification in psychology*. Toronto, Canada: University of Toronto Press, 1970.

Bijou, S. W. A systematic approach to an experimental analysis of young children. *Child Development*, 1955, 26, 161–168.

Bijou, S. W. Methodology for an experimental analysis of child behavior. *Psychological Reports*, 1957, 3, 243–250.

Bijou, S. W. *Child development: The basic stage of early childhood*. Englewood Cliffs, N.J.: Prentice-Hall, Inc., 1976.

Bijou, S. W., and Baer, D. M. *Child development. Vol. 1*. New York: Appleton-Century-Crofts, 1961.

Bijou, S. W., Peterson, R. F., Harris, F. R., Allen, K. E., and Johnston, M. S. Methodology for experimental studies of young children in natural settings. *The Psychological Record*, 1969, 19, 177–210.

Bindra, D. How adaptive behavior is produced: A perceptual-motivational alternative to response-reinforcement. *The Behavioral and Brain Sciences*, 1978, 1, 40–91.

Birge, J. S. Verbal responses in transfer. Unpublished doctoral dissertation, Yale University, New Haven, 1941.

Black, J. A., and Champion, A. L. *Methods and issues in social research*. New York: Wiley, 1976.

Blum, G. S., and Barbour, J. S. Selective inattention to anxiety-linked stimuli. *Journal of Experimental Psychology*, 1979, 108, 182–224.

Blumenthal, A. L. *The process of cognition*. Englewood Cliffs, N.J.: Prentice-Hall, 1977.

Bolles, R. C. *Learning theory* (rev. ed.). New York: Holt, Rinehart and Winston, 1979.

Bolles, R. C. Wundt and after. *Science*, 1980, 208, 715–716.

Boring, E. G. *A history of experimental psychology* (2nd ed.). New York: Appleton, 1950.

Bowers, K. S. Situationism in psychology: An analysis and a critique. *Psychological Review*, 1973, 80, 307–336.

Braithwaite, R. B. *Scientific explanation*. London: Cambridge University Press, 1955.

Brehm, J. W., and Cohen, A. R. *Explorations in cognitive dissonance*. New York: Wiley, 1962.

Breland, K., and Breland, M. The misbehavior of organisms. *American Psychologist*, 1961, 16, 681–684.

Bridgman, P. W. *The logic of modern physics*. New York: Macmillan, 1928.

Bridgman, P. W. *The nature of physical theory*. Princeton: Princeton University Press, 1936.

Briskman, I. B. Is a Kuhnian analysis applicable to psychology? *Science Studies*, 1972, 2, 87–97.

Broadbent, D. E. The role of auditory localization in attention and memory span. *Journal of Experimental Psychology*, 1954, 47, 191–196.

Broadbent, D. E. *Perception and communication*. New York: Pergamon Press, 1957.

Broadbent, D. E. Stimulus set and response set: Two kinds of selective attention. In D. I. Mostofsky (Ed.), *Attention: Contemporary theories and analysis*. New York: Appleton-Century-Crofts, 1970.

Broadbent, D. E., Cooper, P. J., and Broadbent, M. H. P. A comparison of hierarchical and matrix retrieval schemes in recall. *Journal of Experimental Psychology: Human Learning and Memory*, 1978, 4, 486–497.

Brogden, W. J. Sensory pre-conditioning. *Journal of Experimental Psychology*, 1939, 25, 323–332.

Brown, R., and Lenneberg, E. H. A study in language and cognition. *Journal of Abnormal and Social Psychology*, 1954, 49, 454–462.

Bugental, J. F. T. The challenge that is man. In J. F. T. Bugental (Ed.), *Challenges of humanistic psychology*. New York: McGraw-Hill, 1967.

Burian, R. M. More than a marriage of convenience: On the inextricability of history and philosophy of science. *Philosophy of Science*, 1977, 1–42.

Burns, G. L. Indirect measurement and behavior assessment: A case for social behaviorism psychometrics. *Behavioral Assessment*, 1980, 2, 197–206.

Buss, A. R. The structure of psychological revolutions. *Journal of the History of the Behavioral Sciences*, 1978, 14, 57–64.

Byrne, D. Interpersonal attraction and attitude similarity. *Journal of Abnormal and Social Psychology*, 1961, 62, 703–715.

Byrne, D. Response to attitude similarity-dissimilarity as a function of affiliation need. *Journal of Personality*, 1962, 30, 164–177.

Byrne, D. *The attraction paradigm*. New York: Academic Press, 1971.

Byrne, D. Social psychology and the study of sexual behavior. *Personality and Social Psychology Bulletin*, 1977, 3, 3–30.

Byrne, D. Separatism, integration or parallel play? *Personality and Social Psychology Bulletin*, 1978, 4, 498–499.

Byrne, D., and Clore, G. L. A reinforcement model of evaluative responses. *Personality: An International Journal*, 1970, 1, 103–128.

Byrne, D., and Griffitt, W. Similarity and awareness of similarity of personality characteristics as determinants of attraction. *Journal of Experimental Research in Personality*, 1969, 3, 179–186.

Camp, B. W. Remedial reading in a pediatric clinic. *Clinical Pediatrics*, 1971, 10, 36–42.

Carlson, R. Where is the person in personality research. *Psychological Bulletin*, 1971, 75, 203–219.

Carmichael, L. The development of behavior in vertebrates experimentally removed from the influence of external stimulation. *Psychological Review*, 1926, 33, 51–58.

Carnap, R. *Philosophy and logical syntax.* London: Kegan, Paul, Trench, Trubner, 1935.

Carver, C. S. A cybernetic model of self-attention processes. *Journal of Personality and Social Psychology*, 1979, 37, 1251–1281.

Catania, A. C. On citing the literature. *The Behavior Analyst*, 1980, 3, 63–64.

Chandler, M. J., Paget, K. F., and Koch, D. A. The child's demystification of psychological defense mechanisms: A structural and developmental analysis. *Developmental Psychology*, 1978, 14, 197–205.

Chomsky, N. Linguistic contributions to the study of mind. In N. Chomsky (Ed.), *Language and mind.* New York: Harcourt, Brace and World, 1968.

Cialdini, R. B., Darby, B. L., and Vincent, J. E. Transgression and altruism: A case for hedonism. *Journal of Experimental Social Psychology*, 1973, 9, 502–516.

Cialdini, R. B., and Kenrick, D. T. Altruism as hedonism: A social development perspective on the relationship of negative mood state and helping. *Journal of Personality and Social Psychology*, 1976, 34, 907–914.

Cofer, C. N., and Foley, J. P. Mediated generalization and the interpretation of verbal behavior: I. Prolegomena. *Psychological Bulletin*, 1942, 49, 513–540.

Cohen, B. D., Brown, G. W., and Brown, M. L. Avoidance learning motivated by hypothalamic stimulation. *Journal of Experimental Psychology*, 1957, 53, 228–233.

Cole, S., and Cole, J. R. Scientific output and recognition: A study in the operation of the reward system in science. *American Sociological Review*, 1967, 32, 377–390.

Craik, F. I. M., and Lockhart, R. S. Levels of processing: A framework for memory research. *Journal of Verbal Learning and Verbal Behavior*, 1972, 11, 671–684.

Craik, F. I. M., and Tulving, E. Depth of processing and the retention of words in episodic memory. *Journal of Experimental Psychology: General*, 1975, 104, 268–294.

Crane, D. M. The gatekeepers of science: Some factors affecting the selection of articles for scientific journals. *American Sociologist*, 1967, 2, 195–201.

Crown, D. P., and Liverant, S. Conformity under varying conditions of personal commitment. *Journal of Abnormal and Social Psychology*, 1963, 66, 547–555.

Cuber, J. F. *Sociology: A synopsis of principles*. New York: Appleton, 1955.

Cuents, T. E. Discriminación y generalización en letras y palabras. *Aprendizaje y Comportamiento*, 1979, 2, 64–91.

Darden, L. Reasoning in scientific change: The field of genetics at its beginnings. Ph.D. dissertation, University of Chicago, 1974.

Darden, L. Reasoning in scientific change. *Studies in the History and Philosophy of Science*, 1976, 7, 127–169.

Darden, L., and Maull, N. Interfield theories. *Philosophy of Science*, 1977, 44, 43–64.

Davison, G. C., and Neale, J. M. *Abnormal psychology*. New York: Wiley, 1974.

Dawe, H. C. A study of the effect of an educational program upon language development and related mental functions in young children. *Journal of Experimental Education*, 1942, 11, 200–209.

Deese, J. Behavior and fact. *American Psychologist*, 1969, 24, 515–522.

Delgado, J. M., Roberts, W. W., and Miller, N. E. Learning motivated by electrical stimulation of the brain. *American Journal of Physiology*, 1954, 179, 587–593.

Deutsch, J. A., and Deutsch, D. Attention: Some theoretical considerations. *Psychological Review*, 1963, 70, 80–90.

Dollard, J., and Miller, N. *Personality and psychotherapy*. New York: McGraw-Hill, 1950.

Doob, L. The behavior of attitudes. *Psychological Review*, 1947, 54, 135–156.

Dorfman, D. D. The Cyril Burt question: New findings. *Science*, 1978, 201, 1177–1186.

Dorna, A., and Mendez, H. *Ideología y conductismo*. Barcelona: Editorial Fontanella, 1979.

Doszkocs, T. E., Rapp, B. A., and Schoolmon, H. M. Automated information retrieval in science and technology. *Science*, 1980, 208, 25–30.

Douglas, R. J. The development of hippocampal function. In R. Isaacson and K. Pribram (Eds.), *The hippocampus*. New York: Plenum, 1975.

Dunham, P. J. Punishment of mice and men. *Contemporary Psychology*, 1978, 23, 551–552.

Dunnette, M. D. Fads, fashions, and folderol in psychology. *American Psychologist*, 1966, 21, 343–352.

Durkheim, E. *Les régles de la méthode sociologique* (8th ed.). Paris: Alcan, 1927.

Early, J. C. Attitude learning in children. *Journal of Educational Psychology*, 1968, 59, 176–180.

Edsall, J. T. *Scientific freedom and responsibility*. Washington, D.C.: American Association for the Advancement of Science, 1975.

Eiduson, B. T. *Scientists: Their psychological world*. New York: Basic Books, 1962.

Eisman, B. S. Attitude formation: The development of a color preference response through mediated generalization. *Journal of Abnormal and Social Psychology*, 1955, 50, 321–326.

Ekehammar, B. Interactionism in personality from a historical perspective. *Psychological Bulletin*, 1974, 81, 1026–1048.

Ekstrand, B. R., Sullivan, M. J., Parker, D. F., and West, J. N. Spontaneous recovery and sleep. *Journal of Experimental Psychology*, 1971, 88, 142–144.

Ekstrand, B. R., Wallace, W. P., and Underwood, B. J. A frequency theory of verbal-discrimination learning. *Psychological Review*, 1966, 73, 566–578.

Ellson, D. Hallucinations produced by sensory conditioning. *Journal of Experimental Psychology*, 1941, 28, 1–20.

Elms, A. C. The crisis of confidence in social psychology. *American Psychologist*, 1975, 30, 967–976.

Endler, N. S., and Magnusson, D. Toward an interactional psychology of personality. *Psychological Bulletin*, 1976, 83, 956–974.

Erdelyi, M. H. A new look at the new look: Perceptual defense and vigilance. *Psychological Review*, 1974, 81, 1–25.

Ervin-Tripp, S. An overview of theories of grammatical development. In D. I. Slobin (Ed.), *The ontogenesis of grammar*. New York: Academic Press, 1971.

Esper, E. A. *A history of psychology*. Philadelphia, Pa.: W. B. Saunders, 1964.

Estes, W. K. Learning theory and intelligence. *American Psychologist*, 1974, 29, 740–749.

Estes, W. The locus of inferential and perceptual processes in letter identification. *Journal of Experimental Psychology: General*, 1975, 1, 122–145.

Estes, W. K. Intelligence and cognitive psychology. In L. B. Resnick (Ed.), *The nature of intelligence*. Hillsdale, N.J.: Lawrence Erlbaum Associates, 1976.

Evans, P. A visit with Michael Argyle. *APA Monitor*, 1978, 9, No. 8, 6–7.

Eysenck, H. J. (Ed.). *Behavior therapy and the neuroses*. London: Pergamon, 1960. (a)

Eysenck, H. J. *Behaviour therapy and the neuroses*. Oxford, England: Pergamon, 1960. (b)

Farberow, N. L. The crisis is chronic. *American Psychologist*, 1973, 28, 155–156.

Fiegl, H. The "orthodox" view of theories: Remarks in defense as well as critique. In M. Radner and S. Winokur (Eds.), *Minnesota Studies in the Philosophy of Science, Vol. 4*. Minneapolis, Minn.: University of Minnesota Press, 1970.

Feldman, K. A. Using the work of others; some observation on reviewing and integrating. *Sociology of Education*, 1971, 44, 86–102.

Ferster, C. B., and Skinner, B. F. *Schedules of reinforcement*. New York: Appleton-Century-Crofts, 1957.

Feyerabend, P. K. How to be a good empiricist — a plea for tolerance in matters epistemological. In B. Baumrin (Ed.), *Philosophy of science. The Delaware seminar. Vol. I.* New York: Wiley, 1963.

Feyerabend, P. K. Problems of empiricism. In R. Colodny (Ed.), *Beyond the edge of certainty.* Englewood Cliffs, N.J.: Prentice-Hall, 1965.

Feyerabend, P. Consolations for the specialist. In I. Lakatos and A. Musgrave (Eds.), *Criticism and the growth of knowledge.* London: Cambridge University Press, 1970. (a)

Feyerabend, P. K. Against method: Outline of an anarchistic theory of knowledge. In M. Radner and S. Winokur (Eds.), *Minnesota Studies in the Philosophy of Science, Vol. 4.* Minneapolis, Minn.: University of Minnesota Press, 1970. (b)

Finch, G. Hunger as a determinant of conditional and unconditional salivary response magnitude. *American Journal of Physiology,* 1938, 123, 379–382.

Fiske, D. W. The limits for the conventional science of personality. *Journal of Personality,* 1974, 42, 1–11.

Flanery, R. C., and Balling, J. D. Developmental changes in hemispheric specialization for tactile spatial ability. *Developmental Psychology,* 1979, 15, 364–372.

Flavell, J. H. *The developmental psychology of Jean Piaget.* New York: Van Nostrand, 1963.

Fraisse, P. Psychologie générale. *L'Anne Psychologique,* 1976, 76, 280–282.

Frank, P. *Modern science and its philosophy.* Cambridge: Harvard University Press, 1950.

Frederiksen, J., and Kroll, J. Spelling and sound: Approaches to the internal lexicon. *Journal of Experimental Psychology: Human Perception and Performance,* 1976, 2, 361–379.

Gadlin, H., and Ingle, G. Through the one-way mirror: The limits of experimental self-reflection. *American Psychologist,* 1975, 30, 1003–1009.

Gagne, R. M. Learning hierarchies. *Educational Psychologist,* 1968, 6, 1–9.

Garcia, J., Ervin, F. R., and Koelling, R. A. Learning with prolonged delay of reinforcement. *Psychonomic Science,* 1966, 5, 121–122.

Garvey, W. D., and Griffith, B. C. Scientific communication: Its role in the conduct of research and creation of knowledge. *American Psychologist,* 1971, 26, 349–362.

Gaston, J. *Originality and competition in science.* Chicago, Ill.: Chicago University Press, 1973.

Gellner, E. Explanation in history. *Proceedings of the Aristotelian Society,* 1956.

Gentile, R. J. Significance of single-subject studies (and repeated measures designs). *Educational Psychologist,* 1982, 17, 54–60.

Gergen, K. J. Social psychology as history. *Journal of Personality and Social Psychology,* 1973, 26, 309–320.

Gergen, K. J., Greenberg, M. S., and Willis, R. H. (Eds.). *Social exchange: Advances in theory and research.* New York: Plenum, 1980.

Gesell, A., Halverson, H. M., Thompson, H., Ilg, F. L., Castner, B. M., Ames, L. B., and Amatruda, C. S. *The first five years of life.* New York: Harper, 1940.

Gesell, A., and Thompson, H. Learning and growth in identical infant twins: An experimental study by the method of co-twin control. *Genetic Psychological Monographs*, 1929, 6, 1–124.

Gesell, A., and Thompson, H. (assisted by C. Strunk). *The psychology of early growth.* New York: Macmillan, 1938.

Giddens, A. *New rules of sociological method.* New York: Basic Books, 1976.

Giorgi, A., Knowles, R., and Smith, D. L. (Eds.). *Duquesne studies in phenomenological psychology*, Vol. 3. Pittsburgh, Pa.: Duquesne University Press, 1979.

Glad, B. Psychobiography. In J. Knutson (Ed.), *Handbook of political psychology.* San Francisco: Jossey-Bass, 1973.

Glashow, S. L. Toward a unified theory: Threads in a tapestry. *Science*, 1980, 210, 1319–1323.

Goffman, E. *The presentation of self in everyday life.* Garden City, N.Y.: Doubleday Anchor, 1959.

Goldfried, M. R. Toward the delineation of therapeutic change principles. *American Psychologist*, 1980, 35, 991–999.

Goldstein, M. K., and Pennypacker, H. S. Call for papers: APA '79. *Division 25, Recorder*, 1978, 14, 1–19.

Golightly, C., and Byrne, D. Attitude statements as positive and negative reinforcements. *Science*, 1964, 146, 798–799.

Goodstein, L. D., and Brazis, K. L. Psychology of the scientist: XXX. Credibility of psychologists: An empirical study. *Psychological Reports*, 1970, 27, 835–838.

Gore, P. M., and Rotter, J. B. A personality correlate of social interaction. *Journal of Personality*, 1963, 31, 58–64.

Gouldner, A. W. *The coming crisis of Western sociology.* New York: Basic Books, 1970.

Greenspoon, J. The effect of verbal and nonverbal stimuli on the frequency of members of two verbal response classes. Unpublished doctoral dissertation, Indiana University, 1950.

Greenwald, A. G. On defining attitude and attitude theory. In A. G. Greenwald, T. C. Brock and T. M. Ostrom (Eds.), *Psychological foundations of attitudes.* New York: Academic Press, 1968.

Greenwald, A. G., Brock, T. C., and Ostrom, T. M. (Eds.). *Psychological foundations of attitudes.* New York: Academic Press, 1968.

Hage, J. *Techniques and problems of theory construction in sociology.* New York: Wiley-Interscience, 1972.

Hagstrom, W. O. *The scientific community.* New York: Basic Books, 1965.

Hagstrom, W. O. Competition and teamwork in science. Final Report to the National Science Foundation (in mimeo), 1967.

Hanson, N. R. *Patterns of discovery.* Cambridge: Cambridge University Press, 1958.

Hanson, N. R. Observation and interpretation. In S. Morgenbesser (Ed.), *Philosophy of science today*. New York: Basic Books, 1967.

Hanson, N. R. *Perception and discovery: An introduction to scientific inquiry*. San Francisco: Freeman, Cooper and Company, 1969.

Harlow, H. William James and instinct theory. In R. MacCleod (Ed.), *William James: Unfinished business*. Washington, D.C.: American Psychological Association, 1969.

Harms, J. Y., and Staats, A. W. Food deprivation and conditioned reinforcing value of food words: Interaction of Pavlovian and instrumental conditioning. *Bulletin of the Psychonomic Society*, 1978, 12(4), 294–296.

Hearst, F. The behavior of Skinnerians. *Contemporary Psychology*, 1967, 12, 402–404.

Heber, R., Garber, H., and Hoffman, C. *Rehabilitation of families at risk for mental retardation*. Madison: Rehabilitation Research and Training Center in Mental Retardation, University of Wisconsin, 1971.

Heider, F. *The psychology of interpersonal relations*. New York: Wiley, 1958.

Hekmat, H. Systematic versus semantic desensitization and implosive therapy. *Journal of Consulting and Clinical Psychology*, 1973, 40, 202–209.

Hekmat, H., and Vanian, D. Behavior modification through covert semantic desensitization. *Journal of Consulting and Clinical Psychology*, 1971, 36, 248–251.

Hellige, J. B., Cox, R. J., and Litvac, L. Information processing in the cerebral hemispheres: Selective hemispheric activation and capacity limitations. *Journal of Experimental Psychology: General*, 1979, 108, 251–279.

Hempel, C. G. *Aspects of scientific explanation and other essays in the philosophy of science*. New York: Free Press, 1965.

Hempel, W. E., and Fleishman, I. A. A factor analysis of physical proficiency and manipulative skill. *Journal of Applied Psychology*, 1955, 39, 12–16.

Hermann, C. F. *International crises: Insights from behavioral research*. New York: Free Press, 1972.

Hilgard, E. R. *Theories of learning* (2nd ed.). New York: Appleton-Century-Crofts, 1948.

Hill, L. Jr., and Eckberg, D. L. Clarifying confusions about paradigms: A reply to Ritzer. *American Sociological Review*, 1981, 46, 248–252.

Himmelfarb, S. Integration and attribution theories in personality impression formation. *Journal of Personality and Social Psychology*, 1972, 23, 309–313.

Hirsch, J. To "unfrock the charlatans." *Sage Race Relations Abstracts*, 1981, 6, 1–65.

Hobbes, T. Of other laws of nature. In W. T. Jones, F. Sontag, M. O. Beckner and R. Fogelin (Eds.), *Approaches to ethics*. New York: McGraw-Hill, 1969.

Hoffman, M. L. Moral internalization, parental power, and the nature of parent-child interaction. *Developmental Psychology*, 1975, 11, 228–239.

Holden, C. FDA tells senators of doctors who fake data in clinical drug trials. *Science*, 1979, 206, 432–433.

Holsti, O. R. Foreign policy formation viewed cognitively. In R. Axelrod (Ed.), *The structure of decision*. Princeton, N.J.: Princeton University Press, 1976.

Homans, G. C. *Social behavior*. New York: Harcourt, 1961.

Horridge, G. A. Learning of leg position by the ventral nerve cord in headless insects. *Processes of the Royal* (London), Series B, 1962, 157, 33–52.

Hounshell, D. A. Edison and the pure science ideal in 19th-century America. *Science*, 1980, 207, 612–617.

Howell, N. Cultures under stress. *Science*, 1979, 203, 1235–1236.

Hudson, L. *Contrary imaginations*. New York: Schocken Books, 1966.

Hull, C. L. Quantitative aspects of the evolution of concepts. *Psychological Monographs*, 1920, No. 123.

Hull, C. L. Knowledge and purpose as habit mechanisms. *Psychological Review*, 1930, 37, 511–525.

Hull, C. L. Mind, mechanism, and adaptive behavior. *Psychological Review*, 1937, 44, 1–32.

Hull, C. L. The problem of stimulus equivalence in behavior theory. *Psychological Review*, 1939, 46, 9–30.

Hull, C. L. Memoranda concerning behavior theory. (On file in Yale University Library), 1940–1941.

Hull, C. L. *Principles of behavior*. New York: Appleton-Century, 1943.

Hulse, S. H., Deese, J., and Egeth, H. *The psychology of learning*. New York: McGraw-Hill, 1975.

Humphreys, L. G. Interaction. *Monitor*, 1976, 7, No. 7, 2.

Hunt, J. McV. The impact and limitations of the giant of developmental psychology. In D. Elkind and J. H. Flavell (Eds.), *Studies in cognitive development*. New York: Oxford University Press, 1969.

Hymes, D. (Ed.). *Reinventing anthropology*. New York: Pantheon, 1972.

Iltis, H. *Life of Mendel*. New York: Norton, 1932.

Isaacs, W., Thomas, J., and Goldiamond, I. Application of operant conditioning to reinstate verbal behavior in psychotics. *Journal of Speech and Hearing Disorders*, 1960, 25, 8–12.

Jackson, G. B. Methods for integrative reviews. *Review of Educational Research*, 1980, 50, 438–460.

Jackson, M. D., and McClelland, J. L. Processing determinants of reading speed. *Journal of Experimental Psychology: General*, 1979, 108, 151–181.

Jacob, F. Evolution and tinkering. *Science*, 1977, 196, 1161–1166.

Janet, P. (trans. by E. R. Guthrie). *Principles of psychotherapy*. New York: Macmillan, 1924.

Janis, I. L. *Victims of groupthink*. Boston: Houghton Mifflin, 1972.

Janis, I. L., and Mann, L. A conflict-theory approach to attitude change and decision making. In A. G. Greenwald, T. C. Brock and T. M. Ostrom (Eds.), *Psy-*

chological foundations of attitudes. New York: Academic Press, 1968.

Jarvie, I. C. Reviews. *British Journal for the Philosophy of Science,* 1979, 300, 100–104.

Jenkins, J. G., and Dallenbach, K. M. Oblivescence during sleep and waking. *American Journal of Psychology,* 1924, 35, 605–612.

Jensen, A. R. How much can we boost IQ and scholastic achievement? *Harvard Educational Review,* 1969, 39(1), 1–123.

Jervis, R. *Perception and misperception in international politics.* Princeton, N.J.: Princeton University Press, 1976.

Jones, E. E., and Nisbett, R. E. *The actor and the observer: Divergent perceptions of the causes of behavior.* Morristown, N.J.: General Learning Press, 1971.

Jones, R. T. The role of external variables in self-reinforcement. *American Psychologist,* 1980, 35, 102–104.

Kamin, L. J. *The science and politics of IQ.* Potomac, Md.: Erlbaum, 1974.

Kandel, E. R., and Tauc, L. Mechanism of heterosynaptic facilitation in the giant cell of the abdominal ganglion of *Aplysia depilans. Journal of Physiology,* 1965, 181, 28–47.

Kanfer, F. Personal control, social control, and altruism: Can society survive the age of individualism? *American Psychologist,* 1979, 34, 231–239.

Kantor, J. R. *Principles of psychology.* New York: Knopf, 1924.

Katahn, M., and Koplin, J. H. Paradigm clash: Comment on "Some recent criticisms of behaviorism and learning theory with special reference to Breger and McGough and to Chomsky." *Psychological Bulletin,* 1967, 69, 147–148.

Kellas, G., and Butterfield, E. C. Effect of response requirement and type of material on acquisition and retention performance in short-term memory. *Journal of Experimental Psychology,* 1971, 88, 50–56.

Keller, A., Ford, L. H. Jr., and Meacham, J. A. Dimensions of self-concept in preschool children. *Developmental Psychology,* 1978, 14, 483–490.

Keller, F. S., and Schoenfeld, W. N. *Principles of psychology.* New York: Appleton, 1950.

Kelley, J. Attribution theory in social psychology. In D. Levine (Ed.), *Nebraska symposium on motivation.* Lincoln, Neb.: University of Nebraska Press, 1967.

Kessel, F. S. The philosophy of science as proclaimed and science as practiced: "Identity" or "dualism"? *American Psychologist,* 1969, 24, 999–1005.

Kimble, G. A. *Hilgard and Marquis' conditioning and learning* (2nd ed.). New York: Appleton-Century-Crofts, 1961.

Kirkland, K. Frequency of dependent measures in two non-behavioral journals. *Behavior Therapist,* 1978, 1, 14.

Kleiman, G. Speech recoding in reading. *Journal of Verbal Learning and Verbal Behavior,* 1975, 14, 323–340.

Knapp, T. R. A case against the single-sample repeated-measures experiment. *Edu-*

cational Psychologist, 1982, 17, 61–65.

Koch, S. (Ed.). *Psychology: A study of a science*. Volumes 1–7. New York: McGraw-Hill, 1959.

Koch, S. Psychological science versus the science-humanism antinomy: Intimation of a significant science of man. *American Psychologist*, 1961, 16, 629–639.

Koch, S. Comment. In Wertheimer et al., Psychology and the future. *American Psychologist*, 1978, 33, 637–639.

Koch, S. The nature and limits of psychological knowledge. *American Psychologist*, 1981, 36, 257–269.

Kogan, N., and Wallach, M. A. *Risk taking: A study in cognition and personality*. New York: Holt, Rinehart and Winston, 1964.

Kohlberg, L. Stage and sequence: A cognitive-developmental approach to socialization. In D. Goslin (Ed.), *The handbook of socialization theory and research*. Chicago: Rand McNally, 1969.

Krantz, D. L. The separate worlds of operant and non-operant psychology. *Journal of Applied Behavior Analysis*, 1971, 4, 60–70.

Krasner, L. The use of generalized reinforcers in psychotherapy research. *Psychological Reports*, 1955, 1, 19–25.

Krasner, L. Studies of the conditioning of verbal behavior. *Psychological Bulletin*, 1958, 55, 148–170.

Krasner, L., and Ullmann, L. P. (Eds.). *Research in behavior modification*. New York: Holt, Rinehart and Winston, 1965.

Krech, D. Epilogue. In J. R. Royce (Ed.), *Toward unification in psychology*. Toronto, Canada: University of Toronto Press, 1970.

Kretch, D., Crutchfield, R. S., and Ballachey, E. L. *Individual in society*. New York: McGraw-Hill, 1962.

Kruglanski, A. W. On the paradigmatic objections to experimental psychology: A reply to Gadlin and Ingle. *American Psychologist*, 1976, 31, 655–663.

Kuhn, T. S. *The structure of scientific revolutions*. Chicago: University of Chicago Press, 1962.

Kuhn, T. S. *The structure of scientific revolutions* (2nd ed.). Chicago, Ill.: University of Chicago Press, 1970. (a)

Kuhn, T. S. Logic of discovery or psychology of research. In I. Lakatos and A. Musgrave (Eds.), *Criticism and the growth of knowledge*. Cambridge: Cambridge University Press, 1970. (b)

Kuhn, T. S. Second thoughts on paradigms. In F. Suppe (Ed.), *The structure of scientific theories*. Urbana, Ill.: University of Illinois Press, 1977.

Kuhn, T. S. *The essential tension: Selected studies in scientific tradition and change*. Chicago, Ill.: University of Chicago Press, 1979.

Kunen, S., Greene, D., and Waterman, D. Spread of encoding effects within the nonverbal visual domain. *Journal of Experimental Psychology: Human Learning and Memory*, 1979, 5, 574–584.

LaBerge, D., and Samuels, S. Toward a theory of automatic information processing in reading. *Cognitive Psychology*, 1974, 6, 293–323.

Laffal, J., Lenkoski, L. D., and Ameen, L. "Opposite speech" in a schizophrenic patient. *Journal of Abnormal and Social Psychology*, 1956, 52, 409–413.

Lakatos, I. Falsification and the methodology of scientific research programmes. In I. Lakatos and A. Musgrave (Eds.), *Criticism and the growth of knowledge*. London: Cambridge University Press, 1970.

Lakatos, I. History of science and its rational reconstructions. In R. C. Buck and R. S. Cohen (Eds.), *PSA 1970 in memory of Rudolf Carnap*. Dordrecht-Holland: D. Reidel, 1971.

Lakatos, I., and Musgrave, A. (Eds.). *Criticism and the growth of knowledge*. Cambridge: Cambridge University Press, 1970.

Leduc, A. L'apprentissage et le changement des attitudes envers soi-même: Le concept de soi. *Canadian Journal of Education*, 1980, 5, 91–101. (a)

Leduc, A. L'apprendissage et le changement des attitudes: L'approche interactioniste de Staats. *Canadian Journal of Education*, 1980, 26, 345–351. (b)

Lefcourt, H. M. Internal versus external control of reinforcement: A review. *Psychological Bulletin*, 1966, 65, 206–230.

Lefcourt, H. M. and Ladwig, G. W. The effect of reference group upon Negroes' task persistence in a biracial competitive game. *Journal of Personality and Social Psychology*, 1965, 1, 668–671.

Lenneberg, E. H. *Biological foundations of language*. New York: Wiley, 1967.

Lepper, M., and Greene, D. On understanding "overjustification": A reply to Reiss and Sushinsky. *Journal of Personality and Social Psychology*, 1976, 33, 25–35.

Leuba, C. Images as conditioned sensations. *Journal of Experimental Psychology*, 1940, 26, 345–351.

Levine, M. Scientific method and the adversary model. *American Psychologist*, 1974, 29, 661–677.

Levin, M. *A cognitive theory of learning*. Hillsdale, N.J.: Erlbaum, 1975.

Lewin, K. The conceptual representation and the measurement of psychological forces. *Contributions to Psychological Theory*, 1938, 1, No. 4.

Lewin, K. Formalization and progress in psychology. *University of Iowa Studies in Child Welfare*, 1940, 16, No. 3.

Lindsey, D. *The scientific publication system in social science*. San Francisco: Calif.: Jossey-Bass, 1978.

Lindsley, O. R. Operant conditioning methods applied to research in chronic schizophrenia. *Psychiatric Research Reports*, 1956, 5, 118–153.

Lindzey, G., and Borgatta, E. F. Sociometric measurement. In G. Lindzey (Ed.), *Handbook of social psychology*. Cambridge, Mass.: Addison-Wesley, 1954.

Lockhart, R. S., Craik, F. I. M., and Jacoby, L. Depth of processing, recognition and recall. In J. Brown (Ed.), *Recall and recognition*. London: Wiley, 1976.

Logan, F. A. Hybrid theory of operant conditioning. *Psychological Review*, 1979, 86, 507–541.

Logan, F. A., and Ferraro, D. P. From free responding to discrete trials. In W. N. Schoenfeld (Ed.), *The theory of reinforcement schedules*. New York: Appleton-Century-Crofts, 1970.

Long, J. S., and McGinnis, R. Organizational context and scientific productivity. *American Sociological Review*, 1981, 4, 422–442.

Lott, A. J., and Lott, B. E. A learning theory approach to interpersonal attitudes. In A. G. Greenwald, T. C. Brock, and T. M. Ostrom (Eds.), *Psychological foundations of attitudes*. New York: Academic Press, 1968.

Lott, A. J., and Lott, B. The power of liking: Consequences of interpersonal attitudes derived from a liberalized view of secondary reinforcement. In L. Berkowitz (Ed.), *Advances in experimental social psychology*. New York: Academic Press, 1972.

Lott, B. E., and Lott, A. J. The formation of positive attitudes toward group members. *Journal of Abnormal and Social Psychology*, 1960, 61, 297–300.

Lovaas, O. I. A behavior therapy approach to the treatment of childhood schizophrenia. In J. P. Hill (Ed.), *Minnesota symposium on child psychology, Vol. 1*. Minneapolis, Minn.: University of Minnesota Press, 1966.

Luchins, A. S. Mechanization in problem solving: The effect of Einstellung. *Psychological Monographs*, 1942, 54 (6, Whole No. 248).

Lundin, R. W. *Personality: An experimental approach*. New York: Macmillan, 1961.

MacCorquodale, K. and Meehl, P. E. On the distinction between hypothetical constructs and intervening variables. *Psychological Review*, 148, 55, 95–107.

Mackenzie, B. D. *Behaviourism and the limits of scientific method*. Atlantic Highlands, N.J.: Humanities Press, 1977.

Mackintosh, N. J. *The psychology of animal learning*. London: Academic Press, 1974.

Mackintosh, N. J. Limits on reinterpreting instrumental conditioning in terms of classical conditioning. *The Behavioral and Brain Sciences*, 1978, 1, 41–91.

MacLeod, R. B. Psychological phenomenology: A propaedeutic to a scientific psychology. In J. R. Royce (Ed.), *Toward unification in psychology*. Toronto, Canada: University of Toronto Press, 1970.

Maddi, S. R. *Personality theories*. Homewood, Ill.: Dorsey Press, 1972.

Mahoney, M. J. Publication prejudices: Partiality toward confirming data. Unpublished manuscript, 1975.

Mahoney, M. J. Reflections on the cognitive-learning trend in psychotherapy. *American Psychologist*, 1977, 32, 5–13.

Maier, S. F., and Seligman, M. E. P. Learned helplessness: Theory and evidence. *Journal of Experimental Psychology: General*, 1976, 105, 3–46.

Maltzman, I., Raskin, D. C., Gould, J., and Johnson, O. Individual differences in the orienting reflex and semantic conditioning and generalization under different UCS intensities. Paper delivered at the Western Psychological Association meetings, Honolulu, 1965.

Mandelbaum, M. Societal facts. *British Journal of Sociology*, 1955, 6, 305–317.

Mandler, G. Message to Division 3 Members. November 1, 1979.

Marshall, E. Psychotherapy works, but for whom? *Science*, 1980, 207, 506–508.

Marx, J. L. Lasker award stirs controversy. *Science*, 1979, 203, 341.

Marx, M. H. The general nature of theory construction, In M. H. Marx (Ed.), *Psychological Theory*. New York: Macmillan, 1951.

Marx, M. H. Observation, discovery, confirmation, and theory building. In A. R. Gilgen (Ed.), *Contemporary scientific psychology*. New York: Academic Press, 1970.

Marx, M. H., and Hillix, W. A. *Systems and theories in psychology*. New York: McGraw-Hill, 1973.

Maslow, A. H. *The psychology of science*. New York: Harper & Row, 1966. (a)

Maslow, A. H. *The psychology of language*. Chicago: Regnery, 1966. (b)

Massaro, D. Primary and secondary recognition in reading. In D. Massaro (Ed.), *Understanding language: An information processing analysis of speech, reading and psycholinguistics*. New York: Academic Press, 1975.

Masterman, M. The nature of a paradigm. In I. Lakatos and A. Musgrave (Eds.), *Criticism and the growth of knowledge*. Cambridge: Cambridge University Press, 1970.

McCandless, B. R. The effect of enriched educational experiences upon the growth of intelligence of very superior children. Unpublished master's thesis, University of Iowa, 1940.

McGinnies, E. Thoughts from a behaviorist. *Contemporary Psychology*, 1976, 21, 481–482.

McGinnies, E., and Ferster, C. B. (Eds.). *The reinforcement of social behavior*. Boston: Houghton Mifflin, 1971.

Meichenbaum, D. *Cognitive-behavior modification: An integrative approach*. New York: Plenum Press, 1977.

Merton, R. K. Sociology of knowledge. In G. Gurvitch and W. E. Moore (Eds.), *Twentieth-century sociology*. New York: Philosophical Library, 1945.

Merton, R. K. Priorities in scientific discovery. *American Sociological Review*, 1957, 22, 635–659.

Merton, R. K. (Edited and with an introduction by Norman W. Storer). *The sociology of science*. Chicago, Ill.: University of Chicago Press, 1973.

Miller, N. E. Studies of fear as an acquirable drive: I. Fear as motivation and fear reduction as reinforcement in the learning of new responses. *Journal of Experimental Psychology*, 1948, 38, 89–101.

Miller, N. E., and Dollard, J. *Social learning and imitation*. New Haven, Conn.: Yale University Press, 1941.

Mischel, W. Delay of gratification, need for achievement, and acquiescence in another culture. *Journal of Abnormal and Social Psychology*, 1961, 62, 543–552. (a)

Mischel, W. Father absence and delay of gratification: Cross-cultural comparisons. *Journal of Abnormal and Social Psychology*, 1961, 63, 116–124. (b)

Mischel, W. *Personality and assessment.* New York: Wiley, 1968.

Mischel, W. *Introduction to personality.* New York: Holt, Rinehart and Winston, 1971.

Mischel, W. Direct versus indirect personality assessment: Evidence and implications. *Journal of Consulting and Clinical Psychology*, 1972, 38, 319–324.

Mischel, W. Toward a cognitive social learning reconceptualization of personality. *Psychological Review*, 1973, 80, 252–283.

Mitroff, I. I. Norms and counter-norms in a select group of the Apollo moon scientists: A case study of the ambivalence of scientists. *American Sociological Review*, 1974, 39, 579–595. (a)

Mitroff, I. I. *The subjective side of science: An inquiry into the psychology of the Apollo moon scientists.* Amsterdam, The Netherlands: Elsevier, 1974. (b)

Mitroff, I. I., and Kilmann, R. H. *Methodological approaches to social science.* San Francisco: Jossey-Bass, 1978.

Moscovici, S. Society and theory in social psychology. In J. Israel and H. Tajfel (Eds.), *The context of social psychology.* New York: Academic Press, 1972.

Mowrer, O. H. *Learning theory and personality dynamics.* New York: Ronald, 1950.

Mowrer, O. H. The autism theory of speech development and some clinical implications. *Journal of Speech and Hearing Disorders*, 1952, 17, 263–268.

Mowrer, O. H. The psychologist looks at language. *American Psychologist*, 1954, 9, 660–694.

Mowrer, O. H. *Learning theory and the symbolic processes.* New York: Wiley, 1960.

Murstein, B. I. A theory of marital choice and its applicability to marriage adjustment. In B. I. Murstein (Ed.), *Theories of attraction and love.* New York: Springer, 1971.

Musgrave, A. Logical versus historical theories of confirmation. *British Journal for the Philosophy of Science*, 1974, 25, 1–23.

Nagel, E. *The structure of science.* New York: Harcourt, Brace, and World, 1961.

Naitoh, S., and Staats, A. W. Positive and negative transfer of control: Instrumental mediation and response competition. *Bulletin of the Psychonomic Society*, 1980, 15, 317–320.

Neurath, O. Unified science and its encyclopedia. *Philosophy of Science*, 1937, 4, 265–277.

Newman, H. H., Freeman, F. N., and Holzinger, K. J. *Twins: A study in heredity and environment.* Chicago: University of Chicago Press, 1937.

Nisbet, R. A. *Aspects of the Western theory of development.* New York: Oxford University Press, 1969.

Nudler, O. (Ed.). *Problems epistemologic.* Buenos Aires: Siglo XXI, 1975.

O'Donnell, J. M. The crisis of experimentalism in the 1920s: E. G. Boring and his uses of history. *American Psychologist,* 1979, 34, 289–295.

Olds, J., and Milner, P. Positive reinforcement produced by electrical stimulation of the septal area and other regions of the rat brain. *Journal of Comparative and Physiological Psychology,* 1954, 47, 419–427.

O'Neill, P., and Levings, D. E. Inducing biased scanning in a group setting to change attitudes toward bilingualism and capital punishment. *Journal of Personality and Social Psychology,* 1979, 37, 1421–1438.

Oppenheim, P., and Putnam, H. Unity of science as a working hypothesis. In H. Feigl, M. Scriven and G. Maxwell (Eds.), *Concepts, theories and the mind-body problem. Minnesota studies in the philosophy of science. Vol. II.* Minneapolis: University of Minnesota Press, 1958.

Osgood, C. E. *Method and theory in experimental psychology.* New York: Oxford University Press, 1953.

Osgood, C. E., Suci, G. J., and Tannenbaum, P. H. *The measurement of meaning.* Urbana, Ill.: University of Illinois Press, 1957.

Osgood, C. E., and Tannenbaum, P. H. The principle of contiguity in the prediction of attitude change. *Psychological Review,* 1955, 62, 42–55.

Overmier, B. J., and Lawry, J. A. Pavlovian conditioning and the mediation of behavior. In G. H. Bower (Ed.), *The psychology of learning and motivation, Vol. 13.* New York: Academic Press, 1979.

Page, M. M. Social psychology of a classical conditioning of attitudes experiment. *Journal of Personality and Social Psychology,* 1969, 11, 177–186.

Paivio, A. Coding distinctions and repetition effects in memory. In G. H. Bower (Ed.), *The psychology of learning and motivation, Vol. 9.* New York: Academic Press, 1975.

Palermo, D. S. Is a scientific revolution taking place in psychology. *Science Studies,* 1971, 1, 135–155.

Paniagua, F. A. El problema fundamental de la interpretación y del tratamiento efectivo en psicología clínica. *Revista Latinoamericana de Psicología,* 1981, 13, 51–74.

Parish, T., and Fleetwood, R. S. Amount of conditioning and subsequent change in racial attitudes of children. *Perceptual and Motor Skills,* 1975, 40, 79–86.

Parke, R. D. Cognition comes to social learning theory. *Contemporary Psychology,* 1979, 24, 289–290.

Parsons, T. *Societies: Evolutionary and comparative perspectives.* Englewood Cliffs, N.J.: Prentice-Hall, 1966.

Patterson, G. R. Prediction of victimization from an instrumental conditioning procedure. *Journal of Consulting Psychology,* 1967, 31, 147–152.

Pavlov, I. P. *Conditioned reflexes* (Trans. G. V. Anrep). London: Oxford University Press, 1927.

Perin, C. T. Behavior potentiality as a joint function of the amount of training and degree of hunger at the time of extinction. *Journal of Experimental Psychology*, 1943, 32, 37–51.

Peters, C. C. and McElivee, A. R. Improving functioning intelligence by analytical training in a nursery school. *Elementary School Journal*, 1944, 45, 213–219.

Pfaff, D. Parsimonious biological models of memory and reinforcement. *Psychological Review*, 1969, 76, 70–81.

Phillips, L. W. Mediated verbal similarity as a determinant of the generalization of a conditional GSR. *Journal of Experimental Psychology*, 1958, 55, 56–62.

Piaget, J. *The child's conception of number*. New York: Humanities, 1952.

Piaget, J. *The child's conception of time* (Trans. A. J. Pomerans). New York: Ballantine, 1969.

Piaget, J. *The child's conception of movement and speed* (Trans. G. E. T. Holloway and M. J. Mackenzie). New York: Ballantine, 1970.

Piaget, J. and Inhelder, B. *The early growth of logic in the child*. London: Routledge and Kegan Paul, 1964.

Piaget, J., and Kamii, C. (Trans.). What is psychology. *American Psychologist*, 1978, 33, 648–652.

Pines, H. A. An attributional analysis of locus of control orientation and source of informational dependence. *Journal of Personality and Social Psychology*, 1973, 26, 262–272.

Popper, K. R. *The open-society and its enemies*. New York: Harper & Row, 1945.

Popper, K. R. *The logic of scientific discovery*. London: Hutchinson, 1959.

Popper, K. R. *Conjectures and refutations*. New York: Harper & Row, 1963.

Popper, K. R. Normal science and its dangers. In I. Lakatos and A. Musgrave (Eds.), *Criticism and the growth of knowledge*. London: Cambridge University Press, 1970.

Popper, K. R. *Objective knowledge*. Oxford: Clarendon Press, 1972.

Ravetz, J. R. *Scientific knowledge and its social problems*. Oxford: Clarendon Press, 1971.

Rechea, C. El concepto de modelo en psicología. *Análisis y modificación de conducta*, 1980, 6, 109–115.

Reichenbach, H. *The rise of scientific philosophy*. Berkeley, Calif.: University of California Press, 1951.

Rescorla, R. A., and Solomon, R. L. Two-process learning theory: Relationships between Pavlovian conditioning and instrumental learning. *Psychological Review*, 1967, 74, 151–182.

Resnick, L. B. Introduction: Changing conceptions of intelligence. In L. B. Resnick (Ed.), *The nature of intelligence*. Hillsdale, N.J.: Lawrence Erlbaum Associates, 1976.

Ritzer, G. *Sociology: A multiple paradigm science*. Boston: Allyn and Bacon, 1975.

Ritzer, G. Paradigm analysis in sociology: Clarifying the issues. *American Sociological Review*, 1981, 46, 245–248.

Roberts, M. J. On the nature and condition of social science. *Daedalus*, 1974, 103(3), 47–64.

Roe, A. The psychology of the scientist. *Science*, 1961, 134, 456–459.

Rogers, C. R., and Skinner, B. F. Some issues concerning the control of human behavior. *Science*, 1956, 124, 1057–1066.

Rosenthal, R., and Rubin, D. B. Interpersonal expectancy effects: The first 345 studies. *The Behavioral and Brain Sciences*, 1978, 3, 377–415.

Rotter, J. B. *Social learning and clinical psychology*. Englewood Cliffs, N.J.: Prentice-Hall, 1954.

Royce, J. R. Prologue. In J. R. Royce (Ed.), *Toward unification in psychology: The first Banff conference on theoretical psychology*. Toronto, Canada: University of Toronto Press, 1970.

Royce, J. R. Philosophic issues, Division 24, and the future. *American Psychologist*, 1982, 37, 258–266.

Rubenstein, H., Lewis, S., and Rubenstein, M. Evidence for phonemic recoding in visual word recognition. *Journal of Verbal Learning and Verbal Behavior*, 1971, 10, 645–657.

Rubenstein, H., Richeter, M., and Kay, E. Pronounceability and the visual recognition of nonsense words. *Journal of Verbal Learning and Verbal Behavior*, 1975, 14, 651–657.

Rychlak, J. F. *A philosophy of science for personality theory*. Boston, Mass.: Houghton Mifflin, 1968.

Sachs, D. H., and Byrne, D. Differential conditioning of evaluative responses to neutral stimuli through association with attitude statements. *Journal of Experimental Research in Personality*, 1970, 4, 181–185.

Sahlins, M. D. Evolution: Specific and general. In R. A. Manners and D. Kaplin (Eds.), *Theory in anthropology*. Chicago: Aldine, 1968.

Sailor, W. Reinforcement and generalization of productive plural allomorphs in two retarded children. *Journal of Applied Behavior Analysis*, 1971, 4, 305–310.

Sampson, E. E. Scientific paradigms and social values: Wanted — a scientific revolution. *Journal of Personality and Social Psychology*, 1978, 36, 1332–1343.

Samuels, S. J. Effect of distinctive feature training on paired associate learning. *Journal of Educational Psychology*, 1973, 64, 164–170.

Santayana, G. The sense of beauty. In K. Aschenbrenner and A. Isenberg (Eds.), *Aesthetic theories: Studies in the philosophy of art*. Englewood Cliffs, N.J.: Prentice-Hall, 1965.

Sarnoff, I. Psychoanalytic theory and social attitudes. *Public Opinion Quarterly*, 1960, 24, 251–279.

Scheffler, I. *Science and subjectivity*. Indianapolis, Ind.: Bobbs Merrill, 1967.

Scheffler, I. *Four pragmatists*. New York: Humanities Press, 1974.

Schlenker, B. R. Social psychology and science. *Journal of Personality and Social Psychology*, 1974, 29, 1–15.

Schmidt, F. L., Hunter, J. E., Pearlman, K., and Shane, G. S. Further tests of the Schmidt-Hunter bayesian validity generalization procedures. *Personnel Psychology*, 1979, 32, 257–276.

Schopler, J., and Layton, B. Determinants of the self-attribution of having influenced another person. *Journal of Personality and Social Psychology*, 1972, 22, 326–332.

Schopler, J., and Stockdale, J. E. An interference analysis of crowding. *Journal of Environmental Psychology and Nonverbal Behavior*, 1977, 1, 81–88.

Segal, E. M., and Lachman, R. Complex behavior or higher mental process. *American Psychologist*, 1972, 27, 46–55.

Seligman, M. E. P. On the generality of the laws of learning. *Psychological Review*, 1970, 77, 406–418.

Shapere, D. The paradigm concept. *Science*, 1971, 172, 706–709.

Shapere, D. Scientific theories and their domains. In F. Suppe (Ed.), *The structure of scientific theories* (2nd ed.). Urbana, Ill.: University of Illinois Press, 1977.

Shapere, D. The character of scientific change. Unpublished manuscript, 1979.

Shaw, R. Towards continued disunity in psychology. *Contemporary Psychology*, 1972, 17, 75–76.

Shepard, R. N. Message to Division 3 members, 1980.

Shiffrin, R. M., and Schneider, W. Controlled and automatic human information processing: II. Perceptual learning, automatic attending, and a general theory. *Psychological Review*, 1977, 84, 127–190.

Shockley, W. Negro IQ deficit: Failure of a "malicious coincidence" model warrants new research proposals. *Review of Educational Research*, 1971, 41, 227–248.

Sidman, M. *Tactics of scientific research*. New York: Basic Books, 1960.

Siegel, M. Interaction. *Monitor*, 1976, 7, No. 7, 2.

Siegler, R. S., and Richards, D. D. Development of time, speed, and distance concepts. *Developmental Psychology*, 1979, 15, 288–298.

Silberner, J. Cheating in the labs. *Science Digest*, 1982, 90, 38–41.

Sills, D. L., Glock, C. Y., Menzel, H., Glaser, W. A. and Sommers, R. H. The flow of information among scientists: Problems, opportunities, and research questions. Bureau of Applied Research, Columbia University. Prepared for the National Science Foundation, 1958.

Skinner, B. F. The concept of the reflex in the description of behavior. *Journal of General Psychology*, 1931, 5, 427–458.

Skinner, B. F. *Behavior of organisms*. New York: Appleton, 1938.

Skinner, B. F. The operational analysis of psychological terms. *Psychological Review*, 1945, 52, 270–277.

Skinner, B. F. Are theories of learning necessary? *Psychological Review*, 1950, 57, 193–196.

Skinner, B. F. *Science and human behavior*. New York: Macmillan, 1953.

Skinner, B. F. *Verbal behavior*. New York: Appleton-Century-Crofts, 1957.

Skinner, B. F. A case history in scientific method. In S. Koch (Ed.), *Psychology: A study of a science*. Volume 2: New York: McGraw-Hill, 1959.

Skinner, B. F. The operational analysis of psychological terms. In B. F. Skinner (Ed.), *Cumulative record* (2nd ed.). New York: Appleton-Century-Crofts, 1961.

Skinner, B. F. Behaviorism at fifty. *Science*, 1963, 140, 951–958.

Skinner, B. F. Philogeny and ontogeny of behavior. *Science*, 1966, 153, 1205–1213.

Skinner, B. F. *Contingencies of reinforcement*. New York: Appleton-Century-Crofts, 1969.

Skinner, B. F. *Beyond freedom and dignity*. New York: Knopf, 1971.

Skinner, B. F. The steep and thorny way to a science of behavior. *American Psychologist*, 1975, 30, 42–49.

Smith, M. B., Bruner, J. S., and White, R. W. *Opinions and Personality*. New York: Wiley, 1956.

Snow, C. E. Mother's speech to children learning language. *Child Development*, 1972, 43, 549–565.

Spence, K. W. The nature of theory construction in contemporary psychology. *Psychological Review*, 1944, 51, 47–68.

Staats, A. W. Learning theory and "opposite speech." *Journal of Abnormal and Social Psychology*, 1957, 55, 268–269.

Staats, A. W. Verbal habit families, concepts, and the operant conditioning of word classes. *Psychological Review*, 1961, 68, 190–204.

Staats, A. W. (with contributions by C. K. Staats). *Complex human behavior*. New York: Holt, Rinehart and Winston, 1963.

Staats, A. W. (Ed.). *Human learning*. New York: Holt, Rinehart and Winston, 1964. (a)

Staats, A. W. A case in and a strategy for the extension of learning principles to complex human behavior. In A. W. Staats (Ed.), *Human learning*. New York: Holt, Rinehart and Winston, 1964. (b)

Staats, A. W. Outline of an integrated learning theory of attitude formation and function. In M. Fishbein (Ed.), *Attitude theory and measurement*. New York: Wiley, 1967.

Staats, A. W. Social behaviorism and human motivation: Principles of the attitude-reinforcer-discriminative system. In A. G. Greenwald, T. C. Brock and T. M. Ostrom (Eds.), *Psychological foundations of attitudes*. New York: Academic Press, 1968. (a)

Staats, A. W. *Learning, language, and cognition*. New York: Holt, Rinehart and Winston, 1968. (b)

Staats, A. W. Social behaviorism, human motivation, and the conditioning therapies. In B. A. Maher (Ed.), *Progress in experimental personality research.* New York: Academic Press, 1970. (a)

Staats, A. W. A learning-behavior theory: A basis for unity in behavioral-social science. In A. R. Gilgen (Ed.), *Contemporary scientific psychology.* New York: Academic Press, 1970. (b)

Staats, A. W. *Child learning, intelligence and personality.* New York: Harper & Row, 1971. (a)

Staats, A. W. Linguistic-mentalistic theory verus an explanatory S-R learning theory of language development. In D. I. Slobin (Ed.), *The ontogenesis of grammar.* New York: Academic Press, 1971. (b)

Staats, A. W. Language behavior therapy: A derivative of social behaviorism. *Behavior Therapy*, 1972, 3, 165–192.

Staats, A. W. Behavior analysis and token reinforcement in educational behavior modification and curriculum research. In C. E. Thoresen (Ed.), *Behavior modification in education: 72nd yearbook of the National Society for the Study of Education.* Chicago: University of Chicago Press, 1973.

Staats, A. W. Behaviorism and cognitive theory in the study of language: A neopsycholinguistics. In R. L. Schiefelbusch and L. L. Lloyd (Eds.), *Language perspectives: Acquisition, retardation, and intervention.* Baltimore, Md.: University Park Press, 1974.

Staats, A. W. *Social behaviorism.* Homewood, Ill.: Dorsey Press, 1975.

Staats, A. W. Social behaviorism's assessment conception: Behavioral interaction principles, tripartite personality repertoires and abnormal psychology. Paper presented at the meetings of the Association for the Advancement of Behavior Therapy, Atlanta, Georgia, December, 1977.

Staats, A. W. Byrne's social psychology of sexual behavior and the social behaviorism approach: Pre-paradigmatic separatism. *Personality and Social Psychology Bulletin*, 1978, 4, 491–497. (a)

Staats, A. W. About social behaviorism and social learning theory. Unpublished manuscript (mimeographed), 1978. (b)

Staats, A. W. Science standards or separatism: Questions in the methodology of citations. Unpublished manuscript (mimeographed), 1979.

Staats, A. W. 'Behavioral interaction' and 'interactional psychology' theories of personality: Similarities, differences, and the need for unification. *British Journal of Psychology*, 1980, 71, 205–220. (a)

Staats, A. W. Separation in theory construction: Methodological problems exemplified by Bandura's social learning theory. Unpublished manuscript, 1980. (b)

Staats, A. W. Social behaviorism, unified theory, unified theory construction methods, and the Zeitgeist of separatism. *American Psychologist*, 1981, 36, 239–256.

Staats, A. W. Paradigmatic behaviorism: Unified theory for social-personality psychology. In L. Berkowitz (Ed.), *Advances in experimental social psychology.* New York: Academic Press, in press.

Staats, A. W., Brewer, B. A., and Gross, M. C. Learning and cognitive development: Representative samples, cumulative-hierarchical learning, and experimental-longitudinal methods. *Monographs of the Society for Research in Child Development*, 1970, 35 (8, Whole No. 141).

Staats, A. W., and Burns, G. L. Intelligence and child development: What intelligence is and how it is learned and functions. *Genetic Psychology Monographs*, 1981, 104, 237–301.

Staats, A. W., and Burns, G. L. Emotional personality repertoire as cause of behavior: Specification of personality and interaction principles. *Journal of Personality and Social Psychology*, 1982, 43, 873–881.

Staats, A. W., and Butterfield, W. H. Treatment of nonreading in a culturally-deprived juvenile delinquent: An application of reinforcement principles. *Child Development*, 1965, 36, 925–942.

Staats, A. W., Finley, J. R., Minke, K. A., and Wolf, M. M. Reinforcement variables in the control of unit reading responses. *Journal of the Experimental Analysis of Behavior*, 1964, 7, 139–149.

Staats, A. W., Gross, M. C., Guay, P. F., and Carlson, C. C. Personality and social systems and attitude-reinforcer-discriminative theory: Interest (attitude) formation, function, and measurement. *Journal of Personality and Social Psychology*, 1973, 26, 251–261.

Staats, A. W., and Hammond, O. W. Natural words as physiological conditioned stimuli: Food-word elicited salivation and deprivation effects. *Journal of Experimental Psychology*, 1972, 96, 206–208.

Staats, A. W., and Lohr, J. M. Images, language, emotions, and personality: Social behaviorism's theory. *Journal of Mental Imagery*, 1979, 3, 85–106.

Staats, A. W., Minke, K. A., Martin, C. H., and Higa, W. R. Deprivation-satiation and strength of attitude conditioning: A test of attitude-reinforcer-discriminative theory. *Journal of Personality and Social Psychology*, 1972, 24, 178–185.

Staats, A. W., and Staats, C. K. Attitudes established by classical conditioning. *Journal of Abnormal and Social Psychology*, 1958, 57, 37–40.

Staats, A. W., and Staats, C. K. Effect of number of trials on the language conditioning of meaning. *Journal of General Psychology*, 1959, 61, 211–223.

Staats, A. W., Staats, C. K., and Crawford, H. L. First-order conditioning of a GSR. *Journal of General Psychology*, 1962, 67, 159–167.

Staats, A. W., Staats, C. K., and Heard, W. G. Denotative meaning established by classical conditioning. *Journal of Experimental Psychology*, 1961, 61, 300–303.

Staats, A. W., Staats, C. K., Heard, W. G., and Finley, J. R. Operant conditioning of factor analytic personality traits. *Journal of General Psychology*, 1962, 66, 101–114.

Staats, A. W., Staats, C. K., Schutz, R. E., and Wolf, M. M. The conditioning of reading responses using "extrinsic" reinforcers. *Journal of the Experimental Analysis of Behavior*, 1962, 5, 33–40.

Staats, A. W., and Warren, D. R. Motivation and three-function learning: Deprivation-satiation and approach-avoidance to food words. *Journal of Experimental Psychology*, 1974, 103, 1191–1199.

Staats, C. K., and Staats, A. W. Meaning established by classical conditioning. *Journal of Experimental Psychology*, 1957, 54, 74–80.

Sternberg, R. J. *Intelligence, information processing, and anological reasoning: The componential analysis of human abilities.* Hillsdale, N.J.: Erlbaum, 1977.

Stevens, S. S. Psychology and the science of science. *Psychological Bulletin*, 1939, 36, 221–263.

Stevens, S. S. Mathematics, measurement, and psychophysics. In S. S. Stevens (Ed.), *Handbook of experimental psychology.* New York: Wiley, 1951.

Storms, M. D. Videotape and the attribution process: Reversing actors' and observers' points of view. *Journal of Personality and Social Psychology*, 1973, 17, 165–175.

Studdert-Kennedy, G. *Evidence and explanation in social science.* London: Routledge and Kegan Paul, 1975.

Suedfeld, P., and Tetlock, P. E. Integrative complexity of communications in international crises. *Journal of Conflict Resolution*, 1977, 21, 169–184.

Sulzer-Azaroff, B., and Catania, A. C. Report on the meeting of the Council of Representatives. *Division 25 Recorder*, 1978, 14, 4.

Suppe, F. *The structure of scientific theories.* Urbana, Ill.: University of Illinois Press, 1977. (a)

Suppe, F. The search for philosophic understanding of scientific theories. In F. Suppe (Ed.), *The structure of scientific theories* (2nd ed.). Urbana, Ill.: University of Illinois Press, 1977. (b)

Suppe, F. Afterward. In F. Suppe (Ed.), *The structure of scientific theories*, Urbana, Ill.: University of Illinois Press, 1977. (c)

Sweller, J., and Gee, W. Einstellung, the sequence effect, and hypothesis theory. *Journal of Experimental Psychology: Human Learning and Memory*, 1978, 4, 513–526.

Tetlock, P. E. Identifying victims of groupthink from public statements of decision makers. *Journal of Personality and Social Psychology*, 1979, 37, 1314–1324.

Thibaut, J. W., and Kelley, H. H. *The social psychology of groups.* New York: Wiley, 1959.

Thompson, R. Interaction. *Monitor*, 1977, 8, No. 9 & 10, 2.

Thorndike, E. L. *The elements of psychology.* New York: Seiler, 1905.

Thorndike, E. L. *Animal intelligence.* Darien, Conn.: Hafner, 1911.

Thorndike, E. L. *Fundamentals of learning.* New York: Teachers College, 1932.

Thurstone, L. L. The measurement of social attitudes. *Journal of Abnormal and Social Psychology*, 1931, 26, 249–269.

Tibbetts, P. On a proposed paradigm shift in social sciences. *Philosophy of the Social Sciences*, 1975, 5, 289–297.

Tolman, E. C. *Purposive behavior in animals and men.* New York: Century, 1932.

Tolman, E. C. Operational behaviorism and current trends in psychology. In M. H. Marx (Ed.), *Psychological theory*. New York: Macmillan, 1951.

Tolman, E. C. Principles of purposive behavior. In S. Koch (Ed.), *Psychology: A study of a science, Volume 2*. New York: McGraw-Hill, 1959.

Toulmin, S. Does the distinction between normal and revolutionary science hold water? In I. Lakatos and A. Musgrave (Eds.), *Criticism and the growth of knowledge*. London: Cambridge University Press, 1970.

Toulmin, S. *Human understanding*. Princeton: Princeton University Press, 1972.

Toulmin, S. Scientific strategies and historical change. In R. F. Cohen and R. J. Seeger (Eds.), *Philosophical foundations of science: Proceedings of section L, AAAS, 1969. Boston studies in the philosophy of science, Vol. XI*. Dordrecht, Holland: D. Reidel, 1974.

Toynbee, A. J. *A study of history* (abridged by D. C. Somervell). New York: Oxford University Press, 1947.

Treisman, A. M. Strategies and models of selective attention. *Psychological Review*, 1969, 76, 282–299.

Tryon, W. W. A reply to Staats' language behavior therapy: A derivative of social behaviorism. *Behavior Therapy*, 1972, 5, 273–276.

Tulving, E. Episodic and semantic memory. In E. Tulving and W. Donaldson (Eds.), *Organization of memory*. New York: Academic Press, 1972.

Ullmann, L. P., and Krasner, L. *A psychological approach to abnormal behavior*. New York: Prentice-Hall, 1969.

Ulmer, M. J. *Economics: Theory and practice*. Boston: Houghton Mifflin, 1959.

Underwood, B. J. Attributes of memory. *Psychological Review*, 1969, 76, 559–573.

Underwood, B. J., and Lund, A. M. Retention differences as a function of the number of verbal lists learned simultaneously. *Journal of Experimental Psychology: Human Learning and Memory*, 1979, 5, 151–159.

van Hoorn, W. *As images unwind*. Amsterdam, Holland: University Press Amsterdam, 1972.

Verplanck, W.S. Skinner, Burrhus F. In W. K. Estes, S. Koch, K. MacCorquodale, P. E. Meehl, C. G. Mueller, W. N. Schoenfeld and W. S. Verplanck (Eds.), *Modern learning theory*. New York: Appleton-Century-Crofts, 1954.

Verplanck, W. S. The operant conditioning of human motor behavior. *Psychological Bulletin*, 1956, 53, 70–83.

Vinacke, W. E. Variables in experimental games: Toward a field theory. *Psychological Bulletin*, 1969, 71, 293–318.

von Bertalanffy, L. General system theory and psychology. In J. R. Royce (Ed.), *Toward unification in psychology*. Toronto, Canada: University of Toronto Press, 1970.

Wade, N. IQ and heredity: Suspicion of fraud beclouds classic experiment. *Science*, 1976, 194, 916–919.

Wallace, A. F. C. The new culture-and-personality. In T. Gladwin and W. C. Sturtevant (Eds.), *Anthropology and human behavior*. Washington, D.C.: Anthropological Society of Washington, 1962.

Walster, E. The effect of self-esteem on romantic liking. *Journal of Experimental Social Psychology*, 1965, 1, 184–197.

Warren, N. Is a scientific revolution taking place in psychology? Doubts and reservation. *Science Studies*, 1971, 1, 407–413.

Warren, R. E. Time and the spread of activation in memory. *Journal of Experimental Psychology: Human Learning and Memory*, 1977, 4, 458–466.

Watson, J. B. *Behaviorism* (rev. ed.). Chicago: University of Chicago Press, 1930.

Watson, J. B., and Rayner, R. Conditioned emotional reactions. *Journal of Experimental Psychology*, 1920, 3, 1–4.

Watson, J. D. *The double helix*. New York: Atheneum, 1968.

Weigel, R. H. Personality and behavior revisited. *Contemporary Psychology*, 1978, 23, 553–554.

Weimer, W. B. *Notes on the methodology of scientific research*. Hillsdale, N.J.: Erlbaum, 1979.

Weimer, W. B., and Palermo, D. S. Paradigms and normal science in psychology. *Science Studies*, 1973, 3, 211–244.

Weiner, B., Heckhausen, H., Meyer, W., and Cook, R. E. Causal ascriptions and achievement behavior: A conceptual analysis of effort and reanalysis of locus of control. *Journal of Personality and Social Psychology*, 1970, 15, 1–20.

Weiss, R. F. Persuasion and the acquisition of attitudes: Models from conditioning and selective learning. *Psychological Reports*, 1962, 11, 709–732.

Weiss, R. F. An extension of Hullian learning theory to persuasive communication. In A. G. Greenwald, T. C. Brock and T. M. Ostrom (Eds.), *Psychological foundations of attitudes*. New York: Academic Press, 1968.

Weiss, R. F. The drive theory of social facilitation. *Psychological Review*, 1971, 78, 44–57.

Weiss, R. F., Boyer, J. L., Lombardo, J. P., and Stich, M. H. Altruistic drive and altruistic reinforcement. *Journal of Personality and Social Psychology*, 1973, 25, 390–400.

Weiss, R. L. Operant conditioning techniques in psychological assessment. In P. McReynolds (Ed.), *Advances in psychological assessment*. Palo Alto, Calif.: Science and Behavior Books, 1968.

Weisz, J. R. Perceived control and learned helplessness among mentally retarded and nonretarded children: A developmental analysis. *Developmental Psychology*, 1979, 15, 311–319.

Wertheimer, M., Barclay, A. G., Cook, S. W., Koch, S., Riegel, R. F., Rorer, L. G., Senders, V. L., Smith, M. B., and Sperling, S. E. Psychology and the future. *American Psychologist*, 1978, 33, 631–647.

Wertlieb, D., and Rose, D. Maturation of maze behavior in preschool children. *Developmental Psychology*, 1979, 15, 478–479.

Whimbey, A., and Whimbey, L. S. *Intelligence can be taught*. New York: E. P. Dutton, 1975.

White, A. D. *A history of the warfare of science with theology in Christendom*. New York: Braziller, 1955. (Written in 1899)

White, M. G. Historical explanation. *Mind*, 1943, 52, 212–229.

Whitlock, C., and Bushell, P. Some effects of back-up reinforcers on reading behavior. *Journal of Experimental Child Psychology*, 1966, 3, 83–85.

Whittaker, E. T. *A history of the theories of aether and electricity*. New York: Thomas Nelson, 1951.

Whorf, B. L. (Edited by J. B. Carroll). *Language, thought, and reality*. New York: Wiley, 1956.

Wickens, D. Being a general psychologist. *Newsletter*, 1978, 24, 1–2.

Williams, C. D. The elimination of tantrum behavior by extinction. *Journal of Abnormal and Social Psychology*, 1959, 59, 269.

Winter, D. G. *The power motive*. New York: Free Press, 1973.

Wohlwill, J. F. *The study of behavioral development*. New York: Academic Press, 1973.

Woll, S. The best of both worlds? A critique of cognitive social learning. Unpublished manuscript, 1978.

Woodward, W. R. Social behaviorism and social learning theory: Historical origins and contemporary significance. Unpublished manuscript (in draft form), 1979. (a)

Woodward, W. R. The "discovery" of social behaviorism and social learning theory, 1890–1980. Unpublished manuscript, 1979. (b)

Woodworth, R. S. Heredity and environment: A critical survey of recently published material on twins and foster children. *Social Science Research Council Bulletin*, 1941 (Whole No. 47).

Yates, A. J. *Behavior therapy*. New York: Wiley, 1975.

Zajonc, R. B. Family configuration and intelligence. *Science*, 1976, 192, 227–236.

Zanna, M. P. On inferring one's beliefs from one's behavior in a low-choice setting. *Journal of Personality and Social Psychology*, 1967, 26, 386–394.

Zerdy, G. A. Incidental retention of recurring words presented during auditory monitoring tasks. *Journal of Experimental Psychology*, 1971, 88, 82–89.

Zuckerman, H. A. Nobel laureates in science: Patterns of productivity, collaboration, and authorship. *American Sociological Review*, 1967, 32, 391–403.

Zuckerman, H. Interviewing an ultra-elite. *Public Opinion Quarterly*, 1972, 36, 159–175.

Zuckerman, H. A., and Merton, R. K. Patterns of evaluation in science: Institutionalization, structure and functions of the referee system. *Minerva*, 1971, 9, 66–100.

Index

About the Author

Arthur W. Staats, now at the University of Hawaii, has had tenured professorships at Arizona State University and the University of Wisconsin, Madison. Fellow in five APA divisions, member in two others, Fellow in the American Sociological Association and the American Association for the Advancement of Science, on the editorial boards of various domestic and foreign journals, author of many journal articles, book chapters, and books, the author has strived with his theory to unify the divided field of psychology. Professor Staats is also known in various specialized areas for his seminal contributions, for example, to (1) developmental psychology for work in language acquisition and in formulating the first modern, systematic learning theory of intelligence, and in making the first behavioral analyses of early child learning; (2) clinical psychology in helping lay the foundations of behavior modification and behavioral assessment and more recently the turn to language-cognitive behavior therapy, in originating the token-reinforcer or token-economy system, and in presenting the first systematic behavioral abnormal psychology; (3) personality and social psychology for his theories of personality and of social interaction and for his first experiments on attitude acquisition through language conditioning; (4) experimental psychology for his theory of human learning and motivation, for his psychology of language, and for introducing conditioning experimentation on word meaning development; (5) educational psychology in originating the first behavioral analysis of reading and other cognitive skills; (6) general psychology for formulating a unified, comprehensive theory and a new method of theory construction. Since the middle 1950s his theory has had various lines of influence on the development of psychology as a science.

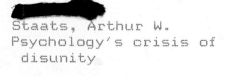